NICHOLAS RIDLEY

A Biography

BY

JASPER GODWIN RIDLEY

LONGMANS, GREEN AND CO
LONDON · NEW YORK · TORONTO

LONGMANS, GREEN AND CO LTD
6 & 7 CLIFFORD STREET LONDON W I
BOSTON HOUSE STRAND STREET CAPE TOWN
531 LITTLE COLLINS STREET MELBOURNE

LONGMANS, GREEN AND CO INC
55 FIFTH AVENUE NEW YORK 3

LONGMANS, GREEN AND CO
20 CRANFIELD ROAD TORONTO 16

ORIENT LONGMANS PRIVATE LTD
CALCUTTA BOMBAY MADRAS
DELHI VIJAYAWADA DACCA

First Published 1957

PRINTED IN GREAT BRITAIN BY
LATIMER, TREND AND CO LTD PLYMOUTH

CONTENTS

PLATES

I

NORTHUMBERLAND AND CAMBRIDGE

Nicholas Ridley was probably born at Willimotiswick Castle in South Tynedale in Northumberland
about the year 1503. We do not know the day or
the month, or even the year of his birth; for he was born at
a time when England was only beginning to emerge from
the intellectual darkness of the Middle Ages and written
records were scanty. We do not know the exact year of the
birth of most of Ridley's famous contemporaries. This is the
last generation in which there is no record of the date of
birth of its famous members; for it was a child of this generation, Thomas Cromwell, who was to order that parish
registers were to be kept after 1538, and to make England
into a sufficiently organised state to ensure that at least in
the case of the gentry the approximate date of birth of the
children should be recorded.

The first recorded date in Ridley's life is 1518, when he
was admitted as a student at Cambridge. We do not know
how old he was, but the average age of students was higher
at this time than it had been a hundred years before;[1] many
students were now older than fourteen when they first went
to the University, and some were as old as eighteen; but
these were for the most part those who had gone to school
in the great Colleges of Eton and Winchester. It is unlikely

that Ridley was older than sixteen when he went to Cambridge, and consequently, although 1500 is usually stated to be the approximate date of his birth, he was probably not born before 1502. Many students, indeed, still went to the University at the age of fourteen, and as Ridley was apparently a precocious schoolboy,[2] he may well have been no older when he first went to Pembroke Hall; but he can hardly have been any younger. It is thus almost certain that he was born in 1502, 1503 or 1504.

The Ridleys had been living in South Tynedale for some three hundred years. In rank, they were gentlemen, and a family of some importance in Northumberland. The head of the family lived in Willimotiswick Castle—a small stone fortress standing on a hill above the South Tyne. Other members of the family lived in their small, fortified houses nearby—at Tecket, at Marley and at Walltown on the Roman Wall.[3] Bishop Ridley's grandfather had four sons. The eldest was Sir Nicholas Ridley of Willimotiswick, who was Sheriff of Northumberland when Bishop Ridley was a child, and had served as one of the English representatives on the commission which preserved the truce between England and Scotland during the closing years of the reign of Henry VII.* The second son was John Ridley, who was the father of Launcelot Ridley; the third son was Christopher Ridley who is supposed to have lived at Unthank Hall, and who was the father of the Bishop; and the fourth son was Dr. Robert Ridley, who entered the Church and became a learned and notable figure in London and Cam-

---

* Sir Nicholas Ridley was Sheriff of Northumberland in 1506–7, and possibly also from 1510 to 1512; see *List of Sheriffs of England and Wales* (*Public Record Office Lists and Indexes*, vol. IX, p. 98). See Rymer, *Foedera*, vol. XIII, pp. 69–73 (29th May–1st June 1503) with regard to Sir Nicholas Ridley's appointment to the Border truce Commission.

bridge.* The Bishop's father Christopher is said to have married Ann Blenkinsop—the castle of the Blenkinsops was some four miles from Unthank—and they apparently had at least four surviving children. They had two sons, Hugh and Nicholas, and two daughters, Elizabeth and Alice. Hugh is supposed to have been the eldest son, for he inherited Unthank Hall, and it therefore appears that Nicholas was a younger son.† Elizabeth was probably about the same age as Nicholas, for when they were children she was particularly attached to him.[4] Alice must have been a good deal younger than Hugh, Nicholas and Elizabeth, for we know that she had several children by her first marriage who were young enough to be still dependent on her and her second husband—George Shipside—when Nicholas was over fifty; and Shipside was a young man at this time.[5]

According to William Turner, who was a pupil and

* Hodgson, *History of Northumberland*, Part II (iii), p. 344. Gloucester Ridley, *Life of Dr. Nicholas Ridley*, pp. 2–3, refers to the four sons, but mentions only John and Robert by name. He states that Launcelot was the son of John, and was therefore Bishop Ridley's cousin. It has often been stated that Launcelot was the Bishop's nephew; but see Cooper, *Ath. Cant.*, vol. I, p. 354. Ridlon, *History of the Ancient Ryedales*, p. 418, seems to be the only authority for the name of Bishop Ridley's mother; but he is an unreliable authority.

† Ridley, *Last Farewell* (Ridley's *Works*, p. 396), shows that Hugh Ridley's widow was living at Unthank in 1555. If his father Christopher lived there, as is generally supposed, Hugh was presumably the eldest son, though it must be borne in mind that a great deal of land in Northumberland descended by gavelkind tenure (Reid, *The King's Council in the North*, p. 6). Neither Christopher nor Hugh is listed as living at Unthank in Bowes' and Ellerker's report or in Bowes' *Book of State* of 1541 and 1550. Ridlon, *History of the Ancient Ryedales*, p. 419, states that Bishop Ridley was the third son, and that the second son was Richard, who went to live in Newcastle; but Bishop Ridley does not mention Richard or his family in his *Last Farewell*. William Ridley was living at Unthank in 1530 (see p. 14), and may therefore have been another brother; he was dead by 1555.

friend of Bishop Ridley at Cambridge, Ridley was born at Willimotiswick.[6] This is probably correct, for Turner was a Northumberland man himself, and much less likely than others to confuse the various residences of the Ridleys. There is, however, a tradition that Bishop Ridley was born at Unthank Hall, though it does not seem to be supported by any evidence other than the fact that his brother's widow was living there in 1555. It is very possible that Christopher Ridley lived at Unthank, as the whole family would hardly have lived with Sir Nicholas at Willimotiswick; and while, in view of Turner's statement, we must accept it that Bishop Ridley was born at Willimotiswick, he may have lived at Unthank during his childhood. Unthank lies some four miles to the west of Willimotiswick on the south side of the still waters of the South Tyne; behind, the rough grass slopes rise rapidly to the wild moor of Plenmeller, where Sir Nicholas Ridley was granted land in 1524, which involved him in a dispute with Lord Dacre and the Keeper of Tynedale.[7] The town of Haltwhistle stood on rising ground across the Tyne within sight of Unthank, less than a mile away; through it ran the road from Newcastle to Carlisle.

Ridley spent the first years of his life in the Ridley country in Tynedale amid scenes of primitive violence. His surroundings were very different from those of the other children who were later to become his colleagues and adversaries in high politics and the Church. Cranmer, Latimer, Gardiner and the rest were born and bred in the Midland plains or in East Anglia. They grew up in the changing England of Henry VII, in a country of small walled towns and a prosperous countryside, in which hardly a trace of feudalism remained either in the economic or in the political sphere. They lived among independent yeomen, contented and well fed on their small holdings. There was hardly a feudal lord left anywhere south of the Trent, and the rising generation was rapidly coming to accept the absolute power of the King as the basis of government, however much they might resent the heavy direct taxation which was imposed to satisfy the inordinate avarice of Henry VII. They were surrounded, too, by signs of the power and influence of the Church—by jovial and immoral priests, by great monasteries and convents with their servants and hangers-on, by villagers who looked on the church along with the inn as the centre of parish life, and to morality plays as their chief entertainment.

Things were very different in Northumberland. Northumberland was nearly three hundred years behind the rest of England in development, and feudalism was still politically, if not economically, as strong as ever. The Percies at Alnwick were as powerful as they had ever been; they had emerged almost unscathed from the Wars of the Roses, and were by far the most powerful family in the North. No one in Northumberland could equal its Earl in importance and influence, though the Dacres at Gilsland in Cumberland, a few miles west of the Ridley country, were rapidly becoming second to the unchallengeable Percies. The feudal privileges of the nobility and the Church existed in Northumberland almost as they had done in the twelfth century. The King's writ ran in only a small part of the county; the Sheriff and the Justices of the Peace had no jurisdiction in the Baronies and Honours of Percy and Dacre and of lesser lords, or in the Palatine see of Durham. The Liberty of Hexham, which lay to the east and south of the Ridley country, belonged to the Archbishop of York. The Liberty was not merely exempt from the jurisdiction of the royal officers, but was also a sanctuary for any criminal who could evade arrest and take refuge in Hexhamshire. The privilege of sanctuary was not

limited to forty days, as it was in the churches and monasteries of the rest of the Kingdom; the fugitive could stay in
the Liberty for as long as he liked, venturing out, if he
dared, to commit fresh crimes and then retreating again for
safety to Hexhamshire. A statute of 1414, which had attempted to restrict the right of sanctuary in Hexhamshire,
had not been enforced in practice, though Henry VII had
ventured, with much hesitation, to prevail upon Archbishop
Rotherham to waive the privilege in cases of high treason.
In all cases except treason, the right of sanctuary was absolute in the Liberty, and gangs of robbers, under the
notorious William Charlton and others, terrorised the whole
neighbourhood from their Hexhamshire refuge, and committed most of their crimes in the Liberty itself, where law
and order were non-existent.[8]

Bad though the situation was in Hexhamshire, it was even
worse in Tynedale. Tynedale was the scene of daily robbery
and violence. There were very few farmers in the district;
apart from the few fields in the narrow valley of the Tyne,
the country was highland moor, and the climate was too
cold for cultivation. The men of Tynedale were cowherds
and robbers. There was hardly any trade, and very little
money in circulation. There were no market towns in Tynedale: a market would have been a target for bands of armed
robbers. The nearest market was at Hexham, but the men
of Tynedale went there less to buy and sell than to compete
with the criminals in the Liberty in raiding the market.[9]
Murder, too, was nearly as common as robbery in Tynedale.

There was no natural barrier to the enforcement of law
and order in Tynedale. Geographically, the country was
remote, but no more so than many parts of the north, and
the district around Haltwhistle, through which ran one of
the six roads which existed in England north of York,[10] was

more accessible than many parts of Yorkshire which had been made to bow to the authority of the Council of the North. Nor was the lawlessness in Tynedale due to the existence of the feudal Baronies, for Tynedale was under the royal authority. It was part of the Middle March,[11] and was directly governed by the Warden-General of the Marches and the Keeper of Tynedale on behalf of the King. The crime and violence in Tynedale was deliberately permitted by the King as a matter of policy. With bands of Scots making inroads across the border, the King was quite satisfied that there should be armed ruffians in the Marches to resist them, though the Bishop of Carlisle protested to Wolsey that far more damage was done by English robbers than by the Scots.[12] During Ridley's childhood, conditions were worse than at any other time in the whole history of the border. In 1511, Lord Dacre was made Warden of the East and Middle Marches, and he made no attempt whatever to check the crime in Tynedale. A semblance of authority was maintained by granting the royal pardon to every man who committed murder in the Marches on condition that compensation was paid by the murderer's family to the relatives of the murdered man.[13] This compensation was often paid, not so much out of respect for the King and the Warden, as because it had become a recognised convention in the Marches.

The Ridleys seem to have been among the more respectable elements in Tynedale, but their outlook and behaviour was nevertheless governed by the moral code of the Marches, and was very different from what it would have been had they lived anywhere else in England. They were not thieves, and were always ready to follow the fray against the escaping robbers. They defended their property with their own strong arm against thieves like William and Hector Charlton, and against Scots marauders like the Armstrongs, who often crossed the border in search of plunder, sometimes apparently with the connivance of Lord Dacre himself.[14] But all the Ridleys—even Sir Nicholas, the former Sheriff —placed loyalty to the family far higher than their duty to their King and country; they were always ready to protect a Ridley from justice, and to avenge wrongs done to their kinsmen in a summary fashion. One member of the family seems to have been really disreputable; this was William Ridley, who was a friend of the Charltons, and one of the leaders of their band of robbers. Sir Nicholas nevertheless received him at Willimotiswick, and in 1524, when William was being hunted down by the authorities, the former Sheriff arranged for him to escape into Scotland. As Sir Nicholas had recently helped another felon to escape, Lord Dacre and Wolsey took a serious view of the situation, and Sir Nicholas was arrested and held for some months in prison.[15] It was apparently another William Ridley who in 1530, along with several other members of the Ridley family, murdered Nicholas Featherstonehaugh. This William Ridley lived at Unthank Hall, and may therefore have been one of Bishop Ridley's brothers. He was killed by the Featherstonehaughs in 1545.*

* William Ridley the outlaw was dead by 1526 (see Sir Christopher Dacre's letter to Lord Dacre, 17th April 1526, *L. & P. Henry VIII,* vol. IV, No. 2110). The murder in 1530 is the incident referred to in the ballad in Scott's *Border Minstrelsy* about Albany Featherstone-haugh. The record of the Coroner's Inquisition on 26th October 1530 (cited by Hodgson, *History of Northumberland,* Part II (iii), p. 359 n.) shows that the murder took place on 24th October 1530. The entry was wrongly transcribed by Sir Walter Scott, and published by him in his Notes to *Marmion,* so as to show that Alexander Feather-stone was killed by Nicholas Ridley of Unthank and others on 21st October. Scott's error has been copied by the Editor of Ridley's *Works,* by Ridlon, *History of the Ancient Ryedales,* and many others, all of whom

These were the conditions in which the future Bishop passed the years of his early childhood. At Unthank he was protected by no king or justice, but owed his life to the courage and ruthlessness of his family and their dependents. Every night, they drove their cattle within the walls of their strong stone houses to protect them from the thieves;[16] but often worse dangers were at hand. A horseman would bring news that the Scottish raiders had crossed the border, and Nicholas saw his kinsmen put on their jacks and seize their spears as they prepared to defend their homes and the lives of the children.[17] It was natural that Ridley should grow to manhood embued with a strong sense of family loyalty, and with a profound respect for the men who fought the robbers and the Scots; but one would hardly have expected the conditions in the Marches to encourage a religious and pious frame of mind, still less to produce distinguished churchmen. Tynedale had none of the active religious life which was so marked in most parishes of England. There were only three churches in the whole of North and South Tynedale, though Nicholas at Unthank was fortunate in that one of them was at Haltwhistle, less than a mile away.[18] Yet in these wild surroundings the Ridley stock was capable of producing, not only fierce fighters like Sir Nicholas, but men of culture and letters, and the family saw to it that the intelligent children were educated for the Church and removed from the Marches to the civilised parts of the realm. Sir Nicholas' youngest brother, Robert, had gone into the Church, and after studying at Cambridge and at the Sorbonne in Paris had become an important

have apparently ignored the fact that the reference to 'Nicholas Ridley of Unthank' directly implicates Bishop Ridley in the murder. The correct entry, however, was to the murder of 'Nicholas Featherstone-haugh' by 'William Ridley of Unthank' and others.

figure in Cambridge and London. Dr. Robert Ridley was made Rector of Simondburn*—the parish lay a few miles to the north of the Ridley country—on the presentation of the King. It is unlikely that he ever visited his wild, enormous parish—he also held two other benefices and two prebends in the diocese of London—but he remained in contact with his family in Tynedale. It was probably Dr. Robert Ridley who suggested that his nephew Nicholas of Unthank, and later that his other nephew Launcelot, who was a few years younger than Nicholas, should enter the priesthood.

Nicholas was sent to school in Newcastle.[19] We have no knowledge of what kind of a school it was. It was now becoming increasingly common for boys to be sent away from home to one of the grammar schools which were being founded all over England. It is certain, however, that Ridley was not educated at a grammar school, for it was only in 1525 that Sir Thomas Horseley, the Mayor, founded the grammar school at Newcastle in his will,[20] and the bequest did not take effect until after the death of both Horseley and his wife some years later. The tradition that Ridley was educated at Newcastle Grammar School is thus clearly wrong. He was almost certainly sent to some establishment organised by one of the monasteries in the town. We know that the Trinitarians had a school in Newcastle which was staffed by three teachers,[21] but it is possible that the Dominicans, the Franciscans, the Carmelites and the Austin Friars also maintained educational establishments of which no record has survived.

---

* Robert Ridley was appointed Rector of Simondburn on 3rd December 1527 (*L. & P. Henry VIII*, vol. IV (ii), No. 3747, p. 1671). Other authorities give the date as 1510 (see *County History of Northumberland*, vol. XV, p. 188).

Wherever he may have gone to school, Ridley almost certainly found himself in quite a small school side by side with the sons of yeomen and merchants as well as boys of noble and gentle birth. We know that he showed great dexterity in his grammar at school, and had almost certainly acquired a sound knowledge of Latin, in which he was later to excel, before he left Newcastle.[22] As most, if not all, of the boys were probably intended for the Church, it was necessary that Latin should become a second mother tongue to them; it was the usual rule in the schools for the boys to be made to speak Latin outside the classroom, and to be well birched if they were caught speaking English in the playground except at certain permitted times.[23] Ridley certainly became completely at home in Latin, and throughout his life was as fluent in the language as he was in English. He may also have learned a little French. Much of his time at school was certainly occupied with the rudiments of divinity. He would also have learned something about English institutions and government, and of the wider world outside England—about the menace of the Turks and the need for a new Crusade, and the wonders of the New World which had been lost to England through the hesitancy and avarice of Henry VII.

In Newcastle, Ridley spent his later childhood in a very different world from that which he had seen in Tynedale. Whatever might be the state of the rest of Northumberland, Newcastle differed from the other county towns of England only in being more important than most of them, and by the fact that it was both a garrison town and a busy port. The old Norman castle housed a permanent garrison to man the walls of the town against the Scots. The port on the Tyne on the south side of Newcastle was very active. Ships arrived laden with grain from the south, and sailed away

B

carrying cargoes of wool and cloth to Flanders, the Hansa towns, Scandinavia and Poland; for Newcastle, in its difficult economic position, was permitted to export wool direct to any part of the world without passing through the Staple at Calais or Antwerp.[24] The departing ships also carried coal, which was sold on the quayside at two shillings a ton.* For the rest, Ridley saw for the first time a typical English town, with its municipal, religious and commercial life. There were the five monasteries and the nunnery of St. Bartholomew, which had been there since the reign of William the Conqueror, and the trading centres— the hundred-year-old building of the Exchange, and the three markets—as well as several hospitals and almshouses.[25]

Ridley was probably in Newcastle during the Scottish invasion of 1513. The march of the Scottish army under King James in person caused panic in Newcastle and throughout the north, for the inhabitants remembered the barbarities of the Scots at the time of the Perkin Warbeck invasion sixteen years before, and it was generally believed that the realm had been denuded of fighting men who had all accompanied Henry VIII in his invasion of France. In Northumberland, men were less perturbed by the absence of the young King that by the fact that the Earl had gone to France with the best warriors amongst his tenants. But the old Earl of Surrey mustered his army in Newcastle on 1st September. The inhabitants of Newcastle could assist only by their prayers as the army marched off to meet the Scots some fifty miles to the north; but by the middle of September they had heard that the Scottish army had been annihilated

---

* Nef, *Rise of the British Coal Industry*, vol. I, p. 10. In 1514, over six thousand tons of coal were exported from Newcastle (Nef, *op. cit.*, vol. II, *Shipments of Coal from North-Eastern Ports*, opp. p. 380).

at Flodden. The corpse of King James was carried to Newcastle on its journey to London,[26] while Sir Nicholas Ridley
and his men of Tynedale earned special commendation for
the zeal with which they performed the agreeable duty
of ravaging the Scottish borders under the command of
Lord Dacre.[27]

The proficiency which Ridley displayed as a schoolboy
made it obviously necessary to send him to the University.
It was equally obvious that he should go to Cambridge
rather than to Oxford. His uncle Robert Ridley was a Cambridge man, and he agreed to pay for Nicholas to go to
Pembroke Hall. He doubtless did not even consider the
possibility of sending Nicholas to Oxford, for apart from
his own connexions with Cambridge, Robert Ridley was a
great scholar—he was a friend and collaborator of Polydore
Vergil*—and must certainly have wished to give Nicholas
every facility for learning Greek. The authorities at Cambridge were far more advanced and progressive in matters
of learning than the authorities at Oxford, where, despite
all the efforts of Wareham as Chancellor, the teaching of
Greek had encountered bitter opposition from the reactionary doctors, whom the Hellenists nicknamed the
'Trojans'.

In 1518, Ridley left Northumberland and took up residence as an undergraduate at Pembroke Hall. We have no
record that he ever returned to Northumberland during the
rest of his life. He certainly remained in close touch with his
brothers and sisters, but this was probably usually by correspondence, and though he seems to have seen them again

* Robert Ridley collaborated with Polydore Vergil in publishing the
works of Gildas (see Polydore Vergil's Dedicatory Epistle to Tunstall
(*Gildas' History*, A.ii). But he was probably not, as has been stated, a
Fellow of Queens' College; see Cooper, *Ath. Cant.*, vol I, p. 530.

from time to time, it is more likely that they came south to visit their successful brother rather than that he found time to travel to Tynedale, which would have involved a two to three months' absence from his duties. It is quite possible, however, that at some time in the next twenty-nine years, between the time when he left the north and his appointment as Bishop of Rochester, he undertook the long journey. After 1547, he certainly did not do so.

If Ridley, who had been thoroughly imbued with all the traditional family ties and regional loyalty of Tynedale, never lost touch with his relatives and never forgot that he was a Tynedale man, he effectively turned his back on the wild life of his homeland, and devoted himself to the life of learning and worship for which he had prepared at school in Newcastle. This intelligent boy was not made to lead a life of robbery and murder among the cowherds and marauders of the Marches, and to end his days in some affray on the moss. It was quite unforeseeable in 1518 that his studies at Cambridge would eventually lead him to a much more horrible death than any that could befall him in Tynedale.

Pembroke Hall was one of the smaller colleges in Cambridge: there were probably less than fifty members of the College in 1518. It was, however, among the wealthier of the colleges, though its wealth did not equal that of really rich colleges like King's College, Queens' College and St. John's.* Pembroke Hall had been founded in 1347, and was one of the eight old colleges in Cambridge; six more had been founded in the last eighty years, and three of

---

* There were forty-eight members of Pembroke Hall in 1564 (Cooper, *Annals of Cambridge*, vol. II, p. 206). For the revenues, see *Valor Ecclesiasticus* of 1535, vol. III, p. 506.

these were less than twenty-five years old.* Apart from the colleges, there were the many hostels, which were part of the University but independent of the colleges, as well as the monastic educational establishments which were not part of the University. In the colleges, there had recently been a tightening of discipline, and order was maintained by a frequent use of the birch.[28] More serious cases were tried before the Chancellor's Court, and punished by imprisonment or excommunication.

Cambridge lay at the heart of the flat and fertile lands of eastern England. To the north was the large expanse of the undrained Fens, where the inhabitants lived on barges, and were generally considered to be primitive and lawless by the people of Cambridge. The population of Cambridge was probably about six thousand, of whom about a thousand were members of the University.† The religious orders had their monasteries in, or just outside, the town; the most important was the great Barnwell Priory of the Austin Friars, which was older than the University. The monasteries were closely linked with the University, and many monks were graduates of a college and active in University life.

Apart from the University and the religious institutions, Cambridge was one of the most important commercial towns in the south of England. The town, with its Mayor and

---

* Peterhouse, Michaelhouse, Clare Hall, King's Hall, Pembroke Hall, Gonville Hall, Trinity Hall and Benets College (Corpus Christi) had been founded by the middle of the fourteenth century; between 1441 and 1518, six more were founded—King's College, Queen's College, Katherine Hall, and Jesus College (1496), Christ's College (1505) and St. John's College (1511).

† In 1586, the population of Cambridge was 6,500, of whom 1,500 were members of the University (Trevelyan, *English Social History*, p. 185).

Corporation and its own privileges, was the home of merchants, artizans and of many farmers who owned land outside the town but preferred to live in Cambridge; and there were many small agricultural holdings within the confines of the town itself.[29] Every year the great Stourbridge fair, which was under the jurisdiction of the Chancellor of the University, was held for three weeks in September; traders came to the fair from all over the north and south of England, and from overseas. Relations between the town and the University were very bad. There were continual conflicts over the extent of the jurisdiction of the Chancellor in Cambridge. The University authorities were ardent in maintaining their right to imprison and excommunicate the townsmen, to inspect the markets and levy dues, and particularly to control the Stourbridge fair, while they were equally determined to assert the immunity of the members of the University from arrest or civil process by the Mayor and bailiffs. The disputes between town and University occasionally led to violence. In 1524, the Junior Proctor was indicted by the townsmen for murder, but was acquitted.[30] In these conflicts, the University was nearly always victorious, for they could rely on the support of the King and Council. During Ridley's first years at Pembroke Hall, both Wolsey and Queen Catherine were entertained by the University, and in 1522 Henry VIII himself paid a visit to Cambridge.[31] With such patrons, the privileges of the University were secure.

The University in Cambridge was the intellectual centre of England. While Oxford stagnated in sullen opposition to Wolsey's projects for the advancement of learning, Cambridge was eagerly assimilating the new culture with optimism and enthusiasm. By the beginning of the century, Erasmus was teaching Greek in Cambridge. The teaching of Greek had encountered bitter opposition from the traditionalists and reactionaries; a knowledge of Greek had enabled scholars to read the originals of many of the writings of the early Fathers of the Church, and had conclusively proved that many of the documents on which the Papacy relied for its claims to spiritual and temporal authority were forgeries. The Hellenists were consequently attacked as something akin to heretics. It was, however, only in the territories of the Holy Roman Empire that authority was on the side of the reactionaries; while the Inquisition was destroying old Hebrew manuscripts which contained doctrines inimical to Christianity, the Popes themselves were sympathetic to the new culture, and encouraged the study of Greek. In England, Henry VIII and Wolsey supported it, while at Cambridge it had a sure friend in the Chancellor, Bishop Fisher, who despite all the calls of Church and State affairs on his time, settled down to learn Greek himself when he was over fifty.

Ridley spent his time as an undergraduate in reading for a degree in Arts, and studying Latin and Greek. He became an outstanding scholar in both languages.[32] He was fortunate in beginning his studies in 1518. In that year, Richard Croke returned to Cambridge from Leipzig, and began giving lectures in Greek. The lectures were still not officially recognised by the University, but it was now possible for the undergraduates to hear lectures from a great Hellenist for the first time since Erasmus had left Cambridge some years before. In the next year, the study of Greek was officially recognised, and Croke continued his lectures as the Reader. The study of Greek had received a further impetus with the publication of Erasmus' New Testament in 1516. After pursuing his form in Arts for three years, Ridley took his degree as Bachelor of

Arts in 1522 when he was probably about eighteen, being the fourth wrangler for the year.* Robert Ridley then offered to continue to maintain him at Pembroke Hall while he completed his course in Arts, and began his studies in philosophy and divinity.[33] Nicholas must have been very grateful to his uncle, for the life of a scholar and the atmosphere of Cambridge were obviously congenial to him.[34] He remained in residence at Pembroke Hall, completing his training for the Church by these further studies.

It was about this time that Ridley was ordained a priest—perhaps by Fisher, or by West, the Bishop of Ely. We have no record of the date of his ordination, but we know that it took place before April 1524. In that month, Ridley was approached by University College, Oxford, with an offer to elect him as a Fellow to the Exhibition founded by Skirlaw, who had been Bishop of Durham in the reign of Richard II and Henry IV. The Exhibition was open to any graduate or undergraduate of either Oxford or Cambridge University, who was in holy orders, with preference being given to those who had been born in the diocese of York or Durham; so it is clear that Ridley was already a priest by this time. Ridley declined the offer.† He had perhaps first made discreet inquiries, and discovered that he was to be offered a Fellowship at Pembroke Hall in the near future. He was deeply attached to Cambridge, and obviously preferred to stay in Pembroke Hall as a Fellow of his own college rather than move to the strange surroundings of Oxford, with its reactionary climate and its suspicion of

---

* *Grace Books* B (Part II), p. 99, and $\varGamma$, p. 198.

† For the conditions of Skirlaw's Exhibition, see MS., University College, Oxford; for a summary, see *Victoria County History of Oxfordshire*, vol. III, pp. 63–4. Ridley did not, as has been stated, accept the Exhibition; nor was he offered it in 1521, but on 13th April, 1524. As to this, see Gloucester Ridley, pp. 62–3.

Hellenism. Less than a year later, Ridley was elected a Fellow of Pembroke Hall, and stayed on in residence pursuing his studies. In July 1525, he took his degree as Master of Arts.*

By this time, the authorities at Cambridge were seriously alarmed over the spread of Lutheranism in the University, and State and Church had begun a great campaign to extirpate heresy in the Kingdom. England had not been seriously troubled by heretics for nearly a hundred years, but the Acts which had been passed to deal with the Lollards were still on the statute book. The statute of 1401† provided that where any person had been condemned as a heretic and excommunicated in the Ecclesiastical Courts, the King had power to order him to be burned without further legal process, while the determination of the issue as to whether or not he was a heretic was still left to the Ecclesiastical Courts. The jurisdiction of the Ecclesiastical Courts was exercised by the Bishop in his diocese, and in Oxford and Cambridge by the Chancellor of the University. In important cases, a special commission was usually issued to several prominent churchmen to conduct the trial of the heretic. The procedure in heresy trials was inquisitorial. As the purpose of the trial was to find out whether the views of the defendant were heretical, the Court was not usually concerned with hearing evidence, but only with questioning the defendant to discover what views he pro-

---

* *Grace Books* B (Part II), p. 122, and Γ, p. 218, show the award of the degree to Ridley during the year 1524–5. The degrees were always finally awarded at the Great Commencement at the beginning of July (see *Grace Book* A, p. xxv). Gloucester Ridley, p. 64, gives the date as 1525, and Cooper, *Ath. Cant.*, vol. I, p. 135, as 1526.

† *Statutes of the Realm*, 2 Hen. IV, c. 15. The other two Lollard statutes of 1382 and 1414 merely made provision for the arrest of heretics and the forfeiture of their property.

fessed. Consequently, a defendant could always save his life by a recantation of his heresy at his trial: in this case, he was merely made to do penance and carry his fagot at a public ceremony where, after publicly recanting his views, the penitent heretic threw a fagot into the flames to be burned in place of his living body. The primary object of the judges was to induce the heretic to recant, and it was only if repeated efforts to do this had failed that they proceded regretfully—in the words of their commission, 'suffering and groaning'*—to pass the sentence of excommunication which sent the heretic to the fire. Even after his excommunication, however, the heretic could still save his life; for it was the almost invariable practice for the King to exercise his prerogative of pardon if he recanted even at the stake itself.† It was only in 1556, after thirty years of bitter religious strife, that this custom was shamefully violated in the case of Cranmer.

By 1430, the Lollards had been crushed, and the number of prosecutions for heresy fell appreciably; but they revived a little towards the end of the century, and a heretic was occasionally burned in the reign of Henry VII and in the early years of Henry VIII. But now the handful of heretics had far more fertile ground on which to breed than had Wyclif and the Lollards; the moral standards of the Church had greatly deteriorated during the previous century, and there was widespread disgust at the corruption and immorality which permeated it at every level. For every heretic who attacked the doctrines of the Church, there were

---

* *'Dolentes et gementes'*; see the words of Bishop White at Ridley's trial (Foxe, vol. VII, p. 539).

† This appears to have been the general practice, except possibly in the case of Bilney, who was a relapsed heretic, and in the special case of Barnes and his colleagues, who were condemned by an Act of Attainder, and in cases under the Act of the Six Articles.

hundreds of faithful Catholics who denounced its abuses. The first-fruits and benevolences and other taxes levied in every country by the Papal see had been paid without demur as long as it was felt that the money was properly used; but now the tithes and the more venal methods of extorting money caused great resentment. The auction of benefices and sees to the highest bidder, the shameless bribery of the officials in Rome, who paid large sums to the Pope to obtain their offices where they could make their fortunes in accepting bribes, the corruptibility of the Judges in the Ecclesiastical Courts, whether in the determination of disputed ecclesiastical claims, in divorces on the grounds of precontract or in criminal proceedings against sinners, were the subject of cynical jokes among the people and of strong condemnation by leading churchmen such as Fisher and even some of the Popes; but it was impossible to root out the corruption. The clergy, and particularly the monks and nuns, were supposed to be more immoral than anyone else, and caused the word 'priest' to be used as an insult in every drunken brawl.

Worst of all was the sale of indulgences and pardons, which had arisen after the Church had adopted the doctrine of Purgatory, and had laid down that in the Sacrament of Penance, absolution was to be given before satisfaction, and that a lack of contrition could be atoned for by attrition combined with the purchase of an exemption from additional satisfaction. The farming out of the grant of pardons to pardoners, who charged a large commission for their labours, served to emphasise the degeneration of the Sacrament of Penance and the corruption of the Church. Nor did the people attribute the corruption merely to the priest or pardoner with whom they came into contact; they placed the blame on the hierarchy and on the Pope. At the begin-

ning of the sixteenth century, the English people were
reciting a rhyme about the Borgia Pope, and Ridley was
later to cite the rhyme, with some apologies for doing so,
in his *Piteous Lamentation*, which he wrote in prison in
Oxford shortly before his death:

> Alexander our Holy Father, the Pope of Rome,
> Selleth for money both right and doom.
> And all kind of holiness the Holy Father doth not stick
> To set to sale, ready money for to get.
> And eke Christ himself, he dare be bold
> To chop and change for silver and gold.
> And why should any think this to be sore?
> For what doth he sell, but what he bought before?*

The year before Ridley went up to Cambridge, Luther
began his campaign against indulgences at Wittenberg University. His theses that the Pope's indulgences served only
to remit the need for satisfaction in penance, and did not
remit the guilt of the sin itself, were sufficient to lead to his
condemnation by the Church for propounding ideas which,
if taken seriously and acted upon, would lead to a serious
reduction in the Papal income. By 1520, Luther had been
excommunicated, and was loudly denouncing the Pope and
challenging his spiritual authority. The contacts between
Cambridge and the Universities of Germany were close,
and it took less than a year for the repercussions of Luther's
stand to be felt. Already in 1517, the year before Ridley first
went to Pembroke Hall, there had come the first affront to
the Pope. Pope Leo's indulgence of 1516 had been affixed
by Fisher's order in some public place in the town; and
somebody wrote across it the words from the fortieth Psalm:
'Blessed is that man that maketh the Lord his trust and
respecteth not the proud, nor such as turn aside to lies'.

* Ridley, *Piteous Lamentation* (Foxe, vol. VII, p. 570; *Works*, p. 54).

In view of the temper of the times, the implication of the words were unmistakable: it was a public affirmation of the worthlessness of Papal indulgences, and therefore heresy. Fisher was incensed; he was shocked at the degeneration of the Church and at the abuse of the power of pardon, but he would not tolerate an open challenge to the authority of the Pope—a challenge which, in his view, could only lead to the disruption of the Universal Church, the hope of salvation, the unifier of all the divers nations in Christendom, the only restraint on the tyranny of Princes, the centre of all culture and learning. The authorities could not discover the identity of the culprit. Many suspected Peter de Valence, a young French undergraduate studying at Cambridge, but it could not be brought home to him. So Fisher had to be content with excommunicating the unknown heretic, whoever he might be.[35]

Soon there were other heretics in Cambridge. As the centre of progressive intellectual activity, the University naturally also became the centre of heresy in England. Copies of Luther's works, in print and manuscript, were circulated secretly in the University; and sympathisers with reform began to meet regularly at the White Horse Inn near St. John's College, which became known as 'Germany'.[36] The authorities grew alarmed. In 1520, Wolsey called a conference at York House in Westminster to discuss measures for counteracting the spread of heresy in the Universities. Dr. Robert Ridley was one of the Cambridge doctors who attended the conference.[37] No useful suggestion seems to have been made, except that it was decided that Luther's books should be ceremonially burned in Cambridge.

Within a few years, a number of doctors in Cambridge were in close touch with the heretics. The leader of the reformers was Thomas Bilney, a Fellow of Trinity Hall, and a priest. Bilney was a very popular man, of a charming, quiet disposition. He strongly repudiated the allegation that he was a Lutheran, as anyone who questioned any of the doctrines of the Church was now promptly labelled. He condemned Luther for challenging the authority of the Pope, whom Bilney held to be the Supreme Head of the Church, with complete authority in spiritual matters; but he criticised the worship of images and prayers for the intercession of the Saints, and the great festivities of the Church, which placed the emphasis on outward form instead of on inner faith. Among the critics of the Church were Coverdale, Foreman, Frith and Lambert. Most of the heretics seemed to come from Gonville Hall, which acquired a very bad reputation as a result; but four of Ridley's colleagues among the Fellows of Pembroke Hall were suspected of heresy. These were John Rogers, John Thixtel, Nicholas Peynel, and no less a man than Dr. Stafford, who had been Senior Proctor of the University in 1523 and was the University Reader in Divinity.[38] But the orthodox doctors were still more shocked and worried to find among the ranks of the heretics a man who was not only a member of the University, but who held a position which made his views even more distressing and alarming. This was Robert Barnes, the Prior of Barnwell. The second greatest man in Cambridge was preaching in his Priory against indulgences, against the feasts of the Church, against the intercession of Saints, against relics and images.

Another of the Cambridge heretics was Hugh Latimer. Latimer was the cross-bearer to the University. He was not outstanding for his learning, but he was a passionate and stimulating personality, always more interested in the rights and wrongs of a question, and in practical results, than in doctrinal argument. He always loved a fight, and would stand out against any injustice—for an innocent man who had been wrongly convicted, or for tenants against enclosures. When Lutheranism first appeared in Cambridge, Latimer attacked it strongly, and became known as one of the most ardent persecutors of heretics in the University; but he too came under the influence of Bilney. On long walks with Bilney on a hill outside Cambridge, which men called in consequence 'Heretics Hill', Latimer became as zealous a reformer as he had formerly been orthodox,[39] and added all his enthusiasm and jovial humour to the quiet gravity of Bilney.

Robert Ridley, who now held several benefices and prebends in the diocese of London, had been appointed an assessor to the Bishop of London—his relative, Tunstall—in proceedings against heretics. Robert Ridley was not only an assessor at the trials, but was also active in discovering heretics and bringing them before the ecclesiastical Courts. In 1526, he denounced Barnes as a heretic,[40] and he was arrested and taken to London. Barnes was eventually induced to recant by Gardiner, who was Master of Trinity Hall, and Wolsey's secretary, and he carried his fagot. Next year, the authorities moved against Bilney and Latimer. Bilney was arrested, and tried for heresy in London before Wolsey, Warham, Tunstall, Fisher and other dignitaries. He too at last recanted, and carried his fagot. Latimer was allowed to go free after an interview with Wolsey. Bilney bitterly repented himself of his recantation, and soon resumed his heretical preaching. In 1531, he was tried for heresy in the court of the Bishop of Norwich, and was burned in Norwich, protesting to the last that he was opposed to Lutheranism.

With all this perturbation about heresy at Cambridge, and with his uncle and patron playing so active a part against it, Ridley must have been fully aware of the menace

of Lutheranism. We have no record of his attitude to the
problem at the time, but there can be little doubt that he
was entirely on the side of authority.* It was not only
that the whole tradition of the Church and the priesthood
to which he belonged, the views of the majority of his
friends and colleagues, and the zeal of his uncle would draw
him to the side of orthodoxy; but Ridley was also by tem-
perament hostile to the whole attitude of the heretics.
Bilney, Barnes and Latimer directed their criticism against
the pomp and glory of the Church, against the outward
show of piety, against the subtleties of dogma, and called
for a simple inner faith based primarily on the Scriptures
alone. They and their followers were the successors of the
old heretic friars who for four hundred years had vexed the
Church with the same line of argument. Their views were
democratic, and anti-intellectual. They rated the simple
faith of the peasant above the sophistry of the scholars. This
was not calculated to appeal to a profound scholar like
Ridley, who delighted in intellectual subtleties, who fully
understood the reason for every point of dogma, including
all the arguments criticising its validity and the answers

* See Foxe, vol. VII, p. 409; Bale's Preface to *Conferences between
Ridley and Latimer* (*Works*, p. 100); Gloucester Ridley, pp. 49, 61.
Janelle, *L'Angleterre catholique à la veille du schisme*, p. 71, states that
Ridley was one of the reformers at Cambridge in the 'twenties; and
Maynard Smith, *Henry VIII and the Reformation*, p. 254, following
Janelle, states that Ridley attended the meetings at the White Horse
Inn. Neither Janelle nor Maynard Smith give any authority for these
statements. It should be noted, however, that Maynard Smith chal-
lenges the traditional view that the meetings at the White Horse Inn
were Lutheran and subversive, and considers that they were merely
meetings of a theological discussion group where Lutheran and other
doctrines were discussed (*op. cit.*, p. 252). If this is so, Ridley may well
have attended the meetings there. There seems to be no evidence that
Ridley held unorthodox religious views at this period, or was in any
way connected with Bilney and Barnes.

Willimotiswick Castle in South Tynedale. The buildings have not been substantially changed since Ridley's time

St. Martin's Church at Herne in Kent, the appearance of which has changed little since it was built in 1360

Ridley's Chair in the Church at Herne

refuting the criticism, and was beginning to acquire a reputation as a masterly debater in theological and other disputations. The Cambridge heretics must have seemed to him a threat to intellectual scholasticism like the bigots who denounced the new culture—a manifestation of the primitive ignorance of the uneducated and prejudice against the culture and learning of the Church, which for a thousand years had stood alone as the guardian of all spiritual and mental values. Ridley was much too learned a scholar to be by instinct a Protestant.

The Church offered a career to men of many different types. While the majority of priests were unambitious men living a comfortable, easy and immoral life, the small number of outstanding personalities amongst them can be divided into three main kinds. There were the politicians—men like Wolsey and Gardiner, who, while neglecting neither their studies nor the pleasures of the world, were primarily interested in public affairs and the struggle for political power. There were the saintly fanatics—men like Bilney, and Latimer for all his rough humour—who challenged convention and complacency, denouncing abuses, hostile to the scholars, and always prepared for martyrdom if not actually courting it. And there were the real scholars, the intellectuals who lived among books and disputations at some University, mastering culture in all its forms, but especially the dogmas of theology. Ridley was one of these. He was neither a politician nor a fanatic. Had he been ambitious for political power, he would not have remained in residence at Pembroke Hall. He was now nearly twenty-five, an age at which many of his contemporaries already held important positions in the State; he could easily have obtained through his uncle's influence some appointment at Court or in the household of the Cardinal or of some other great dignitary. If he had been a fanatic, he would probably have joined with Bilney and Latimer. But he preferred to stay and study quietly in Cambridge.

In July 1526, Ridley was appointed to act for his college in a vexatious matter which was a perpetually recurring source of trouble. Pembroke Hall claimed the advowson of three benefices in the diocese of Norwich—Soham, Tilney and Saxthorpe; but in the case of Soham, their claim was disputed by the Bishop of Norwich, who argued that there was a technical flaw in the deed in which King Henry VI had purported to grant the advowson to the College in 1441. Whenever the necessity arose for preferring a new incumbent, the dispute with the Bishop flared up again; and it seems that this had occurred in 1526. Ridley was appointed along with twelve other members of the College to act as agent for Pembroke Hall in all matters arising in connexion with the three Norwich benefices.* We have no record as to whether Ridley was engaged in any negotiations with the Bishop of Norwich on this occasion, but the quarrel was apparently settled amicably for the time being, for two years later the Vicar of Soham, who had been appointed by Pembroke Hall in 1502, agreed to exchange his cure for another with a priest who was presumably the nominee of the Bishop of Norwich. This post appears to be the only office which was entrusted to Ridley at this time; apart from this, he seems to have devoted himself to a study of divinity.

It was probably during these years at Cambridge that Ridley struck up his friendship with Thomas Cranmer, who was a Fellow of Jesus College. Cranmer was nearly fifteen years older than Ridley. He may already have had his

* On 14th July 1526 (MS. in Pembroke College, Cambridge). Gloucester Ridley, p. 64, gives the correct year. Cooper, *Ath. Cant.*, vol. I, p. 135, wrongly states that it was in the year 1527.

doubts as to whether all was well with the state of the Church, and may even have been in contact with Bilney and the so-called Lutherans; but if so, he was very cautious, and kept his views to himself. He did not have the same strength of character as Ridley, nor did he enjoy the same reputation for purity with regard to his private life;* but Ridley probably found the quiet and studious Cranmer a more sympathetic companion than any of the ambitious politicians or the fanatical heretics among the Fellows in Cambridge. Ridley now had another friend in the University—his cousin Launcelot, who like Nicholas had been picked out by Robert Ridley to be trained for the Church, and was now an undergraduate of Clare Hall.

After he had been in residence at Pembroke Hall for about nine years, Ridley decided to pursue his studies in foreign Universities. Robert Ridley agreed to pay for him to go to the Sorbonne,[41] where Robert himself had studied in his younger days. We have no definite record of the date of Ridley's foreign visits, but they can be placed with absolute certainty as having been between 1527 and 1530,† and as we know that he was abroad for some years, they probably filled the whole of these three years. The Univer-

---

* With regard to Ridley's reputation for purity in his private life, see Foxe, vol. VII, p. 407. The chief proof of his purity is that no allegations to the contrary were ever made by his enemies. Cranmer's reputation for lasciviousness may well have been due merely to the fact that he married twice, which would be quite sufficient to account for the accusations.

† See Gloucester Ridley, p. 94, for the evidence as to the dates of Ridley's visit to Paris and Louvain. Foxe, vol. VII, p. 407, is certainly wrong in stating that Ridley visited the foreign Universities after he had been appointed Master of Pembroke Hall and before his appointment as a chaplain to Henry VIII. These two appointments were conferred on him within a few weeks of each other in 1540, and Robert Ridley, who paid for Nicholas to study abroad, was dead by that date.

sity of Paris was one of the oldest in Europe, and stood high
in learning and reputation. Ridley could want nothing
better than to complete his studies of divinity at the theological school of the University—the Sorbonne. It was almost certainly in the year 1527 that he travelled to Paris.

Paris was the second greatest city in Europe. With its
population of some three hundred thousand, it had about
five times as many inhabitants as London. The citizens were
crowded together in the narrow streets, which were so full of
filth that it was nearly always difficult to move along them;
even the four bridges which crossed the Seine were so
crowded with buildings, and stood so close together, that it
was hardly possible to see the water of the river from either
bank. Ridley ran an even greater risk of catching plague in
Paris than he did in Cambridge, though he was fortunate to
miss the fierce epidemics which regularly struck the city
every three or four years.[42] There was much commercial activity, and a great deal of building going on; in 1528, to the
dismay of many Parisians, workmen began pulling down the
Louvre and filling in the moat which surrounded it, in order
to erect a modern palace on the site. We do not know where
Ridley stayed in Paris; he may have managed to find accommodation in one of the many colleges which were crowded
together on the south bank, or he may have been obliged,
like so many other students, to stay in lodgings in the University quarter. Ridley was not, like the English students
of the Arts in Paris, a member of the 'German Nation'
of the University; as a Master of Arts and student of
divinity, he was a member of the Sorbonne,* and in a

---

* Only those theological students who had obtained a doctor's
degree were members of the Theological Faculty; Bachelors remained
members of their 'Nation' (Crevier, *Histoire de l'Université de Paris*,
vol. I, p. 469).

privileged position in matters of discipline to the students of the Arts.

The danger of Lutheranism and heresy was as burning a topic at the Sorbonne as it was at Cambridge. The University had in the past played a great part in the struggle of the Gallican Church against Rome, but since the Concordat of 1516 it stood firmly with the Papacy against heretics, and had duly condemned the works of Luther. When Ridley first arrived in Paris, the campaign against heresy at the Sorbonne was held in check by the opportunist policy of the King. Francis altered his attitude towards heretics to suit the needs of his foreign policy, and alternatively encouraged and burned them according to the state of his relations with the Pope. In 1527, he was encouraging heretics; Lefèvre d'Etaples, whose translation of the New Testament had been condemned and burned at the instigation of Cardinal Duprat, had been appointed tutor to the King's son; and Francis had quashed the prosecution of Berquin, who had been arrested as a Lutheran. Béda, at the Sorbonne, was profoundly disturbed at the royal policy; but in the summer of 1528, there came another change in Francis' line. The excuse was provided at the end of May, when someone desecrated an image of the Virgin which stood at a street corner on the north bank. The offender could not be found, but his act was made the opportunity for a drive against heresy. A great exhibition of public penitence for the outrage was staged, and day after day all the dignitaries in Paris, including the doctors of the Sorbonne, as well as thousands of the common people, made their way to the spot where the image had stood, to expiate the sacrilege. It is very likely that Ridley went along with the other doctors of the University on the Tuesday after Trinity.[43] The proceedings culminated in a great procession in which Francis and all his courtiers went barefoot to receive absolution from Cardinal Duprat, while a new image was raised into the niche where the old one had stood. Some months later, Berquin was excommunicated as a heretic, and strangled and burned in Paris.

Ridley was probably still in Paris during this time, for twenty-six years later he wrote about his experiences at the Sorbonne in terms which suggest that he was referring to the period after May 1528, rather than to the previous year when heresy was almost tolerated.* The change in Francis' attitude enabled the University to launch a violent attack on Protestantism without the need for any hesitation or caution. On 23rd June, Béda proposed that the Colloquies of Erasmus should be immediately condemned and banned. A few of the doctors at the Sorbonne were prepared to oppose the suggestion, but it was carried by a substantial majority[44] after a keen disputation which Ridley most probably attended. As a student of the classics, he would certainly have been interested in the matter, and may well already have been concerned and anxious over the decision of the Theological Faculty. We know that he attended a number of disputations at the Sorbonne, and it seems likely that many of them were on theological subjects. He may, indeed, sometimes have been chosen to take part in the disputations, for he had probably already become recognised at Cambridge as a brilliant disputant, and as the disputations at the Sorbonne, as at Cambridge, were always held in Latin, the language prob-

* 'The Sorbonnical clamours which at Paris (where Popery most reigns) I in times past have seen' (Ridley, *Account of the Disputation at Oxford*, Foxe, vol. VII, *App.*, Document No. IV). In *Works* (p. 303), the passage is published in Bradford's incorrect translation as 'when Popery most reigned' (see Moule, *Bishop Ridley on the Lord's Supper*, p. 37).

lem was no difficulty. But Ridley was evidently displeased
with the violent tone in which the disputations were conducted.[45] The disputations at the Sorbonne were in any case
notorious for the shouting and excitement and noisy interruptions which they produced, and it is easy to appreciate
the insults which must have been thrown at anyone who
ventured to express the mildest criticism of orthodoxy in
religion in a disputation at the Sorbonne at the end of
1528. Ridley, by nature quiet and courteous, was always
perfectly calm in debate, though he was quite prepared
to snub a presumptuous or arrogant opponent;[46] and the
heated atmosphere of the disputations at the Sorbonne
seems to have made a very unfavourable impression upon
him.

Ridley had decided to imbibe the learning of another
foreign University before returning to Cambridge, and after
leaving the Sorbonne he went to Louvain, in Brabant. We
do not know at what date he left Paris for Louvain, but it
seems likely that it was not before the autumn of 1529, for
the war between England and the Empire probably prevented his journey to Louvain. Wolsey, alarmed at the unchallengeable position of the Emperor in Europe after his
victory at Pavia and his seizure of Rome and the Pope,
negotiated in the strictest secrecy an alliance with Francis,
and a complete reversal of England's foreign policy; and in
January 1528, France and England declared war on the
Empire. Charles V was so enraged at Wolsey's duplicity
that he arrested the English merchants in his dominions. In
these circumstances, it seems unlikely that Ridley would have
left Paris for Brabant. It was perfectly possible for an English-
man to obtain a licence to visit enemy territory in time of
war, and as a student of divinity in Louvain he would have
been spared the internment to which the English merchants

in Spain were subjected. But in view of the unusually bitter relations between England and the Empire, he probably did not go to Louvain until after peace was signed at Cambray in August 1529.

If this conjecture is right, Ridley's stay in Louvain was much shorter than his sojourn in Paris; he probably resided there for only a little more than six months. Louvain was a quiet town, and was rapidly declining in population and commercial activity; but the University was flourishing. It had been founded a hundred years before under the patronage of the Pope, and was famous as a bastion of orthodoxy. The teaching of Greek had for long been frowned upon in Louvain, but Erasmus had eventually induced the University to adopt a more sympathetic attitude towards it, and the famous College of Three Languages—Latin, Greek and Hebrew—was now one of the twelve colleges of the University. But if somewhat less rigid than formerly in matters of culture, the University was as orthodox as ever in theological questions. The doctors of Louvain had condemned the works of Luther and the Paraphrase of Erasmus.[47] Ridley must also have heard from them of a new kind of heresy—the most horrible which had yet appeared anywhere in Christendom—which was said to exist among the weavers and labourers, among the poorest sections of the people, where the atrocious doctrine was spread in the strictest secrecy. It was probably in Louvain that Ridley first learned to shudder at the mention of Anabaptism, and was told that the Anabaptists denounced infant baptism, and in many cases questioned the divinity of Christ, while they worked for the immediate establishment of the Kingdom of God on earth in which all property should be held in common. Five years later, all Europe would watch in horror their revolt in Germany, which was to make the word

'Munster' a fearful warning for the remainder of the century.

Ridley cannot have spent much more than six months in Louvain, for he must have returned to Cambridge before the end of the summer of 1530. He was nearly thirty, and as learned in divinity as in philosophy and in the classics. In Cambridge he would now be among the most learned of the Fellows, and eligible for important offices in Pembroke Hall and in the University.

NOTES

[1] Trevelyan, *English Social History*, p. 79.

[2] Foxe, vol. VII, p. 407.

[3] Bowes and Ellerker's Report to the Council of 2nd December 1541 (cited in Hodgson, *History of Northumberland*, Part III (ii) where the year is wrongly given as 1542) mentions Willimotiswick and Tecket (at pp. 216–17); Bowes, *Book of State of the Frontiers and Marches*, 1550, refers to Marley and Walltown (Hodgson, *op. cit.*, Part III (ii), p. 247).

[4] Ridley, *Last Farewell* (*Works*, p. 396).

[5] Ridley's letters to Queen Mary, 16th October 1555, and to Cranmer and Latimer (*Works*, pp. 428, 362).

[6] Turner's letter to Foxe (*Works*, p. 492).

[7] See *L. & P. Henry VIII*, vol. IV (i), No. 213, p. 82; Lord Dacre's letter to Wolsey, 1st April 1524 (*L. & P. Henry VIII*, vol. IV, No. 219).

[8] *County History of Northumberland*, vol. III, pp. 40–9.

[9] Leland's *Itinerary*, vol. V, p. 68; Bishop of Carlisle's letter to Wolsey, 17th June 1522 (*L. & P. Henry VIII*, vol. III, No. 2328).

[10] Reid, *The King's Council in the North*, p. 2 and map opposite p. 532.

[11] See Bowes, *Book of State of the Frontiers and Marches* (Hodgson, *History of Northumberland*, Part III (ii), pp. 246–7).

[12] Bishop of Carlisle's letter to Wolsey, 17th June 1522 (*L. & P. Henry VIII*, vol. III, No. 2328).

[13] Reid, *The King's Council in the North*, p. 93.

[14] Articles of Accusation against Lord Dacre (Hodgson, *History of Northumberland*, Part III (i), p. 34).

[15] Lord Dacre's letters to Sir William Lisle, 13th May 1524, and to Wolsey, 20th May 1524, and Wolsey's letter to Lord Dacre, 11th June 1524 (*L. & P. Henry VIII*, vol IV, Nos. 329, 346, 405); Hodgson, *History of Northumberland*, Part II (ii), pp. 478–9.

[16] Bishop of Carlisle's letter to Wolsey, 17th June 1522 (*L. & P. Henry VIII*, vol. III, No. 2328).

[17] Ridley, *Conferences Between Ridley and Latimer* (*Works*, p. 145); Ridley, *Last Farewell* (*Works*, p. 398).

[18] Leland's *Itinerary*, vol. V, pp. 61-2.

[19] Foxe, vol. VII, p. 407.

[20] Brand, *History of Newcastle*, vol. I, p. 86 n.

[21] Brand, *History of Newcastle*, vol. I, p. 401.

[22] Foxe, vol. VII, p. 407; Bale, cited by Gloucester Ridley, p. 49.

[23] Trevelyan, *English Social History*, p. 75.

[24] *Rot. Parl.*, vol. IV, p. 379; Mackenzie, *History of Newcastle*, p. 664; *L. & P. Henry VIII*, vol. I, No. 289 (25); *Statutes of the Realm*, 5 & 6 Edw. VI, c. 7.

[25] Mackenzie and Dent, *History of Northumberland*, vol. II, pp. 627-41, 711.

[26] Hall's *Chronicle*, p. 564.

[27] Lord Dacre's letter to Henry VIII, 13th November 1513 (Hodgson, *History of Northumberland*, Part I (ii), pp. 159-61.

[28] Trevelyan, *English Social History*, pp. 78-9.

[29] Trevelyan, *English Social History*, pp. 185-6.

[30] Cooper, *Annals of Cambridge*, vol. I, p. 310.

[31] Cooper, *Annals of Cambridge*, vol. I, pp. 303-5.

[32] Bale, cited by Gloucester Ridley, p. 49.

[33] Gloucester Ridley, p. 61.

[34] Ridley, *Last Farewell* (*Works*, p. 406).

[35] Bass-Mullinger, *History of Cambridge University*, vol. I, pp. 556-7.

[36] Foxe, vol. V, p. 415.

[37] Gloucester Ridley, pp. 48-9.

[38] Bass-Mullinger, *History of Cambridge University*, vol. I, p. 573; Gloucester Ridley, pp. 58-9.

[39] See Latimer's first sermon on the Lord's Prayer to the Duchess of Suffolk (Latimer's *Sermons*, pp. 334-5); Foxe, vol. VII, pp. 437-8, 452.

[40] Gloucester Ridley, pp, 59, 61.

[41] Turner's letter to Foxe (*Works*, p. 492).

[42] Franklin, *Paris et les Parisiens au Seizième Siècle*, pp. 24, 32-3, 58-9, 82.

[43] Michelet, *Histoire de France*, vol. X, pp. 319-21; Crevier, *Histoire de l'Université de Paris*, vol V, p. 212.

[44] Crevier, *Histoire de l'Université de Paris*, vol. V, p. 209.

[45] Ridley, *Account of the Disputation at Oxford* (*Works*, p. 303).

[46] Turner's letter to Foxe (*Works*, p. 493).

[47] De Ram, *Anecdotes pour servir l'histoire de l'Université de Louvain*, No. 10, pp. 52-60; Namèche, *Cours d'Histoire Nationale*, vol. X, p. 813.

II

THE BREAK WITH ROME

It was about the time when Ridley left England for Paris
that Henry VIII decided, after nearly twenty years of
married life, that in view of the charms of Ann Bullen,
his conscience would no longer permit him to cohabit with
his deceased brother's wife. Ridley was abroad during the
years when the King moved slowly and timidly towards a
rupture with a Pope who dared not oblige Henry and
offend the Emperor by declaring that the dispensation of
1503, which had enabled Henry to marry Catherine, was
invalid. Ridley was certainly well informed as to the progress of the divorce proceedings, for it was the talk of every
university in Europe; and while he probably hesitated to
express an opinion amongst his foreign colleagues on an
issue in which his Prince was a party, there is every reason
to believe that his sympathies at this time were fully on the
side of Catherine. Though the interests of Francis' foreign
policy eventually led the Sorbonne, in July 1530, to give
judgment in Henry's favour, the prevalent opinion at the
Sorbonne when Ridley was there was against the divorce;
while at Louvain, in the Emperor's territories, the doctors
were even more strongly against it. The views which Ridley
heard expressed in Paris and Louvain were almost certainly
reinforced by any letters which he received from home, for
public opinion in England was strongly sympathetic to
Catherine. Moreover, Ridley's family connexions linked
him more closely than most with the Queen's party, for

43

Robert Ridley appeared as proctor for Catherine at the trial before the Legates at Blackfriars. Yet there were men among the younger doctors who, both from conviction and self-interest, were in favour of the divorce. It was Ridley's Cambridge acquaintance, Cranmer, who first suggested to Gardiner that the question of the validity of the Papal dispensation of 1503 should be submitted to the judgment of the Universities. Gardiner mentioned Cranmer's suggestion to the King, and thus ensured the progress of the Reformation which he was later to oppose so strongly, and the rise from obscurity of the man who was to be his bitterest enemy during the last twenty years of his life.

Cambridge was the first University to be asked to answer the King's question, which was submitted to the doctors in February 1530. Gardiner succeeded, with considerable difficulty, in inducing the doctors to give the answer which the King required, and the University of Cambridge gave judgment that if the marriage of Prince Arthur and Catherine had been consummated in 1501, the Pope had no power, by the laws of God, to grant a dispensation which would permit the marriage between Henry and his deceased brother's wife. In order to please their Prince, the Cambridge doctors had taken a step which nearly all of them would have denounced as heretical a few years before. Luther's first move, when he challenged the efficacy of indulgences, had been much less subversive than this.

We do not know whether Ridley was in Cambridge at the time of the University's answer to the King's question, or whether he was still at Louvain, and only returned to Pembroke Hall a few months later. It seems most likely that he had not yet returned from abroad. If the conjecture is right that Ridley did not go to Louvain until the autumn of 1529, it is unlikely that he had already left it by February

1530. He probably returned to England during the summer of 1530, when travelling conditions would be somewhat easier than in the winter. But he was back in Cambridge within a few months of the great pronouncement there, to find himself in an atmosphere which was radically different from that which had prevailed when he had left for France three years before. Cambridge would never be the same again after the decision of February 1530.

By the end of 1530, Ridley was home at Pembroke Hall, and had been given his first important office by his College. He was appointed Junior Treasurer of Pembroke Hall.[1] He seems to have had no ambitions for political life, and settled down to study his books, to take part in disputations, to act as a tutor to undergraduates and to younger boys who were sent to him by noblemen and gentlemen for tuition. Ridley is said to have been small in stature,[2] though Foxe, who knew him, describes him as being handsome and well built;[3] his keen, intelligent face was probably still clean shaven at this time, as beards and short hair were only just coming into fashion. Ridley was in the habit of strolling in the gardens of the College in an avenue which later became known as Ridley's Walk. As he paced up and down, he learned by heart the whole of the Epistles in Erasmus' New Testament in Greek, except the Apocalypse. These days at Pembroke Hall were evidently the happiest in his life.[4]

It was probably about this time that Ridley acted as tutor to one of his fellow-countrymen from Northumberland, William Turner, who later became the personal physician of the Duke of Somerset, and also Dean of Wells. He came to Ridley at Pembroke Hall for further tuition in Greek. He developed a great affection and admiration for his tutor. Ridley was very patient, and his knowledge of Greek was profound. Turner was also struck by his remarkable memory. He was often Ridley's opponent in disputations, and was impressed by his skill and patience in debate. Ridley regularly visited some hospital in Cambridge, where he gave generously to the poor, and encouraged Turner to do the same; when he felt that Turner could not afford to give generously, he would himself give money to Turner for him to give to the hospital. Ridley also had his recreations. He often competed with Turner at archery, and played handball with him.[5] This was a variety of tennis which at this time was played both with the hand and with a racket.

Two years after his return to Cambridge, Ridley was appointed to his first University office. Early in 1532, he was elected Chaplain to the University. The office had previously been held by Heath, but he resigned in February, and Ridley was elected to succeed him in an election by private scrutiny.* His chief duty as chaplain was periodically to read out the names of all those who had, in the last three hundred years, made benefactions to the University, and then to offer a prayer for their souls. The office apparently also involved the duty of acting as librarian and cross-bearer to the University.[6] Ridley held the office of chaplain for at least four years, including the year in which he served as Senior Proctor, and resigned it some time between Michaelmas 1535 and the summer of 1537.†

* *Grace Book Γ*, p. 263. The entry, which is dated during the year 1531–2, states that Ridley was elected chaplain on the resignation and departure of Heath. Heath was appointed Rector of Hever on 17th February 1532 (Cooper, *Ath. Cant.*, vol. I, p. 402). Gloucester Ridley incorrectly states that Ridley became Chaplain when he ended his term as Proctor, though he is right in that Ridley was still Chaplain at this time.

† The last entry in the *Grace Books* with regard to Ridley as University Chaplain is in *Grace Book* B (Part II), p. 191, in the year 1534–5, Gloucester Ridley, p. 135, implies that Ridley vacated all his University offices when he left Cambridge in the summer of 1537, and this is probable.

Ridley was now recognised as one of the best debaters in the University, and frequently took part in disputations with other Fellows. One of these disputations aroused more than usual interest in Cambridge. Two young undergraduates from Oxford named Throgmorton and Askwell arrived in Cambridge, and challenged the University authorities to provide their most eminent disputants to dispute with them on two subjects which they had selected. The first was whether medicine or civil law was the higher subject of study by scholars; the second was whether, when a woman had been sentenced to death, and two attempts to hang her had failed owing to the breaking of the rope, she should be pardoned, or whether a third attempt should be made to carry out the sentence. It was generally considered that the two young Oxford men were guilty of great presumption in challenging the most eminent doctors of Cambridge to a disputation; but the University authorities felt bound to accept the challenge. They therefore selected Ridley and four other doctors to meet Throgmorton and Askwell. Ridley's colleagues were John Redmayne, Rokesby, Elizeus Price and Griffith Tregarn, who was famous as a teacher of civil law, although in the disputation as to the superiority of medicine or civil law, the Cambridge men were arguing in favour of medicine.

The adversaries met in Regents' Hall before a large audience. Throgmorton was to dispute first on the merits of medicine and civil law, and afterwards Askwell was to dispute on the hanging of the woman. The Cambridge doctors soon got the best of the argument. They were evidently annoyed at the impudence of the challengers, for they pressed them ruthlessly, holding up Throgmorton and his arguments to ridicule, as Ridley, despite his well-known courtesy in debate, was always prepared to do when confronted with an arrogant opponent. When the time came to pass to the disputation about hanging the woman, Askwell announced that he was feeling ill, and the discomfited undergraduates left the hall without ever debating the second question at all. All Cambridge rejoiced at their humiliating defeat, while Throgmorton and Askwell, on their return to Oxford, were punished by the University authorities. They had gone to Cambridge without the consent of the authorities at Oxford, and had made their University a laughing stock. If Oxford was to hold a disputation with Ridley and the leading disputants of Cambridge, it should be represented by its foremost doctors, not by two boastful young undergraduates.[7]

The most important event in Ridley's life during the four years after his return from Louvain was one of which we have no record whatever, except that we know it happened: his transformation from an orthodox Catholic into a Protestant. It was a development which he shared with many other men at Cambridge, and to some extent with nearly all his colleagues, though he was soon to go far beyond many of them. The mental climate of Cambridge during these four years led nearly all the doctors to move from their reluctant condemnation of the Pope's power of dispensation in the divorce issue in 1530 to their unhesitating repudiation of Papal supremacy in 1534. Ridley spent these years amid this atmosphere, and shared in the development.

Until 1530, all the doctors except the heretics around Bilney and Latimer had been zealous in hunting Lutherans, in condemning any deviation in doctrine as Lutheran, and above all in denouncing any challenge to the authority of the Pope. As for questioning the Papal power of dispensation, this was the cardinal heresy, the first step which had led Luther to excommunication and damnation. Their esteemed Chancellor, Fisher, still strongly adhered to his old views; he was writing one treatise after another in support of Catherine on the divorce question. Yet as soon as the King required it, it was possible, though with difficulty, to induce the University to give an opinion which challenged in one circumstance the validity of a Papal dispensation.

The explanation lies in the application by Henry of the weapons with which all absolutist governments obtain the support and submission of men of learning: the weapons of flattery and hope of advancement combined with concealed threat. When these weapons are applied, theoreticians who have been trained to see both sides of any question can always persuade themselves that that argument is right which coincides with their own advantage. Every doctor in Cambridge had long since realised that the Pope's dispensing power had been shamefully abused; but they also knew that to challenge the validity of dispensations was to undermine the authority of the Pope and the Universal Church, to disrupt the unity of Christendom, to subvert religious discipline and authority, and to open the door to anarchy and Anabaptism. For the sake of unity and authority, they had closed their eyes to the abuses and stood firm against the Lutherans and heretics who attacked the Church, who wished to make every ploughboy as well versed in Scripture as the most learned doctor, and to glorify the faith of a peasant while denigrating dogma and learning. But now things were very different; now Authority itself was in revolt against Authority. Authority armed with prisons and men at arms was in revolt against Authority armed only with Papal bulls. And they were flattered and elevated, not insulted and degraded, by the new revolt against Rome. Their King was submitting to them, as the most learned and esteemed of his subjects, the crucial

D

questions of doctrine which would decide the future of the Church in England; they had been chosen, on account of their wisdom and learning, to judge between Pope and King. The doctors now remembered the scandalous misuse of the powers of dispensation, and were prepared to hold that no Pope could dispense with the observance of the laws of God, while stoutly protesting, just as Luther had done ten years before, that they fully acknowledged the spiritual supremacy of the Holy See. Men who before had doubted, but kept quiet out of fear, now openly spoke their minds about the Pope; men who had formerly denounced all heretics who criticised the Papacy now kept quiet out of fear; while others again who had been amongst the most ardent persecutors of Lutherans were now loudest of all against Rome. Only a handful, like Fisher, remained firm in their old beliefs, and opposed the King and the divorce.

There were many arguments with which the doctors could justify their change of front. There were many quotations from the Scriptures and from the works of the early Fathers, which they knew so well, which could be interpreted in a very different way from that in which they had always interpreted them until now. They could persuade themselves that by pretending to submit they were pursuing clever tactics: by yielding to Henry, they could retain his confidence, and thereby exercise a restraining influence on him. This was probably the argument which induced old Archbishop Warham to support the King, and Sir Thomas More to accept the Great Seal at Wolsey's fall, And there was one supreme justification for their actions: the duty of obedience which every Christian owed to his Prince. The duty to render unto Caesar the things that are Caesar's was one of the chief tenets of their faith; it could be used to justify, and indeed to glorify, every submission to Henry. Cranmer was to use this argument most plausibly in his attempt to get More to swear the Oath of Succession. There might be some doubt, said Cranmer, whether the King or the Pope was right in the issue between them; but it was certain that a subject must obey his Prince. Doubt should give way to certainty, and More should conform.[8] The argument failed to convince More, but it persuaded nearly everyone else.

By 1533, Henry was prepared, in order to marry Ann, to repudiate the Papal supremacy, and to proclaim himself the Supreme Head of the Church of England. He had no intention that the revolt against Rome should go any further than this. There was to be no challenge to any of the doctrines of the Catholic Church; apart from the break with Rome, the Church of England was to be as orthodox and Catholic as ever. During these years when the nation was being prepared for the overthrow of Papal supremacy, the authorities had not relaxed their persecution of reformers. In 1531, Bilney was finally burned; in the same year, Latimer got into trouble again, and saved himself by a recantation. In 1533, Cranmer, who had been made Archbishop of Canterbury for the purpose of divorcing Henry from Catherine, excommunicated Frith for questioning the importance of the doctrine of the Real Presence in the Sacrament, and handed him over to the secular power to be burned. But doubts had been sown in the minds of many of the learned doctors in the universities; and once doubts had been recognised as permissible, there came further doubts which were not so easily suppressed as the old doubts had been. Ten years ago it had been heresy to deny the validity of Papal dispensations; now all good men admitted that in certain circumstances they were powerless to dispense with the necessity of observing God's law. What of those other questions of doctrine which the heretics had challenged—the invocation of the Saints, prayers for the dead, the value of images and holy water, and even the truth of transubstantiation itself? It was still heresy to question these doctrines in England—but would it be in ten years' time? One thing at least was certain: it was for them, the learned doctors, to determine these questions on the basis of their interpretation of the Bible and the works of the early Fathers; and they would pay no attention at all to any command from the Pope prohibiting them from discussing these things.

During these years in Cambridge, Ridley's attitude changed along with that of most of his colleagues, and by 1533 he was quite prepared to renounce the Papal supremacy. It seems likely that his uncle Robert was much less ready to change his opinions; but Robert, whatever his private feelings, can hardly have dared to press his views on his nephew, and Nicholas was obviously more likely at such a time to be influenced by the attitude of the great majority of the younger doctors than by his uncle or the lonely Chancellor of the University. Yet by 1534, or within a very few years afterwards, Ridley had advanced far beyond the position of most of his colleagues. He was not content to adopt the fashionable and safe position of a zealous Catholic anti-Papist, conforming in every respect to the official line. He had become a reformer, a member of the Protestant party, though he was still very cautious and discreet about expressing his views. After 1537, when he became Cranmer's chaplain, he was throughout in the closest contact with the Archbishop, and he may well have been in touch with Cranmer and his circle before he left Cambridge. It is probable that his religious development at every stage was very similar to Cranmer's own.

There has been a great deal of controversy and speculation on the sincerity of the attitude of Cranmer and his
followers during the last fourteen years of Henry's reign.
The official view, which has been put forward by their bio-
graphers during the last four hundred years, is that Cranmer and Ridley, starting as devout Papists, gradually saw
the light, and by 1547 had advanced to a Protestant position.
Less friendly historians have interpreted their actions in a
different light:[9] they believe that Cranmer had been a Protestant at heart since 1530, if not earlier, and deliberately
dissembled his views, celebrating the Mass which he regarded as blasphemous, and burning men who advocated
the opinions which he secretly held himself, until it was safe
at Henry's death openly to proclaim himself a Protestant.
The truth is probably not so simple, and is perhaps easier
for us to understand today, with our knowledge of totali-
tarian régimes, than it was for the historians of the nineteenth century. Cranmer almost certainly held Protestant
views on many subjects at the time of his appointment
as Archbishop; he certainly married a German wife in
1532, at a time when priests were forbidden to marry, and
successfully concealed the fact for sixteen years. He probably concealed many other heretical views as well. On the
other hand, his views did not develop all at once; it was a
gradual process. What is true of Cranmer is also true of
Ridley. Ridley probably did not doubt the truth of transubstantiation until 1545, and it was Ridley who soon
afterwards converted Cranmer to a belief in the spiritual
Presence. But it is not true to say, as Bale did, that Ridley
came to Protestantism at the eleventh hour of his life;[10] by
1543, he was already sufficient of a Protestant to be in
danger.

Cranmer and Ridley were one step in front of the official

policy during Henry's reign. This makes their policy understandable, if not excusable. They had no wish to suffer a horrible death for being a little in advance of a government which was moving in their direction; they knew that a heretic today might be an honoured prelate tomorrow if he managed to survive for twenty-four hours. It was of incalculable advantage to the Reformation that the Archbishop of Canterbury was a secret Protestant. If Cranmer was obliged to divorce one Queen after another whenever Henry required it, and sometimes to play his part in burning Protestants as heretics, he could justify this to himself as good tactics designed to further the Reformation, and as he and Ridley were always honestly opposed to extremism and Anabaptism, it was easy for Cranmer to persuade himself that the heretics he condemned were akin to Anabaptists. Moreover, there was always the greatest justification of all for his actions: he was obeying his Prince.

In October 1533, Ridley was appointed Senior Proctor of the University.* Simon Haynes was the Vice-Chancellor, and Richard Wilkes the Junior Proctor. The system of selecting the Proctors had been revised in 1514 with the object of avoiding the ill-feeling and bitterness which had previously been aroused at proctorial elections. The new system provided that each College, and the Hostels acting as one unit, should be entitled to nominate the Proctors every year in rotation.[11] In 1533, it was the turn of Pembroke Hall to nominate the Senior Proctor, and of the Hostels to choose the Junior Proctor. The Master and Fellows of Pembroke Hall decided to nominate Ridley, and the Hostels nominated Wilkes.

A few days before the election of the Proctors, there was a demonstration by Papist sympathisers in Cambridge which

* *Grace Book* B (Part II), p. 179.

was presumably intended as a warning to the new Proctors not to collaborate in any future measures which the King might take against the Pope. There had been a riot in the town at the time of the University's judgment on the divorce question, and there were still members of the University who strongly supported Catherine and opposed the break with Rome. The centre of resistance to Henry's policy was the Franciscan monastery in Cambridge, and its leader was Henry Standish. Standish was a very old man; he was the Provincial of the Franciscan Order, and Bishop of St. Asaph, and was probably a Doctor of Divinity of Cambridge University.* He evidently had a certain amount of support among the lawyers in the University. The Pope's decree of excommunication against Henry had just come into force, and everyone was expecting the King to take violent counter-measures, and probably to strike at Standish. On two successive evenings, a group of lawyers called at several colleges and houses, and demonstrated in favour of Standish, warning anyone whom it might concern that if they did any wrong to Standish they would have to take the consequences. Perhaps the Papists in the University had particular misgivings about what Ridley would do when he was Proctor, for by this time Ridley's views were almost certainly sufficiently far advanced for him to be considered a heretic by supporters of Papal supremacy.

On the second evening, about eighty lawyers took part in the demonstration. They ended up at the Vice-Chancellor's house, where they called for Haynes to make an appear-

---

* Cooper, *Ath. Cant.*, vol. I, p. 55. Meers' diary does not directly state that the lawyers' demonstration was a pro-Papist one; but this seems the most probable explanation, in view of the references to heretics during the incident before Haynes' house. It seems clear that the reference to Standish was to Henry Standish, and not to Richard Standish.

ance, and adopted a most threatening attitude; they shouted out slogans about knaves, cowards and heretics. The Vice-Chancellor's servants and other persons attempted to disperse the rioters by pelting them with stones, and the demonstrators shouted out that they would set fire to the Vice-Chancellor's house; but they eventually departed, and moved on to Christ's College, where they assaulted a member of the College. Next morning, the Masters and leading Fellows of every College assembled for a meeting which had been hastily convened by the Vice-Chancellor. They decided that every College should provide a number of men to preserve order at the election, and forbade any further demonstrations. There was no further disorder.[12]

This was hardly a pleasant beginning to Ridley's year as Proctor, and his term was to be marked by unusual difficulties and friction. On taking office, he inherited from his predecessors a quarrel with the town which had already reached the earlier stages of litigation. In the summer of 1533, the Mayor and corporation had served a bill of complaints against the University, accusing them of exceeding their jurisdiction with regard to the inspection and seizure of fish, soap and cloth, of wrongfully exacting dues, of intervening in the Stourbridge fair and hampering the merchants there with their regulations, and with excommunicating the Mayor for disobedience. The University's legal advisers denied some of these allegations, and justified the others by claiming that their charters entitled them to act as they had done; and while the University authorities agreed to relinquish their right to excommunicate the townsmen, they put forward a demand that in future they should be entitled to exercise the jurisdiction of a Justice of the Peace over the townsmen in Cambridge. The Vice-Chancellor and the Proctors did not have the assistance of

their Chancellor in their dispute with the town: Fisher was
in disgrace, the target for insult and villification by all who
wished to curry favour with the authorities. But Haynes,
Ridley and Wilkes set out with great determination to
defend and extend the privileges of the University against
the town.

In the summer, the Vice-Chancellor and the Mayor had
made a serious attempt to reach an amicable settlement of
the dispute; but soon after Ridley took office as Proctor in
the Michaelmas term, the corporation decided to pursue
the matter further, and again served their bill of complaints,
with an additional clause inserted, on the Proctors. Ridley
and Wilkes called a meeting of the University authorities
on Friday, 7th November. The University had already
decided to send the Vice-Chancellor to London, where he
could use his influence with the right people; and Haynes
quickly realised that the right person for all purposes was
now the Chancellor of the Exchequer, Thomas Cromwell.
At the meeting on 7th November, Buckmaster, who was
acting as Vice-Chancellor in Haynes' absence, was able to
read out a letter from Haynes informing them that the King
and Queen and the peers, and especially Master Cromwell,
were prepared to defend and even to extend the privileges
of the University. The University authorities immediately
decided to grant an annuity of forty shillings to Cromwell.[13]

The quarrel with the corporation took a turn for the
worse at Candlemas. On that day the Mayor sent his
officers to serve writs on several members of the University,
including Ridley's Pembroke colleague Peynel, who had
formerly been close to Bilney. The writs apparently demanded the payment of certain fines under threat of legal
process. When Peynel was served with the writ in church,
he struck the process-server with a processionary. That

same evening, Ridley and Wilkes sent their servants out to Castle End, on the northern outskirts of Cambridge, to arrest a woman who had been accused of immoral behaviour. When they tried to apprehend her, the town bailiffs intervened, supported by several of the townsmen; one of the bailiffs assaulted the Proctor's servants with his staff, whilst the townsmen struck at them with sticks and flails. On Shrove Tuesday, a mob of townsmen chased Buckmaster through the streets. A month or so later, Buckmaster summoned the bailiff and townsmen who had assaulted the Proctor's servants at Castle End to appear before him: but the bailiff refused to submit to the jurisdiction of the Vice-Chancellor.[14]

Meanwhile the corporation were continuing to badger Peynel, Taylor and others with threats of legal proceedings. Peynel and Taylor began to think that it might be better to pay their fines to avoid all this trouble; but the University was very anxious to make it a test case on the question of the Mayor's jurisdiction. Haynes was still in London, along with Thirlby, but as the University authorities had heard that several of the Cambridge aldermen were in London lobbying the courtiers, they decided to send Ridley to London, along with Peynel and Taylor.[15] The dispute was eventually heard at Lambeth Palace on 24th July 1534, before Cranmer, Sir Thomas Audley the Lord Chancellor, the Duke of Norfolk, and the Marquis of Exeter. The University's case was presented by Haynes, Thirlby, Shaxton and others. Judgment was given in favour of the University: the Commission ruled that Stourbridge fair, being in the suburbs of Cambridge, was within the Chancellor's jurisdiction, and that consequently the University was entitled to regulate the merchandise and the conduct of the fair. They also decided that the Chancellor's Court had jurisdiction to try every civil action where either the plaintiff or the defendant was a member of the University. This successful litigation was highly expensive to the University, costing nearly eighty pounds.[16]

The burgesses of Cambridge had no chance at all in their disputes with the authorities of the University, who, as a result of the recent religious and political developments, stood higher in the King's favour than ever before. But the doctors were expected in return, not merely to give gratuities to Cromwell, but also to render important political services. In 1533, as soon as Henry had tricked the Pope into consenting to Cranmer's appointment as Primate, Cranmer divorced Henry from Catherine; soon afterwards, Henry announced that he had married Ann Bullen. The Pope thereupon excommunicated Henry, and the sentence came into force in October. In November, the Council proclaimed that the Pope had no more jurisdiction in the realm of England than any other foreign bishop, and was henceforth to be known as the Bishop of Rome. But the King was determined to obtain a solemn opinion to the same effect from the Universities, to bolster up the new order with the moral weight of the doctors' judgment, and to flatter the doctors again. He asked the Universities of Oxford and Cambridge to decide, from their great learning and knowledge of books, without fear or favour, whether or not, by the laws of God, the Pope had any authority in England. The Chancellor of Cambridge took no part in the proceedings; Fisher was arrested in the spring of 1534 along with Sir Thomas More. The duty of answering the King's question devolved primarily on the Vice-Chancellor and the Proctors. With their Chancellor in prison, Ridley and his colleagues set out to peruse the Scriptures and the works of the early Fathers, well knowing what the consequences might be if they answered the King's question in the affirmative.

The University of Cambridge gave its decision to the King on 2nd May 1534. It pronounced that after a diligent examination of all the authorities, it was fully satisfied that by the laws of God the Bishop of Rome had no more jurisdiction in the realm of England than any other foreign bishop. The University's opinion was signed by Haynes, Ridley and Wilkes. The reasons for the decision were not stated; but they were apparently formulated chiefly by Day, who had been consulted along with several other doctors by the Vice-Chancellor and the Proctors.[17]

The current arguments against Papal supremacy followed two main lines: on the one hand, all the traditional authorities in favour of the Pope's supremacy were either rejected as forgeries, or re-interpreted as meaning no such thing, while on the other the duty of obedience to Caesar, and the supremacy of the Prince in his realm, were emphasized with authority from Scripture. Many of the old documents such as the Donation of Constantine, on which the Popes relied for their claims, were forgeries: some of them had been universally recognised as such among scholars for the last hundred years. There was the well-known passage of Augustine: 'All the Christian countries beyond the sea and far regions are subject to the see of Rome'; but the phrase 'beyond the sea'—*transmarinis*—was now interpreted as meaning only the mainland of Europe, and not England—a conclusion which would hardly have appealed to Luther, but which satisfied King Henry. In Augustine's time, the Patriarchs of Alexandria, Constantinople and Antioch had held an independent and equal jurisdiction in their provinces to that of the Patriarch of Rome in his province. In any case, when the early Fathers spoke of the supremacy of the Bishop of Rome, they meant no more than a preeminence in status, and not an authoritative power. The greatest authority of all—the '*Tu es Petrus*' passage in Matthew's Gospel—was interpreted anew. The rock upon which the Church was to be built was not the mortal man Peter, but Peter's confession of Christ's divinity; it now stood firm, not on the rock of Peter's mortal successors in the see of Rome, but on the rock of the Christian belief in the divinity of Christ which was shared by King Henry and all his subjects.

The doctors also stressed the duty of the Christian to obey his Prince, and the supremacy of Caesar in his realm. The leading treatise on the subject was Gardiner's book *De Vera Obedientia*. He showed by Scriptural authority that the supremacy of the Prince over the priest was recognised by God's law. Solomon had sat in judgment on Abiathar the High Priest, and had condemned him to death; he made ordinances for the regulation of religion, as did Hezekiah, by virtue of his regal power. In the Maccabees, King Alexander appointed Jonathan to be High Priest, and Demetrius likewise appointed Simon. Christ did not call his disciples to an earthly Kingdom; he did not incite to sedition against Caesar, but submitted to be crucified by Caesar; and Gardiner even went so far as to suggest that if the Pope were as true a Christian as he professed to be, he would surrender to King Henry and show himself ready to suffer death at his hands.[18]

Ridley's year of office as Proctor came to an end in October 1534. At about the same time he was appointed Master of the Glomery. Apparently the duties of the Master of the Glomery were to approve the lists of candidates who had applied to take degrees, to regulate and announce the results of University elections in the absence of the Proctors, and to keep the University Register; but the further duty

of delivering orations on formal occasions had been transferred to the Public Orator when this office was created
for Croke in 1520. It seems perfectly clear that Ridley was
never Public Orator, and that Day continued to hold this
office.* Ridley continued as Chaplain to the University for
at least another year. He was also now the Treasurer of
Pembroke Hall. This office must have involved Ridley in
considerable anxiety, for the finances of his College were in
a precarious state. Its expenditure was exceeding its annual
income of £154,† and the Fellows were compelled to sell
some valuable land and to pawn some of the College plate;
but Ridley seems to have handled the finances of Pembroke
Hall with care, for in 1536 he was able to redeem the plate
which had been pawned.[19] As Fellow of Pembroke Hall,
Ridley probably received £4 1s. for commons, £1 for livery,
and 8s. for his scholastic habit, every year,‡ and he had, in

---

* See Gloucester Ridley, pp. 133–4, for this very probable explanation and for the reasons for believing that Ridley was never Public
Orator. Day continued as Public Orator until succeeded by Red-
mayne in 1537. The suggestion that Ridley was at some time Public
Orator seems to be based on his statement in his *Last Farewell* that he
had held the office of 'a common reader' in Cambridge (see Gloucester
Ridley, p. 133); but it is much more likely that Ridley was referring, in
this passage, to some office connected with his duties as University
Chaplain or Master of the Glomery. For the duties of the Master of the
Glomery, see Gloucester Ridley, p. 134; Peacock, *Statutes of Cambridge
University*, App., pp. xxxii–iii.

† *Valor Ecclesiasticus* (1535), vol. III, p. 506, gives the income. In
the survey pursuant to the Chantries Act in 1546, the annual expenditure of Pembroke Hall was shown as being nearly £188; but by this
time—after the inflation—the income was higher than in 1535. With
regard to the financial difficulties of Pembroke Hall in the 'thirties,
see Attwater, *Pembroke College Cambridge*, pp. 32–3.

‡ These are the figures for the year 1546, as recorded in the survey
taken pursuant to the Chantries Act; but the College authorities had
a motive to supply inaccurate accounts in their return. See Cooper,
Annals of Cambridge, vol. I, p. 433.

addition, his salary of £2 a year as Chaplain to the University, which was paid him from the Chair of Canon Law.[20]

The University was closely affected by political developments. Cambridge, too, felt the iron hand of Cromwell. In 1534 and 1535, all the doctors, like everyone else in public life, were required to take the Oath of Succession and the Oath of Supremacy; those who refused to swear the oath 'purely and of my own voluntary accord' were guilty of high treason.* Fisher refused, and lost his head on Tower Hill. The office of Chancellor of Cambridge University thereupon became vacant; and the doctors elected Cromwell himself as their new Chancellor. Cromwell was determined to ensure that Cambridge should no longer be a training school for Papist theologians. In 1535, he promulgated new injunctions in the King's name, which were presented to the University by Dr. Legh on 22nd October. In future, canon law was no longer to be taught as a separate subject from civil law; the teaching of the two subjects was to be merged, and no separate degree of Doctor of Canon Law, but only one degree of Doctor of Laws, was to be given. Every undergraduate was to read the Bible. They were also to read Aristotle, Rudolphus Agricola, George of Trebizond, Melanchthon and other suitable works; they were not to read Duns Scotus, Burley, Trombeta, Bricot, Brulifer and other mischievous Popish writers. The Injunctions also directed that no lectures should be given on Peter Lombard's Books of the Sentences, which had laid down the doctrines of the Church in the middle of the twelfth century, or on any doctor who had developed

---

* This was the combined effect, as interpreted by the authorities, of the three statutes (*Statutes of the Realm*, 26 Hen. VIII, c. 1, c. 2, and c. 13) which enacted that the King was Supreme Head of the Church of England, required all subjects to swear to this when so ordered, and made it high treason to deny the King's titles.

Lombard's doctrines.[21] This necessitated a revision in the form of words used in the ceremony of conferring the degree of Bachelor of Divinity, for hitherto all candidates awarded a degree had been admitted for the purpose of reading the Four Books of the Sentences. Ridley was among the first to be admitted under the revised formula, for in the summer of 1537 he took his degree as Bachelor of Divinity.* His younger cousin Launcelot had taken the degree in 1535.

In June 1536, Robert Ridley died.† He had lived to see Nicholas rise to high office in Cambridge, and his other nephew Launcelot prove himself to be a learned divine. Robert Ridley had attracted unfavourable attention by appearing for Queen Catherine at the trial at Blackfriars; but he had conformed with the rest, and took the Oath of Supremacy. His friend Tunstall, who had been translated from London to Durham, was a loyal supporter of the King's policy. No doubt Robert Ridley had his own views on the new developments, but he would hardly have expressed them to his nephew, who had played so leading a part in the University's repudiation of Papal supremacy. Nicholas, on his side, would not have told his uncle of his own views on Catholic doctrine, and of the opinions which he was formulating with the Archbishop of Canter-

* *Grace Book* Γ, p. 310. Gloucester Ridley, p. 133, states that Ridley took his B.D. degree in 1534. This error is probably caused by the fact that Launcelot Ridley took his B.D. degree in the year 1534–5, and Nicholas in 1536–7, and Gloucester Ridley doubtless assumed that, as Nicholas was older than Launcelot, it was Nicholas who took the degree at the earlier date. The list of Bachelors of Divinity in *Grace Book* B (Part II), pp. 188, 230 does not distinguish between the two Ridleys; but the full entry in *Grace Book* Γ makes it clear that Launcelot took the degree in 1534–5 (p. 298), and Nicholas in 1536–7 (p. 316).

† On 12th June 1536 (Gloucester Ridley, p. 134).

bury and his circle about many fundamental tenets of
the Faith.

It was in 1537, when Ridley was about thirty-five years
old, that he at last took the step which dragged him into the
dangerous world of high politics. Cranmer invited Ridley
to become his chaplain.[22] This meant that he would have to
leave Cambridge. Ridley probably hesitated before accepting the offer; he loved Pembroke Hall, and the quiet life of
a university. But he decided to accept the post. This decision
is a strong indication that Ridley was by now in full agree-
ment with the Protestant policy of Cromwell and Cranmer.
It is difficult otherwise to account for his decision to leave
Cambridge. He was clearly not ambitious for high ecclesiastical or political office; had he been, he would not have
remained at Pembroke Hall until he was thirty-five. The
honour of the University offices which he held must have
meant more to him than the position of chaplain to the
Archbishop of Canterbury. The only explanation as to
why he accepted the post was his desire to help Cranmer in
furthering the Reformation. Here he would certainly be of
great assistance to the Archbishop. Few of the reformers
were as learned as Ridley; Cranmer himself was not his
equal in disputation.

So in the summer of 1537, Ridley vacated his University
offices, and left Cambridge, where he had lived, apart from
his sojourn in foreign Universities, for the past nineteen
years. This year the plague was worse than usual; it was
widespread in Cambridge, where the beginning of the
Easter term was postponed till Corpus Christi day. Cranmer
had been compelled to leave Lambeth Palace on account of
the plague, which had spread from London to the village of
Lambeth, and he was in residence at his manor of Ford,
near Herne, in Kent. It seems that it was to Ford that

E

Ridley first went when he took up his office as Cranmer's chaplain.*

At Cranmer's side in Lambeth and Ford, and at his many other houses in Surrey and Kent, Ridley was in daily touch with the political and religious developments in the highest councils of the State. He went there at the height of the Protestant advance under Cromwell. It is difficult to believe that this student of Macchiavelli was actuated in the smallest degree by religious motives; but he believed that the Papists were the greatest enemy of royal absolutism, and in order to crush them he was ready to enlist the support of their bitterest enemies—the Lutheran Princes of Germany and the reformers at home. Cranmer's religious beliefs went hand in hand with Cromwell's cynical policy, and the Vicar-General and the Primate accomplished much during these years. When Ridley became Cranmer's chaplain, the smaller monasteries had already been suppressed; shrines and valuable images had been pillaged; relics had been paraded for mockery, and suppressed; most important of all, at the time when Ridley first went to Ford, an English translation of the Bible had been published by the King's command, and disseminated in all the churches throughout the realm, though only a small circle around Cromwell and Cranmer—of whom Ridley was probably one—knew that it was based on the work of Tyndale. All resistance had been ruthlessly suppressed. In the north, the Pilgrimage of Grace, which had bestirred even Tynedale to rise for the Percy and demand the dismissal of Cromwell and Cranmer and

* 'From Cambridge I was called into Kent by the Archbishop of Canterbury, Thomas Cranmer'—Ridley, *Last Farewell* (*Works*, p. 407). Cranmer was in residence at Ford during August, September and October 1537. He did not reside at any of his other manors in Kent during the year (see Cranmer's correspondence, Cranmer's *Works*, vol. II, pp. 332–58).

the heretic bishops, had been defeated by trickery and mass hangings.

Cromwell had also taken steps to infiltrate ardent Protestants into high office in Church and State. Men like Latimer, who only a few years before had been denounced as heretics, now sat with their former inquisitors on the Bench of Bishops. Latimer was appointed Bishop of Worcester in 1535 in the place of an Italian Cardinal who had never set foot in England; at the same time, the reformer Shaxton was appointed Bishop of Salisbury in place of Campegio. Among Cromwell's Protestant appointees to the episcopal Bench was Bonner, who was made Bishop of Hereford in 1538, and translated to London next year. Bonner was suspected of Lutheran tendencies, but, as he had written to Cromwell when Haynes was suspected of Lutheranism, this was a sure sign that he was loyal to the King. Bonner ingratiated himself with Cromwell by reporting to him some disloyal remarks which he alleged that Gardiner had made in private conversations with him.[23] Yet even during this period, when the Reformation was advancing far beyond the repudiation of Papal supremacy, a Protestant extremist was occasionally burned under the statute of 1534, which, while repealing as Papist the heresy statute of 1401, had re-enacted its provisions with some procedural alterations.*

In April 1538, Cranmer appointed Ridley to be Vicar of Herne.[24] The village was about a mile west of the Archbishop's manor of Ford, and a little further from the priory

---

* *Statutes of the Realm*, 25 Hen. VIII, c. 14. The statute provided that suspected heretics were to be indicted before a jury, who could remit the case to the Bishop's Court for trial. After excommunication, the heretic was to be burned by the secular powers as before. The statutes of 1382 and 1414 were not repealed in 1534.

of Reculver on the coast, to which it had formerly been closely linked. The living brought Ridley a net income, after payment of all rents and dues, of more than twenty pounds a year,* on which he could live quite comfortably. He could easily have obtained a licence exempting him from the duty of residing in his parish; but it seems certain that he spent a considerable amount of time in Herne. He had got to know the district the previous summer, when he was staying with Cranmer at Ford, and probably had already made the acquaintance of some of the parishioners. He was presumably able to enjoy the use of Ford Manor when he was in residence in Herne, though he probably lived in the vicarage nearly opposite the church. The inhabitants of Herne were mostly agricultural labourers and fishermen, and they were evidently a prosperous community. They were able to supplement their diet with excellent mussels, which were found in abundance on the shore.†

The most important person in Herne was Lady Fyneux. She was the widow of Sir John Fyneux, who had been Chief Justice of the Court of King's Bench, and she lived in her splendid manor house up on the hill between Herne and Ford. The Fyneux family did everything that could have been expected of them in the way of benefactions to the parish church, and presented an Easter Sepulchre to the church. Ridley became very friendly with Lady Fyneux. She was an old woman, and she died just over a year after

---

* This was the income of Ridley's predecessor three years earlier (*Valor Ecclesiasticus*, vol. I, p. 34). In 1535, the Vicar received an income of £29 16s. 9d., and his outgoings were £9 1s. 8d., leaving a net income of £20 15s. 1d., on which he paid his tenth of £2 1s. 7d.

† Ridley, in his *Last Farewell*, calls Herne 'thou worshipful and wealthy parish' (*Works*, p. 407). Leland's *Itinerary*, vol. IV, p. 69, refers to the mussels.

Ridley became Vicar;* but during the first year after his preferment, Ridley evidently spent a great deal of time in Herne. Whenever he preached in Herne, people came from the neighbouring parishes to hear him;[25] he obviously had much more interesting things to say than the ordinary vicars of the neighbourhood. At the end of 1538, Cromwell was at the height of his power, and with the tide of reformation flowing strongly in his favour, Ridley had no need to hesitate in advancing more radical Protestant views than any which he had advocated hitherto. He still fully believed in the doctrine'of transubstantiation,[26] but he was probably already expressing his opinion on confession which was to lead him into trouble five years later—that while auricular confession was a beneficial practice, it was not necessary to salvation, as there was no authority for it in Scripture. He already believed that the Church services should be conducted in English rather than in Latin, and directed that the *Te Deum* should be sung in English in the church at Herne[27]. It seems that Ridley discussed theological questions with Lady Fyneux, and found that she had markedly Protestant views; and when she died on 22nd August 1539, she bequeathed a legacy of four marks—£2 13s. 4d.—to Ridley.†

For the first two years after Ridley became Cranmer's chaplain, the Reformation continued to advance. In 1538, the larger monasteries were suppressed; the monks usually

* Lady Fyneux's brass at Herne records her death as occurring on 22nd August in the year 'One Thousand Five Hundred and Forty ave One'. Lady Fyneux was obviously old, because her husband was nearly ninety when he died in 1527, and Lady Fyneux's son had a grandchild when he died in 1557. The name Fyneux is also written—presumably phonetically—as Fiennes, or Phines.

† Ridley, *Last Farewell* (*Works*, p. 407); Leland's *Itinerary*, vol. IV, p. 43; Buchanan, *Memorials of Herne*, p. 62. The mark was worth 13s. 4d.

received handsome pensions, but the servants and beggars in the houses were turned adrift as vagrants. The shrine of St. Thomas of Canterbury—who was now considered to have been nothing but a pestilent priest—was suppressed, to the horror of all Catholic Europe. To crown the achievements of the reformers came the Great Bible of 1539. No one in the past had objected more than Henry to the publication of an English Bible which would make the most ignorant ploughboy as learned in the Scriptures as the most learned clerk; yet Cromwell and Cranmer and the march of events had induced the King to authorise the translation in his own name. The Great Bible was handed to the people as the gift of the most absolute autocrat who has ever ruled in England; but few acts have been more subversive of authoritarianism. The Bible in English was the food of the movement which rose against the supremacy of the ecclesiastical hierarchy; and if for a century this movement strengthened the tyranny of the Crown, it would in due course overthrow it, drawing its inspiration in this second struggle too from the English Bible.

But in the summer of 1539 the Reformation was brought to a sudden halt. The danger of foreign intervention had never loomed larger than at this moment when Charles V and Francis I had made peace and were negotiating an alliance, and when the efforts of Cardinal Pole to launch the Crusade against the heretic realm seemed to be nearing fruition. Faced with the danger of invasion and with seething discontent at home, Henry decided to pursue his opponents' policy while exterminating their leaders. While the relatives of Pole—the impotent heirs of the House of York— were executed, along with several Abbots, Henry gave proof to all Europe, and to his Catholic subjects, that a King whom the Pope had excommunicated as a heretic could be as savage a persecutor of Protestants as the Pope himself. In June 1539, Parliament passed the Statute of the Six Articles.

The Act laid down six fundamental articles of Catholic doctrine, all of which were still accepted in the Church of England, but had been challenged by some heretical sect or other. The first article proclaimed the doctrine of transubstantiation. The second article prescribed that it was unnecessary for salvation that the Sacrament of the Altar be administered to the laity in both kinds and that the flesh and blood of Christ were both present in the bread and the wine. The third article laid down that priests after ordination were forbidden by the laws of God to marry, and the fourth that vows of chastity or widowhood taken by any man or woman ought to be observed by the laws of God. The fifth article stated that private Masses were approved by the laws of God, and the sixth that auricular confession was expedient and useful and ought to be retained. The statute enacted that it was heresy to dispute the truth of the first article, and felony to do likewise as regards the other five articles. The Act contained certain novel features. It laid down, for the first time, a statutory definition of heresy, whereas hitherto it had been left to the unfettered discretion of the Ecclesiastical Courts to determine whether or not a defendant was guilty of heresy. The Act laid down that a denial of transubstantiation was to be punished by death at the stake for the first offence, notwithstanding the subsequent recantation of the heretic, though it was not interpreted as restricting the royal prerogative of pardon. A denial of the truth of any of the other five articles was to be punished with death by hanging if the criminal opinions had been expressed in a sermon or public meeting, and otherwise with imprisonment during the King's pleasure and by confiscation of goods for the first offence, and on the second offence with death by hanging. A Protestant who questioned the truth of the doctrines expressed in the last five articles could nevertheless still be burned as a heretic, for the Statute of the Six Articles did not prevent proceedings being brought against him for heresy in the Ecclesiastical Courts under the statute of 1534, which remained in force. Priests who married after the Act came into force, or who, being married at this date, did not put away their wives within a month, were, together with their wives, to suffer death as felons.[28]

The reformers did not submit without a struggle to the Statute of the Six Articles. Cranmer had been at pains to engratiate himself with Henry, but he now felt bound to take great risks in his resistance to the project. There has been much controversy as to the attitude which Cranmer adopted at the time of the enactment of the Act of the Six Articles, but there appears to be convincing evidence both of his open resistance and of his compliance in the House of Lords. On 5th May 1539, the King asked the House of Lords to draft a bill which would safeguard he unity of the Church of England and lay down principles of religious doctrine to be observed by his subjects. Cranmer was appointed, along with Latimer and Cromwell and Goodrich and five of the catholic prelates, to the commission which examined the question, and was able to prevent any obnoxious proposals from being recommended. On 16th May, however, the Duke of Norfolk informed the House of Lords of the six articles which the King desired them to incorporate in the bill. The articles had probably been drafted by Gardiner. Norfolk's statement in the House could only mean that Henry had decided on a complete reversal of policy; and this placed Cranmer in a dreadful dilemma. He was strongly opposed to the articles, while the measures proposed against married priests affected the Archbishop himself; but it was absolutely necessary, both for his own safety and for the interests of the Reformation, that he should retain the confidence of the King. He nevertheless made private representations to the King in an attempt to dissuade him from his policy, and even opposed it openly, though in a very mild and conciliatory manner, in the House of Lords. He was supported in his opposition by Latimer and Shaxton and three other Bishops; but the bill was ruthlessly pressed by Gardiner and the Duke of Norfolk, supported by Tunstall and the other bishops, while Cromwell cynically supported the measure. During the debate, the King entered the House, and peremptorily ordered the peers to pass the bill without further discussion. Cranmer could do no more, and assented to the bill.*

There can be little doubt that Ridley was as alarmed as Cranmer at the prospect of the bill becoming law. It is certain that he was convinced of the truth of transubstantiation, and consequently had no criticisms to make with regard to the first article; but it seems likely that he already had doubts as to the doctrines prescribed in all the remaining articles. His associations with Cranmer had probably led him to oppose the prohibition on the marriage of priests, though he had no intention of marrying himself, and to favour, along with Cranmer's Lutheran friends in Germany, the administration of the cup to the laity; and he may well already have been opposed to private masses. As to auricular confession, he was to preach a sermon only twelve

---

* See Letter by an Unknown Member of Parliament (Strype, *Cranmer App.*, p. 743), which gives a first-hand account, both of Cranmer's initial opposition, and of his final submission, in the debates on the bill in the House of Lords.

months later in which he criticised the orthodox doctrine on this point. But the political significance of the Statute of the Six Articles went far beyond that of a mere affirmation of doctrines which had never been officially challenged in England; it was a triumph for Norfolk and Gardiner's party, and in so far as it showed that Henry was not over eager to conciliate the German Princes, it was a signal defeat for Cromwell's foreign policy, and threatened his position.

On 2nd May 1539, Convocation met at St. Paul's. Ridley preached a sermon in Latin at the opening of Convocation. His text was: 'Fear of the Lord is the beginning of wisdom', and he spoke for a long time. We do not know exactly what he said, but he apparently dealt with the abuses in spiritual matters, and the necessity for reforming them.[29] It was three days before the King first instructed the House of Lords to draw up a bill to regulate the unity of the Church, and it was therefore still possible for Ridley to preach in favour of reform; but he may already have heard rumours of what was in the wind, and probably spoke with a certain amount of discretion. There can be little doubt that Cranmer received the full support of his chaplain during his resistance to the bill of the Six Articles during the next month; but it is much more doubtful if Ridley preached any sermon against the Six Articles. He is said to have attacked the Six Articles in the pulpit;* but if he did so, it is surprising that his action was completely overlooked by the authorities and by his Catholic oppo-

* Gloucester Ridley, p. 136, states that Ridley 'bore his testimony in the pulpit' against the Act of the Six Articles, but he gives neither the date, the place nor his authority. Cooper, *Ath. Cant.*, vol. I, p. 135, repeats Gloucester Ridley's phrase, and states that it was in 1539. No reference to this sermon was made by the Catholic Prebendaries and Preachers of Canterbury in 1543 (see Chapter III); but this is by no means conclusive that the sermon was not preached.

nents. In any case, we can be sure that if Ridley preached this sermon, it was during the month when the bill was before Parliament, for he would not have dared to attack the Act once it was on the statute book. After 28th June 1539, he was obliged to show the greatest caution, and certainly read out the statute once every three months from the pulpit in Herne, as he was required to do by the Act itself.

Ridley was now to enter upon a most difficult and dangerous period. The years which followed were perhaps the hardest of his life. Fifteen years before, at Cambridge, he had been an orthodox scholar, and had been untouched by the persecution of the heretics in the University; fifteen years later, when he encountered the full fury of the Marian terror, he was one of the most eminent of the Protestant leaders, and was ready to go to a martyr's death at the hands of Antichrist. But the position was not so clear in the seven years which followed the enactment of the Statute of the Six Articles. During this time, Ridley was a respected priest, holding several important offices in the Church and at Cambridge, and was indeed one of Henry's chaplains. He still believed in transubstantiation, and was consequently in no danger of being burned as a heretic under the statute; but he had almost certainly begun to doubt the truth of the other five articles. He had brought himself to accept, during the previous nine years, the supreme authority of the King over the Church, and with the inherent respect for his Prince which he shared with nearly all his contemporaries, he cannot have found it easy to condemn, even in his own mind, the laws which Henry laid down for the governance of religion; but neither could he forget the other doctrines which he had assimilated since the break with Rome, and return to the secure and orthodox opinions which he had held in the 'twenties. This made the situation a highly complex one for Ridley, and one which called for both courage and caution.

NOTES

[1] Gloucester Ridley, p. 94.

[2] Faulkner, *History of Fulham*, p. 207.

[3] Foxe, vol. VII, p. 407.

[4] Ridley, *Last Farewell* (*Works*, pp. 406–7).

[5] Turner's letter to Foxe (*Works*, pp. 492–3).

[6] Cooper, *Annals of Cambridge*, vol. I, p. 97; see Dr. Stokes' lecture to Cambridge Antiquarian Society, cited in Editor's Introduction to *Grace Book* B (Part II), p. xxii.

[7] Caius, *De Antiquitate Cantebrigiensis Academiae*, pp. 17–18 (published in *Works of John Caius*); Fuller, *History of Cambridge*, pp. 208-9. The disputation was held during the academic year of 1532-3. Fuller, who places it in the year 1531–2, is mistaken as to the date of the proctorship of Taylor and Cake.

[8] More's letter to Margaret Roper of (probably) 17th April 1534 (*Correspondence of Sir Thomas More*, p. 505).

[9] See Gairdner, vol. III, pp. 73–8; Belloc, *Cranmer*, pp. 112–13.

[10] Bale's Preface to *Conferences between Ridley and Latimer* (*Works*, p. 100).

[11] Cooper, *Annals of Cambridge*, vol. I, pp. 296–7.

[12] The Diary of Meers the Beadle (published in *Grace Book* A, pp. 222-3).

[13] Meers' Diary (*Grace Book* A, pp. 225-7); Lamb's *Collection*, pp. 28-33.

[14] Meers' Diary (*Grace Book* A, pp. 227-9). Cooper, *Annals of Cambridge*, vol. I, p. 365, states that the Proctors themselves were involved in the brawl at Castle End; but it is clear from Meers' account that Ridley and Wilkes were not present in person.

[15] *Grace Book* B (Part II), p. 184.

[16] Lamb's *Collection*, p. 40; Cooper, *Annals of Cambridge*, vol. I, p. 369.

[17] Fuller, *History of Cambridge*, p. 211n.

[18] Gardiner, *De Vera Obedientia* (published by Janelle, *Obedience in Church and State*, pp. 128–32).

[19] MS., Pembroke College, Cambridge; Attwater, *Pembroke College Cambridge*, pp. 32–3.

[20] *Grace Book* B (Part II), p. 173.

[21] Cooper, *Annals of Cambridge*, vol. I, p. 375.

[22] Gloucester Ridley, p. 135.

[23] Foxe, vol. V, pp. 151, 154–60.
[24] On 30th April 1538 (Gloucester Ridley, p. 135).
[25] Gloucester Ridley, p. 142.
[26] Ridley, *Last Farewell* (*Works*, p. 407).
[27] *Cranmer and the Heretics in Kent* (*L. & P. Henry VIII*, vol. XVIII (ii), No. 546, p. 306).
[28] *Statutes of the Realm*, 31 Hen. VIII, c. 14.
[29] Wriothesley's *Chronicle*, vol. I, p. 94.

III

THE DANGEROUS YEARS

For a year after June 1539, the fate of the Reformation in England hung in the balance; Henry was watching the international situation, while he mercilessly crushed the Papist peers and abbots at home. By the spring of 1540, Cromwell was fighting for his life. He counter-attacked against the Catholic faction, and struck at the Bishop of Chichester. As the spring turned to the hottest summer which the people of England had known for many years,[1] Ridley, who was probably staying at Herne, rode to Hackington—a village just outside Canterbury on the road to Herne. There, during Rogation week, he preached a sermon in St. Stephen's Church which shows that Ridley, if he appreciated the political situation, had not been intimidated by it. He was later accused of saying in this sermon that there was no better way of describing the ceremonies of the Church than to call them beggarly ceremonies; it is much more likely that he said that Church ceremonies conducted and attended without faith, or that certain specific ceremonies in the existing services, were beggarly. He also dealt with the very delicate question of confession. He stated that he believed auricular confession to the priest was a beneficial practice, and urged all sinners to come to confession; but he added that he could find no authority in Scripture to support it.* A month later, Cromwell was arrested.

* See MS. 128, Corpus Christi College Cambridge. A very full summary of this document is published in *L. & P. Henry VIII*, vol.

The fall of Cromwell ushered in a most difficult and dangerous period for Ridley and his Protestant colleagues. It made the Duke of Norfolk and Gardiner the most powerful figures in the State—a fact which was emphasized by Henry's marriage to Katherine Howard a fortnight after Cromwell's execution. Norfolk and Gardiner represented a powerful section of the nobility and gentry and of the clergy. They were genuinely anti-Papist, but they were Catholic. They were prepared to arrest, torture and execute the supporters of the Papacy, and were still more ready to take their share in the loot of the suppressed monasteries; but they were resolved that the independent Church of England should be a Catholic Church, and that except for the repudiation of Papal supremacy, everything should continue the same as it had been for centuries. They were far stronger than their Protestant opponents; apart from the fact that they had far more support among the people of all classes, they also had the only thing that really mattered—the sympathy of Henry himself. The King had given his subjects a grim illustration of his future policy when he arranged for Barnes and two of his colleagues to be dragged to Smithfield, each with a Papist traitor alongside him on his hurdle, and for the three heretics to be burned alive a few yards from the spot where the three Papists were being hanged, drawn and quartered.

XVIII (ii), No. 546, pp. 291–378, sub. tit. *Cranmer and the Heretics in Kent*. Strype, *Cranmer*, pp. 143–68, contains a shorter and somewhat inaccurate summary. The MS. merely states that the sermon was preached in St. Stephen's Church, but it is obvious that it was at St. Stephen's Church in Hackington. Strype, *Cranmer*, p. 153, gives the date of the sermon correctly as 1540. Gloucester Ridley, pp. 153–4, gives no indication of the date, and therefore implies incorrectly that it was given during Rogation week in 1543. In 1540, Rogation Sunday was 2nd May.

The one hope for Cranmer and the reformers was that Henry had no intention of permitting Norfolk to attain an unchallengeable position in the State. He was not prepared to entrust a Howard with the power of a low-born minister like Wolsey or Cromwell, and he did not now need a strong adviser to overawe all opposition. Henry wished only for peace and order at home while he turned his attention to international affairs, and pursued a traditional foreign policy in which religious issues played no part. He therefore tried his best to check doctrinal controversy, while ensuring that the dominant Catholic faction of Norfolk and Gardiner did not become too powerful. He consequently refused to allow the Catholics to get rid of Cranmer and his Protestants; the Protestants might be needed when the occasion arose. In July 1540, they had been betting in London as to the date of Cranmer's arrest;[2] but the Archbishop remained free, though he withdrew into seclusion for several months. Some of the more notorious heretics who had been elevated by Cromwell had to go; Latimer and Shaxton had been compelled to resign their bishoprics when they opposed the Statute of the Six Articles. Latimer was arrested in trying to leave the country,[3] and he and Shaxton were confined in house arrest in the palaces of the Bishops of Chichester and Bath and Wells. But for the rest, the Protestants in the Church were left alone as long as they made no move to disrupt the religious settlement. They were quite prepared, in this difficult situation, to remain passively on the defensive, and to try to safeguard as much as possible of the gains which had been won under Cromwell. They were able to gain the support of the Seymours, for Hertford, alarmed at the influence of the Howards, drew close to Cranmer at Court.

For Ridley, these dangerous years did not at first bring

any personal set-back. On the contrary, the year 1540 brought him new offices and honours. In July he took his degree as Doctor of Divinity at Cambridge;* and in October he received an appointment which he was probably to value above all others that he was given throughout his life. The Fellows of his College elected him Master of Pembroke Hall.† It was twenty-two years since Ridley had gone to Pembroke Hall as an undergraduate; and now, when he was nearly forty, he became the head of the College where he had spent the greater part of his adult life. He would probably have wanted nothing better than to take up residence in the Master's lodgings; but he was now definitely committed to helping Cranmer in the struggle for a Protestant Reformation. Ridley was a useful man to his party; there was no one among them, not even Cranmer himself, who could compete with him in debating ability; and Ridley was not yet generally suspected of any marked Protestant leanings. He could be appointed to positions in the Church which were absolutely closed to notorious heretics like Latimer and Shaxton.

It was about this time that Ridley was appointed to be one of the royal chaplains.[4] His most prominent colleague was Thirlby, the Dean of the Chapel Royal, who had just been made Bishop of the new see of Westminster. Thirlby

---

* *Grace Book* Γ, pp. 348, 358, which gives the full entry, shows clearly that Nicholas Ridley was given his D.D. degree in 1539–40, and that Launcelot Ridley received the same degree in 1540–1. The lists in *Grace Book* B (Part II), pp. 224, 230, do not distinguish the two Ridleys, and the Index is wrong in showing that Nicholas received the degree in 1540–1.

† Gloucester Ridley, p. 142, gives the date as October 1540. Attwater, *Pembroke College Cambridge*, pp. 34–5, states that Ridley was elected Master at the death of Folberry, which he places in December 1540; but the entries in the College MSS. show that Ridley was already Master on 17th November 1540.

F

had attached himself to the Catholic party after the fall of Cromwell, but he remained on terms of the closest friendship with Cranmer, who had conferred many favours and benefits upon him. As Cranmer's friend Ridley could rely upon Thirlby's friendship, and had no reason to fear that Thirlby would be over eager to discover any of his heretical tendencies.

In 1541, the Cathedral Church of Canterbury was re-organised, and it was decided to appoint twelve prebendaries and six preachers to the Cathedral. The appointments were made by Cranmer, but the King had no intention of allowing him to fill all these offices with his own supporters. He probably made it clear to Cranmer that he would not tolerate any heretic canons, but he ordered him to see to it that the advanced and conservative elements in the Church were evenly represented among the preachers.[5] In view of the King's directive, Cranmer proceeded very cautiously; of the twelve prebendaries, eleven were orthodox Catholics, and only one had any leanings towards Protestantism. This was Ridley, who in April 1541 was appointed to the fifth stall.* With regard to the preachers, however, Cranmer did not hesitate to ensure that three of the six were reformers. He appointed Scory, Drum and Ridley's cousin Launcelot. The other three preachers were Catholics.

It is clear that Ridley spent a considerable amount of time in Canterbury during the next five years—or at least in the earlier part of this period. He found the atmosphere exceedingly unpleasant. The Catholic and Protestant canons and preachers were perpetually at loggerheads. This was no doubt what Henry had intended, as they were both very ready to denounce any Papistical or heretical devia-

* The letters patent were dated 22nd March 1540/1, and delivered on 8th April 1541 (*L. & P. Henry VIII*, vol. XVI, No. 779 (5)).

tions in the others, as well as similar delinquencies by Protestant and Papist vicars in the diocese. Ridley made a few friends in Canterbury, but these friendships were quite insufficient to compensate for the suspicion and fear in the Cathedral,[6] as the canons and preachers eyed each other under the shadow of the Act of Supremacy and the Statute of the Six Articles. Nor was the ill-feeling confined to doctrinal matters. Ridley became involved in a dispute with Wooton, the Dean, over the boundaries of his living accommodation and of the garden allotted to him as Canon; the quarrel was eventually settled by Cranmer, apparently in Ridley's favour, in December 1546.*

The Protestants were naturally as careful to avoid transgressing against the Statute of the Six Articles as were the Catholics to stress their loyalty to the King and their abhorrence of the Bishop of Rome. But the reformers were prepared to suggest that certain reforms should be introduced in the services of the Church in matters which the statute did not touch, and were eager to denounce their opponents for reluctance to carry out the decrees against Popish superstition which had been promulgated in Cromwell's day, and were still in force. They were prepared to criticise prayers for the intercession of the Saints, and particularly the worship of images; and they also urged that Church services should be held in English and not in Latin. The Catholics disapproved of services in English as strongly as they did of the reading of the Bible, which they

* Strype, *Cranmer*, pp. 197–8, refers to the dispute and the settlement of it by Cranmer, and publishes Cranmer's letter to the Vice-Dean and Prebendaries of 12th December 1546; but this does not give the name of the Prebendaries involved. Hasted, *History of Kent*, vol. XI, pp. 497–500, cites from another document and shows that one of the points in dispute was the boundary of the garden between Dean Wooton's quarters and Ridley's.

soon afterwards succeeded in prohibiting by statute in the
case of the lower orders;[7] but the Protestants believed that
services should be conducted in a language which all the
congregation could understand. Scory and Launcelot
Ridley declared that if the services were conducted in a
foreign language, they became nothing better than babbling.*

At the end of September 1541, Gardiner returned home
after his secret negotiations with the Pope at the Diet of
Ratisbon. On his way from Dover to London he stayed at
Canterbury. During his stay, he was approached by William
Gardiner, one of the Catholic Prebendaries, who was not
related to the Bishop of Winchester, and had never met him
before.[8] William Gardiner complained to the Bishop of the
conduct of Scory and Launcelot Ridley, reporting what
they had said about the service in Latin being babbling; he
also said that the Protestants were continually criticising
him and his colleagues, and distorting what they had said in
their sermons. Bishop Gardiner, with his strong sense of
propriety and discipline, told the canon that he was sure that
if Cranmer knew about this he would take action to prevent
it; but he advised him in the meanwhile to write out his
sermons in full, and to hand a copy to those members of the
congregation who could read, so that they could bear witness to the fact that he had not deviated from the script in
his sermon.[9]

It so happened that during Gardiner's stay in Canterbury, Nicholas Ridley had been selected to preach the
sermon at matins. The Bishop of Winchester naturally
attended the service, and was distressed to find that the
congregation was very small, as scarcely a hundred of the
citizens of Canterbury had troubled to attend. Ridley dealt

* *L. & P. Henry VIII*, vol. XVIII (ii), No. 546, p. 339.

with gluttony in his sermon. About this time, new regulations were promulgated by Cranmer prescribing how much the various ranks in the ecclesiastical hierarchy were permitted to eat for dinner. The Archbishops were limited to six, and Bishops to five, different dishes of meat—or fish on fish days—and respectively to four and three different courses of pudding, cheese and fruit; the number of different dishes was lower for archdeacons, deans and other priests. Bishops were not permitted to have more than two partridges, or four blackbirds, in a pie.[10] In his sermon, Ridley urged the bishops to suppress the tendencies to gluttony amongst the clergy; but Bishop Gardiner considered Ridley's sermon to be a most inappropriate one to deliver to a congregation composed largely of the ordinary laity of Canterbury, and was thankful that the congregation was not larger. He doubtless considered the sermon to be by implication subversive. After the service, Gardiner had a private talk with Ridley and criticised his sermon.* Gardiner doubtless behaved in a civil manner to a fellow Master of a Cambridge College, but nevertheless made it perfectly clear that he was displeased with the sermon. As for Ridley, he was probably tactful, respectful and evasive.

The disputes at Canterbury were more bitter than ever during the winter. The Catholic Canons acted as Gardiner

* Gardiner's letter to Cranmer, July 1547 (*Letters of Stephen Gardiner*, p. 356). We know that Gardiner was in Canterbury at the end of September 1541, in October 1545, and at Ascension 1546. This sermon of Ridley's was not preached at Ascension 1546 (see Gardiner's letter, *op. cit.*, p. 356) and it seems more likely that it was preached on the occasion of the 1541 visit rather than in 1545, because the order regulating the fare was issued during the year 1541 (old style). This is probably the sermon by Ridley on the occasion of Gardiner's 1541 visit referred to in *Cranmer and the Heretics in Kent* (*L. & P. Henry VIII*, vol. XVIII (ii), No. 546, pp. 339, 368), which makes it clear that the sermon was preached by Nicholas, not Launcelot, Ridley.

had advised, and denounced Scory and Launcelot Ridley
to Cranmer whenever he came to Canterbury.* Cranmer
naturally took no action against the Protestant Preachers; indeed, next year he took steps against the Catholics at Canterbury. By this time, Cranmer's position had
been somewhat strengthened by his exposure of Katherine
Howard, and while Norfolk retained his position and influence at Court by the zeal with which he prosecuted the
inquiries against his adulterous niece—denouncing his
stepmother to the King into the bargain—the fortunes of
the Protestants had risen a little from the nadir which they
had reached in the summer of 1540. On Trinity Sunday
1542, Cranmer called a meeting of the Prebendaries and
Preachers of Canterbury, and took a firm attitude with the
Catholics.[11] His commissary Nevinson now proceeded to
suppress several images in the diocese, and when Serles, one
of the Catholic preachers, objected to this policy, the Archbishop had him arrested, and confined for a short time in
prison.[12] The Catholics then consulted with their friends in
London, and decided to strike at the Archbishop.

In Passion Week 1543, Serles rode through the bitter
cold[13] to London to consult with Dr. London, a zealous
persecutor of heretics, on the drafting of an accusation of
heresy against Cranmer. The Catholics at Canterbury were
now in touch with the Bishop of Winchester himself.
Gardiner, with his great political experience and ability,
realised the need to proceed with the utmost caution. He
had apparently warned London and Serles in the first place,
of the risks involved in a direct attack on Cranmer; once
they had initiated the proceedings themselves, he gave them
all possible assistance, instructing his secretary German
Gardiner to improve the form of their articles against the

* *L. & P. Henry VIII*, vol. XVIII (ii), No. 546, p. 304.

Archbishop, while taking care not to make any open move himself in the affair. He seems to have warned London and Serles that the case against Cranmer and his chaplains was weak, and it was apparently because of this that the proceedings were not prosecuted more promptly.[14] By the summer of 1543, however, they were ready to proceed and presented the articles against Cranmer to the King on his barge in the Thames.

The King, however, had no intention of allowing Gardiner and his faction to destroy Cranmer and his party. As soon as he received the articles, he summoned Cranmer to his presence, showed him the articles, and, after turning the whole matter into a joke, assured him of his continued support. He granted a commission to the Archbishop to inquire into the charges against himself, and to investigate the whole affair along with other commissioners.[15] At the end of August, Cranmer went to his diocese, and began an exhaustive inquiry. But the Catholics of Canterbury were not prepared to accept defeat. While Cranmer was energetically collecting the evidence of seditious utterances by the Catholic prebendaries and preachers, they themselves indicted two of his chaplains—Turner and Bland—at the Sessions of the Six Articles on 27th September; and Cranmer was obliged to order the arrest of Scory, who was accused of spreading heretical views about the Sacrament of the Altar.[16] The Catholics also complained to Cranmer of all the Protestants in the diocese against whom they could find anything to say. Nicholas Ridley was denounced along with all the others; but he had obviously been far more cautious than Scory and his cousin Launcelot. The only accusation which could be brought against Ridley related to his sermon on confession and his references to the 'beggarly ceremonies' of the Church at Hackington

more than three years earlier—before the fall of Cromwell—
and to his action in ordering the *Te Deum* to be sung in
English in Herne. These charges could not be lightly regarded by Ridley, for one of the charges against Bland in
the indictment at the sessions accused him of having said
almost exactly the same things about confession that Ridley
had said at Hackington; but Ridley was not prosecuted
along with Bland and Turner.* The sermon at Hackington could not be the basis of criminal proceedings against
Ridley himself, for even if his statement that confession,
though beneficial, had no authority in Scripture could
be construed as denying that it was 'expedient and necessary to be retained and continued, used and frequented',
the Statute of Pardons of 1540 had barred all proceedings in respect of offences committed before 1st July 1540;
for while denial of the truth of transubstantiation had
been excepted from the pardon, all other offences against
the Statute of the Six Articles, and all other kinds of heresy,
were included in it.[17] The singing of the *Te Deum* at Herne
while irregular, could hardly be said to constitute heresy,
while it was certainly not an offence against the Statute of
the Six Articles.

The Protestant Prebendaries and Preachers now had the
opportunity to make their own accusations against the
Catholics in Canterbury and throughout the diocese, and
were not slow to do so. Ridley himself was a party to only
one of these denunciations: he reported that Shether, one of
the Catholic Preachers, had said in a sermon that for a long

* *L. & P. Henry VIII*, vol. XVIII (ii), pp. 320–1, where it is stated that
Bland and Turner and others were prosecuted. There is no suggestion
that Nicholas Ridley was one of those indicted. Bland was charged
before the justices with saying similar things about confession to what
Ridley had said, but presumably after 1st July 1540 (see *op. cit.*, p. 320).
Nicholas Ridley was denounced to Cranmer on 22nd September 1543.

time men had kept to the right road in religion, but had recently strayed from the road, and must now return to join the road at the point where they had left it, as there was no short cut which they could take. Ridley pointed out that this statement showed that Shether supported Popery, and that he had made no mention in his sermon of the splendid religious innovations introduced by the King.[18] Cranmer and his fellow commissioners had finished their inquiries by December. They ordered the arrest of several of the Catholic prebendaries and preachers, and took no action at all against Ridley and his colleagues; Scory was released from prison, and the prosecution against Turner and Bland was eventually abandoned after the King had intervened to stop it.[19] But Henry would no more permit Cranmer to destroy the Catholics than he would allow Gardiner to get rid of the Protestants. The Catholics were released after a few months, and were able to extricate themselves from the affair by writing a full confession and retraction to Cranmer. As for the Bishop of Winchester, he was in no way involved, and was as correct as ever to Cranmer in the Council chamber. Dr. London, however, had not learned his lesson. Soon afterwards, he denounced Sir Philip Hobby, with whom the King was friendly, as a heretic, and was sentenced to the pillory and to prison for perjury.

This signal demonstration of the royal favour to Cranmer and Ridley and the Preachers was quite sufficient to put an end to the disputes in Canterbury Cathedral. The next conspiracy against Cranmer was carried on at a higher level, and Ridley was in no way involved in it. In Canterbury, the Catholics had been effectively frightened, while the Protestants were wise enough to realise that if they took as many risks in future as they had done in the past, they might find the King in a less favourable mood. But the relationships in Canterbury Cathedral can hardly have been pleasant, and Ridley must have been very pleased whenever he could get away from Canterbury. He was certainly much happier in Cambridge; but there is no reason to believe that he was often in Cambridge during these years. He went to Cambridge in November 1540, immediately after he had been elected Master of Pembroke Hall, and was probably there again in April 1541. It is likely that he was in residence at Pembroke Hall for a more prolonged period at the beginning of 1542. He was in Cambridge on 2nd January,* and during the academic year which began at Michaelmas 1541 he was appointed by the University, together with the Vice-Chancellor Standish, and Dr. Edmunds, to draft and seal letters to be sent to Gardiner, who had succeeded Cromwell as Chancellor of the University. They were not to send the letters, however, until they had been read out to the Senate.[20] This suggests that Ridley stayed in Cambridge for several months at the beginning of 1542. There is no record of any further visit by Ridley to Cambridge in the next five years, but he probably went there from time to time.

If Ridley was in Cambridge during the late winter of 1541–2, he must have been there during the height of the controversy over the pronunciation of Greek. In any case, Ridley, as an eminent Hellenist, must certainly have interested himself in the matter; but we have no record whatever of his views on the question. We would certainly suppose that he agreed with Thomas Smith and Cheke, who was a friend of Ridley, in pronouncing Greek in the new way which Erasmus had suggested was that used by the ancient

* MSS., Pembroke College, Cambridge, show that Ridley was engaged in transactions which indicate that he was in Cambridge on 17th November 1540, on 13th April 1541, and on 2nd January 1541/2.

Greeks, and in challenging the recognised pronunciation of Reuchlin, by which Greek was pronounced like Latin and Italian. The Chancellor, Gardiner, was not prepared to tolerate innovation even in the realm of pronunciation, and in June 1542 he put an end to the dispute by ordering that the Reuchlinian pronunciation was to be used, and that any undergraduate who used the Erasmian was to be birched.[21] Ridley was probably as incensed as Smith and Cheke at Gardiner's order, and as much opposed on this academic issue as on all others to the Bishop of Winchester.

There is no period of Ridley's adult life of which we know so little as of the three years which followed the defeat of the Catholic conspiracies in Canterbury in the autumn of 1543. There is some indication, however, that he may have spent a considerable part of the time in London and at the Court, carrying out his duties as a royal chaplain. His experiences in 1543 may have convinced him that he could more profitably spend his time, not in quarrels at Canterbury Cathedral, but in winning favourable notice from the King. Unfortunately, we know nothing of his personal relationship with Henry VIII, but it is clear that he must often have officiated at the royal Mass, and have given absolution to Henry after confession. There is no reason to doubt that Ridley treated Henry with the obsequiousness which the King demanded, and was at pains to avoid raising any doubts in Henry's mind as to the orthodoxy of his own opinions. He could hardly have survived had he done otherwise.

In 1543, Ridley preached the sermon at the marriage of Sir Anthony Browne to Elizabeth Fitzgerald at Hampton Court. The wedding was a great occasion. Sir Anthony Browne, who was just on sixty, was high in favour with the King. He was an ardent Catholic, and a supporter of Norfolk and Gardiner, though he had not scrupled to profit largely from the dissolution of the monasteries. The bride was a girl of fifteen. She was the daughter of Lord Kildare, who had died in confinement under suspicion of treason in 1534, and her brother had been executed as a traitor a few years later for leading the Papist revolt in Ireland; but Elizabeth had been brought up at Court, and was a lady-in-waiting to the Lady Mary. She had attracted the attention of Lord Surrey, the wild and gallant son of the Duke of Norfolk, and was his 'fair Geraldine.'[22] The King himself was present at the wedding, as was the Lady Mary and the whole of the Court. There is no record as to whether Ridley performed the marriage ceremony, but his sermon at the wedding was much praised on all sides.[23] Presumably he dealt with the duties of matrimony in his sermon, and took good care to say nothing which could by any stretch of the imagination be condemned as heretical.

There is, indeed, some reason to believe that Ridley was particularly eager at this time to live down the reputation which he had acquired of being a heretic. He was now in no danger of being called to account again for his sermon at Hackington in 1540, or for any other indiscretion which he had committed at Canterbury; it was perfectly clear that he was safe provided that he behaved himself in future. This was certainly not the time to take the slightest risk. Ridley seems to have succeeded in establishing himself in Henry's favour, and in acquiring the reputation of being a respectable, if not strictly orthodox, priest; and he certainly impressed his associates with his great ability and learning. In December 1544, Cox wrote to Paget that the quality of the King's chaplains was of a high order, and that Ridley was the most worthy of them all.[24] Cox's letter is some indication that Ridley had spent a considerable amount of time at Court in the latter half of 1544.

In January 1545, Ridley offered himself as a candidate for the office of Vice-Chancellor of Cambridge University. Thomas Smith was vacating the office, and his successor was to be elected on 25th January. Ridley was opposed by three other candidates—Atkinson, Standish and Matthew Parker, the new Master of Corpus Christi College. Ridley's friends engaged in a considerable amount of canvassing on his behalf in Cambridge before the election, though they could not equal the efforts of the supporters of Dr. Atkinson. Parker was elected by a large majority; he received seventy-nine votes against eight for Standish, six for Atkinson and five for Ridley, who received the lowest number.[25] The Chancellor of the University must have been very pleased that Ridley had not been elected as his Vice-Chancellor; Gardiner did not as yet have much reason to suppose that Parker would become another heretical archbishop.

Ridley probably paid fairly frequent visits to his parish of Herne. It was only eight miles from Canterbury, and Ridley could easily go there when he was in residence at Canterbury to escape from the hateful atmosphere of the Cathedral. We do not know whether the *Te Deum* was still being sung in English in Herne; it is not unlikely that Ridley had discontinued the practice as early as 1540, already before he had been accused of this offence by the Canterbury Prebendaries. He had his enemies in Herne as well as at Canterbury, for several of his parishioners had been prepared to subscribe the articles against him which the Catholics in Canterbury had presented to Cranmer.[26] Herne was not remote enough to make it safe to forget the Statute of the Six Articles; it was well within the range of the whip with six strings. By 1545, however, Ridley was able to hold cer-

tain prayers in English for the success of the war against
France, which Henry himself had specially ordered at a
time when throughout the country—and especially at
Herne—men were hourly expecting a French invasion.[27]

It was probably in Herne in 1545 that Ridley reached the
decision which was to dominate the rest of his life, to make
him a famous figure in the Church and in English history,
and to lead him to a martyr's death. We cannot know for
certain when Ridley changed his mind on the question of
transubstantiation; in the circumstances, he naturally took
the greatest care to make it impossible for anyone to know.
He did not make a public declaration against transubstantiation until December 1548; as late as November or
December 1547, he was preaching sermons which conveyed
the impression to all who heard him that he believed in the
corporal Presence in the Sacrament. This is no reason whatever to believe that he in fact held the opinions which he
was expressing in public. As long as Henry lived, he would
have been burned for questioning the truth of transubstantiation; and in the first two years of Edward's reign, he had
sound tactical reasons for not doing so. We have, moreover,
the statements of both Cranmer and Ridley which make it
almost certain that he had come to believe that the Presence
was spiritual, and not carnal, as early as 1546, in Herne.

At his trial in Oxford in September 1555, Cranmer told
his judges that he had become converted to a belief in the
spiritual Presence as a result of hearing Ridley's arguments
after he had assisted at the trial of Lambert in 1538 and
before he published the Catechism of 1548; and there is
good reason for believing that it was in 1546.[28] This is also
confirmed by Ridley's statement, in his *Last Farewell*, that he
was a debtor to Herne for the doctrine of the Lord's Supper,
which can probably be interpreted as meaning that he be-

came converted to this doctrine in Herne.* Ridley certainly did not stay any appreciable length of time in Herne after the end of 1546; indeed, it is unlikely that he ever visited his parish after the death of Henry VIII. It should also be noted that Ridley, while ready to admit that he had once believed in transubstantiation, always denied most strongly that he still believed in it at the time of his sermon at Paul's Cross in November or December 1547. It is therefore clear that Ridley had already repudiated transubstantiation by the end of 1546.

But if Ridley had abandoned his belief in the corporal Presence before 1547, there remains the possibility that he first did so, not in 1546, but at a very much earlier date. His statement that he had been converted at Herne is perfectly compatible with it having occurred in 1538 or 1539, when Lady Fyneux was alive and Ridley was certainly often in Herne; even if—which is by no means certain—Ridley did not discuss the matter with Cranmer until 1546, it is nevertheless possible that he himself had been converted several years before he ventured to impart his heretical opinions to Cranmer. On the whole, however, this is unlikely. Ridley had no incentive whatever to adhere to the tiny sects who were the chief target for persecution under Henry VIII; and he was no more susceptible now than he had been twenty years before, at Cambridge, to the simple appeal of the extremists. Ridley could only be converted by irrefutable doctrinal arguments. It was probably only after the renewal of the controversy between the Lutherans and

* 'And yet I must knowledge me to be thy debtor for the doctrine of the Lord's Supper, which at that time, I acknowledge, God had not revealed unto me.' (Ridley, *Last Farewell*, Foxe, vol. VII, p. 558, *Works*, p. 407). But these words may merely mean that Ridley was in debt to Herne on account of his failure to teach the doctrine of the Lord's Supper when he was Vicar there.

Zwinglians in 1544 that Ridley turned to consider the
question at issue between them,* and thus came to study
the treatise of Bertram of Corbie, which we know first
caused him to doubt the truth of transubstantiation.[29]

Bertram's treatise on the Sacrament had been published
by Vadianus at Cologne in 1532. Bertram had written the
treatise for the Emperor Charles the Bald in about 840,
though the Papists and Catholics denounced the document
as a forgery by Œcolampadius. Bertram had expressed the
view that the change in the consecrated bread was a change,
not in deed, but in figure; he believed in the Mysterious
and Figurative Body and Blood in the Sacrament, which
still remained bread and wine in substance.[30] This treatise
somehow came into Ridley's hands—probably in 1545. It
would be interesting to know how Ridley obtained possession of it. It was, of course, prohibited in England, and there
is no record that Ridley had any connexions with foreign
Protestants at this time. It is very likely that he obtained
a copy of the treatise from Cranmer, who some years before
had been in correspondence with Vadianus as well as with
the German Lutherans. However that may be, it is certain
that Ridley read it. The importance of Bertram's work was
not so much for the views which he expounded in it, as the
fact that he had been able to write the treatise for the Emperor in the ninth century and had not been excommunicated. This was a clear indication that his doctrines were not
regarded as heretical at that time, and consequently that it

* Gloucester Ridley, p. 162, states definitely that Ridley spent
most of the year 1545 in Herne, studying Bertram and the early
Fathers, and there became converted to the doctrine of the Lord's
Supper; but he does not cite any authority for his statement. See
Gloucester Ridley, pp. 163–75, for an examination of the attitude of
the Catholics and Lutherans to Bertram's book, and for the circumstances in which he considers that Ridley studied it.

was at best highly doubtful whether transubstantiation had been a fundamental doctrine of the Church in the time of the early Fathers. After reading Bertram, Ridley decided that he must make a far more exhaustive examination of the works of the early Fathers on the matter than he had done hitherto.[31] As a result of this further study, and above all of an examination of Scripture, he came to the heretical conclusion that there was no change in the substance of the consecrated bread and wine, and that the flesh and blood of Christ were not corporally present in the Sacrament of the Altar. This was an opinion which led straight to the fire.

In 1554, while he was awaiting death in his Oxford prison, Ridley wrote a pamphlet in which he explained, in simple language, the views which he held on the question of the Sacrament. There is little doubt that he had already formed these opinions nine years before in Herne. He strongly repudiated the ideas of the Messalians or Euchites that the Sacrament could do neither good nor harm, and those of the Anabaptists who alleged that there was no difference between the bread and wine of the Lord's table and that of any other table. He similarly condemned the view that the consecrated bread and wine were merely a bare sign or figure of Christ. He believed that Christ's body was present in the bread and wine by grace; but he denied that it was present in the natural substance of Christ's human and assumed nature. The natural substance of Christ's body and blood, being united in the divine nature of the Second Person of the Trinity, had not only life in itself, but was able to give life to the partakers in the Sacrament; consequently, while the natural body remained in Heaven, it was in the Sacrament by grace, just as the sun, while never moving from its place in the heavens, was present by its beams, light and influence on earth.[32] His opposition to the Figurists

G

was not of the slightest importance from the point of view of the Statute of the Six Articles. Ridley no longer believed that the natural body and blood of our Saviour Jesus Christ, conceived of the Virgin Mary, was present really, under the form of bread and wine, in the Sacrament of the Altar, and that no substance of bread and wine remained. He was therefore guilty of the supreme heresy.

Ridley's *Treatise on the Lord's Supper*, while it was intended to serve as an explanation of his doctrines for the simple layman, is an interesting example of the way in which he formulated his ideas on the matters in issue. There were five questions to be answered: firstly, does a transubstantiation take place in the Sacrament of the Altar; secondly, is the body and blood of Christ carnally present in the bread and wine; thirdly, ought adoration, which should only be given to God, to be given to the consecrated Host; fourthly, is the Mass a sacrifice of the flesh and blood offered up to the Heavenly Father; and fifthly, does a sinner—an unrepentant murderer or adulterer—receive the body and blood of Christ when the Sacrament is administered to him? The answer to all the other questions, he thought, depended on the answer to the second question. If the body and blood were present in substance, there must have been a transubstantiation in the bread and wine; but if they were not carnally present at all, then the original substance of the bread and wine remained unaltered; then it followed that the bread and wine ought not to be adored, and that the elevation of the Host was idolatrous; that the priest did not make any oblation or sacrifice, and that the Mass was only a commemoration of the Lord's Supper; and that the sinner who received the Sacrament did not receive the flesh and blood, whereas if the flesh and blood were present in substance, then everyone who received the Sacrament, however great a sinner he might be, must necessarily receive the body and blood of Christ.[33]

In support of his opinions against transubstantiation, Ridley relied primarily on the passages in the Gospels themselves describing the Last Supper. Two passages from his later treatise on the Lord's Supper well illustrate his method of reasoning:

First, let us repeat the beginning of the institution of the Lord's Supper, wherein all the three Evangelists and St. Paul almost in words do agree, saying, that 'Jesus took bread, gave thanks, brake, and gave it to the disciples saying, Take, eat, this is my body'. Here it appeareth plainly, that Christ calleth very bread his body. For that which he took was very bread. In this all men do agree. And that which he took, after he had given thanks, he brake; and that which he took and brake, he gave to his disciples; and that which he took, brake, and gave to his disciples, he said himself of it: 'This is my body'. So it appeareth plainly that Christ called very bread his body. But very bread cannot be his body in very substance thereof. Therefore it must needs have another meaning. Which meaning appeareth plainly, what it is, by the next sentence that followeth immediately, both in Luke and in Paul. And that is this: 'Do this in remembrance of me'. Whereupon it seemeth unto me to be evident, that Christ did take bread, and called it his body, for that he would thereby institute a perpetual remembrance of his body, specially of that singular benefit of our redemption, which he would then procure and purchase unto us by his body upon the cross. But bread, retaining still his own very natural substance, may be thus by grace, and in a sacramental signification, his body: whereas else the very bread, which he took, brake, and gave them, could not be in any wise his natural body. For that were confusion of substances; and therefore the very words of Christ, joined with the next sentence following, both enforceth us to confess the very bread to remain still, and also openeth unto us how that bread may be and is thus by his divine power, his body which was given for us.[34]

He used a similar argument in connexion with the wine:

And this shall be my third argument, grounded upon Christ's own words. The natural substance of the sacramental wine remaineth still, and is the material substance of the sacrament of the blood of Christ: therefore it is likewise so in the sacramental bread.

I know that he that is of a contrary opinion, will deny the former part of mine argument: but I will prove it thus, by the plain words of Christ himself, both in Matthew and in Mark. Christ's words are these, after the words said upon the cup: 'I say unto you (saith Christ), I will not drink henceforth of this fruit of the vine tree, until I shall drink that new in my Father's kingdom'. Here note how Christ calleth plainly his cup the fruit of the vine tree. But the fruit of the vine tree is very natural wine. Wherefore the natural substance of the wine doth remain still in the sacrament of Christ's blood.[35]

It was probably some time in 1546 that Ridley discussed the question of transubstantiation with Cranmer, and told him of the opinions which he had formed. It says much for the friendship and trust between the two men that Ridley was prepared to tell the Archbishop of Canterbury that he was a heretic. He knew how Cranmer had played his part in condemning as heretics those sectaries who had publicly expressed the same opinions that Ridley was now expounding to him in private; but perhaps Cranmer had already given Ridley hints that even on this fundamental point he was beginning to doubt the orthodox doctrines himself. Ridley's conversion to the doctrine of the spiritual Presence is conclusive proof of his courage and sincerity. He had been an orthodox Papist at Cambridge in the 'twenties when Bilney and Barnes were suffering for their opinions; he had changed his views on Papal supremacy at a time when everyone else was doing the same, and had conformed to Henry's will when Fisher and More were dying for their old beliefs. But this change, in Ridley's case, as in the case of many others, had been an honest change of mind under the pressure of public opinion rather than a cynical desire for self-advancement; and now he was prepared, with no hope of material gain, to adopt a belief which led to nowhere except the stake.

There was no need for Cranmer to impress upon Ridley the importance of keeping his new ideas a close secret. It would have been fatal, not only to Ridley but to the whole future of the Reformation, if the criminal views of the Primate and the royal chaplain had become known to Gardiner and his supporters. Ridley obviously took good care not to give the slightest indication that he had weakened in his orthodoxy on the Sacrament of the Altar, and he remained in favour at Court carrying out his duties as a royal chaplain. It has been said that in January 1547, Ridley preached a sermon at .Paul's Cross in which he announced the King's decision to grant the old church of the Greyfriars in London to be used as a school by the poor orphans of Christ's Hospital; but it is unlikely that Ridley preached this sermon, as there is every reason to believe that it was preached by Holbeach, the Bishop of Rochester.*

In October 1545, Ridley was given another preferment; he

---

* Wriothesley's *Chronicle*, vol. I, p. 177, gives the date as 30th January 1546/7; this was two days after Henry VIII died. Stow gives the date as 3rd January 1546/7 in his *Annals* (p. 1034), and as 13th January 1546/7 in his *Survey* (vol. II, p. 24). Holinshed, vol. III, p. 861, follows Stow's *Survey*. All these authorities state that the sermon was preached by the Bishop of Rochester, giving no name; and Holbeach was Bishop of Rochester until August 1547. The statement that the sermon was preached by 'Bishop Ridley of Rochester' only appears in the works of historians of a later date. The deed of grant in respect of the church had been executed by Henry on 27th December 1546. (Trollope, *History of Christ's Hospital*, *App.*, pp. xiii–xxix.)

was made the Eighth Prebendary in the Cathedral Church at Westminster.* The old abbey had been converted into a cathedral in 1540, when the see of Westminster was carved out of the diocese of London with Thirlby as its first bishop. We have no knowledge of any activities in which Ridley engaged in virtue of his position here. In his *Last Farewell*, he seems to imply that his experiences as a Canon of Westminster were as disagreeable as those which he had undergone as a Prebendary of Canterbury;† but it is difficult to believe that this was really the case, for there is no record of any attempt being made to denounce Ridley as a heretic for any of his sermons in Westminster.

Yet if Ridley was referring, not to his experiences as a Canon of Westminster, but to the conditions in general which applied in the first few months after his presentation to the stall, it is easy to believe that he felt as unhappy as he had done four years before in Canterbury. In the spring of 1546, the Catholics, under the Lord Chancellor, Wriothesley, launched a new campaign against heretics. Latimer and Shaxton, who had been released from confinement some years before, were now once more arrested. Latimer, who was nearly sixty and had been crippled in an accident, was sent to the Tower.[36] The authorities also arrested a heretic whose case attracted unusual attention, and who became a famous martyr of the Protestant cause. Ann Askew was a gentlewoman of Lincolnshire; she had said that it was better to read five lines of the Bible than to

* The appointment was made under the privy seal at Windsor on 29th October 1545. The grant is dated 31st October, and was delivered on 13th November (*L. & P. Henry VIII*, vol. XX (ii), Nos. 706 (91), 910 (35)).

† 'To Westminster other advertisement in God I have not now to say than I have said before to the Cathedral Church of Canterbury.' —Ridley, *Works*, p. 408.

attend five Masses, and had denounced all private Masses; but the main charge against her was a denial of transubstantiation. Ann's account of her examination and torture, which she wrote in Newgate and smuggled out of prison, aroused much sympathy for her and her cause; the Lieutenant of the Tower had refused to put her back on the rack after prolonged torture, and Wriothesley and Rich had thereupon racked her with their own hands.[37] Wriothesley had his reasons for enforcing the torture; he wanted a confession from Ann Askew incriminating Shaxton and Latimer, and eminent ladies at the Court, for his campaign was in fact directed against Queen Katherine Parr herself. In these circumstances, Ridley was careful to make no false move; and far from being charged with heresy, he was himself appointed to take part in the examination of a suspected heretic.

The culprit concerned was Dr. Crome. He was an eminent and learned doctor, whom Cranmer had unsuccessfully recommended for the position of Dean of Canterbury in 1541. He had got into trouble in 1539 for attacking private Masses, and had saved himself by a recantation; but he now ventured to express his true opinions once more. He preached a sermon in which he stated that Christ's sacrifice on the Cross was sufficient for the redemption of mankind, and that he was not sacrificed again in the Sacrament of the Altar. Crome was promptly brought before the Council on a charge of heresy; but he was close to Cranmer, and in favour with the King himself, and was leniently dealt with. He was ordered to preach a sermon at Paul's Cross, in which he was to retract the statements which he had made in his previous sermon. Crome preached at Paul's Cross, and read out the statement which he had been required to read, and then ended his sermon without further

comment.[38] This submission was deemed to be quite insufficient. Crome had been expected to expatiate on the
mercy of the King in forgiving him for his sin, to endorse
the statement which he had read out with fulsome praise
of Henry, and to grovel in his recantation. The Council
decided to inquire into his conduct, and invited two bishops
and five other prominent churchmen to assist in his examination before the Council. Ridley was selected as one of
them, along with Bonner and Heath, who had succeeded
Latimer as Bishop of Worcester, May and Cox, Redmayne,
the Master of Trinity College Cambridge, and Robinson.

Ridley and his colleagues attended a meeting of the Council at Greenwich on 10th May.[39] Ridley rebuked Crome for
the inadequacy of his recantation at Paul's Cross, though the
leading part in the examination was played by Cox, who
elicited the information from Crome that he had been a
friend of Lassels, who four years before had discovered the
adultery of Katherine Howard, and was now in prison as a
confederate of Ann Askew. The Council ordered Crome to
make a better recantation, and he preached a sermon at
Paul's Cross in which he stated that he sincerely repented
of having uttered heretical opinions, and that he was not
recanting under pressure or duress.[40] Ridley can hardly have
relished his share in the proceedings, but it had at least
enabled him to prove his orthodoxy. Two months later, the
same opportunity was given in a far more dramatic fashion
to a much more notorious heretic. Shaxton recanted his
heresies under repeated examinations, and was selected to
preach the sermon against heresy when Ann Askew and
Lassels and two other heretics were burned at Smithfield.

It was in July 1546 that Ann Askew and her colleagues
were burned. What happened in the course of the next six
months has never been clearly understood; but for some

reason Henry decided on a strong turn of policy against the Catholics. We have no means of knowing the reasons which led Henry to adopt this sudden change in his attitude. Perhaps he was influenced by considerations of foreign policy; perhaps he was annoyed at the Catholic machinations against Katherine Parr; perhaps he began to believe the rumours which the Protestants spread that the Catholic faction was too close to the Papists. Perhaps he was annoyed at the continual attacks by the Catholics on Cranmer and the Protestants in the Church; the Catholics had been on the offensive in recent years, and had been much more responsible than the Protestants for the never-ending controversies which endangered the unity of Church and State. Perhaps he was annoyed that Gardiner had not agreed to an exchange of lands with him.[41] The most likely explanation, however, is simply that Henry thought that the Catholic faction had become too powerful, and that, with the instinct of a tyrant, he looked around for the most powerful potentate in order to strike him down. After Buckingham, Wolsey and Cromwell, it was at last the turn of the Duke of Norfolk.

The Howards were arrested on 12th December. Surrey's action in displaying, in the privacy of his own house, a shield on which the arms of Edward the Confessor were quartered with the Howard coat was a sufficient excuse to charge him with high treason, and as Norfolk failed to denounce his son, he was to die for the only decent action in his life. A fortnight later, on St. Stephen's Day, Henry made his will, and devised the Crown to Edward, under the statutory powers which had been given to him. Of all the members of his Council, only Gardiner and Thirlby were excluded from the number of the Executors whom Henry appointed to act as regents for his son during his infancy.

With Norfolk in prison awaiting death, and Gardiner in disgrace, Wriothesley was the only prominent Catholic leader who remained in Henry's favour, and the influence of Hertford and Cranmer was for the time being preponderant at Court; and it is probable that Henry intended to accompany his new policy with Protestant innovations in religion. It is therefore very likely true that Henry had decided during the winter of 1546–7 to appoint Ridley to be the next Bishop.[42] He would certainly have intended to select one of Cranmer's Protestant nominees to fill any vacancy on the episcopal Bench, and Ridley was much the most likely person to be chosen by the Archbishop. As Bishop Longland of Lincoln was old, the project of translating Holbeach from Rochester to Lincoln and appointing Ridley as Bishop of Rochester may well have been contemplated by Henry before he died. Ridley now knew that the seven years of danger were over, and that he could at last move on to the high preferments in the Church to which his learning and abilities entitled him. But the death of the King was to open up a far more splendid prospect.

NOTES

[1] *London Chronicle*, p. 15.

[2] Morice, *Anecdotes of Archbishop Cranmer* (*Narratives of the Reformation*, p. 249).

[3] Warley's letter to Lord Lisle, 6th July 1539 (*L. & P. Henry VIII*, vol. XIV (i), No. 1219).

[4] See Gloucester Ridley, p. 143.

[5] *Cranmer and the Heretics in Kent*, (*L. & P. Henry VIII*, vol. XVIII (ii), No. 546, p. 348).

[6] Ridley, *Last Farewell* (*Works*, pp. 407–8).

[7] *Statutes of the Realm*, 34 & 35 Hen. VIII, c. 1.

[8] Gardiner's letter to Cranmer, July 1547 (*Letters of Stephen Gardiner*, p. 328).

[9] *L. & P. Henry VIII*, vol. XVIII (ii), No. 546, p. 339.

[10] Wilkins, *Concilia*, vol. III, p. 862.

[11] *L. & P. Henry VIII*, vol. XVIII (ii), No. 546, p. 352, etc.

[12] *L. & P. Henry VIII*, vol. XVIII (ii), No. 546, pp. 325, 346, etc.

[13] See *London Chronicle*, p. 17.

[14] *L. & P. Henry VIII*, vol. XVIII (ii), No. 546, p. 353.

[15] Morice, *Anecdotes of Archbishop Cranmer* (*Narratives of the Reformation*, pp. 252–3).

[16] *L. & P. Henry VIII*, vol. XVIII (ii), No. 546, pp. 339, 347, 366–7.

[17] *Statutes of the Realm*, 32 Hen. VIII, c. 49.

[18] *L. & P. Henry VIII*, vol. XVIII (ii), No. 546, pp. 302–3.

[19] Morice's letter to Butts and Denny, 2nd November 1543 (Foxe, vol. VIII, pp. 31–4, where the date is wrongly given as 1544. See *L. & P. Henry VIII*, vol. XVIII (ii), pp. l–lii.

[20] *Grace Book Γ*, p. 368.

[21] Gardiner's Edict of 18th June 1542 (Strype, *Memorials*, vol. I (ii), pp. 479–81).

[22] Leinster, *The Earls of Kildare*, p. 128.

[23] Strype, *Memorials*, vol. II (ii), p. 166.

[24] Cox's letter to Paget, 10th December 1544 (*L. & P. Henry VIII*, vol. XIX (ii), No. 726).

[25] Meers' letter to Parker, 26th January 1544/5 (Parker's *Correspondence*, pp. 17–18).

[26] *L. & P. Henry VIII*, vol. XVIII (ii), No. 546, p. 306.

[27] See the Council's letter to Cranmer, 10th August 1545 (*Cranmer's Works*, vol. II, pp. 495–6). For the preparations taken against a French landing near Herne, see *L. & P. Henry VIII*, vol. XX (i), No. 672 (2).

[28] Foxe, vol. VIII, pp. 56–7. In 1551, Cranmer wrote in his *Answer to Smith* that he had been converted from his belief in the Real Presence only a short time before he published the Catechism of 1548 (see Cranmer's *Works*, vol. I, p. 374). The Preface to the Latin edition of Cranmer's *Defence of the True and Catholic Doctrine of the Sacrament*, published at Emden in 1557, states that Cranmer changed his views in 1546. (See Cranmer's *Works*, vol. I, *App.*, p. 6.) If, as is probable, this Preface was written by Cheke, the statement is of great authority. Cranmer had already had doubts about transubstantiation, though not about the Real Presence, as early as 1538 (see his letter to Cromwell of 15th August 1538 about Damplip, *Cranmer's Works*, vol. II, pp. 375–6); but the distinction between these two doctrines is ignored here, as it played very little part, in the great controversy in England, and was completely ignored by Ridley (see Ridley, *Brief Declaration of the Lord's Supper, Works*, p. 11).

[29] See the statement which Ridley intended to read out in the disputation at Oxford in 1554 (Foxe, vol. VI, p. 477).

[30] For Bertram's views, see his treatise *On the Body and Blood of the Lord*, cited in Stone, *Doctrine of the Holy Eucharist*, vol. I, pp. 227–32.

[31] Ridley's intended statement in the Oxford disputation (Foxe, vol. VI, p. 477).

[32] Ridley, *Brief Declaration of the Lord's Supper* (*Treatise against the Error of Transubstantiation*) (*Works*, pp. 9, 13).

[33] *Works*, pp. 11–12.

[34] *Works*, pp. 15–16. The passages cited are taken from the 1555 edition, with the spelling modernised.

[35] *Works*, p. 17.

[36] Foxe, vol. VII, p. 463. See Darby, *Latimer*, pp. 163–4, for the date of the accident and arrest.

[37] Foxe, vol. V, pp. 537–49.

[38] Strype, *Memorials*, vol. III (i), p. 160.

[39] The Council's letter to Petre, 11th May 1546 (*State Papers of Henry VIII*, vol. I, p. 843).

[40] Crome's Recantations (published in Foxe, vol. V, *App.*, Document No. XVI); Strype, *Memorials*, vol. III (i), p. 161.

[41] See Muller, *Stephen Gardiner and the Tudor Reaction*, p. 140.

[42] Foxe, vol. VII, p. 407.

IV

BISHOP OF ROCHESTER:
THE SUPPRESSION OF IMAGES

From the Protestant point of view, Henry died at the best possible moment. He had lived just long enough to destroy the Catholic faction, and to place Hertford and the Protestants in the saddle; but he did not survive to initiate a change in policy, and to strike down the Seymours and their supporters. His attempt to entrust the government of England during Edward's minority to sixteen Executors was easily brushed aside by Hertford, who now became Duke of Somerset. Of all the Catholic leaders, only Wriothesley had been retained in office by Henry; and Somerset was able to oust him from the woolsack, and compel him to retire into private life after a few months in prison. With Somerset Protector, the way was clear for Cranmer to press forward the religious reformation far beyond the furthest point which it could ever have reached under Henry VIII.

The Reformation, in origin, had been a democratic movement. It was the successor to the old movements of the heretic friars who had first raised their voice against the dogma and authority of the Church. Its feeding ground was the popular discontent with the corruption and moral degeneration of the Church. Its chief purpose, in the days of Bilney and Tyndale, was to elevate the personal faith of the ordinary man above the formal ceremonies of the Church, to make every ploughboy as well read in Scriptures as the most learned clerk, and to encourage every man to interpret the Bible for himself rather than to accept without question the conclusions reached by the schoolmen. Yet the historical accident which led to the rupture between Henry VIII and Clement had caused it to be closely associated with royal absolutism. If it had not been for the divorce, there would still have been Protestant martyrs consigned to the flames at the orders of Henry and Wriothesley; but there would never have been an Archbishop of Canterbury who secretly sympathised with the martyred heretics. As long as Henry was alive, the Reformation could only advance as far as he wished it to go; but in so far as it did advance, it did so by virtue of his royal absolutism, and was inextricably entangled with it.

A very different situation arose during the night of 27th January 1547. Edward VI was a King, as his father had been, and the Protestants and the Protector did all they could to enhance the boy's position as the sole source of power in the Kingdom; but a nine-year-old boy was not the same as the formidable Henry. Gardiner and the Catholics immediately challenged the authority of the Protector and the Council to wield in the name of an infant King the absolute power which they admitted could be exercised by an adult King in person. This theoretical argument was sustained by the practical example of the men in power, and encouraged by the policy of the Protector.

The character of Edward Seymour was a curious mixture of good and evil which in the ruler of England was a fatal one. Hertford had spent his life till now in the struggle for power at Court, and as a successful general in the field; he had done nothing to distinguish himself from any of the other scheming courtiers except by the measure of success which he had attained. Yet now that the supreme power was vested in him, he had his own ideas as to what to do with it. He intended to use it primarily for amassing enormous wealth, though he was already very rich; but he also decided to put into practice some of the Humanist ideas which he had imbibed. Thirty years before, Sir Thomas More had entertained the King and the Court with his story of the island of Utopia in the New World, where the rulers were elected by the people, where savage punishments were unknown, where the people owned goods in common, and where toleration was accorded to all religious sects, including atheists. More himself did not take this kind of thing too seriously, and would have been the first to denounce anyone who did as an Anabaptist; as Lord Chancellor in England, he acted very differently from the magistrates in Utopia. But the Humanist ideas which he and his friends had spread, and which absorbed the attention of idealists while more practical men were concerning themselves with religious controversies and the realities of the struggle for power, had taken root in Seymour's mind. He was as vainglorious as he was covetous; he wanted all the trapperies as well as the realities of power, and behaved to his colleagues in the Council with an arrogance which his far less scrupulous rival, Warwick, was careful to avoid. But he wanted to be a benevolent despot, to be loved rather than feared by the people of all classes, including the artizans and labourers. He would pardon criminals, and release prisoners; he would divest the King and himself of the autocratic powers which had been voted to Henry VIII; he would mitigate the rigours of the law of treasons and felonies; he would accord religious toleration to all heretics; and he would ensure justice for the poorer classes, and champion their cause. To his contemporaries, both Catholic and Protestant, this was nothing but a contemptible desire to court popularity among the ignorant multitude. It was as unrealistic as his offer to the Scots that England and Scotland should be united to form one realm on the basis of equality, and that King Edward, after marrying Mary Queen of Scots, should bear the title of Emperor of Great Britain. He certainly acquired a popularity among the people, but his policy of inciting popular discontent, while setting his face against disorder and revolution, led to his downfall and ruin.

If the character of Somerset was complex, those of his colleagues in the Council were very simple. They were out for power and money, and were prepared to do anything to get it. They looted the monasteries, the chantries and the colleges, and some of them amassed enormous fortunes. In religion and politics, they were quite unprincipled. These men came to power under Edward VI, and the Reformation, which had earlier been associated with the tyranny of Henry, became linked with the greed of the new nobility.

The historians who oppose the Reformation have eagerly stressed these vices of the champions of the Protestant cause. They are perfectly entitled to do so; but they have been less than fair in failing to point out that Cranmer and Ridley and most of their colleagues in the Church had nothing to do with this covetousness, though accusations of corruption and greed were made against some of the Protestant Bishops.* For the most part, the Bishops did not share in any of the gains of the rapacious nobles; on the contrary, the lords enriched themselves largely out of their sees. The reformers were always denouncing the covetousness of the nobles; no Catholic spokesman ever equalled the energy of

---

* Ferrar was accused of covetousness by the Canons in his diocese of St. David's (Foxe, vol. VII, pp. 6–7), but seems to have been guilty merely of eccentricity. For the accusations against Cranmer, see Strype, *Cranmer*, pp. 401–6. See Burnet, vol. III, p. 344, with regard to Archbishop Holgate.

Latimer and Knox in attacking it. Cranmer was prepared
to vote in the House of Lords with the Catholic Bishops
against Somerset's Chantries Act. The worst that can be
said of Cranmer and Ridley is that they did not expressly
denounce the great peers, who were the worst offenders, by
name; but the logic of events had forced them into a position
where they were absolutely dependent on the support of
these careerists to carry through the Reformation. Their
policy was inevitable; but it certainly carried its Nemesis. If
the Protestant cause had not become identified with the
greedy nobles and landowners, there might never have been
the rising which put Mary on the Throne. When that day
came, the spoilers were the first to become Catholics and
Papists, and they prospered almost as much under Mary as
they had done before. It was the Bishops who had denounced the covetousness who were sent to the stake.

The attitude of the common people was a more important
factor than could have been expected. It is impossible to
determine the controversial question as to the number of
Catholics and Protestants in the Kingdom. It seems likely
that in London and the south-eastern counties, the Protestants formed a substantial minority of the people, and as
they attracted the most ardent and enthusiastic elements
among all classes, their influence was out of all proportion
to their numbers; but even in the south-east it is probable
that there were more Catholics than Protestants. In the
north and west, there were hardly any Protestants at all. It
is quite certain that a large majority of the people of England were Catholic in 1547. It could hardly have been
otherwise; the Protestants had been condemned as heretics
and punished by a dreadful death, and had never been
allowed to propagate their views and disseminate their
literature openly. The mass of the people still believed in

H

the doctrines of the old Church, and many of them were probably distressed at the break with Rome, as they had certainly disapproved of Henry's action at the time of the divorce from Catherine; and the suppression of the monasteries had caused dissatisfaction among the dependants of the houses who had been turned adrift to be hounded and mutilated as vagabonds. But the people were no more devout than they had been fifty years before, and however much they might disapprove of innovations in religion, they would not, in the ordinary way, have bestirred themselves to prevent them.

It never occurred to either the Protestant or the Catholic leaders to attach any importance to the views and feelings of the people. It was only the economic and social unrest which made it an important factor in the political and religious struggle. The inflation and the enclosures caused widespread discontent, and as these evils grew worse under a Protestant government, it was not difficult for the Catholic priests to associate the social unrest with opposition to the heretic bishops. For the last fifty years, the landowners had been enclosing common land, surrounding the fields with hedges and fences, and converting arable land into pasture or pleasure gardens. They were buying up land from smaller freeholders, and after ejecting their leasehold tenants were refusing to let the land again, but were retaining it in their possession for hunting and hawking, putting sheep to graze in the fields. As a result of this, the small freehold, and the tenant farmers found themselves without land, while the agricultural labourers were often out of work; and they began to drift into the towns, and to swell the numbers of vagabonds. The proportion of enclosed land was still very small in the country south of the Trent, and in the north the process had hardly even begun; while only a small part of the countrymen had gone into the towns. But these developments nevertheless caused much alarm and resentment. The royal officials warned their superiors of the danger to the agriculture of the Kingdom and the risk of depleting and weakening the class of small freehold and tenant farmers—the yeomen of England—who were the backbone of the King's armies in time of war, though this argument, in the days of mercenaries, was somewhat out of date. The clergy preached against the immorality of enclosures and ejectments, and the disregard of long-standing traditions and customs by the landowners. The people, exasperated by the recent rise in prices, complained bitterly about conditions. Henry VIII and Wolsey had been largely thwarted by the landowners in their attempts to check the growth of enclosures and the pastoralisation of land by statutes and proclamations. Now King Henry was dead, and an age of freedom had dawned. If every heretic was free to preach his heresy, the nobles and the country gentlemen felt free to defy the old restrictions on enclosures and pastoralisation of land; and if there was now to be no restraint on the greed of the landowners, their tenants felt free to proclaim their discontent, and to speak of forcible resistance to enclosures and ejectments.

The liberal ideas of the Protector, though they immediately led him to abolish the heresy laws and to give freedom and toleration to Protestants, were to some extent an obstacle to Cranmer's policy. The action of Somerset in relaxing the rigour of Henry's absolutism weakened the royal authority at a time when the reformers wished to see it strengthened. They intended to use the royal power to carry through the Reformation. The break with the Papacy had firmly established that the King was the Supreme Head of the Church of England; and now the King—and during his infancy, the Lord Protector—would use his supreme authority over the Church to make it a Protestant Church. The Reformation would be introduced by the force of the royal command. The Protestant leaders had never considered reaching their aim by any other means. They had never thought of fermenting a Protestant revolution. Their religion taught them that it was a sin for the people to revolt against their Prince; if he were unjust, his subjects must bear his government as a punishment ordained on account of their sins, and as a trial to test their patience. The whole weight of official teaching for the last sixty years had taught them that the will of the King was absolute, and that no one could gainsay him. Experience had taught them that a revolt was never successful, but was always cruelly crushed. Nor did the Protestants have sufficient support among the people to attempt a rising. As revolt was therefore out of the question, the reformers relied solely on the royal authority; and 'Render unto Caesar the things that are Caesar's' became one of the favourite texts of Protestant preachers.

This Protestant ideology was plainly stated in Cranmer's address to the King at the Coronation on 20th February, in which he set forth the philosophy that was later to become known as the divine right of Kings. The Archbishop exhorted the King to rule justly, for God had always condemned those evil Kings who tyrannised over their subjects and oppressed the poor; but he emphasized that he was not threatening the King with excommunication if he failed to follow his exhortation, and that neither the Bishop of Rome nor anyone else had the power to excommunicate or depose the King. Cranmer said that Pope Innocent had purported to depose King John on account of his tyranny, but that Innocent had had no right to do so, and that he, as

Archbishop of Canterbury, did not have that right. He was urging Edward to be a good ruler so as to please God, but if he were to be a bad king none of his subjects would have any right to condemn him. His hands were not bound in any way by the Coronation ceremony, for Cranmer declared that he had no power to draw up the terms of a contract between God and the King.[1]

Cranmer had now no need to hesitate in appointing reformers to the highest offices in the Church, and among his supporters he had marked out Ridley for immediate promotion. It is probable that Henry had approved the suggestion shortly before his death. It was now arranged that Longland, the Bishop of Lincoln, should resign, and that Holbeach should be translated from Rochester to Lincoln, while Ridley was to be appointed Bishop of Rochester. As it happened, Longland died in May 1547 and the way for Ridley's elevation was clear: it now waited only on the formalities of Holbeach's election to Lincoln, and Ridley's election to Rochester. But Cranmer had no intention that Ridley should be inactive in the meanwhile, and he was immediately appointed to be the royal preacher during Lent. He could now say what he thought without fear; only on the matter of transubstantiation must he still go carefully. This was not because he feared a prosecution for heresy, for though the Acts against the Lollards and the Statute of the Six Articles were still in force, everyone knew that they would be repealed as soon as Parliament met, and that Somerset would not allow any proceedings under these Acts to take place in the interval. But the Mass was the most fundamental and sacred tenet of the Catholic faith, in which the great majority of the English people still believed, and to attack the doctrine of the corporal Presence was considered to be the worst kind of heresy.

Cranmer had therefore decided to prepare the way by attacking on all the lesser points of doctrine before challenging the Mass.

But it was not Cranmer who was to select the first issue to be raised in the struggle. This was to be done by the Protestant rank and file. Within a few days of Henry's death, the Vicar and churchwardens of St. Martin's Church in Ironmonger Lane in London removed the images in the church, and replaced them with the royal arms. The Council immediately investigated this wholly unauthorised innovation;[2] but Cranmer decided to throw the weight of the Protestant leadership behind the movement against images. In his address at the Coronation, he urged the King to remove images throughout his kingdom; and three days later, on Ash Wednesday, 23rd February, Ridley dealt with the matter at greater length in his first sermon before Edward as preacher during Lent.

In his sermon to the King, Ridley began with a strong attack on the Pope, stating that by the laws of God he had never had any authority in England, and attacking the Papal abuse of the grant of pardons and dispensations. He then turned to the question of images. We have no record of what Ridley said in this sermon apart from the criticisms of it in Gardiner's letter; but it is clear that he expressed himself very cautiously. He said that as far as he could see from his studies of the question, it was wrong that images should be displayed in churches and throughout the country, and he evidently referred to the images as idols; but he was not at all dogmatic about the matter, and emphasized that he was perfectly open to persuasion that he was wrong. Ridley then proceeded, equally cautiously, to criticise the use of holy water for exorcising devils. Ridley was obviously testing the reaction of the dignitaries at Court to his opinions,

and was careful to do no more than make a tentative suggestion that images and holy water be suppressed.*

The nine-year-old King, who was being brought up as a
Protestant by his tutor Cheke, was probably impressed by
the sermon. But the Bishop of Winchester was also among
Ridley's congregation at Court. A year before, Gardiner
would have reacted violently to such a sermon, and would
perhaps have contemplated prosecuting Ridley for heresy;
but now he knew the weakness of his position. Realising,
however, that this sermon threatened to be the forerunner
of a heretical attack on all the doctrines of the Church, he
decided that he could not let it pass without a protest. He
therefore wrote a long letter to Ridley,[3] and sent a copy of
the letter to the Lord Protector. The letter was couched in
courteous terms. Gardiner wrote that he completely agreed
with everything that Ridley had said about the Pope and
the King's supremacy over the Church; but he was surprised that Ridley had criticised images and the use of holy
water. He complimented Ridley on the moderation with
which he had expressed his opinions, and wrote that as
Ridley had said that he was willing to be persuaded that he
was wrong, he was writing to show him his error. He en-

* According to Foxe, Ridley wrote a *Treatise on the Worship of Images*
(Foxe, vol. VIII, pp. 701-7), which was presented to Edward VI on
behalf of the whole clergy. There is, however, no record of any such
memorial being presented to Edward, and as the document appears to
be identical with that presented by some of the bishops to Elizabeth I
in 1560 (Collier, *Ecclesiastical History*, vol. VI, pp. 310-12), it seems that
Foxe was mistaken in attributing the authorship of the treatise to
Ridley, unless the treatise, which is in the form of notes, was found
among Ridley's papers in Elizabeth's reign and then presented to the
Queen. It is certain that Ridley did not refer to any of the authorities
cited in the treatise in his sermon on Ash Wednesday 1547, for had he
done so, Gardiner would certainly have dealt with them in his letter
to Ridley.

closed a treatise by Eusebius, which he was sure that Ridley
had read, which showed that the use of images in the
Church was of great antiquity, and he argued at length that
Ridley had been wrong to confuse the words 'image' and
'idol'. If images were wrong, so was the Cross of St. George
which the King wore around his neck. With regard to holy
water, Gardiner enclosed a further work which showed how
Marcellus the Bishop had told his deacon to cast forth water
which he had blessed, and wrote that the power of the holy
water, like the healing power of the rings which were distributed by the King, was the faith in the word of God. In
the new situation, Gardiner was prepared to enlist the support of Luther: he wrote to Ridley that Luther had not condemned images, and that he himself, on his visits to Germany,
had seen images displayed in Lutheran churches there.

Gardiner concluded his letter by warning Ridley of the
value of tradition, and the dangers of innovation, in religion,
and by telling him that though he had never included Ridley among his friends, and had never pretended to do so, he
was writing to him because he respected Ridley for his
learning, and had availed himself of Ridley's offer to accept
correction of his views. Gardiner's statement that he had
never pretended to be a friend of Ridley was a good deal
less than the truth: if he had never pretended friendship, he
had tried his best to conceal his connexion with the intrigues
of the Canterbury Canons against Ridley in 1543. We do
not know whether Ridley replied to this letter. Foxe states
that he did, but he based his conclusion on a passage in a
letter from Somerset to Gardiner which appears to be somewhat ambiguous.* It is very likely that Ridley sent a reply

---

* 'And because we have begun to write to you, we are put in
remembrance of a certain letter or book which you wrote unto us
against the Bishop of St. David's sermon, and Dr. Ridley's, to the

containing his views on images. At any rate, he had no cause for anxiety. The time was passed when Ridley had reason to fear Gardiner; soon it would be not Ridley, but Gardiner himself, who would be called to account for his sermons.

Ridley had preached his sermon against the background of a violent attack on images all over London and the south-eastern counties. Within a month of King Henry's death, Protestant pamphlets, rhymes and ballads were everywhere in circulation, as all the restrictions on their publication were no longer enforced. In accordance with the usual practice at the beginning of a new reign, the Protector pardoned all convicted criminals, and released all prisoners from the gaols, though the pardon excepted some political prisoners in the Tower, such as Norfolk, and the traitors abroad, like Pole. Latimer amongst others was released from the Tower. Apart from these traditional pardons, it was generally realised that as soon as a new Parliament had assembled, it would be asked to repeal all the laws against heresy, and greatly to relax the treason laws. Gone was the fear which had held everyone in its grip during the last fourteen years.

The news of the new era in England spread rapidly throughout the country, and abroad throughout Europe. In England, men who had been silent, or who had only whispered, during Henry's reign, now suddenly began to shout from the roof-tops their detestation of the doctrines of the Catholic Church. The influx of foreign Protestants added

which answer being immediately made, it was by negligence of us forgotten to be sent. Now we both send you that, and also the answer which the Bishop of St. David's wrote to the same book of yours.'— Somerset's letter to Gardiner (Foxe, vol. VI, p. 64). It seems doubtful whether the answer which was 'immediately made' was a letter written by Ridley or by Somerset.

to the violence of the agitation. Many Protestants fled to England from the persecution in the Netherlands, including some Anabaptists, who may fondly have imagined that they would be accorded some measure of toleration in heretic England, where in view of the repeal of the heresy statutes they could at least not be burned for the time being. Most of the refugees were artizans, and the government welcomed them, especially the weavers, as useful subjects; but several leading Protestant theologians were among the immigrants. During the course of the next two years, Ochino, Utenhove, Tremellius, Knox, Micronius, and the Polish noble John à Lasco, came to England. The most eminent of the foreign Protestants were Peter Martyr and Bucer, who were appointed to the chairs of Divinity at Oxford and Cambridge. The English Catholics loathed the foreign heretics, and complained that England had become a harbour for all infidelity.

The immigrants were in many cases among the most violent of the Protestants who now denounced fasting in Lent, the doctrine of transubstantiation, and all kinds of superstitious practices. They also began to attack priests in the streets, and to pelt them with stones and offal, and to jeer at them. But it was above all against images that the Protestant fury directed itself. Ridley's sermon at Court may have encouraged the agitators to believe that on the issue of images they would have official support; and in this they were not mistaken. All over London and south-eastern England, mobs were destroying images, or throwing them out of the churches. Gardiner strongly protested to the Protector against such outrages at Portsmouth, in his diocese of Winchester, and against the failure of the government to check these disorders and the circulation of heretical pamphlets, or to enforce the laws as to fasting in Lent. This

anarchical violence was not to the liking of either the Protector or of Cranmer and Ridley and their supporters; but
while setting their face against violence, they welcomed the
opportunity provided by the outrages to deal authoritatively
with images. The Council ordered that all attacks on
priests, and all removal and desecration of images by mobs,
must be suppressed at once; but they also directed that all
images which had been abused by being the object of
idolatrous worship should be removed.

While the movement against images, which had received
its first official support from Ridley, was winning this success, Ridley had been involved in a controversy of a less
public nature. The benefice of Soham had fallen vacant.
Ridley was only waiting for the formalities to be completed
before he was elected Bishop of Rochester; but the trustees
who had been appointed by Pembroke Hall to make the
presentment to Soham decided to nominate the Master of
the College as vicar. The Bishop of Norwich, however, who
still challenged the claim of Pembroke Hall to the advowson,
had some years before promised Dr. Miles Spencer that he
would be the next vicar; and this time neither Repps nor
the College was prepared to give way. The Bishop informed
Ridley that he would never consent to his taking office as
Vicar of Soham, and intended to present Spencer to the
cure; and Ridley thereupon started an action in the Court
of King's Bench against Repps and Spencer, asking for a
declaration that Pembroke Hall held a valid advowson and
that he was entitled to be admitted as Vicar of Soham.
Ridley apparently went to Cambridge in the spring of 1547,
and while there rode over to Soham, where he contrived to
preach a sermon in the parish church; and he also succeeded,
presumably through the medium of Cranmer, in interesting
the Council in the matter. The Council wrote to Repps,

ordering him to admit Ridley to Soham, or to appear before
the Council and explain his conduct. Soon afterwards, in
the Easter term, the Court of King's Bench gave judgment
in Ridley's favour, and thereupon the Council wrote again
to the Bishop, ordering him to admit Ridley as vicar immediately. On 17th May, Ridley was admitted by a proxy;
he did not go himself to Soham for the ceremony. He never
resided in the parish.*

In March, King Francis of France had died. France had
been a friendly power since the peace treaty of 1546, and
Somerset had signed a treaty of friendship with Francis
shortly before Francis' death. The Council therefore ordered
a requiem Mass for the late French King to be held in St.
Paul's on 19th June. Cranmer and eight bishops officiated
at the ceremony. All the dignitaries of the realm attended
the service, and Ridley may well have sat among them in
the heavily draped cathedral; but the suggestion that he
preached the sermon appears to be an error. The contemporary records state that the sermon was preached by the
Bishop of Rochester, and as Holbeach was still Bishop of
Rochester in June 1547, there seems no reason to doubt
that the sermon was preached by Holbeach.† The sermon

---

* Ridley, *Last Farewell* (*Works*, p. 536, and notes). With regard to
the dispute about Ridley's presentation to Soham, see Repps' letter to
Ridley, 21st February 1547, and other documents in MSS., Pembroke
College, Cambridge, and Gloucester Ridley, p. 207. Attwater, *Pembroke College, Cambridge*, p. 37, states that Wren found among the
Pembroke College accounts, in the seventeenth century, an item for
the cost of hiring Ridley's horse for him to ride to Soham at the time
of the dispute with regard to his admission as vicar, and references to
his preaching a sermon at Soham at this time.

† The accounts in the Lord Chamberlain's office (L.C. 2/1/180) and
Wriothesley's *Chronicle*, vol. I, p. 184 (where the date of the service is
wrongly given as 29th June) state that the sermon was preached by the
'Bishop of Rochester'. In June 1547, this was Holbeach, who was not

was apparently a eulogy of Francis for having permitted the publication of a French translation of the Bible. The sermon was no doubt necessary in the interests of Somerset's foreign policy, but it seems clear that it was not Ridley who was required to glorify Francis, who, as he himself must have witnessed in Paris, had burned men for denouncing images, and who shortly before his death had ordered the massacre of three thousand people in Provence because it was a region of heretics.

During the summer, the Council promulgated a Book of Homilies, which Cranmer had compiled. The greater part of the book was not controversial; but one section of it aroused the opposition of Gardiner and the Catholic clergy. Charity was omitted from the requirements for salvation.* The Council also ordered that Erasmus' Paraphrase of the New Testament, which had been translated into English, should be distributed to every church in the Kingdom. This decision likewise aroused the opposition of the Catholics. But the Council had no intention that the bishops and

translated to Lincoln until August; Ridley was not appointed Bishop of Rochester until September. Strype, *Cranmer*, p. 225, likewise states that the sermon was preached by the Bishop of Rochester. Heylin, Part I, p. 40, and Gloucester Ridley, p. 210, state that the sermon was preached by Ridley, who was already referred to at the time as the Elect of Rochester; but they give no authority for this. The French Ambassador, Selve, does not refer to the preacher in his letter to Henry II of 23rd June 1547 (*Correspondance Politique de Odet de Selve*, pp. 152–3); nor does the *Greyfriars Chronicle* (p. 54).

* The Homilies dealt with the use of the Scriptures; with sin; with salvation by Christ; with true and lively Faith; with good works; with Christian love and charity; with swearing and perjury; with apostasy, and declining from God; with fear of death; with obedience; and with the beneficial effects of marriage, and the sin of whoredom and adultery. It also contained an exhortation to the people to refrain from religious controversy (Burnet, vol. II, pp. 72–3). For the Homily of Salvation, see Cranmer's *Works*, vol. II, pp. 128–34.

priests who were opposed to their policy should be allowed to thwart their designs. The Protector ordered a royal visitation throughout the realm. The duty of the Visitors was to ensure that the royal supremacy over the Church was fully recognised, and the Papal supremacy rejected; that the Book of Homilies was accepted; that the people were well acquainted with the English Bible; and that they should be disabused of the prevalent idea that it was wrong to work on holy days. The Visitors were to see that the order for the removal of every image which had been abused had been carried out, but the images were only to be removed by the clergy, and not by unauthorised persons and mobs. Pilgrimages, the sprinkling of beds with holy water, and the superstitious use of blessed candles were to be prohibited. Every Sunday, one chapter from the New Testament was to be read in English at matins, and one chapter from the Old Testament in English was to be read at evensong. The Visitors were also to ensure that every bishop preached four times a year in his diocese—once in his cathedral, and three times elsewhere; that all priests preached personally twice a year in their parishes;* and generally that the clergy performed their duties and led moral lives, and that taxes and tithes were paid.[4]

For the purpose of the visitation, the country was divided into six circuits; on every circuit, a preacher was sent to accompany the Visitors. Ridley was appointed preacher to the northern circuit.[5] The Visitors were the Dean of Westminster and Sir John Horseley. The northern circuit comprised the whole of the province of York except the Isle of Man—the dioceses of York, Durham, Carlisle and Chester.

---

* Priests could be exempted from the duty to preach twice a year in their parishes by special licence. Ridley undoubtedly received such a licence with regard to his parishes of Herne and Soham.

On no other circuit was the task of the Visitors more difficult. Archbishop Holgate was a Protestant, but was more concerned with furthering his personal interests than those of the Reformation. Ridley's kinsman, Bishop Tunstall of Durham, had capitulated to Henry on the question of Papal supremacy, but in all other respects was as Catholic now as he had been twenty years before, when he had sat, with Robert Ridley as an assessor, to try the first Lutheran heretics. As for the priests, the large majority of them were Catholics, and among the people there were virtually no Protestants at all. Even the injunction to suppress all traces of Papistry was no formality on the northern circuit. Papist sympathies were strong throughout the north, which still retained, beneath the surface, the emotions which had caused the Pilgrimage of Grace ten years before.

In other respects, however, Northumberland had changed at last in the previous fifteen years. The Percies had been attainted and had lost their title for their part in the Pilgrimage of Grace. The abbey of Hexham had been suppressed, and the Liberty of Hexhamshire, with all its privileges and sanctuary, had been surrendered to the Crown. Only the Marches had not changed. The Ridleys and the Featherstonehaughs and all their neighbours would be permitted to continue their feuds, and the thieves would be left to rob, unmolested by the most tyrannical monarch as long as a hostile state lay just across the border, even if Somerset preferred to rely on foreign mercenaries for his great campaign against the Scots. But Ridley was not destined to see for himself the changes which had taken place in his homeland. It had been intended to begin the visitation in May, but in fact it was postponed until the autumn. The visitation began on 1st September, and continued throughout October and November. It is therefore certain that Ridley did not go to the north with the Visitors, for he was in London continuously after 25th September. Evidently another preacher was appointed to take his place on the northern circuit.

In September, Ridley was ordained a bishop. The formalities had at last been completed: Holbeach had been installed as Bishop of Lincoln, and the Chapter of Rochester had elected Ridley as their Bishop on 4th September. On Sunday, 25th September 1547, Ridley was consecrated in the chapel of the Dean of St. Paul's.* The consecration was most appropriately performed by Holbeach, assisted by the Suffragan Bishops of Bedford and Sidon. There is very little doubt that Ridley was consecrated in accordance with all the requirements of the old ritual, being anointed with oil and receiving the vessels of the Eucharist; and there seems no reason whatever to believe that any part of the old ceremony was surreptitiously dispensed with at Ridley's consecration.† Ridley's diocese of Rochester was one of the smallest in the country. It was about thirty-five miles long, stretching from the Thames estuary to the diocese of Chichester to the south, and lay between the dioceses of Canterbury and Winchester. It covered most of the western part of Kent, but a large part of the diocese was subject to the peculiar jurisdiction of the Archbishop of

* The *congé d'élire* was sent to the Chapter of Rochester on 31st August, and the King's consent and the mandate for the consecration was sent to Cranmer on 14th September (Rymer, *Foedera*, vol. XV, pp. 163–4). The date of Ridley's consecration is given as Sunday, 5th September in Cranmer's Register, and this has been followed by Strype, *Cranmer*, p. 250, and generally; but 5th September was a Monday. See Gloucester Ridley, pp. 211–2, for the strong reasons for concluding that the date in Cranmer's Register is a clerical error, and that Ridley was consecrated on Sunday, 25th September. Ridley's Rochester Register begins on 29th September (see the Register).

† See Chapter X, p. 391.

Canterbury. The annual net income of the see probably amounted to about £700, of which Ridley paid his usual tenth in tax.*

His preferment to the see of Rochester did not make it necessary for Ridley to resign any of his other offices in the Church. He continued to be Vicar of Soham and Vicar of Herne, and to hold his prebends in Canterbury and in Westminster Cathedrals, for he was granted a licence to hold all these offices *in commendam* until Christmas 1552.† He was still a chaplain to Edward VI, as he had formerly been to Henry VIII. His position as royal chaplain was a remunerative one, for he received twenty shillings whenever he preached before the King.‡

Things had changed indeed since that other September when Ridley's colleagues at Canterbury had been prosecuted, and the Catholic prebendaries and preachers were reporting to Gardiner that Ridley was a heretic who had caused the *Te Deum* to be sung in English in the little village of Herne. A week before Ridley became a bishop, the Council ordered the *Te Deum* to be sung in English in every church throughout the country to celebrate the Protector's victory over the Scots at Pinkie; and on the very day of his consecration, Gardiner was arrested. He had protested against the royal visitation on the grounds that the powers of the King over the Church, under which the visitation had been held, could not lawfully be exercised on behalf of

---

* In 1535, the revenues of the see of Rochester amounted to £411 0s. 11d. net, and the tenth to £41 2s. 1d. (see *Valor Ecclesiasticus*, vol. I, p. 100); but the inflation of 1542–6 had almost certainly increased the revenues by about 80 per cent by 1547.

† On 16th November 1547 (Rymer, *Foedera*, vol. XV, p. 165).

‡ Ridley received twenty shillings for preaching to the King on 27th February 1548 (*Household Book of Edward VI*, published in *Trevelyan Papers*, vol. I, p. 203).

I

an infant King by his Protector. He had opposed Cranmer's
Book of Homilies for omitting good works as a means to
salvation. He had attacked the issue of the Paraphrase of
Erasmus: Erasmus, he said, laid the eggs and Luther
hatched them. Bonner also criticised the royal visitation,
and while he ordered the removal of images in his diocese
of London, and the acceptance of the Book of Homilies, in
compliance with the royal injunctions, he made a public
declaration that he accepted the injunctions on condition
that they were not contrary to God's law and the statutes of
the Church. The Council decided to take action against
both Gardiner and Bonner. The visitation had been ordered
in a royal proclamation, and by the Statute of Proclamations of 1539, which was still in force though Somerset intended to repeal it, a royal proclamation had the force of
law as if it were contained in a statute. In opposing the
visitation, Gardiner and Bonner had resisted a law of the
realm, and had consequently been guilty of a misdemeanour. On 25th September, Gardiner was arrested and sent
to the Fleet. On learning of the Council's resolve to brook
no opposition, Bonner promptly withdrew his statement and
admitted that he had been at fault in suggesting that there
was any possibility that the royal injunctions might be
contrary to God's laws and the statutes of the Church. He
was nevertheless arrested and sent to the Fleet, but in view
of his submission he was released in a few weeks.

A few days after he became a bishop, Ridley was chosen
by the Council, together with Cranmer, Holbeach, May
the Dean of St. Paul's, Cox, Aire and others, to examine
Gardiner. Gardiner was brought from the Fleet prison to
May's house, and there Cranmer reprimanded him for his
opposition to the royal visitation and the Book of Homilies.
Gardiner said that to claim that Faith excluded Charity

seemed to him to be directly contrary to the words of Scripture. When Cranmer proceeded to argue the point, Gardiner stated that he would repeat that he was opposed to the Homilies, but would add nothing more, as he would not waste his arguments on his examiners; he would reserve them until such a time as there were others present. Ridley does not seem to have taken any part in the discussion, leaving the matter entirely to Cranmer.[6] Gardiner was taken back to the Fleet, and remained there; he indignantly rejected Cranmer's offer of a place on the Council if he abandoned his opposition to the Protestant religious policy.

On 4th November, the new Parliament assembled at Westminster. Ridley preached the sermon at the state opening by the King, when the service was conducted partly in English.[7] He was now a Lord of Parliament, and he attended the House of Lords with great regularity; as far as we know, he was present at every one of the thirty-eight sittings during the session, except at the prorogation ceremony on 24th December, for though there are no records of attendances at two of the sittings, Ridley was present on every other occasion.* During the session, a large number of far-reaching measures were enacted. These repealed the Statute of the Six Articles, and the heresy statutes of 1382, 1414 and 1534; there was thus no longer any statutory power to burn heretics. They repealed all statutes enacted since 21st April 1509, when Henry VIII came to the throne, which created any new treasons or felonies; but the provisions of the Act of Supremacy, which made it high treason to assert the Papal, or deny the royal, supremacy over the Church were re-enacted in a milder form. It was still to be

* *House of Lords Journal*, 4th November–24th December 1547. The record of attendances has not been preserved for the sittings of 17th November and 14th December.

high treason to do this in writing, but to do it by spoken words was to be punishable as a misdemeanour, and only to be treason at the third offence. The Statute of Proclamations of 1539 was repealed, as were all statutes passed in the reign of Henry VIII which regulated the doctrines of religion and the practice of the Church.[8] By thus making a clean sweep of all existing laws on these matters, the way was open for Cranmer to begin afresh.

While the peers and gentlemen of the House of Commons were quite ready to pass any bill which the Protector required of them in the matter of religion or the treason laws, they were not prepared to vote for anything which was against their own economic interests. They rejected all the measures which Somerset put forward for relieving the agrarian and social distress. Instead, they passed a bill dealing with vagabonds which re-introduced slavery into England in the middle of the sixteenth century, in the first year of Somerset's free and benevolent government. The statute of 1536, which punished vagabonds with flogging and mutilation, had utterly failed to stamp out the scourge of vagabonds, and the new statute, while providing a system of relief for paupers who could not work on account of age or health, laid down a novel and drastic method of dealing with able-bodied vagabonds.

The Statute of Vagabonds enacted that every able-bodied vagabond, who had not obtained a licence to beg, must offer himself as a servant to some gentleman, and work for him for no renumeration except food and shelter. If he failed to do this, or if, having begun to work, he ran away, he was to be branded with a V for vagabond, and become the slave of his master for two years. If he ran away during this time, he was upon recapture to be branded with the letter S for slave, and become the slave of his master for life. The

statute expressly provided that a master might compel a
slave to labour at any task, however vile it might be, with
whip and chain, and anyone who removed an iron from the
neck of a slave could be fined ten pounds. The Act directed
that the master was to feed his slave on nothing but refuse
meat. The children of an enslaved vagabond were to be
slaves of the master until they reached the age of twenty-
four if males or twenty if females, and any children of any
vagabonds could at any time be seized and held as slaves
until they reached this age. If these children ran away, or
married without their master's consent, or attempted to see
their parents, they were to become the slaves of their master
for life. Slaves who injured their masters in resisting chastise-
ment, or otherwise, were to be hanged as felons.[9] The bill
passed the House of Lords unanimously, without the opposition of a single peer or Bishop, and Ridley was in his place
on 8th December to vote in favour of the bill at the third
reading.* There is no doubt that the vagabonds were a
very real menace to law-abiding people of all classes, and
on the whole deserved little sympathy; but the remedy
adopted by Ridley and his colleagues apparently seemed
somewhat drastic to most of the local justices, for the preamble of the Act of 1549, which repealed the statute of 1547,
stated that the statute had not been generally enforced.

Among the measures introduced in Parliament was a
second Chantries bill, to reinforce and extend the provisions of the Chantries Act of 1545. The bill recited that all
gifts for the establishment of chantries to offer up prayers
for souls were superstitious, as denoting a belief in Purgatory,
and that all chantries and colleges were to be suppressed;

* *House of Lords Journal*, 8th December 1547; the names of those
voting against a bill are always given, and it is clear that those not
named voted in favour.

their funds could much more profitably be used for the establishment of schools. But while the bill abounded in references to schools, its operative sections provided merely that all chantry property was to vest in the King, and that all gifts which were payable to the suppressed chantries were henceforth to be paid to the King, who could sue or distrain to enforce his claim. It was left entirely to the discretion of the King's commissioners whether compensation was paid, for a limited period, to those who were deprived of their livelihood by the suppression of the chantries. The bill also suppressed all colleges, and provided that all the college lands and plate should vest in the King; but the Colleges of Oxford, Cambridge, Eton and Winchester were expressly excepted from the operation of the statute.[10] The Catholic Bishops were strongly opposed to the bill, which condemned the practice of private masses for souls, and gave over the endowments of the pious as spoil to the courtiers. Cranmer felt unable to support this project, and joined with seven of his opponents—Bonner, Tunstall, Skyp, Day, Heath, Repps and Aldrich—to vote against the bill at the fourth reading; but Ridley did not follow him, and along with all the other reforming Bishops, and all the happy peers, voted in favour of the Chantries Act.*

While Parliament was in session, a meeting of Convocation was also in progress. It was the first that had been held since King Henry's death, and in the new situation the Protestants were able to secure the support of the majority of the members. The Protestant leaders put forward a proposal that the Sacrament should be administered to the laity in both kinds. The second article in the Statute of the Six Articles had condemned the doctrine that the administration of the Sacrament of the Altar to all persons in both

* *House of Lords Journal*, 15th December 1547.

kinds was necessary to salvation; but Cranmer did not now attack this doctrine directly. The resolution merely stated that henceforth both the bread and wine should be administered to the congregation except where this was impracticable; and the Catholics, who had never directly condemned the administration of the wine to the laity, but had merely denied its necessity, were able, in the different situation which they now faced, to accept the resolution without compromising their doctrine. The resolution was carried unanimously. The same did not apply to another resolution which the Protestants moved in Convocation. This was to permit the marriage of priests. The Catholic bishops strongly opposed the motion; but the Protestant tide was now flowing with growing force, and Cranmer's position in the Church and the State was too strong to be resisted. The resolution was carried by a substantial majority.

Neither Cranmer nor Ridley had so far given any indication that they no longer believed in the doctrine of transubstantiation. On the question of the Mass, they had not as yet made the slightest move. But the Protestant fanatics in the streets of London were not as cautious as their bishops. In the autumn, there began a series of attacks on the Sacrament in which the foreign Protestants in England played a leading part. Pamphlets and broadsheets appeared denouncing the Mass as idolatry; it was the subject of ribald rhymes; the Host was ridiculed as a round Robin and Jack in the Box, and the Sacrament of the Altar as the Sacrament of the Halter. The Protestant fanatics had seen how their attacks on images in the spring had resulted in the Council's order for the removal of many images throughout the country; and this success encouraged them to believe that by attacks on the Mass they would likewise compel the Council to take action against idolatry.

In this matter, however, they did not achieve so rapid a success. Cranmer and his bishops were not prepared to tolerate the attacks on the Sacrament. They had three reasons to resist the clamour of the Protestant mobs. In the first place, they did not wish to see the issue of the Mass raised before they had carefully prepared the way and judged the situation ripe for action on the most fundamental of all questions. Secondly, they abhorred mob violence, and were determined that no one, not even their supporters, should violate the cardinal principle of their ideology—that religious innovation, and all religious policy, was a matter for the Lord Protector alone as regent for the King. Lastly, and most important, they did not approve of the doctrine of the fanatics. Cranmer and Ridley, believing in the spiritual Presence, were outraged by the sects who reviled the Sacrament of the Lord's Supper, and condemned them as Euchites and heretics. But it is not surprising, in view of the fact that they had not yet condemned the doctrine of the Real Presence, that their attitude was misunderstood both by their contemporaries and by scholars in the future.

To check the outrages on the Sacrament, it was arranged that Ridley should preach a sermon on the subject at Paul's Cross in November or December 1547. The Cross was the most famous pulpit in England. It stood in the churchyard at St. Paul's, right up against the north-east wall of the Cathedral; stone steps led up to the pulpit, which was covered by a roof made of lead, on the top of which was the wooden cross; but it was largely open at the sides.[11] Ridley preached to the people standing in the open air in the churchyard to hear him, and denounced the blasphemers who mocked and reviled the Sacrament of the Altar. It was a holy Sacrament, because the Flesh and Blood of Christ were present in the consecrated bread and wine. He ordered all those who did not revere the Sacrament to leave the church while it was administered; the early Fathers had always excluded heretics and doubters from the commemoration of the Lord's Supper. Ridley said that the blasphemers were worse than the Devil: the Devil had believed that Christ could transform stones into bread, but they did not believe that the bread could be transformed into his body.* It is clear that Ridley gave no indication in his sermon as to whether he believed that Christ's Presence in the Sacrament was corporal or spiritual; and in view of the fact that none of the Protestant leaders had so far given any sign of unorthodoxy on this point, there is no doubt that all his congregation, both the Catholics and the Protestant sectaries whom he was attacking, were firmly convinced that the Bishop of Rochester believed that the Presence was corporal. For the immediate purpose there was no need to go into this question: whether the Presence was corporal or spiritual, it was equally blasphemous to revile the Sacrament. But Ridley was to be reminded of this sermon in after years, and when on trial for his life would have some difficulty in explaining it consistently with the views for which he was prepared to suffer.

The Protector and the Protestant bishops were not prepared to rely on sermons alone to suppress the Euchites; and as Parliament was still in session, a bill was presented for this purpose. This provided Cranmer with the opportunity of killing two birds with one stone, and while sup-

* See Feckenham's speech against the Uniformity Bill in the House of Lords in 1559, cited by Strype, *Annals*, vol. I (ii), p. 435; Ridley's statements as to the content of his sermon in his *Conference with Secretary Bourn and others* (Foxe, vol. VI, p. 437, *Works*, pp. 162–3), and at his trial in 1555 (Foxe, vol. VII, p. 523); and Gloucester Ridley, pp. 215–16. Gloucester Ridley gives the date of the sermon as November 1547, and it was evidently in either November or December.

pressing the Anabaptist attacks on the Sacrament, to ensure that the Sacrament should be administered in both kinds. The two questions were dealt with in the same bill, and this skilful strategy ensured the passage of the bill, despite the opposition of Bonner, Skyp, Heath, Day and Repps. The last clause of an eight-clause bill provided that the cup should be administered to the laity except where it was necessary to do otherwise.

The Act made attacks on the Sacrament a misdemeanour punishable by imprisonment during the King's pleasure.[12] On 27th December, the Council issued a proclamation, which was probably drafted by Cranmer and Ridley, which drew the attention of the people to the statute, and prohibited any attacks on the corporal Presence or any discussion about transubstantiation.* This, too, could be used by the Protestant leaders against two sets of opponents: it could prevent all premature and Euchite attacks on the Mass, and also any further propagation of the doctrine of the Real Presence. The statute and the proclamation were successful in putting a stop to the outrages on the Sacrament.

The Protector had not abandoned his policy of benevolence. He now decided to deal leniently with Gardiner, who had been in prison for three and a half months. In January, he was brought before the Council, and told that he would be released on condition that he ceased his opposition to the Book of Homilies and the royal policy. Gardiner agreed to this, but stated that he was still convinced that the omission of good works as a requirement of salvation was wrong. He was thereupon released from the

---

* For the text of the proclamation, see Wilkins, *Concilia*, vol. IV, pp. 18–19; and see Cranmer's *Works*, vol. II, pp. 505–7, where the authorship is attributed to Cranmer; Strype, *Memorials*, vol. II (i), p. 126, states that it was drafted by Cranmer and Ridley.

Fleet, but ordered to stay confined in his house; and as the Council were by no means satisfied with his statement, they sent Ridley to argue with Gardiner, about the beginning of February, on the question of the exclusion of Charity. Ridley called on Gardiner at his house in Southwark. He did not persuade him to change his views, but soon afterwards Cecil, who was just starting his career as one of Paget's assistant Secretaries to the Council, was able to induce Gardiner to submit.*

During his conversation with Gardiner, Ridley raised the question of the attacks on the Sacrament. Here at least was a matter on which he could agree with Gardiner; they were at one where the Euchites and the Anabaptists were concerned. They discussed the case of two Anabaptists in Kent, though it seems very unlikely that they had been granted any commission to deal with the two Anabaptists.† This

* See Gardiner's answer to the articles at his trial in 1550 (Foxe, vol. VI, p. 65); this makes it clear that Cecil did not accompany Ridley on his visit to Gardiner, as stated by Gloucester Ridley, p. 221, but that Gardiner was visited first by Ridley, then by Smith, and finally by Cecil. All these visits took place between 19th January and 20th February 1548 (see Muller, *Stephen Gardiner and the Tudor Reaction*, p. 171).

† Ridley stated at his trial in 1555, with regard to his visit to Gardiner in January or February 1548: 'At that time my Lord of Winchester and I had to do with two Anabaptists in Kent' (Foxe, vol. VII, p. 523). This is probably the only evidence on which Strype based his statement that Ridley and Gardiner were 'appointed . . . to examine two Anabaptists in Kent' (*Cranmer*, p. 297); he is followed by Gloucester Ridley, p. 221. Ridley probably meant no more, by these words at his trial, than that he had discussed the case of the two Anabaptists with Gardiner during this conversation in Southwark; for it seems very unlikely that Gardiner would have been entrusted with the task of examining Anabaptists when he was confined in house arrest. At any rate, as Gardiner's movements in the spring of 1548 are quite well known, it is hardly possible that he could have travelled into Kent at this period. Strype is certainly wrong in placing the date of this incident in 1549.

conversation with Gardiner was cited against Ridley at his
trial more than seven years later. Gardiner's version of the
talk was rather different from Ridley's. According to Gardiner, Ridley urged him to be zealous in defending the
Sacrament, which he said was a much more important
question than that of Justification by Faith; and Gardiner
apparently interpreted this as meaning that Ridley wished
him to defend the doctrine of transubstantiation. According
to Ridley, he tried to persuade Gardiner not to indulge in
opposition to the Book of Homilies on so comparatively
minor a matter as the exclusion of Charity at a time when
the Church was endangered by the attacks of the Anabaptists on the Sacrament. Ridley stated at his trial that he had
said: 'Why, my Lord, what make you so great a matter
herein? You see many Anabaptists rise against the Sacrament of the Altar; I pray you, my Lord, be diligent in
confounding them.'[13]

Despite the very different interpretations which Ridley
and his Judges in Oxford were to place on Ridley's words
to Gardiner, it is not difficult to reconcile the two versions
of this conversation. Ridley was concerned with inducing
Gardiner to subscribe to the Book of Homilies, and cease his
opposition to the exclusion of Charity from the requirements
for salvation; he was also strongly opposed to the Anabaptists, and may well have wished to emphasize to Gardiner
the orthodoxy of himself and Cranmer and the Council
where Anabaptism was concerned. Nor had the Protestant
Bishops made any overt move against the doctrine of transubstantiation. Ridley may therefore have gone as far as to
suggest to Gardiner that he could have understood his
defiance of the Council if the issue of transubstantiation had
been involved, but that Gardiner had no excuse for refusing
to give way on an unimportant point like Justification by

Faith. He obviously used the argument that Gardiner should not weaken the unity of the Church by his opposition to the Book of Homilies at a time when it was menaced by Anabaptist attacks on the Sacrament; and if Gardiner, who certainly suspected the Protestant leaders of heresy on the subject of the Real Presence, tried to turn the conversation to his own advantage by saying that he was glad that Ridley was an orthodox believer in transubstantiation, Ridley would have been unable, in February 1548, to avoid a non-committal answer.

Gardiner was allowed to remain at liberty, and he left London and travelled to his diocese. There he preached two sermons—one at Farnham, and one in the cathedral at Winchester. In these sermons, Gardiner said that it was a solemn duty for Christians to submit to evil without resistance, and they must therefore either comply with the Book of Homilies or submit to the punishment inflicted by the Council. When the Council was informed of his thinly veiled defiance, they were incensed, and ordered Gardiner to appear before them. He was then required to preach before the King on the Feast of St. Peter; in the sermon, he was to approve the Book of Homilies without equivocation. Gardiner duly preached his sermon; he denounced Papal supremacy, agreed to the Homilies and the removal of images, and to the administration of the Sacrament in both kinds. He spoke against the marriage of priests, and spent some time in urging the importance of belief in the Real Presence. This was a contravention of the proclamation which forbade discussion of this question. Next day, on 30th June, Gardiner was arrested and sent to the Tower. He remained a prisoner for over five years.

Early in 1548, Ridley was required, along with most of his brother bishops, to reply to a number of questions about the nature of the Sacrament of the Altar. It is not certain whether the prelates and doctors who were consulted on this matter were members of any Commission, or whether Cranmer merely selected them himself for consultation. But it is clear that at some time during the winter of 1547–8 —and probably in January 1548 *—Cranmer formulated a number of questions as to the doctrine and practice of the Mass for himself and the Bishops to answer. The Archbishop of York and most of the Bishops, as well as five other leading churchmen, replied to the ten questions which Cranmer put to them. Most of the questions were not controversial, and the answers were virtually unanimous; but four of them touched on matters of bitter dispute between the old Church and the Protestant extremists. These were those that dealt with the nature of the oblation in the Mass, with the practice of hanging up the Host, with private Masses for the dead, and with whether the Liturgy should be in English or in Latin.

The answers which Ridley gave to the questions have been preserved, and are of great interest. They are the earliest of his writings which we can read in their original form, and when compared to the things which Ridley was saying and writing two years later, are remarkable for the caution with which his views are expressed. On the question of transubstantiation, Masses for the dead and of the language of the Liturgy, Ridley formulated his answers in most

* Burnet, vol. II, pp. 128–9, points out that the answers to these questions may equally well have been given after, as before, the enactment of the statute authorising the administration of the cup to the laity 'except where necessity otherwise requireth' (*Statutes of the Realm*, 1 Edw. VI, c. 1.); and it was almost certainly after Christmas 1547 that the questions were put to the bishops. See Gasquet and Bishop, *Edward VI and the Book of Common Prayer*, pp. 82–5, for the reasons indicating that it was in January 1548.

moderate language. His answers were, indeed, considerably more cautious than those which Cranmer gave himself. In reply to the question 'What is the oblation and sacrifice of Christ in the Mass?' Ridley said nothing about idolatry, but merely answered: 'The representation and commemoration of Christ's death and passion, said and done in the Mass, is called the sacrifice, oblation or immolation, of Christ; "*non rei veritate*", as learned men do write, "*sed significandi mysterio*".'[14]

Cranmer was prepared to say: 'The oblation and sacrifice of Christ in the Mass is not so called because Christ indeed is there offered and sacrificed by the priest and the people (for that was done but once by himself upon the Cross); but it is so called because it is a memory and representation of the very true sacrifice and immolation which before was made upon the Cross.'[15]

To the question as to whether Masses Satisfactory should continue, Ridley replied very shortly that he thought it was not convenient that they should continue.[16] He replied to the question as to the language in which the Liturgy should be held by saying that it should be held in a language which the people understand, and should be spoken in an audible voice, but that the words of consecration might be spoken in silence on the authority of Dionysius and Basil.[17] Cranmer went no further than Ridley on this point, while Bonner and the Catholic bishops stated plainly that the Mass should be held in Latin, though Tunstall suggested that part of the service might be in English.[18]

The caution of the Protestants in their answers to the questions was matched by the restraint with which the Catholics defended the existing doctrines and practices. These answers could only have been given during this period of twenty months between the death of Henry VIII and the publication of the Book of Common Prayer, when the Catholics were on the defensive and the Protestants still hesitated to attack on the vital issue of the Mass. It was apparently as a result of these consultations between the Bishops that the Order of Communion was published in March 1548. Ridley was almost certainly one of the Commissioners who met at Windsor to draft the book.[19] It was a bitter disappointment to the Protestant extremists. It made no changes in the traditional service of the Mass; but it provided for the insertion of certain prayers to be said in English, though the words of consecration were still to be spoken in Latin. This proposal had actually been put forward by Tunstall in his reply to Cranmer's questions, and was the most that the Catholics could reasonably hope for in the present situation. The book directed all priests to continue to administer Mass in all other respects exactly as they had done hitherto until they received instructions to the contrary; but this was an unmistakable hint that further changes were in the offing, and the King's proclamation promulgating the book was clearly intended to restrain the zeal of the Protestants until their leaders thought that the time was opportune for a further advance.[20] But if Cranmer still hesitated on the issue of transubstantiation, the Reformation was carried a step forward in other fields. In February 1548, the Council finally ordered the removal of all images from every church in the Kingdom. They also directed that no one should use candles at Candlemas, ashes on Ash Wednesday, or palms on Palm Sunday, and prohibited the practice of creeping to the Cross on Good Friday, and the use of holy bread and holy water.[21]

Ever since the previous May, Ridley had been a member of a Commission which had been set up to determine a matter which would decide what was to be the attitude of

Thomas Cranmer during the reign of Edward VI

Stephen Gardiner

Hugh Latimer

the Church of England towards divorce. A divorce case had arisen which involved one of the great dignitaries of the realm. The Marquis of Northampton, who was the brother of Katherine Parr and had been one of the Executors of Henry's will, had obtained a separation in the ecclesiastical Courts on the grounds of the adultery of the Marchioness. He did not, however, content himself with a separation, but asked for a divorce *a vinculo* which would enable him to marry Elizabeth Brooke, the daughter of Lord Cobham. This raised for the first time since the break with Rome the question of the attitude to be adopted to divorce since the repudiation of Papal supremacy. A decree of divorce *a mensa et thoro* did not permit re-marriage during the lifetime of the spouse, and it was now no longer possible to re-marry with a Papal dispensation as had been done before 1533. Lord Northampton's case would therefore be a precedent to meet a completely new situation. In view of the great importance of the case, it was decided to appoint a special commission of ten leading churchmen to determine whether, when a divorce *a mensa et thoro* had been obtained on the grounds of adultery, either or both the spouses could re-marry during the lifetime of their spouse. The commissioners were Cranmer, Tunstall and Holbeach, who was still Bishop of Rochester at the time of his appointment to the commission, and seven others, of whom Ridley was one. Smith, May, Haynes, and Redmayne were also commissioners.*

The commissioners sat from time to time for eleven months. They were in no hurry to come to a decision in a very difficult case in which many issues were involved. Apart from the religious aspect of the matter, there were

* *Cal. Pat. Rolls Edw. VI*, vol. I, pp. 137, 261 (19th April and 7th May, 1547). The Commissioners were first appointed on 19th April 1547.

political interests concerned: if they denied the Marquis the right to re-marry, they would not only be offending a powerful noble, the brother of the Queen Dowager, but would be absolutely prohibiting, in every case, the re-marriage of divorced persons during the lifetime of their spouses, except in cases of nullity. Such a decision might not only annoy powerful personages like Lord Northampton, but even, in certain circumstances, embarrass the interests of the State. To permit Northampton to re-marry, however, would not only lay them open to attack from foreign Papists and English Catholics, but would cause much resentment among many of their most ardent Protestant supporters. It is clear that the commissioners were divided in their opinion, because Cranmer's copious notes on the case contain the arguments both for and against permitting the marriage of the spouses after a divorce for adultery. They carefully considered whether Christ's prohibition on the re-marriage of the spouses except after a divorce for adultery was to be interpreted as permitting a re-marriage in such a case, and examined the conflicting views of the early Fathers and of the Councils of the Church.[22] The commissioners decided to refer the question to some learned men, who were pre-sumably canon lawyers.

Northampton grew more and more impatient at the long delay, and in January 1548, he married Elizabeth Brooke, and openly cohabited with her. The adulterous Marchion-ess protested to the Council against the Marquis' second marriage. Somerset had no personal objection to the re-marriage of a divorced person. He had been divorced from his first wife, and had married his handsome Duchess in 1530 during the lifetime of the first Lady Seymour, at a time when the Pope was prepared to grant to every English knight the dispensation to re-marry which the Emperor prevented him from granting to King Henry. But Somerset had no reason at the moment to love the Parrs. He was highly displeased that his brother Thomas had married the Queen Dowager without his consent, and was involved in a bitter quarrel with him as to whether Katherine Parr should have precedence over the Protector's wife; besides, the Protector was always eager to show that he administered justice with impartiality, and that the greatest dignitary of the realm could not defy the law with impunity. The Council therefore summoned Northampton before them, and ordered him to put away his second wife; and she was confined to the household of her would-be sister-in-law, Katherine Parr, and forbidden to have any communication with Northampton.[23] With Thomas Seymour in the household, Elizabeth Brooke can hardly have found the moral discipline very irksome.

This incident may well have served to hasten the deliberations of the commissioners, for soon after they pronounced their judgment. They decided that both Lord and Lady Northampton were free to marry again during each other's lifetime. Northampton and Elizabeth Brooke were thereupon received at Court as husband and wife. There seems little doubt that some of the commissioners disagreed with the majority decision, although the lawyers whom they consulted gave their opinion that the re-marriage of the parties was lawful.[24] We have no knowledge as to what attitude Ridley took in the matter. It has been suggested that there is some indication that he was in favour of allowing Lord Northampton to re-marry from the fact that in 1550 Hooper, in the midst of his controversy with Ridley over vestments, sent to Bucer a copy of a document which he had written about divorce three years before.[25] As Hooper was against the re-marriage of a divorced person, it is suggested that Ridley, his opponent in the vestments' controversy, was likewise opposed to Hooper on the divorce issue.* This seems quite insufficient evidence on which to ground a conclusion that Ridley supported the majority view in Lord Northampton's case; and there is, on the contrary, some evidence—though admittedly almost as slight—that he was one of the minority of the commissioners who were against permitting Northampton to re-marry. In March 1552, the judgment of the commissioners was strengthened by an Act of Parliament which enacted that Northampton's marriage to Elizabeth Brooke was valid. Ridley absented himself from the House of Lords when the bill was before the House. Indeed, Ridley, who was extraordinarily regular in his Parliamentary attendances, was nearly always absent from the House of Lords whenever any bill relating to divorce was under discussion.† This may of course have been merely coincidence; but it would also be explained by the fact that he was opposed to the official policy on divorce, and not wishing to oppose the Council and his Protestant colleagues in public as the ally of the Catholic bishops and peers, he stayed away from the House on these occasions. Apart from this, there appears to be no other indication of Ridley's attitude to divorce except the mathematical probability that he was one of the majority, rather than of the minority, on the Northampton Commission.

In the summer of 1548, Ridley was about forty-five, and was therefore considered, in the sixteenth century, to be

---

* See Gloucester Ridley, pp. 208–10.

† See *House of Lords Journal*, 9th and 19th March 1551/2, and 12th April 1552. Ridley was present for the first and second reading of Lord Northampton's divorce bill on 7th and 8th March 1551/2, but was absent on the 9th, when the House divided on the third reading. He was absent from the readings of the bills relating to unlawful divorces on 9th and 19th March 1551/2 and on 12th April 1552.

well advanced into middle age. His academic abilities, his profound learning in divinity, and his skill in disputation had not led to rapid advancement in the Church; it was only at the end of 1547 that he had been made a bishop, and only a few months earlier that he had been entrusted with any important duties in Church and State. There were probably two reasons for this: on the one hand, his absorbing interest in his studies, and his fondness for the life at Cambridge, had led him to neglect and avoid the path of political intrigue which alone led to promotion in the Church; and on the other, he had already by 1543 become suspect as a heretic, and though he had succeeded in living this down to some extent, it undoubtedly prevented his rise during the last years of Henry VIII. But the accession of Edward VI had entirely altered the position. In the last eighteen months, Ridley had been given the opportunity to serve in many positions of the greatest importance; he was now generally recognised as standing second only to Cranmer among the leaders of the Reformation. He had seen the campaign against images, in which he had given the initial lead, carried to a triumphal conclusion when the Protector had ordered the removal of every image throughout the realm. He was about to play the chief part in a still more important victory—the overthrow of transubstantiation.

NOTES

[1] Strype, *Cranmer*, pp. 205–7.

[2] *Acts of the Privy Council*, vol. II, pp. 25–7 (10th February 1546/7).

[3] Foxe, vol. VI, pp. 58–63.

[4] For the Injunctions to the Visitors, see Wilkins, *Concilia*, vol. IV, pp. 3–9.

[5] Strype, *Cranmer*, p. 209.

[6] Foxe, vol. VI, p. 45.

[7] Wriothesley's *Chronicle*, vol. I, p. 187.

[8] *Statutes of the Realm*, 1 Edw. VI, c. 11, c. 12.

[9] *Statutes of the Realm*, 1 Edw. VI, c. 3.

[10] *Statutes of the Realm*, 1 Edw. VI, c. 14.

[11] Stow's *Survey*, vol. I, p. 331; Strype, *Stow's Survey*, Part III, pp. 148-9; Simpson, *St. Paul's Cathedral*, p. xv.

[12] *Statutes of the Realm*, 1 Edw. VI, c. 1.

[13] Ridley's statement at his trial in Oxford in 1555 (Foxe, vol. VII, p. 523).

[14] Queries put concerning some abuses of the Mass; Answer of Roffen. to Question 4 (Burnet's *Records*, vol. V, p. 205. Ridley's answers to Questions 3 and 4 have obviously been transposed.)

[15] Answer of Cantuarien. to Question 3 (Burnet's *Records*, vol. V, p. 201).

[16] Answer of Roffen. to Question 7 (Burnet's *Records*, vol. V, p. 210).

[17] Answer of Roffen. to Question 9 (Burnet's *Records*, vol. V., p. 213).

[18] Answers of London., Hereford., Cicestren., Worcester (*sic*), Norvicen. and Assaven., and Answer of Dunelm., to Question 9 (Burnet's *Records*, vol. V, p. 212).

[19] Foxe, vol. V, p. 716, states that the divines who drafted the Order of the Communion met at Windsor. There is no record of the names of these divines, but it is very likely, as Heylin (Part I, pp. 57-8) suggests, that they were the same as those mentioned by Fuller as having drafted the First Book of Common Prayer.

[20] *The Order of the Communion* (*Liturgies of King Edward VI*, pp. 1-8).

[21] See the Council's proclamations of 6th and 21st February 1547/8 (Burnet's *Records*, vol. V, pp. 188-92); Cranmer's letter to Bonner, 27th January 1547/8 (Wilkins, *Concilia*, vol. IV, p. 22).

[22] For a somewhat inaccurate summary of Cranmer's notes on the Northampton divorce, see Burnet, vol. II, pp. 117-22.

[23] *Acts of the Privy Council*, vol. II, pp. 164-5 (28th January 1547/8).

[24] Burnet's *Records*, vol. V, pp. 183-4.

[25] Hooper's letter to Bucer, 17th October 1550 (Gorham, *Reformation Gleanings*, p. 185).

V

THE BOOK OF COMMON PRAYER AND
THE CAMBRIDGE VISITATION

There was a lull in the religious and political struggle from July to November 1548. This was partly due to the plague, which drove all important people away from London and Westminster. It was probably also because Cranmer and the Protestants were carefully preparing the way for the next and most critical step in their campaign. The Archbishop was preparing the draft of the first Book of Common Prayer. As for Ridley, we know comparatively little of his movements during 1548, but it seems likely that he spent the greater part of the summer at Rochester.* In September, he assisted at the consecration of the Protestant Ferrar as Bishop of St. David's by Cranmer at Chertsey†—a ceremony at which a number of innovations were made in the prescribed ordination service.

There is no record as to who were the authors of the first Book of Common Prayer. It seems unlikely that any large number of divines were consulted in the early stages of preparation.[1] The book bears every mark of both the Protestantism and the timidity of Cranmer, and it is virtually certain that the Archbishop played by far the most important part in drafting it. It has often been suggested that Cranmer consulted closely with Ridley in this work.

* It is not, however, possible to obtain any proof of this from Ridley's Register as Bishop of Rochester.

† On 9th September 1548 (Strype, *Cranmer*, p. 261).

This is very probable; there was no one else to whom he was more likely to show his draft and disclose his ideas than to Ridley. The most far-reaching provision in the book—the prohibition on the elevation of the Host—was the logical conclusion of the doctrine of the Lord's Supper which Ridley had first persuaded Cranmer to accept. But it is quite possible that Ridley played no part in the actual drafting of the Book of Common Prayer. He would probably already have preferred to see a more radical reform introduced than that which was laid down in Cranmer's draft.

Cranmer had for some years been engaged in preparing a new form of service which would be common to the whole kingdom. Over most of the country, the Church services were held in accordance with the Sarum Use; but in other districts the York Use, the Lincoln Use, the Hereford Use and the Bangor Use were in force. The difference between these various Uses was small, and of no great importance; but in the days of Henry VIII, uniformity was required in even the smallest matters. In 1543, Henry had consequently instructed Cranmer to prepare a new form of service to replace the differing Uses and to be applied throughout the realm; but the task was not considered to be important or urgent, and Cranmer did not allow this duty to distract his attention from the urgent business with which he was confronted during these dangerous years.

It was probably soon after the accession of Edward that the idea came to the Archbishop to use the new Prayer Book as a formidable weapon in the religious struggle. Instead of producing a form of service which was based on the most common factors of the five existing Uses, he intended to draft a document which contained practices which had never been known in any of them, and which, moreover, by implication made alterations in matters of doctrine. At the meeting of Convocation in November 1547, he announced that his draft was not yet ready. This may have been true, but in any case the time was not suitable, from a tactical view point, for putting forward the book which he had in mind. By the summer of 1548, things were different. Cranmer evidently decided that the time had come to present a document containing a new form of service which would advance the Reformation as far as he thought it wise to go, and would appease the impatience of the Protestants without arousing the resistance of the Catholics.

This dual purpose was evident in the Preface to the Book of Common Prayer, and in a note at the end explaining why some ceremonies had been abolished and some retained. While this stated, on the one hand, that the object of the new service was to replace the diversity of Uses with a service common to the realm, it also declared the necessity of eliminating the ritual and traditions which had crept into the Church since the days of the early Fathers, though the need to retain a certain amount of ritual was emphasized. The Note on Ceremonies was equally careful not to offend either the foreign Papist Kings or the Protestant Princes and republics; it stated that the Book did not intend to criticise the form of service used in other countries, as the regulation of church services in every land was a matter for the rulers of each nation.[2] The Book stressed the need to read the Lessons from the Bible, and to sing the Psalms, and made a number of alterations in practices. The most important were in the service of the Mass. A great deal of ritual by the priest was abolished. The Book contained an exhortation to the people to come to Communion, which had already been published in the Order of Communion of March and which was to be read out during the service unless the priest had made his own exhortation in his sermon; this exhortation contained all kinds of ambiguous phrases which were equally applicable to a corporal or a spiritual Presence. The whole of the service, was henceforth to be in English. The priest was to make the sign of the cross twice over the elements—as he spoke the words 'bless' and 'sanctify'—but these were the only occasions on which the sign of the Cross was to be made in place of the twenty-seven occasions in the existing service. Most important of all, alterations were to be made in the Prayer of Consecration; and the new form of words was of such a nature that it was perfectly applicable to a belief in the spiritual Presence— 'Hear us, O merciful Father, we beseech thee, and with thy blessed spirit and word vouchsafe to bless and sanctify these thy gifts and creatures of bread and wine that they may be unto us the body and blood of thy most dearly beloved Son Jesus Christ, who in the same night that he was betrayed took bread'. The priest was not to elevate the Host or show it to the people as he spoke the words of consecration.[3]

Cranmer was supposed to be preparing a common form of service to replace the slightly different Uses in accordance with the orders given to him by King Henry in 1543. But in the eyes of the Catholic bishops the service which Cranmer had prepared, though superficially resembling the Sarum Use, was radically different in spirit from any which had ever been found in any Use hitherto, and by implication put forward a doctrine which men were burned for advocating in 1543. Only two years before they had burned as a dangerous heretic any preacher who denied the truth of transubstantiation to a handful of rustics or artizans; now the Archbishop of Canterbury, while not openly making any change in doctrine, was proposing to force every priest in every parish in England to abandon the old service of the

Mass and to substitute a form of service in which the doctrine of the corporal Presence was undermined at its very foundations. Only a few months earlier, the Order of Communion had left the Liturgy in its traditional Latin tongue; now the whole service was to be in English, and the vital words of consecration were associated with an ambiguous phrase which would be equally applicable to a spiritual as to a corporal Presence. The exhortation to come to Communion which was to be printed in the book was not made compulsory; but though the learned Catholic bishop or priest was to be entitled to substitute his own exhortation in his sermon, the ordinary happy-go-lucky priest, who was no more ardent in his religion than he had been thirty years before, would obviously adopt the easy course of reading out the exhortation in the book. Worst of all, the priest was now to be forbidden to elevate the Host. The condemnation of the elevation of the Host could only be right if the presence of the flesh and blood in the bread and wine was spiritual and not corporal.

It is probable that Cranmer submitted his draft in the first place to Ridley and eleven other bishops and divines who met at Chertsey and Windsor in September. Later he presented it to all the bishops.[4] The retention of so much of the traditional practices did not placate the Catholic bishops; they strongly opposed the book, and prepared to resist the Archbishop's project of enforcing it upon the people. The Council nevertheless decided to obtain statutory authority for the adoption of the Book of Common Prayer as soon as Parliament reassembled.

Parliament met on 24th November. The Protector submitted a bill of Uniformity to provide for the adoption of the Book of Common Prayer. It provided that the book should come into operation at Whitsun, 9th June 1549, and thereafter was to be used and followed in every church throughout the realm. The priest who refused to apply it, or who used any other form of service, was liable to six months' imprisonment and to forfeiture of the revenues of his benefice for one year, for the first offence; for the second offence, he was liable to one year's imprisonment and to forfeiture of all ecclesiastical preferments; for the third offence, he was to suffer imprisonment for life. Any layman who criticised the book in writing, or who interrupted the service prescribed by the book or who procured the use of any other service, was to be subject to the heavy fine of £10 for the first offence and £20 for the second, and was to suffer imprisonment for life and confiscation of all his goods for the third offence.[5] The Act did not impose any penalty on people who refused to go to church, but non-attendance at the new service was punishable by ecclesiastical censures and excommunication in exactly the same way as the failure to attend the old service had been.[6] By comparison with the heresy laws of Henry VIII, the penalties were very light; but the severe punishment on the third offence for priests who refused to conform, and for persons who wrote against the book, were sufficient to ensure that there should be no organised opposition to the new services.

In putting forward the bill, the Council and the Protestant leaders professed to be adopting a conservative, rather than a revolutionary, position. The preamble to the bill stated that it aimed at purging the Church of all modern innovations in order to revert to the practices which had been in use in the primitive Church, and brazenly stated that all the commissioners had been unanimous in approving the book. In the House of Commons, where the members were busy in bitter opposition to the Protector's bills for agrarian reform, the bill was passed almost without discussion; but it was another matter in the House of Lords. The Catholic bishops were not deceived by the pretence of uniformity and conservatism which the Protestant leaders had adopted; they recognised that the Book of Common Prayer was undermining the very foundations of transubstantiation, and consequently prepared to fight the bill with all possible vigour. In view of the attitude of their opponents, Cranmer and Ridley decided to throw aside the mask, and come boldly out into the open. They therefore arranged for a disputation to be held in the House of Lords on the question of transubstantiation a few days before the Uniformity bill was introduced in the House of Commons.

The disputation began on 15th December. It was resumed on the 17th, and continued on each of the next two days. The Protector himself presided, and Warwick and Sir Thomas Smith disputed along with the bishops. The members of the House of Commons came to the bar of the House to hear the disputation. It caused a great sensation. The Catholic bishops were probably much less surprised than were the ardent Protestants to hear Cranmer declare himself opposed to the doctrine of the corporal Presence; the zealous reformers had no idea that Henry's Archbishop, who for nearly two years since the tyrant's death had firmly checked all sign of extremism, was prepared to lead them to the overthrow of the Mass. They were equally impressed by the attitude of Ridley, who was at his most brilliant in the disputation, and in the eyes of his supporters completely confounded Heath, who argued in favour of transubstantiation. In this, however, Ridley's task was made easier by Warwick, who assisted the learned arguments of Ridley with the mocking interjections with which he interrupted Heath, and prevented him from developing his case. Ridley also refuted the arguments of Day, the Bishop of Chichester.[7]

Next month the issue came up again in the debate on the bill of Uniformity. Bonner, Tunstall, Thirlby, Skyp, Heath, Repps, Aldrich and Day voted against the bill;* they were joined by three of the Lords temporal, one of whom was Ridley's relative, Lord Dacre of Gilsland, who since the attainder of the Percies was the most powerful figure in Northumberland. The bill passed the House, and became law; the old forms of service were to be used until Whitsun, but thereafter the Act of Uniformity would be in force.

The Protector presented another bill to Parliament to enable priests to marry. Since the repeal of the Statute of the Six Articles, married priests were no longer guilty of felony; but the practice was still prohibited by the canon law. Parliament was now asked to carry out the recommendation of Convocation in the previous year. The bill provided that priests might marry after ordination, and that married men might be ordained as priests, while it retrospectively validated any marriage of priests which had already been performed.† The House of Commons readily passed the bill. In the House of Lords, Ridley was probably one of the spokesmen for the Council, for he is said to have been among the foremost advocates of the measure in general, along with Redmayne, Taylor and Benson.[8] Ridley was certainly an excellent person to put up to support the bill, for his private life was above reproach; there was no breath of scandal abroad about Ridley, as there was about Cranmer and Gardiner and many other bishops. The attitude of the Protestant leaders was that it was eminently

* *House of Lords Journal,* 15th January 1548/9.
† *Statutes of the Realm,* 2 & 3 Edw. VI, c. 21; the Act provided that where the wives of priests, who had been put away by the priest (as was done in many cases after the passing of the Act of the Six Articles) had re-married, their marriage to the priest was not deemed to be subsisting.

desirable, as was stated in the preamble to the bill, that priests should remain unmarried, both because chastity was a worthy moral state, and because a priest should not be troubled with the cares and distractions of a wife and family, but should give his whole attention to his flock; but it had unfortunately been found that priests, being subject to human frailty, had frequently indulged in fornication. As a remedy against fornication, it was right that priests who were unable to resist the temptation should be permitted to marry. Even Pope Aeneas Silvius had suggested this reform nearly a hundred years before on the same grounds. The marriage of priests had not been forbidden in the early Church; Peter and several of the Apostles were married, and so, probably, was Paul; and the celibacy of the clergy had only been generally introduced by Hildebrand in the eleventh century. As to the argument that priests who married were breaking their vows of chastity, the reformers replied that the oath to follow chastity meant that the priest would refrain from adultery and fornication, and did not compel him to abstain from lawful matrimony.[9] The bill was before the House of Lords for more than two months; it finally passed on 19th February 1549. Eight bishops and four of the Lords temporal voted against the bill.[10] The Archbishop of Canterbury, who had been hiding his wife for nearly seventeen years, was now able to admit that he was a married man, and so could Archbishop Holgate, who had also married secretly a year or so before.

The Protestant leaders also introduced legislation to deal with the controversial question of fasting during Lent. In the two years since the death of Henry VIII, Lent had been a season of bitter dispute, and had witnessed a flood of pamphlets attacking the laws which enforced fasting. It had long been an issue between many Protestants and the

Church, and there had been many convictions under Henry for violations of the fasting laws. But Cranmer was not prepared to yield to the extremists on this question. In March, a statute was passed which made some alterations in the existing laws, but which enforced fasting during Lent as before. The preamble to the Act declared that while no day and no food was purer than any other, it was virtuous to indulge in abstinence and necessary to assist the fishing industry; and the statute enacted that, subject to the usual exemptions, no one should eat meat during Lent, or on any Friday, Saturday or Ember Day, or on any other fish day that might be proclaimed, on pain of imprisonment for ten days without any meat at all.*

Soon after the prorogation of Parliament, Ridley visited his diocese. He seems to have stayed in Rochester for about a month in March and April 1549; he was evidently there for Easter.[11] His chief concern was probably to ensure that his clergy were ready and willing to receive the Book of Common Prayer, when it came into force at Whitsun. The book and the Act of Uniformity had caused widespread resentment throughout the country, and this could be expected to increase when the new services actually came into operation. Most of the priests in England were Catholics, if not very zealous ones, and many of them did not hesitate to agitate amongst their parishioners against the Book of Common Prayer. Nor had the book been received with approval by many of the Protestants. The extremist sects and the less shrewd among the Protestant rank and file did not appreciate the significance of the changes in the Liturgy; they were indignant that the sign of the Cross was

* *Statutes of the Realm*, 2 & 3 Edw. VI, c. 19. There were exemptions in favour of the aged and sick, pregnant women, soldiers, and those obtaining a special licence.

still retained in two places in the service, and that the book did not contain an express repudiation of transubstantiation. But there was probably less opposition in Protestant Kent than elsewhere, for Ridley was fully satisfied with the obedience which he met with in his diocese.[12]

The opposition to the Book of Common Prayer was developing against the background of the rising social discontent. The landlords had obstructed the Protector's plans for appeasing it both inside and outside Parliament, though under the pressure of the Protector and of popular opinion two of Somerset's measures had been passed by Parliament in the winter of 1548–9.[13] In the main, however, the nobles and landowners paid no heed either to the sermons of Latimer at Court or to the economic arguments of Hales and his 'Commonwealth's men'. Somerset had only succeeded in arousing hatred on all sides by his social policy. The landlords thought of him as a dangerous demagogue, and bitterly resented his denunciations of the greed of the new nobility which had 'sprung from the dunghill'. These were certainly strange words to hear from Somerset; his patent of nobility dated back only twelve years, and during this time he had himself amassed an enormous fortune, more than ten times larger than the total revenues of Ridley's see of Rochester. The tenants, on the other hand, were rapidly realising that the Protector's speeches and good intentions had not brought them any solution to their complaints, and were beginning to look to other means to achieve their ends. Riots had broken out in Hertfordshire in the spring of 1548. When at last the Protector took action, and set up a Court of Requests, under the presidency of Cecil, to hear complaints against enclosures and evictions, he succeeded in alienating the support of the great majority of the lords of the Council, as well as bitterly antagonising the nobles and

L

landowners and incurring the disapproval of the common lawyers; while he made himself most unpopular with the people by ordering the execution of his brother Thomas, the popular Lord Admiral, for high treason. Cranmer was one of the lords of the Council who signed Lord Seymour's death warrant, and in the House of Lords Ridley voted, together with all his colleagues, in favour of the Act of Attainder, and condemned to death the Admiral who had been sitting with them in the House only a month before.*

While Ridley was in Rochester, ensuring that no Catholic priest in his diocese should obstruct the Book of Common Prayer, he was suddenly required to go into action against a very different kind of enemy. In April 1549, the Council received letters from the Justices of the Peace in Kent informing them of the activities of Joan Bocher. Joan was an old heretic; she had been a friend of Ann Askew, and had been brought before Cranmer in the diocese of Canterbury in 1542, when, according to the Catholic Prebendaries and Preachers in Canterbury, she had been released with Cranmer's connivance. She had now been spreading extraordinary opinions in Kent, and had apparently succeeded in disseminating her pamphlets at Court.[14] The justices in Kent found Joan Bocher's views very hard to understand, but as far as they could make out she was asserting that Christ had not taken flesh of the Virgin, but had miraculously passed through Mary as through a glass.[15] Of one thing, however, the Justices were sure: she was an Anabaptist. It was obvious that Joan Bocher was propagating a serious heresy, but in view of the repeal of all the Acts against heresy, the Justices were in doubt as to what action

* *House of Lords Journal*, 25th, 26th and 27th February 1548/9. Thomas Seymour last attended the House of Lords on 17th January (see *House of Lords Journal*).

they should take. The Council promptly set up a commission to repress Anabaptism. The commissioners were Cranmer, Ridley, Goodrich, Holbeach, Day, Thirlby, Heath, May, Latimer, Haynes, Sir Thomas Smith, Petre, Cecil and others.[16] Day, Thirlby and Heath could be trusted to work hand in hand with Cranmer and Ridley in the matter of Anabaptism, and could profitably be employed on the commission rather than be left with more time on their hands to thwart the Archbishop's policy in other fields. The Council also ordered the justices to arrest Joan Bocher, and to send her to London to appear before the commissioners.

These events immediately started a campaign against Anabaptism throughout London and Kent. The Anabaptists denounced infant baptism on the grounds that it was not expressly authorised in the Gospels, and as Christ had directed his disciples to go out and baptise and teach the people, they argued that teaching should in all cases accompany baptism, and that no child should be baptised until he was old enough to understand the teachings of Christianity. But Cranmer and Ridley and the Protestant bishops were now using the term 'Anabaptist' as loosely as Fisher and Warham had used the term 'Lutheran' thirty years before —to denote anyone who propagated religious doctrines which were more unorthodox than those which they held themselves. It was particularly applied to anyone who denied the divinity of Christ. The Protestant leaders were at one with the Catholics in considering Anabaptism to be a dreadful threat to both Church and State, to be subversive of the royal authority, of the privileges of the nobility and gentry, and of the rights of private property itself. They were convinced that if Anabaptism were not sternly suppressed, there would soon be a repetition of the Munster horror on English soil. The rumour also spread that the Pope and Cardinal Pole had sent their agents to England disguised as Anabaptist refugees to disrupt the unity of the Protestant Church of England.[17]

Ridley was apparently still in Rochester when Joan Bocher was tried before the commissioners. Joan was examined, and behaved with defiance before the commission; all attempts to induce her to recant were unsuccessful, and she was excommunicated as a heretic. So quickly did the commissioners deal with Joan Bocher that though Ridley must have returned to London within little more than a fortnight after her arrest, her case had already been concluded before he was able to take any part in it.* Her excommunication now raised most serious difficulties for Cranmer and the Council. She was the first person to be excommunicated for heresy since the accession of Edward VI and the repeal of the heresy statutes; but now that the Act of 1534 was no longer in force, there was no longer any statutory power to burn heretics. It therefore seemed that Joan could be sentenced to no greater punishment than imprisonment, which could still be imposed by any ecclesiastical court or by a commission exercising its powers; yet the fight against Anabaptism would be hamstrung if this were the severest penalty which could be imposed on the greatest enemies of society. But Lord Rich and the common lawyers were able to give the Council some welcome legal advice. The Lord Chancellor disclosed that a study of the old law reports made it plain that heretics had been burned in England

---

* Joan Bocher was excommunicated by the Commissioners on 30th April 1549; the sentence was signed by Cranmer, Smith, Cooke, Latimer and Lyell (Sentence on Joan Bocher, Burnet's *Records*, vol. V, pp. 246–9). Ridley was in Rochester just before Easter, which was on 21st April (*Works*, p. 328); he had already arrived in Cambridge by 5th May (Lamb's *Collection*, p. 109).

before the statute of 1401 had been passed.* It therefore followed that the King had power at common law, independent of any statute, to order the burning of excommunicated heretics under the royal prerogative.

The Council then decided that Joan Bocher should be burned unless she could be induced to recant; but they hesitated to proceed to execution. It is at least possible, as Foxe states, that the eleven-year-old King was shocked at the idea of burning her.† According to Foxe, it was Cranmer who at last succeeded in persuading Edward to agree to her death. The Archbishop pointed out that Moses had ordered blasphemers to be stoned; he argued that the burning of Anabaptists could not be compared to the action of the Catholics in burning Protestants, for the Protestants had merely wished to reform the doctrines of the Church, whereas the Anabaptists had blasphemed against the Apostles' Creed. Cranmer told the King that in conscience he had no choice in the matter; it was the duty of a king, as God's representative on earth, to punish offences against God, just as it was the duty of the magistrates, as the King's representatives, to punish all crimes against the King's person. Edward finally agreed, with great reluctance, to

* Apart from doubtful cases where Albigensian heretics, and a case where a deacon who had married a Jewess, were burned in the thirteenth century, Henry IV had ordered the burning of Sawtre in 1401, a fortnight before the statute of 1401 came into force (see Holdsworth, *History of English Law*, vol. I, pp. 616–7.

† Foxe, vol. V, p. 699. For the arguments against the authenticity of Foxe's story, see Editor's Biographical Note in Hutchinson's *Works*, pp. iii–v, and Pollard, *Thomas Cranmer*, p. 262. These arguments do not appear to be very convincing. The fact that the entry in Edward's Journal shows no trace of regret is hardly conclusive, in view of the fact that the entry refers to 2nd May 1550, when Joan was finally burned; Edward may well have opposed the idea when it was first broached in May 1549, and yet have become reconciled to it a year later. See also Burnet, vol. II, p. 204.

sign the warrant; but Cranmer assured him that it would not be carried out at once, and that every attempt would still be made to convert Joan Bocher before she was burned. Joan remained in prison under sentence of death for a whole year.

In May 1549 the commission for the suppression of Anabaptism sat in judgment on a number of small London tradesmen. The defendants were all classed as Anabaptists, but they held widely differing views. Some asserted, like Joan Bocher, that Jesus had not been born to the Virgin by the ordinary human processes of birth; some denied that Christ had been born to the Virgin at all; others, on the contrary, asserted that he was not divine, but was merely a great religious teacher and prophet. Most of them were opposed to infant baptism. With the warrant signed for Joan Bocher's burning, the commissioners could now threaten the London Anabaptists with the stake; the heretics all recanted, and Cranmer was spared the embarrassment of asking the King for authority to burn them. The Anabaptists carried their fagot at Paul's Cross.[18]

In the trial of the London Anabaptists, as in that of Joan Bocher, the commissioners were deprived of the assistance of the Bishop of Rochester; for Ridley had hardly returned from Rochester before he again left London to perform another important duty. In November 1548, Ridley had been appointed as one of the Visitors to Cambridge University, and in April 1549, the Protector ordered the Visitors to go to Cambridge to begin the visitation. The other Visitors were Goodrich, who was the diocesan Bishop at Cambridge; Paget, the Secretary of State; Sir Thomas Smith and John Cheke, who had both been professors of Greek in Cambridge before they left to perform more important duties at Court; May, the Dean of St. Paul's; and the King's physi-

cian, Dr. Wendy.[19] Cheke was a great friend of Ridley, who
declared that Cheke was 'one of Christ's special advocates
and one of his principal proctors'.[20] Ridley had also been
appointed as one of the Visitors to Oxford, where a similar
visitation was held at the same time; but he did not go to
Oxford, or play any part at all in the deliberations of the
Oxford Visitors.[21]

The King's Injunctions to the Visitors required them to
purge the Universities of all traces of popery and superstition, and to see that the royal supremacy over the Church
was fully recognised. The visitation was primarily intended
to ensure that no officer of the University would frustrate
the religious policy of Cranmer and the Protector; but the
Visitors were also required to enforce academic discipline,
and to found a Chair of Medicine at Cambridge. Moreover,
they had another duty to perform. The Protector had
decided to close Clare Hall, and to merge it with Trinity
Hall. He had originally intended to suppress Trinity Hall
as well as Clare Hall, and to merge both Colleges into a new
College; but Gardiner, the Master of Trinity Hall, naturally
refused to collaborate from the Tower in suppressing his
own college,* and on reflection the alternative plan was
adopted. Clare Hall was a college to which Northumberland men were particularly apt to go, and Ridley's cousin
Launcelot was a member of Clare Hall. It had been
founded for the purpose of studying the canon law, but the
Council had decided that the undergraduates of Clare Hall
could far more profitably be employed in studying civil law
at Trinity Hall, for there was a need for trained civilians in
the King's service. Nothing was said as to what would happen to the lands and property of Clare Hall; but in view of

* Fuller, *History of Cambridge University*, p. 242; but against this
view, see Cooper, *Annals of Cambridge*, vol. II, p. 32 n.

the usual practice in such cases, it must have been clear to everyone that the assets of the College would be appropriated by the King, and then handed over as a gift to the Lord Protector and the members of the Council.

The Vice-Chancellor and the officers of the University, together with the heads of Colleges and the Fellows, had been summoned to appear before the Visitors in the new chapel of the University between eight and ten in the morning of Monday, 6th May. Ridley, Cheke, Paget, May and Wendy had all arrived in Cambridge by Sunday the 5th, and Ridley took up residence in Pembroke Hall. Goodrich arrived in time for the opening of the proceedings next morning. Smith apparently stayed at Court. For some reason, the Visitors and the University authorities did not go to the new chapel, as arranged, but assembled in Christ's College, which was used by the Visitors as their headquarters throughout the visitation; they then proceeded to St. Mary's Church, where Ridley preached a sermon. When Ridley had finished, they went to King's College chapel, where the commission to the Visitors was read. All the University and College officers present were then required to swear the oath of supremacy, and any who had been summoned to appear and had failed to do so were pronounced to be in contempt of the Visitors. Cheke then read out the new statutes of the University which the Protector had promulgated, and Goodrich made a speech about the need to obey the King before the Visitors went to St. John's College for dinner.[22]

The business of the visitation began next day. The Visitors spent the day at St. John's, and then four days at Trinity. They then proceeded to Gonville Hall, and next to Trinity Hall. At the Colleges, the Visitors interviewed the Master and every Fellow, graduate and undergraduate in turn, talking to them in private and requiring them to subscribe to the articles which they had drafted relating to the good order of the College and obedience to the King. At the end of the day's work, they were invariably entertained to supper by the Master of the College in question. On 15th May, it was the turn of Clare Hall.[23] The Visitors impressed on the Master and Fellows the need for closing down the College so that it could be merged with Trinity Hall and the students put to studying the civil, rather than the canon, law. But the Master and Fellows refused to surrender their charters. They told the Visitors that they had sworn an oath to maintain the College and its privileges, and would never collaborate in suppressing it. The Visitors spent two whole days at Clare Hall, but at the end of this time had been quite unable to persuade the Master and Fellows to surrender their charters.[24]

The Visitors then met in private to discuss what to do. Some of them suggested that in view of the intransigeance of the Master and Fellows, the Visitors should forthwith issue an order dissolving Clare Hall; and they now told Ridley, for the first time, that they had been given powers by the Protector, before they left London, to suppress the College by royal command if Clare Hall refused to surrender its charters voluntarily. Ridley strongly opposed the proposal. He argued that to suppress a Cambridge College by order of the King without the consent of the Master and Fellows of the College was a breach of the privileges of the University, and he refused to be a party to the project. Ridley's colleagues were surprised at his attitude; it had been made perfectly clear to them when they had been appointed Visitors that they were to dissolve the College if the charters were not surrendered. They strongly criticised Ridley, and suggested that his unwillingness to suppress

Clare Hall was due to the fact that many of the Fellows and undergraduates were Northumberland men. But in view of the vigour of Ridley's opposition, the Visitors finally agreed to take no action for the present; instead they wrote a letter to the Protector on 18th May.* In this letter, they reported on the progress of the visitation to date, and on the refusal of Clare Hall to surrender its charters, and asked for instructions as to what they should do next.

On the same day, Ridley wrote a personal letter to Somerset. He reminded the Protector that he had authorised Ridley to approach him at any time if he had important matters to raise with him. Ridley wrote that he had grave doubts as to the propriety of dissolving a great College which was devoted to the study of canon law. It was not that he had any consideration for the members of Clare Hall—many of them, indeed, had misbehaved themselves, and ought to be expelled; it was his respect for the institution and for the canon law which made him oppose the plan to suppress the College. He referred to the story of Naboth's garden, and reminded the Protector that many eminent scholars had been educated at Clare Hall in the past; he expressly mentioned Latimer, whose sermons at Court had attracted so much attention the previous year. Ridley wrote that if Alexander the Great could spare a city from destruction because Homer had lived there,†

* Bradford's *Works*, vol. II, pp. 369–70. The letter is signed by Goodrich, Ridley, Cheke, May and Wendy. Smith apparently never came to Cambridge, and Paget had evidently already returned to Court. The word 'Canterbury' on p. 370 is of course a misprint for 'Cambridge'.

† Ridley, for all his profound knowledge of Greek and his excellent memory, was of course wrong in thinking that it was on account of Homer's house that Alexander had spared Thebes; it was because of Pindar's house. Ridley, however, implied in the letter that he was not certain that he had remembered the incident correctly.

surely the Council could spare Clare Hall for the sake of Latimer. He ended by asking that if the Protector insisted nevertheless on suppressing Clare Hall, he might be permitted to absent himself from the meetings of the Visitors at which this action was taken, or to remain silent when the matter was discussed, as his conscience would not allow him to be a party to the dissolution of the College.[25]

The Lord Protector was probably less impressed by the example of Alexander than by the prospect of acquiring a large share of the revenues of Clare Hall for himself or his friends. He was incensed at Ridley's attitude; this was a quarter from which he had not expected defiance. Somerset apparently also received another letter from some of the Visitors, who complained that Ridley had frustrated their aims by his barking. When Somerset heard about the attitude that Ridley was adopting, he sent for Cranmer, and demanded an explanation of Ridley's conduct in frustrating the King's decision to dissolve Clare Hall. Ridley had obviously written to Cranmer about the matter, for the Archbishop explained that Ridley was motivated by the importance which he attached to the study of the canon law.[26] Somerset then wrote a letter to Ridley in which he expressed his indignation at Ridley's behaviour; he stated that if Ridley had not approved of the injunctions to the Visitors to suppress Clare Hall if the charters were not voluntarily surrendered, he ought to have refused to accept the appointment as a Visitor.

On 1st June, Ridley replied to the Protector in a letter from Pembroke Hall. He explained the circumstances in which he had come to Cambridge. Just before Easter, while he was still in Rochester, he had received letters from Smith and May informing him that he was to go to Cambridge, and stating that he would be required to preach a sermon at the opening of the Visitation; but Smith had not mentioned the purpose of the Visitation, nor had he made any reference to Clare Hall. Ridley had therefore sent his servant from Rochester to London to discover what was the purpose of the Visitation, in order that he might prepare an appropriate sermon; he had then received a letter from May informing him of the general objects of the Visitation, but stating that he could learn about his duties in greater detail after he returned to London. It was not until after the Visitors had reached Cambridge, and the Visitation had been in progress for two days, that he had learned about their duties in connexion with Clare Hall. He had tried his best to induce the Master and Fellows of Clare Hall to surrender their charters voluntarily; but when he had found out that the Visitors were intending to revoke the charters, under authority of the King's command, and to suppress the College, he had felt bound in conscience to protest. He had, however, taken care to do this in private with the other Visitors, and to do nothing which savoured of a public condemnation of the Visitors' injunctions. He denied that he had been in any way influenced by the fact that many members of Clare Hall were his fellow countrymen from Northumberland. He had been accused of barking, but it was his profession to bark to give warning of the wrath of God.

In this second letter, Ridley made no attempt to renew his plea for the preservation of Clare Hall; but while his letter was full of expressions of devotion to Somerset, he made it clear that he was if necessary prepared to resist and offend the Protector.

Before God, there is no man this day living (the King's Majesty for his honour only excepted) whose favour or displeasure I do either seek or fear, as your Grace's favour or displeasure; for of God, both your Grace's authority, and my bounded duty for your Grace's benefits, bind me so to do. So that if the desire of any man's favour, or fear of displeasure, should weigh more with me than godliness and reason; truly if I may be bold to say the truth, I must needs say, that I am most in danger to offend herein, either for desire of your Grace's favour, or for fear of your Grace's displeasure. And yet I shall not cease (God willing) daily to pray God so to stay and strengthen my frailty with holy fear, that I do not commit the thing for favour or fear of any mortal man, whereby my conscience may threaten me with the loss of the favour of the living God, but that it may please him, of his gracious goodness (howsoever the world go) to blow this in the ears of my heart, *Deus dissipabit ossa eorum qui hominibus placuerint.*[27]

He ended his letter by again asking the Protector to give him leave either to absent himself or to remain silent when his fellow Visitors suggested anything which was against his conscience.

Somerset replied in a letter from Richmond on 10th June. The letter was not unfriendly in tone, but the Protector showed plainly that he did not accept Ridley's excuses. He probably did not believe Ridley's story that he had not realised until he reached Cambridge that the Visitors would be expected to suppress Clare Hall; and it is indeed a little difficult to accept, in view of the fact that it was plainly stated in the commission appointing the Visitors in November 1548—long before Ridley went to Rochester— that the Visitors were to dissolve two or more colleges in order to found a college of civil law.[28] Somerset wrote that he had no intention of forcing Ridley to do anything against his conscience, but that he was shocked to find that Ridley was suggesting that his fellow Visitors, who were prepared to carry out the King's wishes, were less conscientious than Ridley himself. He was surprised that Ridley's conscience did not enable him to see how much the King needed the services of trained civil lawyers in negotiating treaties with foreign princes, and how necessary it was that Clare Hall should be merged with Trinity Hall. He was sure that the Master and Fellows of Clare Hall would not have been so intransigeant unless they had known that Ridley was supporting them in their attitude, and he blamed Ridley for the failure to achieve the desired result. If Ridley's conscience did not permit him to assist the Visitors in performing their duty, he ought, as he himself had suggested, to absent himself or keep silent.[29]

Though the displeasure of the Protector was not to be lightly regarded, Ridley had continued to use his influence in favour of Clare Hall even after he had received Somerset's first letter in May. On Whit Sunday, 9th June, the Registrar of the University, Rogers, who had been employed to send reports of the Visitors' proceedings to Smith, wrote to Smith that Ridley was still resisting any attempt to revoke the charters of the College; and Smith and the Council apparently decided to recall Ridley from Cambridge. But on the very day when Somerset wrote his second letter, Ridley realised that he could do no more, and told the other Visitors that he was prepared to do what they wished. On Friday the 14th, Rogers wrote to Smith that Ridley had agreed to suppress Clare Hall.[30] On Tuesday the 11th, Ridley had left Cambridge to spend a few days at Soham; it was certainly appropriate that he should visit his own parish two days after the inauguration of the Book of Common Prayer. He only returned to Cambridge late on the Friday evening,[31] and doubtless found Somerset's letter of the 10th waiting for him at Pembroke Hall. As Rogers had written on the same day to tell Smith that Ridley had capitulated in the matter of Clare Hall, it is obvious that

Ridley must have told his colleagues of his decision on Whit Monday, before he left for Soham. On Saturday the 15th, the other Visitors wrote to Smith asking him not to recall Ridley.[32] These developments were sufficient to appease the Protector, and Ridley remained in Cambridge.* In fact, by his attitude he had saved Clare Hall. The Visitors returned to the College again on 17th June, and expelled the Master and one of the Fellows, and on two further occasions they summoned the Fellows of Clare Hall to appear before them at Christ's College;[33] but Clare Hall was not suppressed for the time being, and the whole matter was allowed to lapse.

Meanwhile the Visitors had been examining the state of the other colleges. On 22nd May, they were at Pembroke Hall where Ridley entertained his colleagues to supper. They had trouble at St. Peter's and at Jesus. The Fellows of Peterhouse denounced their Master for misconduct to the Visitors, but after several hearings they cleared him of the charge; on one occasion, they called unexpectedly at the College to investigate a theft of plate. At Jesus College, matters were more serious: they ordered some altars to be removed, and they found, in one of the rooms, a number of images, which they ordered to be destroyed. They expelled the Master and one of the Fellows; another Fellow they excommunicated, but released him from the sentence two

---

* Bass-Mullinger, *History of Cambridge University*, vol. II, p. 137, Cooper, *Ath. Cant.*, vol. I, p. 136, etc., state that Ridley was recalled from Cambridge during the visitation; but this appears to be wrong, for Ridley was in Cambridge throughout the visitation, and as late as 2nd July—two days before the end of the visitation; on that day, he attended the reading of the Law Act at Christ's College, and signed the Visitors' Injunctions (Lamb's *Collection*, p. 118, *Collection of Statutes of Cambridge University*, p. 37). With regard to the erasure of Ridley's name from the signatures to the Statutes of Trinity College, see Bass-Mullinger, *op. cit.*, vol. II, p. 137 n.

days later. Nor did the Visitors limit their activities to the Colleges and Hostels, for they examined the Vicar of Steeple Morden, who had omitted the words 'He descended into Hell' from the Creed.[34]

In the course of the visitation, Ridley was engaged on a matter of the utmost importance. This was no less a task than to make a public pronouncement against transubstantiation. All discussion on transubstantiation was still prohibited under the royal proclamation, but this had hardly checked the attacks on the doctrine by the Protestant sects, and these had been renewed with increased vigour after the publication of the Book of Common Prayer, and the disputation on the Real Presence in London in the previous December. An attempt to dispute on the subject at Cambridge in February 1549 had been banned by the Vice-Chancellor; but soon after, Peter Martyr had been permitted to take part in a disputation on transubstantiation at Oxford. A licence was now granted for a similar disputation at Cambridge. Goodrich, Cheke, May and Wendy were appointed as commissioners, along with Ridley, to hear the disputation; but Ridley was to preside as Prolocutor, and he alone of them all played an active part, though the other Visitors, and the Marquis of Northampton and other dignitaries, sat at Ridley's side during the disputation.[35]

The commissioners were to hear argument in favour of the corporal and spiritual Presence, and to give their decision as to which was correct. The decision would not have any legal effect, but it would be an authoritative pronouncement under the royal authority, and consequently would carry the greatest moral weight. Two propositions were to be debated at the disputation. The first was: 'Transubstantiation cannot be proved by the plain and manifest words

of Scripture; nor can thereof be necessarily collected, nor
yet confirmed, by the consents of the ancient Fathers these
thousand years past'.* The second proposition was: 'That
in the Lord's Supper is none other oblation or sacrifice than one only remembrance of Christ's death and of
thanksgiving'.[36] The two propositions were to be discussed
together. Twelve doctors of the University were to take
part in the disputation, which was to last three days, with
different disputants on each day.

The disputation opened in the Philosophy Schools after
dinner on Thursday, 20th June. It was then adjourned till
the afternoon of 24th June, when it was resumed, and then
adjourned again till next day, when it was concluded.†
The propositions were asserted for the Protestants by
Madew on the opening day; on the second day, Edmund
Grindal and Pilkington were among the Protestant disputants. The Protestants put forward the argument that
Christ had called the wine at the Last Supper the 'fruit of
the vine'; that the consecrated bread, when consumed, had
the nutritive value of bread; that as Jesus had ascended into
Heaven, he could not be corporally present in the Sacra-

* Foxe, vol. VI, p. 306, where, however, the wording of the first
proposition is given with the word 'for' inserted before 'these thousand
years past', thereby altering the meaning, which according to Pilkington, who took part in the disputation, was that transubstantiation could
not be proved by the writings of the ancient Fathers existing a thousand
years ago, i.e. in A.D. 500; Pilkington, *The Burning of Paul's Church in
London* (Pilkington's *Works*, p. 523).

† Lamb's *Collection*, pp. 114–15. Gloucester Ridley, p. 276, gives the
first two dates correctly, but wrongly states that the last day of the
disputation was on 27th June. He is almost certainly confusing the last
day of the disputation with the incident on the 27th when Ridley engaged in a long argument with Glyn at Christ's College during the
Visitors' examination of the disputes of Peterhouse (Lamb's *Collection*,
p. 116). Foxe gives the correct date of the first two days, but does not
state the final date of the disputation (vol. VI, pp. 305, 319, 327).

M

ment on earth; and that it was stated in the Gospels that Christ was sacrificed once for our redemption. The Catholics replied that Christ's reference to the fruit of the vine was to the wine before consecration; if the passages in Luke were compared with those in Matthew, it was clear that Christ had said that he would drink no more of the fruit of the vine before he blessed the wine, and yet had drunk after he had blessed it, and this proved that after the blessing it was no longer wine, else Christ would have been a liar. The Catholic spokesmen argued that if the bread had the nutritive value of bread, this was miraculous; that Christ's presence in the Sacrament was of a different kind from his presence in Heaven, because he was present visibly and circumspectively in Heaven, and invisibly and sacramentally in the bread and wine. As for the argument that Christ was only sacrificed once, they replied that his sacrifice on the Cross was visible, mortal and bloody, whereas in the Sacrament of the Altar he was sacrificed invisibly, spiritually and sacramentally, and in an unbloody manner.

During the first two days, Ridley intervened on many occasions in the disputation, as he was perfectly entitled to do, putting forward points against Glyn, Young and the other Catholic disputants. On the question of the presence of Christ in Heaven and in the Sacrament, he asserted that he was corporally present only in Heaven, whereas he was spiritually and figuratively present in the Sacrament. To illustrate his point, Ridley was able to give an example which he no doubt considered was a most instructive one: the King's royal person was present at only one place in his Kingdom at any given time, yet his mighty power and authority was present at all times in every part of his realm. On the third day, Ridley completely took over the presentation of the Protestant case; Perne, the Protestant respondent, hardly said a word all day while Ridley argued with Vavasour and Young. He showed his usual patience with Young, but he became impatient with Vavasour, whose tone was perhaps offensive, and indulged in some heavy sarcasm at his expense, as he had done with Glyn at the previous hearing. Vavasour was much too wise to attempt to retaliate, and apologised for his rudeness when Ridley declared that Vavasour would move a saint with his irrelevant reasons.[37]

As soon as the disputation had finished, Ridley gave his decision. There was enormous interest in the University. No one, of course, thought that Ridley and the Visitors had made up their minds after hearing the twelve disputants; Ridley's views on the question had been well known since the previous December. But the doctrine of transubstantiation, which it had until so recently been death to challenge, was now to be publicly condemned in the University by the Bishop of Rochester with the authority of the King and the Protector. The hall was crowded with members of the University, who stood bare-headed for an hour while Ridley, on behalf of all the other commissioners, delivered his judgment.[38]

In his judgment, Ridley declared that he had reached his conclusions on the basis of five reasons. The first was the words of the Gospels. Jesus had called the contents of the cup the fruit of the vine after the supper was finished, and the fruit of the vine was wine, not blood; and he relied also on the words of Christ with regard to the bread. In the second place, there were passages in the works of the early Fathers where the words used by them in reference to the bread clearly showed that the bread remained bread in substance in the Sacrament; he quoted Dionysius, Ignatius, Irenaeus, Tertullian, Chrysostom, Cyprian, Theoderet and Gelasius, and apparently also Augustine and Cyril;* and he referred to the works of Hesychius and Bertram. Thirdly, the doctrine of transubstantiation destroyed the sacramental nature of the Sacrament, which consisted of Unity, Nutrition and Conversion; for transubstantiation would destroy the unity of the particles of bread, and the nutritive value of the bread, and the conversion of the bread into the substance of our bodies which symbolised our conversion to Christ. Fourthly, those who believed in transubstantiation denied the truth of Christ's manhood, like Eutyches, by attributing to his natural body that which was peculiar to his divine nature. Fifthly, Christ had ascended into Heaven and sits at the right hand of God the Father, and if his body was in Heaven it could not be corporally on earth. For these five reasons, Ridley decided that the first Protestant proposition was sound; transubstantiation could not be proved by the plain and manifest words of Scripture. The truth of the second proposition, as Ridley stated, followed from the truth of the first; but he nevertheless gave two further reasons which had led him to the conclusion that there was no oblation or sacrifice of Christ in the Sacrament of the Altar, but only a commemoration of the Lord's Supper. In three different passages, St. Paul stated that Christ was sacrificed once, and consequently there had never been any oblation of Christ except when he suffered on the Cross. Secondly, Ridley relied on the works of the early Fathers, and referred to several passages from Augustine, and one from Fulgentius.[39]

Ridley's judgment made a profound impression on his

---

* Foxe, vol. VI, p. 334, states that Ridley also cited passages from Augustine and Cyril which were not recorded in the transcript of his judgment. The transcript is certainly by no means complete, as it could not have taken anywhere near as long as an hour to read.

audience, and on all the members of the University. Even
the Catholics admitted that it was a splendid technical per-
formance, while the Protestants were enthusiastic about the
judgment.[40] On 30th June, Ridley preached a sermon in St.
Mary's Church, in which he again dealt with the question
of transubstantiation, and pronounced the doctrine to be
false.[41] Two days later, the Visitors promulgated their Injunctions for the governance of the University and the
Colleges. These concerned the regulation of graduation
ceremonies, lectures and disputations, and the fines and
punishments to be inflicted for absence from the Colleges
and for non-attendance at divine service. They prescribed
the dress to be worn by all ranks in the University, and laid
down rules for good order and discipline. The members of
the University must never play at dice, or play or watch the
game of shields; and they were only to play cards at Christmas. They were not to loiter in the town, or go there un-
necessarily. No dicing tavern, or wrestling or fencing school,
was to be permitted anywhere in Cambridge. It is clear
that by the time these injunctions were drafted, the Visitors
had abandoned any idea of suppressing Clare Hall immediately, as they directed that Clare Hall was to be
administered along the same lines as Jesus College, Corpus
Christi College and Gonville Hall 'until some other plan
shall be prescribed for them by the King's Majesty'.[42] On
4th July, the Visitation ended with another ceremony. Then
Goodrich left by boat for Ely, and Cheke rode to Huntingdon, while Ridley, May and Wendy rode back to London.[43]

In the last days of his sojourn in Cambridge, Ridley must
have viewed the situation with the greatest satisfaction,
which his estrangement from Somerset did little to diminish.
It was now three weeks since Whitsun, when the Book of
Common Prayer had come into force; and to cap this

achievement, it had fallen to Ridley to proclaim the truth
of the doctrine of the spiritual Presence in the Sacrament as
the King's Commissioner in his own University. Four years
before, in Herne, he had furtively studied the illegal tracts
and had secretly adopted the criminal doctrine; but he had
converted the Archbishop of Canterbury to his new belief,
and had then slowly moved forward, under Cranmer's
leadership, to enforce his opinions on the kingdom. Today,
in Cambridge, he himself had pronounced his doctrine to be
the truth which all men ought to believe to the applause
of nearly all the University. For Ridley, it was the hour of
triumph.

Yet it was also the hour of danger. When Ridley left
Cambridge, on 4th July 1549, he had probably already
heard the news from the west which made his judgment on
transubstantiation a declaration of faith and an act of defiance in face of mortal peril. The men of Cornwall were in
arms, and at the gates of Exeter. At the same time, riots
against enclosures broke out all over the south of England.
These riots were quickly suppressed; but in Oxfordshire and
the neighbouring counties, the movement took the form of
an organised revolt, in which Catholic priests played an
active part and framed demands for the restoration of the
old services and the withdrawal of the Book of Common
Prayer. The petition of the western rebels left no doubt as
to their intentions: the Cornishmen demanded that Cardinal Pole should be recalled from exile and appointed a
member of the Council because he was of royal blood. They
demanded that Church services should be held in Latin—
they said that many Cornishmen could not speak English
—and that the service of the Mass should be restored in its
old form, with the elevation of the Host; they demanded the
abolition of the administration of the Sacrament in both

kinds, and indeed that the Sacrament should only be administered to the laity—and in one kind—at Easter; they
demanded the restoration of holy bread and holy water,
and that priests should be forbidden to marry. They demanded that the Statute of the Six Articles be re-enacted,
and enforced against heretics. They also demanded that no
gentleman should be permitted to have more than one servant for every hundred marks' worth of land that he owned,
and that half of the confiscated abbey lands should be used
to found two abbeys in every county.[44]

The Council in London, who had no standing army at
their disposal, were in great alarm. They declared a day of
fasting, and prohibited all stage plays, lest these should be
used as a cloak for seditious propaganda. An army of German mercenaries was hastily collected, and sent against the
men of Cornwall and Oxfordshire. Lord Grey was able to
stamp out the rising in Oxfordshire without much difficulty; he hanged the rebels on trees along the highway, and
left many priests to hang alive from their church steeples.
While the Council were anxiously awaiting the outcome of
the campaign in the west, another revolt broke out in Yorkshire, while in Norfolk thirty thousand men rose in arms
against enclosures under Ket. The Protector sent the Marquis of Northampton to suppress the rising in Norfolk; but
his force fell back in confusion, and Ket entered Norwich.
Then suddenly on 8th August, King Henry of France, who
a fortnight earlier had assured the English Ambassador of
his friendship on his word of honour as a King and a gentleman, declared war, and sent his troops against Boulogne;
and the Scots attacked the English fortresses in Scotland.
As the news of these disasters reached London, Catholic
priests began to celebrate the old Mass in their churches
and to defy the Act of Uniformity.

In this grim crisis, it was of paramount importance to the State and to the Protestant Church that the Emperor should remain neutral in the conflict. They could hardly have survived if the strongest military power in Europe had now joined with its hated enemy against the heretics in London, and everything possible had to be done to dissuade Charles from intervention. Somerset accordingly decided to use the services of Ridley in a delicate piece of diplomacy. At the beginning of August, the Protector received the Imperial Ambassador, van der Delft, and assured him that the English government was far less heretical than was generally supposed. He told him that the Communion service of the Book of Common Prayer was almost identical with the Mass, and drew his attention to the measures which had recently been taken against the Anabaptists. He explained that many people in England were clamouring for alterations in the doctrine of the Church, and that the Council had thought it wise to introduce a few reforms in religion in order to prevent the extremists from carrying out more radical innovations. Somerset then suggested that he should send Ridley to visit van der Delft to explain to him the religious policy of the leaders of the Church of England, and he assured van der Delft that Ridley was a most learned and persuasive doctor. He presumably hoped that the Ambassador would be favourably impressed to discover how far removed was the Bishop of Rochester from the foreign Catholics' conception of a ranting heretic. Van der Delft declined the Protector's suggestion, although Somerset pressed him strongly to accept. He said that he thought that no useful purpose would be served by his having a talk with Ridley; he was well aware that Ridley was a most learned doctor, but he was an adherent of the new religion, and as he himself was not a divine or learned in theology, he felt that he would be quite incapable of discussing religious matters with Ridley.[45]

In these weeks, the whole future of the Protestant Reformation, and the lives of its leaders, hung in the balance. Then news came that Russell had defeated the Cornishmen, who had fled in disorder into Cornwall, and the Yorkshire rising was easily suppressed. By the end of August, Lord Warwick and his German mercenaries had defeated Ket on Mousehold Hill, and the last revolt was over. In France and Scotland, the fortunes of war continued to go against the English, but there was no longer any danger of the overthrow of the government in London. Somerset proclaimed a general pardon to all except a handful of ringleaders; but Warwick and the commanders in the field were less disposed to mercy than the Protector, and many rebels were tried by court martial and hanged in Norfolk and Cornwall. In London, the Protestants could now sing their songs of triumph, and declare that while the priests had been responsible for the risings by refusing absolution to those who did not revolt, 'yet God hath given our King the victory'.*

The Protector and the Council had been confronted simultaneously with a Catholic and with a social revolution. The two movements were very largely distinct from each other. In the south-eastern counties, the rioters had not clearly formulated any religious demands, but had been concerned wholly with enclosures and other agrarian injustices. In Warwickshire, Oxfordshire and Buckinghamshire, the revolt had been almost entirely Catholic, and no social demands had been put forward. In Cornwall, where enclosures had not met with the same degree of opposition as they had done elsewhere in the country, there were no

---

* See Rose-Troup, *The Western Rebellion of 1549*, pp. 336-8, citing a contemporary ballad.

agrarian demands; but the rebels demanded that no gentleman should have more than one servant for every hundred
marks' worth of land which he held. In Norfolk, Ket and
his men had not put forward any Catholic demands. Only
in Yorkshire had the religious and the social question gone
together: here the rebels demanded that England should be
divided into four republics, each under a Governor and with
a Parliament elected by the people. The Protestant bishops
feared above all the Catholic risings in Cornwall and Oxfordshire; but they were also greatly alarmed by the Norfolk
rising, and were firmly convinced that Ket was in secret
contact with the Lady Mary at Kenninghall. As regards the
social revolts, the Protestant leaders adopted the line which
they had always held: the revolts were a just punishment on
the masters for their oppression and covetousness, but the
rebels had sinned against God by rebelling against Caesar.
Cranmer sternly rebuked the Cornishmen for demanding
that no gentleman should have more than one servant for
every hundred marks' worth of land. He wrote to them that
in no country in the world had servants ever presumed to
regulate the mode of life of their masters, and if men were
ever to tolerate this, God would not. He was particularly
shocked that they should seek to take from the King half
the abbey lands in his possession.[46] There can be no doubt
that Ridley, whose views on obedience to the temporal
powers seem to have been even more authoritarian than
those of Cranmer, entirely accepted this position.

Faced with revolt at home and war abroad, the Council
grew less tolerant of opposition and criticism, and resolved
to deal firmly with the Catholic bishops who were obstruct-
ing their religious policy. For over a year, Gardiner had
been safely confined in the Tower where he could do no
harm; but no action had been taken against Bonner since

his release from his short imprisonment in the autumn of 1547. He had opposed the Act of Uniformity in Parliament, and since it had come into force at Whitsun he had not preached any sermon or officiated in any way in his diocese of London. Towards the end of July, when the Cornish revolt was at its height, the Council decided to enforce his submission. Bonner was accused of having connived at the violations of the Act of Uniformity in his diocese; he had done nothing to restrain the Catholic priests in London from celebrating the old Mass in their churches as they eagerly watched the successes of the rebels in the west. The Council ordered Bonner to prevent these breaches of the law. Bonner complied with the order with apparent enthusiasm, and directed his clergy to obey the orders of the Council;[47] and his action, combined no doubt with the defeat of the Cornishmen, put an end to the breaches of the Act of Uniformity. There seems little doubt, however, that Cranmer had already decided to get rid of Bonner, and to take the hitherto unprecedented step of depriving him of his see.

On 11th August, Bonner was summoned before the Council, and charged with responsibility for the adultery and immorality which flourished in London. He was also accused of dereliction of duty in failing to officiate at feast days in his diocese. The Council ordered him to preach a sermon at Paul's Cross, and gave him precise instructions as to what he should say in his sermon. He was to condemn the rebels, and to say that they were guilty, by their rebellion, of the sin of Lucifer, and to point out that Korah, Dathan and Abiram were swallowed alive into Hell for rebellion against Moses; he was to say that in prayer the exact form of ceremonies and of the service was unimportant, and that consequently it should be regulated by the temporal powers; but that any person who worshipped in a manner contrary to that prescribed by law was guilty of disobedience, and that this would make the ceremonies worthless in the eyes of God. He was also to state that the King had as much royal authority during his infancy as he would have if he were of full age, as was shown by the example of Josias, who was only eight when he began to reign and was therefore younger than King Edward, who was now twelve.[48]

On 1st September, Bonner preached at Paul's Cross. He spoke as he had been ordered on the sin of rebellion, and on the duty of attending those services which had been prescribed by the magistrates; but he said nothing as to the authority of an infant king. He spent the greater part of his sermon in speaking about the Real Presence, and asserted the truth of transubstantiation in his usual vigorous style. The Council thereupon appointed a commission to examine the conduct of Bonner, and to consider whether he ought to be suspended, excommunicated, imprisoned or deprived of his see on the grounds of disobedience to the King. The commissioners were Cranmer, Ridley, May, Smith and Petre.[49]

The commission to the commissioners was quite unprecedented. In the special circumstances of 1534, the Italian Cardinals had been deprived of their English sees by an Act of Parliament which enacted that no alien could hold an English bishopric; and at the time of the passing of the Statute of the Six Articles, Latimer and Shaxton had been compelled to resign their sees. But no bishop had ever yet been deprived by the King's command. Moreover, it was felt that a bishop should only be deprived, if at all, by an ecclesiastical court;[50] but two of the five commissioners— Smith and Petre—were laymen.

The proceedings opened in public at Lambeth Palace on 10th September 1549.[51] From the start, Bonner adopted a defiant attitude, and in view of the complete lack of precedent for the deprivation of a bishop, he used all his abilities as a trained civil lawyer to challenge the jurisdiction of the commissioners and to take every technical objection which was open to him. Bonner did not dare to challenge the authority of the King to deprive him; this might have been construed as an offence under the Act of Supremacy. But he challenged the authority of the five commissioners to form a court for the purpose, and appealed to be heard by the King himself. The chief witnesses against Bonner were William Latimer and Hooper, who had heard his sermon at Paul's Cross; Bonner denounced both of them as notorious heretics, and abused them in his usual fashion. He stated that he was only being treated in this manner because he believed in the corporal Presence, and he reproved Cranmer for no longer believing in this truth. This provoked the Archbishop into engaging in long wrangles with Bonner over transubstantiation, and at the end of the first day's hearing the commissioners had made no progress at all with the business in hand.

The commission resumed its sittings on 13th September. Sir Thomas Smith had not been present on the first day, but he now took his seat with the commissioners. Bonner immediately objected that no one could sit as a commissioner if he had not been present at the reading of the King's commission on the opening day; but after animated discussion, this plea was overruled. Smith was a skilful lawyer, and with him present the proceedings were a trifle more orderly. Bonner repeatedly tried to draw Cranmer into arguments about transubstantiation; but Cranmer—perhaps at the suggestion of Smith—refused to discuss the matter as being outside the scope of the commission. Bonner continued to argue that the commissioners had no jurisdiction; but Smith replied by laying down that to challenge the jurisdiction of commissioners appointed by the King was itself an act of defiance of the royal authority, and refused to discuss the matter at all. To the accusations that he had failed to deal with the authority of the King during his infancy in his sermon at Paul's Cross, Bonner put forward the defence that this was simply due to a lapse of memory. He told the commissioners that he had prepared notes for his sermon, in which he intended to refer to the example of infant kings in English history, as well as to those in the Old Testament, but that unfortunately his notes slipped from his hand and he forgot to mention this matter. The commissioners can hardly be blamed for refusing to believe this story, and they rejected his defence as frivolous. Bonner became involved in angry altercations with the commissioners, especially with Cranmer and Smith. Matters came to a head at the fifth session on 20th September. The commissioners asked Bonner to state his defence to the accusations which had been made against him. Bonner did so, and stated that he was addressing his remarks to Cranmer, Ridley and May—Petre was not sitting at this session —as he did not recognise Smith as being a member of the commission. He was then ordered to address all the commissioners, and agreed to do so; but soon afterwards he refused to reply to a question from Smith. Smith then sent for the Knight Marshal, and ordered that Bonner should be sent to the Marshalsea for contempt. Bonner was promptly arrested, but still showed defiance; his parting words were a reprimand to Smith for having committed him when the Archbishop, as Smith's superior in rank, should have done so.

The sixth session of the commission was held on 23rd September. Bonner was brought before the commissioners under guard. He told the commissioners that they had vitiated the terms of their commission by displaying bias against him, and that consequently they had no jurisdiction to continue with the hearing. At this, Ridley intervened by citing two texts; one of them was from St. John—'He that doeth evil hateth the light'. Bonner replied by citing another text from John.* The commissioners warned Bonner that they would proceed to give their judgment at the next session, on 27th September, and the commission adjourned. The session of the 27th, however, was postponed to 1st October. The commissioners probably wished to make quite sure that everything was in order before they proceeded to deprive a bishop for the first time; they had taken the precaution, in view of Bonner's arguments as to their jurisdiction, to arrange for a second commission, correcting certain points of detail in the first, to be issued to them by the King.†

On 1st October, the commissioners met for the seventh time. Cranmer told Bonner that they had not sat on the 27th because they were reluctant to deprive him, and had made approaches to the King in Council to urge him to show mercy to Bonner, despite the disgraceful conduct of which he had been guilty. But they had now decided that for his wilful disobedience to the King he must be deprived of the see of London, and they pronounced sentence. Bonner then said that he had appealed to the King, and to the

---

* Ridley's Register as Bishop of London, f. 241d. This passage is omitted from the report in Foxe. Gloucester Ridley, p. 284, refers to it, but implies that it occurred after the sentence of deprivation had been pronounced.

† Rymer, *Foedera*, vol. XV, pp. 191–2; the first commission was issued on 8th September, and the second on 17th September 1549.

Lord Chancellor, and again denied the authority of the commissioners to deprive him, and attacked the commission. He also argued that as they had now ceased to exist as a body, they could not, being *functus officio*, keep him imprisoned for contempt; but he was sent back to the Marshalsea, and remained there for nearly four years. His appeal to the King and to the Lord Chancellor was of course rejected, and a commission of lawyers, which sat under Rich, decided that the commission which deprived Bonner was properly established and had jurisdiction to do so.

From the verbatim report of the proceedings in the deprivation of Bonner, it seems that apart from interjecting the two texts at the sixth session, Ridley's part in the proceedings was a wholly passive one. He was present at every session of the commission, and no doubt lent his advice to his colleagues in private when they retired; but he apparently never intervened to put questions to Bonner, and never became entangled in angry exchanges with him. Ridley may have felt that as the proceedings were legal rather than theological in their nature, he had no individual contribution to make to the discussions, and that the conduct of the trial had best be left to Smith. He was wise enough not to allow himself to be provoked, as Cranmer was at the first sitting, into entering into a discussion about transubstantiation with Bonner.

Hardly had Bonner been deprived of his bishopric, and sent back to the Marshalsea for an indefinite sojourn, when it suddenly seemed for a moment as if the hour of deliverance had arrived for him and for all the Catholics, and that the reign of Cranmer and the Protestants was over. While the commission had been in session, the plot against Somerset had been maturing. Ket's revolt and the other agricultural disturbances had convinced the nobles and landowners that the Protector must be driven from power; they held him responsible for provoking the outbreaks by his demagogic policy, and they were enraged that he had pardoned the rebels and thwarted the vengeance of the landlords. They now looked for a leader against the Protector. Two men were very ready to offer themselves for the part—Warwick and Southampton. Dudley was a brilliant soldier and an able and unscrupulous politician, who had risen to influence at Court under Henry VIII, and since his death had been an important member of the Council. No sooner had he returned in triumph from his victory over Ket than he prepared to seize power in the interests of the nobles and landlords. He entered into secret contact with Southampton, who had been living quietly at his house in Holborn ever since he had been released from prison after Somerset had driven him from the woolsack, and it was here that the conspiracy was hatched. In September 1549, all the members of the Council, except Cranmer and a few others, gathered around Warwick in London while the Protector and his friends were with the King at Hampton Court. At the beginning of October, Warwick seized the Tower and called on Somerset to resign. The Protector fled to Windsor with the King, accompanied by Cranmer and Paget, and issued an appeal to the people to rise in his support against Warwick and the landlords; but at this, Russell and Herbert, at the head of their Landsknechts, who were returning from their campaign in the west, threw their decisive weight into the scales against the Protector. Somerset resigned, and was sent to the Tower, along with Sir Thomas Smith.

The Protestants, who had been rejoicing at the defeat of all the Catholic and Papist risings, were suddenly confronted with a situation which seemed to sound the knell of all their hopes. Warwick had supported the Protector's religious policy in the Council, but his personal beliefs in religion had been more Catholic than Protestant in the past; and here, at his right hand, was Southampton, the hated Wriothesley, the leader of the Catholic party, who had returned to power and took his place in the Council, while their great helper, Smith, was arrested. Gardiner and Bonner and the old Duke of Norfolk at once took heart, and petitioned Warwick for their release from prison. The Protestants were daily awaiting the arrest of Cranmer.

All October they waited for the worst; then came the deliverance. Warwick had spent the month in cold political calculation. The recent revolts had shown the strength of Catholic feeling in the country; but Warwick had set himself up as the leader of the nobles and gentlemen against the people, and did not seek the support of the defeated rebels. Moreover, he had no intention of sharing power with Southampton, and he preferred to gain the support of the Protestants against both Southampton and the Catholic populace. He therefore decided to adopt a Protestant policy in religion. Nor was he merely content, as Somerset had been, to encourage Cranmer and his supporters; he played for the support of the extreme Protestant sects and their adherents among the people of London and the south-east. Warwick knew that among the tenants and smallholders he was the most hated man in England, and that he could never hope to win their affection; but by being more Protestant than Somerset had ever been he could build for himself a party among the substantial minority of the people who were now Protestants. John Hooper was one of the most popular preachers among the Protestants in London, and Warwick appointed Hooper to be his chaplain. He leaned on Hooper more than on Cranmer for advice in his religious policy. This made Hooper a zealous propagandist for Warwick, whom he called 'that most faithful and intrepid soldier of Christ'.[52]

In November, Warwick told Southampton that he would be wise to stop attending the meetings of the Council and to confine himself to his house in Holborn; and the Council continued with much the same composition as before. Warwick did not take the title of Protector, but he was in practice in complete control of the Council, while leaving priority in point of precedence to Cranmer. A few months later, Southampton was expelled from the Council, and soon afterwards died in despair; it was rumoured that he had committed suicide. Southampton had lost, and Warwick had won, the struggle for power. In November, a new Parliament met to greet the Earl of Warwick, who had rid the landowners of the mob's man Somerset. Parliament enacted a drastic new treason statute, which made it high treason to kill, imprison or dismiss from office any member of the Council. It repealed the two Acts which Somerset had forced through in 1548 for relieving the grievances of the tenants, and passed bills which made it felony, and in certain cases treason, to resist the enclosure of land, to enforce a right of way, or to combine to reduce rents or the price of corn. Ridley and the other Protestant bishops voted in favour of these bills in the House of Lords.[53] The victory of the landlords was as complete as the victory of the Protestants.

Cranmer and the reformers, after a few months of great anxiety, now found themselves more securely in power than ever before. On Christmas Day, 1549, the hopes of the Catholics were finally destroyed when the Council sent a letter to all the bishops, informing them that there was no truth whatever in the lying rumour that a change in the religious settlement was contemplated, and directing the bishops to unearth and destroy all Popish books.[54] Warwick was determined to be a better Protestant than Somerset, and the Reformation was henceforth to be linked with the interests of the nobles and landowners to an extent which it had never been when Somerset was Protector. The Protestant preachers had now more occasion than ever to lament the covetousness of the nobility and gentry, and did so in innumerable sermons; but if it was sinful for the lords and masters to covet wealth and oppress the poor, the poor must patiently submit to oppression as an evil sent to try their patience, and must render unto Caesar the things that are Caesar's, and obey the King and his Council. The King, advised by the Lord President, Warwick, that intrepid soldier of Christ, would now not hesitate to use his power as Supreme Head of the Church to press on with the Reformation. With the Book of Common Prayer in force in every church and the doctrine of transubstantiation officially condemned in the disputation at Cambridge, with the fate of Gardiner and Bonner as a warning to their opponents, with the rebels scattered and punished from Bodmin to Scarborough, Cranmer and Ridley were now to be more disturbed by the demands of the Protestant extremists than by the resistance of the Catholics.

NOTES

[1] See Strype, *Memorials*, vol. II (i), p. 134; Gasquet and Bishop, *Edward VI and the Book of Common Prayer*, pp. 180–1.

[2] *The First Book of Common Prayer* (*Liturgies of King Edward VI*, pp. 17–19, 155–7).

[3] *The First Book of Common Prayer* (*Liturgies of King Edward VI*, pp. 88–9).

[4] The earliest authority for the names of the thirteen Commissioners

is Fuller's *Church History* (p. 354), written in 1655. He names Cranmer, Day, Goodrich, Skyp, Holbeach, Ridley, Thirlby, May, Taylor, Haynes, Robertson, Redmayne and Cox. See Gasquet and Bishop, *Edward VI and the Book of Common Prayer*, pp. 143–6, for the evidence that the Commissioners met at Chertsey and Windsor in September 1548.

[5] *Statutes of the Realm*, 2 & 3 Edw. VI, c. 1.

[6] With regard to the punishment for failing to attend the Communion Service, see the *First Book of Common Prayer* (*Liturgies of King Edward VI*, p. 98).

[7] The matter was first raised in the House of Lords on 14th December, but the disputation itself was held on 15th, 17th, 18th and 19th. For the verbatim report of the disputation, containing Ridley's arguments on the last three days, see Gasquet and Bishop, *Edward VI and the Book of Common Prayer*, pp. 397–443. See also Traheron's letter to Bullinger, 31st December 1548 (*Original Letters*, p. 323).

[8] Burnet, vol. II, p. 175.

[9] Burnet, vol. II, pp. 170–3.

[10] *House of Lords Journal*, 19th February 1548/9.

[11] See Ridley's letter to Somerset, 1st June 1549 (*Works*, p. 328).

[12] Ridley, *Last Farewell* (*Works*, p. 408).

[13] *Statutes of the Realm*, 2 & 3 Edw. VI, c. 5, c. 36.

[14] Strype, *Memorials*, vol. II (i), p. 335; *Cranmer and the Heretics in Kent* (*L. & P. Henry VIII*, vol. XVIII (ii), No. 546, p. 314).

[15] See Sentence of Excommunication on Joan Bocher (Burnet's *Records*, vol. V, pp. 246–7).

[16] Rymer, *Foedera*, vol. XV, pp. 181–3 (12th April 1549).

[17] Sir Henry Sidney, *The Popish Policies*, referred to by Strype, *Cranmer*, p. 297.

[18] Wriothesley's *Chronicle*, vol. II, pp. 10, 12–13.

[19] Rymer, *Foedera*, vol. XV, pp. 178–80 (12th November 1548).

[20] Strype, *Life of Cheke*, p. 47.

[21] See Mallet, *History of the University of Oxford*, vol. II, pp. 82, 87 n. Ridley was again appointed a Visitor to Oxford University in another commission in October 1551 (see Dixon, vol. III, p. 384); but he does not seem to have gone to Oxford at this time.

[22] Lamb's *Collection*, pp. 109–10.

[23] Lamb's *Collection*, p. 110.

[24] The Visitors' letter to Somerset, 18th May 1549 (Bradford's *Works*, vol. II, pp. 369–70).

[25] Ridley's letter to Somerset, 18th May 1549 (Bradford's *Works*, vol. II, pp. 370–2).

[26] See Somerset's letter to Ridley, 10th June 1549 (*Works*, pp. 505–6).

[27] Ridley's letter to Somerset, 1st June 1549 (Burnet's *Records*, vol. V, pp. 349–50; *Works*, pp. 327–30).

[28] Rymer, *Foedera*, vol. XV, pp. 178–80 (12th November 1548).

[29] Somerset's letter to Ridley, 10th June 1549 (*Works*, pp. 505–6).

[30] Lemon, *Calendar of State Papers (Domestic) Edward VI*, etc., vol. I, p. 18.

[31] Lamb's *Collection*, p. 113.

[32] Lemon, *Calendar of State Papers (Domestic) Edward VI*, etc., vol. I, p. 18.

[33] Lamb's *Collection*, pp. 113, 116.

[34] Lamb's *Collection*, pp. 111–12, 114.

[35] Lamb's *Collection*, pp. 114–15.

[36] Foxe, vol. VI, pp. 306, 308.

[37] See Foxe, vol. VI, pp. 306–32, for the arguments in the disputation; and see Langdale, *Catholica Confutatio*, p. 7, for an account of Ridley's behaviour as seen by one of the Catholic disputants.

[38] Lamb's *Collection*, p. 115; Pilkington, *The Burning of Paul's Church in London* (Pilkington's *Works*, p. 523).

[39] Ridley's *Determination Concerning the Sacrament*, Foxe, vol. VI, pp. 332–5 (*Works*, pp. 171–9).

[40] Pilkington, *The Burning of Paul's Church in London* (Pilkington's *Works*, p. 523).

[41] Lamb's *Collection*, p. 117.

[42] *Collection of Statutes of Cambridge University*, pp. 26–37.

[43] Lamb's *Collection*, pp. 118–19.

[44] See the first petition of the Western rebels (Strype, *Cranmer App.*, pp. 801–39).

[45] Van der Delft's letter to Charles V, 13th August 1549 (*Calendar of Spanish State Papers* vol. IX, pp. 429–30).

[46] Cranmer, *Reply to the Rebels of Devon* (Strype, *Cranmer App.*, pp. 835–9).

[47] Wilkins, *Concilia*, vol. IV, p. 36.

[48] Foxe, vol. V, pp. 745–6.

[49] Rymer, *Foedera*, vol. XV, pp. 191–2 (8th September 1549). Foxe, vol. V, p. 746, and *Greyfriars Chronicle*, p. 63, state that the sermon was preached on 1st September. Wriothesley's *Chronicle*, vol. II, p. 24, gives the date as 8th September, but not as part of the day to day record of the diary. This can hardly be correct, as the commission for the trial of Bonner was issued on 8th September.

[50] Burnet, vol. II, p. 227.

[51] See Foxe, vol. V, pp. 749–96, for the proceedings against Bonner.

[52] Hooper's letter to Bullinger, 27th March 1550 (*Original Letters*, p. 82).

[53] *Statutes of the Realm* 3 & 4 Edw. VI, c. 5; *House of Lords Journal*, 11th, 14th, 16th and 18th November, and 27th December 1549.

[54] The Council's letter to the Bishops, 25th December 1549 (Burnet's *Records*, vol. V, pp. 287–8).

VI

BISHOP OF LONDON: THE ALTARS AND VESTMENTS CONTROVERSIES

When Bonner was deprived of his bishopric in October 1549, the see of London fell vacant. Cranmer decided to bestow it on Ridley. It was not, however, until February 1550 that Ridley was appointed, and he was not installed until the beginning of April. At first, the appointment was probably held up by the political and religious uncertainty that followed the overthrow of Somerset; but when it became clear that the Protestants were to remain in power under Warwick, and that Cranmer could safely proceed to appoint his supporters to all vacant offices in the Church, other matters arose to postpone the issue of the Letters Patent nominating Ridley as Bishop of London. Bonner had appealed to the King against the judgment of the commissioners, and as the idea of depriving a bishop was of very doubtful legality, the Council were determined to proceed with all proper formalities. Ridley was therefore not appointed as Bishop of London until Bonner's appeal had been heard and dismissed.

Ridley was not inactive during the winter while he was awaiting his translation to London. He was busily engaged in attending the House of Lords. He was present to support the statute which imposed the enormous fine of £2,000 on the Duke of Somerset,[1] and all the measures which Warwick introduced to strengthen his power and the interests of the landlords. He also voted in favour of another bill dealing with vagabonds. This modified the rigour of the statute of 1547, and enacted that vagabonds and their children who were held in forced labour were no longer to be called slaves, though it reimposed the penalties of flogging and mutilation for vagabonds, and provided that any labourer who refused to work for the usual wage in force in his district was to be deemed to be a vagabond.[2] Apart from assisting the landowners, Warwick put forward a number of measures designed to further the Protestant cause. A statute was passed which directed that all missals, Latin primers and antiphoners throughout the country, and all painted or graven images in churches, were to be defaced and handed in this condition to the mayor and bailiffs, who in their turn were to hand them in to the bishops. The Primer of Henry VIII could still be used, but the passages in it which dealt with invocations to the Saints must be cut out or erased in every copy in the kingdom. Failure to comply with these provisions was punished, at the third offence, with imprisonment during the King's pleasure.[3] The bill was carried against the votes of the Catholic bishops and temporal peers.

The Protestant leaders had now decided to press forward with another innovation which was to shock their Catholic opponents. They had decided to introduce far-reaching alterations in the service of ordination of bishops, priests and deacons. A bill was presented to Parliament providing that the King was to appoint twelve divines, six of whom were to be bishops, to draft a form of ordination service, and that in April the new service should have force of law and replace the existing service.[4] The bill was forced through the House of Lords at a special mid-day session on the day before Parliament was prorogued, against the votes of Tunstall, Thirlby, Heath, Day and Aldrich.[5] There is no record of the names of the twelve commissioners who were appointed by virtue of the statute, but it is very likely, as has been suggested, that Ridley was one of the six bishops on the commission.* Heath was certainly one of the commissioners. He had been placed on the commission despite his opposition to the statute under which it was set up, presumably in order to identify him with its recommendations, and to enforce his submission on this issue. Probably the commissioners had already begun their work before they were officially appointed under the statute, and they may well have been considering the matter as early as November 1549. Alternatively, it is possible that the meetings of the commissioners were a mere formality, and that the draft of the new service had already been prepared by some of the Protestant leaders before the commissioners ever met at all. It is certain that within a week of the third reading of the bill in the House of Lords, all the commissioners, except Heath, had agreed on a new ordinal.†

The majority of the Commissioners decided that the only part of the ordination ceremony for which authority could be found in Scripture was the imposition of hands, and prayer. They therefore decided that all other parts of the ceremony could be altered, and proceeded to promulgate

---

* Gloucester Ridley, p. 373, states that Ridley was one of the commissioners. Heylin (Part I, pp. 82–3) thought it likely that the twelve commissioners who drafted the ordinal were the thirteen commissioners, with the exception of Day, named by Fuller as having drafted the First Book of Common Prayer (see pp. 196–7). See Dixon, vol. III, p. 195.

† Burnet, vol. II, pp. 246–7, states that the commission met when Parliament assembled in November 1549. The bill setting up the commission passed the House of Lords on the fourth reading on 31st January 1550, and the commissioners were formally appointed by the Council on 2nd February. Heath was summoned before the Council for refusing to approve his colleagues' draft on 8th February (see *Acts of the Privy Council*, vol II, pp. 379, 388).

many changes in the ordinal. They extended the system of questions and sponsions, by which the person to be ordained was interrogated as to his fitness to be a priest or bishop. They abolished the anointing with holy oil and the donning of consecrated vestments; and most important of all, they abolished the ceremony of handing the vessels to the priest who was ordained which was accompanied by words denoting that he was now competent to offer up a sacrifice of the consecrated Host. The commissioners also decided that no one could be ordained a deacon until he was twenty-one, a priest until he was twenty-four, or a bishop until he was thirty.[6]

The alterations in the ordination service aroused the opposition both of the Catholics and of the Protestant extremists. Many Protestants, under the leadership of Hooper, objected to the ritual in the ceremony,[7] while the Catholics were indignant that any alterations at all had been made. As we do not know who were the members of the commission, we cannot say whether any of the Catholic bishops, other than Heath, were among the commissioners; but if so, they were somehow induced to subscribe the book of the ordination service. Heath was the only commissioner who was prepared to stand firm in defence of the old ordinal. The Bishop of Worcester informed his colleagues that he would not sign the book. On 8th February, Heath was summoned before the Council, and ordered to sign the book; but he declared in his usual quiet manner that his conscience did not permit him to do so. On 4th March, he was arrested, and sent to the Fleet, where he remained for two and a half years.[8]

On 7th February 1550, Bonner's appeal against his deprivation was dismissed. By this time, it was widely known that Ridley was to succeed him, and when the Council wrote to Ridley, on 21st February, and summoned him to appear before them on business about which he would be notified on his arrival, he must have been well aware what this business would be. On 24th February, the King announced that Ridley was to be appointed Bishop of London;[9] but another month was to pass before he was formally appointed and installed. It was first necessary to reorganise the dioceses of London and Westminster. It was decided to suppress the see of Westminster, which had been founded ten years before, and to merge it once again in the diocese of London. Thirlby, the Bishop of Westminster, had been a Catholic ever since the fall of Cromwell, and he had opposed the Book of Common Prayer, and every other Protestant measure—except the marriage of priests—during the last three years; but he had a pleasant and ingratiating disposition, and was on friendly terms with Cranmer. It was almost certainly because of this personal friendship that Thirlby was retained on the episcopal bench; but it was decided to get rid of Repps, who had been as persistent as Thirlby in his opposition to the Council. Repps was induced to resign, and Thirlby was translated to Norwich. The see of Westminster was then dissolved.

On 1st April, Ridley was appointed Bishop of London by Letters Patent. Three days later he took the oath. On 12th April, he was installed as Bishop of London in St. Paul's. For some reason, Ridley was not present at the ceremony, but was represented by a proxy; his proxy was Richard Wilkes, who sixteen years before had been Ridley's brother proctor at Cambridge.* Ridley's diocese, since the

---

* Rymer, *Foedera*, vol. XV, pp. 222–6 (1st April 1550); Strype, *Cranmer*, p. 297; Strype, *Memorials*, vol. II (i), p. 339. Burnet, vol. II, p. 260, is wrong in stating that Ridley was appointed Bishop of London and Westminster.

fusion with Westminster, comprised the City of London, with its population of some seventy-five thousand souls, the whole of the counties of Middlesex and Essex, and that part of Hertfordshire which was not in the diocese of Lincoln. Territorially, the diocese was a good deal larger than Rochester, and its revenues were considerably larger. On the day of his installation, Ridley was granted a licence to hold his cure at Soham, and his stalls in Canterbury and Westminster Cathedrals, *in commendam* until midsummer 1553.[10] He had, however, resigned his benefice at Herne in January.* Cranmer decided to fill the vacancy on the bench of bishops with one of his supporters. He appointed Ponet to succeed Ridley as Bishop of Rochester, and in June Ridley assisted at Ponet's consecration by Cranmer at Lambeth Palace.†

On taking office as Bishop of London, Ridley found that his first duty was to place his seal on a series of transactions which had all been conveniently arranged during the time when the see was vacant. The property of the suppressed see of Westminster, which comprised most of the lands which had belonged to the old abbey of Westminster, was now to be transferred to the see of London. In view of the fact that these assets, added to the revenues of the diocese of London, were more than sufficient for the needs of London, the Bishop was to grant some of the most valuable property in the diocese to the King. The King would then grant this property to influential courtiers.

On 12th April—the very day when he was installed—Ridley granted the manors of Stepney, Hackney, Southminster and Braintree as a gift to the King. He also granted

---

* Ridley's successor was collated to Herne on 16th January 1550 (Gloucester Ridley, p. 291).

† On 29th June (Strype, *Cranmer*, p. 363).

him the advowson of the vicarage of Coggeshall in Essex.[11]
Four days later, the King granted the manors of Stepney
and Hackney to Lord Wentworth, the manor of Southminster to Sir Thomas Darcy, and the manor of Braintree
and the advowson of Coggeshall to Lord Rich.[12] The manors
of Stepney and Hackney, which included some of the best
residential property on the fringe of London, were highly
valuable: they brought in a revenue of £246 a year. The
manor of Southminster brought in revenues of £195 a year,
and these manors, combined with the less valuable manor
of Braintree and the advowson, gave the four manors a total
yearly value of £480 3s. 9d.[13] Before he granted these manors
to the King, Ridley had already received some of the property of the see of Westminster, on 1st April. On the 22nd,
he was granted the rest. The King granted, for no consideration, the lands of the dissolved see in thirteen counties
to the Bishop of London. It had originally been intended to
grant lands to Ridley which would bring him an income of
£1,000 a year;[14] but he only received a little over half this
sum. The total value of these lands was £526 19s. 9d.
Ridley was required to pay £100 a year in first fruits and
tenths, in return for which he was released from the obligation to pay the first fruits and tenths hitherto due from the
see of London, which amounted to £111 18s. 10½d., and
from all other dues and rent charges on the property of the
see except for sundry charges amounting in all to £26 1s. 8d.
He was also granted an annuity of £3 6s. 8d.[15]

It is thus clear that the see of London benefited as a
result of this series of transactions. Ridley has nevertheless
been subjected to considerable criticism by hostile historians for his part in the business. He certainly cannot
avoid his share of responsibility for it, despite the fact that
in the case of the wealthy manors of Stepney and Hackney

the manors had already been granted by the Dean and Chapter of St. Paul's during the period when the see was vacant,[16] because the grants were in every case confirmed and executed by Ridley immediately upon taking office. If the matter is considered, not from the viewpoint of the see of London alone, but from that of the Church as a whole, then the Church was the poorer by the transaction, for Ridley gave away to three courtiers, for no consideration, nearly one-fifth of the total revenues of the see of London, and received in exchange lands which, though not the property of London, had belonged to the Church for centuries. The income of the see of London was probably about £1,900— nearly three times as large as the revenues of the see of Rochester.* The value of money had fallen by about half in the past eight years, but £1,900 a year was still a very large income at a time when the unskilled labourer was earning 4½d. a day. Ridley, unlike the labourer, could afford to buy meat even now that the price of a body of a calf had risen to fourteen shillings.[17]

From a political aspect, Ridley's new diocese was an important and difficult one. In no other part of England were the Protestants so numerous and determined, while the Catholic resistance was far from broken. The many Catholic vicars in the city were strongly opposed to the Reformation, and had done all they could to frustrate and impede it; under the sympathetic eye of Bonner, they had been able, with some success, surreptitiously to evade the provisions of

---

* This is an approximate estimate, based on the *Valor Ecclesiasticus* of 1535 (vol. I, pp. 100, 357), when the net revenues of the sees of Rochester and London (including the future diocese of Westminster) were £411 and £1,119 respectively, but allowing for an increase in the figures during the inflation of 1542–6, calculated on the basis of the increase of about 80 per cent in the revenues of the manors of Stepney, Hackney and Southminster between 1535 and 1550.

the Act of Uniformity. On the other hand, the Protestants
in London were among the most extreme in the country,
and as most of the foreign immigrants had settled in the
capital, it was, along with Kent, the principal centre of
Anabaptism in the realm. Ridley was resolved to crush all
Catholic resistance, and also to stamp out Anabaptism,
while he was equally determined to prevent the Protestant
rank and file from dictating to the King and Council.

On entering into the see, Ridley had to settle some financial matters with Bonner. During the months when the see
was vacant, Bonner had been permitted to appoint agents
to deal with his affairs, and to remove his personal property
from his houses and elsewhere in the diocese; and after
Ridley had entered, he raised no objection to Bonner's
agents removing any goods of Bonner which still remained.
There was a quantity of lead which Bonner had purchased
while he was bishop, and Ridley decided to use this for
repairing the roofs of houses and churches in the diocese. He
paid Bonner's agents the full value of the lead. He found
that some of the servants in his palaces had not been paid
their wages, or the cost of their liveries, by his predecessor,
and he paid these debts to the servants, which amounted to
£54. A few days before his death, Ridley wrote about this
matter to Queen Mary, stating that he could not remember
whether the sum involved was £53 or £55.[18] In this letter,
Ridley certainly gives the impression that he paid this
money from his own pocket, and it has always been assumed
that he did so; but a fortnight before Ridley was installed as
Bishop of London, the Council had issued a warrant for the
payment of £54 in respect of the servants' livery and wages,
to the Bishop of London's receiver.[19] We can disregard the
possibility that Ridley, a few days before his death, deliberately lied to Queen Mary about a matter which Mary's

officers could quite easily have checked from the Council records. Perhaps Ridley meant no more than that he had transmitted the money which he received from the Council to the servants; but it is possible that the Council, after issuing the warrant, did not in fact hand over the money to Ridley's receiver, or that Ridley was somehow cheated in the matter by one of his officers, and that consequently he paid the money himself.

Ridley also showed great consideration for Bonner's old mother, and for his sister, Mistress Mungey, who lived near Fulham Palace. Ridley invited them to dine with him on many occasions when he was in residence in Fulham, and treated old Mistress Bonner with great respect, calling her 'my mother Bonner'; he placed her to sit at the head of the table, and would not allow her to move lower down the table even when a member of the Council was dining with him.[20] Ridley was later to complain of the very different treatment which Bonner meted out to Ridley's relatives when he returned to office in Mary's reign, and subsequent Protestant historians have frequently contrasted Ridley's kindness with Bonner's malice in their hour of triumph. But Bonner may perhaps have resented the fact that his mother and sister were accepting the hospitality and cultivating the friendship of the man who had usurped his see while Bonner was confined in prison at the orders of Ridley and his fellow commissioners.

Soon after he was installed as Bishop of London, Ridley saw the unsuccessful culmination of his efforts to induce Joan Bocher to recant her Anabaptist heresies. Joan was kept alive in prison for a whole year after the warrant for her execution had been signed. During this time, the Protestant leaders made every effort to persuade her to recant, and carry her fagot. In this, they were only emulating the

o

Catholic bishops in the old days, who had always tried hard to obtain a recantation from every Lutheran who had been excommunicated for heresy before finally consigning him to the fire. But in Joan Bocher's case, there were special reasons why the Protestant Bishops wished to induce her to recant. They did not want to burn Joan Bocher. The young King had been highly opposed to the idea. It was by no means certain that Rich and the lawyers were right in their opinion that it was legal to burn heretics at common law without statutory authority; and as long as Somerset was Protector, he was most unwilling to take an action which would be in such flagrant contrast to the liberal policy on which he prided himself, and to the policy of religious tolera-tion which had led to the repeal of the heresy statutes, and which had made England famous throughout Europe as a haven of refuge from persecution. It was unheard of to keep a condemned heretic for as long as a year before carrying out the order for his execution; but from May 1549, to May 1550, Joan Bocher was spared. Ridley had been unable to assist at her trial on account of his absence from London; but as he was considered to be the ablest disputant among all the Protestants, he was chosen to play the leading part in attempting to induce Joan Bocher to recant.

Every day for a week, Ridley and Cranmer visited Joan Bocher at the house of the Lord Chancellor, Rich, where she was confined. Later Joan was brought to Ridley's house for further discussions with him.[21] Ridley apparently did not find it easy to argue with her, for Joan was defiant and abusive. He evidently tried hard to persuade her that there was neither authority nor reason in support of her view that though the Word was made flesh in the Virgin's belly, Christ did not take flesh of the Virgin, as the flesh of the Virgin, being the outward man, was sinfully gotten and born in sin, and that the Word, by the consent of the inward man of the Virgin, was made flesh.[22] But Joan Bocher would not be shaken in her opinion, and ridiculed the attitude of Ridley and Cranmer. She could not see that her position was so very different from that of Ann Askew, who was now revered as a noble martyr. 'It was not so long ago', she told them, 'that you burned Ann Askew for a piece of bread, yet came yourselves to believe the doctrine for which you burned her; and now you will burn me for a piece of flesh, and in the end you will come to believe this also'.[23] Ridley was forced to report that he had completely failed in his mission. On 27th April 1550, the Council signed a warrant fixing the date of Joan Bocher's execution for 2nd May; but one last attempt was made to convert her. On 30th April, Ridley and Goodrich visited her in prison, and argued with her once again; but she was adamant. Two days later, Joan Bocher was burned at Smithfield. Scory, who had been one of the preachers at Canterbury in 1541, and had been imprisoned there as a heretic, preached the sermon at the burning; but Joan interrupted him with shrieks and curses. The spectators in the crowd said to each other that it would have been better to send her to Bedlam rather than to burn her.[24]

The revolts of 1549 had been the watershed of the Reformation. Before the revolt, the fear of its outbreak had restrained the Protestant leaders; now the revolt had been broken, there was nothing to hold them back. Once it was clear that Cranmer really meant business, a number of prominent English exiles returned from foreign Protestant states, along with increasing numbers of alien refugees from Papist persecution in Europe; the returning exiles, who had not stayed in England, like Cranmer and Ridley, to compromise their Protestantism after the fall of Cromwell, were

resolved to urge the Reformation forward beyond the stage
which it had so far reached under Cranmer's leadership.
The most able of these men was John Hooper. Hooper had
originally been a monk and a Fellow of Oxford University,
but he had been deprived of his Fellowship, and had fled
abroad, after the passing of the Statute of the Six Articles.
On his return from Switzerland in 1549, he became chaplain, first to Somerset and then to Warwick. Hooper was a
man of absolute integrity, who made no concession to weakness in himself or in others, though he was obviously a most
affectionate husband and father. He was later to be ruthless
in stamping out all traces of Popery in his diocese, and
would punish the greatest dignitary in the land for immorality or other misconduct. He was indulgent only to
Warwick, who had completely deceived him into believing
without question in his religious sincerity. Hooper now
became the leader of the Protestant extremists.

The first issue which now arose was that of altars. With
the official proclamation of the doctrine of the Lord's
Supper, and the condemnation of transubstantiation, by
Ridley in the Cambridge disputation, the Protestants began
to demand the abolition of altars. An altar was used for a
sacrifice, and to retain it was to imply that the Body of
Christ was sacrificed in the Sacrament of the Altar. As the
Sacrament was not an oblation, but a commemoration of
the Lord's Supper, an altar should not be used; for a supper
a table, not an altar, was required; and the table should not
be set apart at the end of the church, but must be in the
midst of the congregation, and moved about from time to
time, to symbolise that all the people could eat and drink
from the table as partakers in the Lord's Supper.

The first attack on altars had occurred in the summer of
1549, in the heart of Catholic Wales. The Archdeacon of

Carmarthen, who was a zealous Protestant, removed the altar from the church at Carmarthen and replaced it by a wooden movable table. This was at the height of the insurrection, and this highly provocative action came near to starting off another revolt in Wales to add to all the other troubles of the Council; but Bishop Ferrar immediately intervened, and insisted that the table should be put in the place where the altar had been.[25] By the winter the revolts had been crushed, and Ridley, in the more sympathetic and Protestant atmosphere of Kent, was ready to proceed; he ordered the altar to be removed from Rochester Cathedral, and replaced with a movable wooden table, though he presumably set it down in the place where the altar had stood.* Early in 1550, Hooper preached a sermon at Court, in which he called for the removal of altars throughout the realm. When he heard that Ridley was soon to be appointed Bishop of London, he had every hope that Ridley would be ready to give a lead to the kingdom in the matter of altars; but he was nevertheless a little afraid that this higher office might have a restraining effect on Ridley, for he was probably conscious of the moderation and half-heartedness which Ridley, along with Cranmer, had shown in the first two years after King Edward's accession. On 27th March, Hooper wrote to Bullinger: 'There has lately been appointed a new Bishop of London, a pious and learned man, if only his new dignity do not change his attitude. He will, I hope, destroy the altars of Baal, as he did heretofore in his church when he was Bishop of Rochester'.[26]

---

* The only reference to the removal of the altar by Ridley at Rochester appears to be in Hooper's letter to Bullinger, 27th March 1550 (*Original Letters*, p. 79). We can presume that the altar at Rochester was not removed before September 1549, and that Ridley placed the table in the place where the altar had stood, as he did when he first removed the altar in St. Paul's in the next year.

Hooper had no reason to be disappointed. Ridley lost no time, after entering into his new bishopric, in solving the question of altars in a manner which was to satisfy the most ardent of the Protestant extremists, though he proceeded by stages towards his objective—to have a portable table which was moved about in the middle of the church. On the first occasion when he entered St. Paul's after he became Bishop of London—a week after he had been installed by proxy— he ordered the light on the altar to be put out as he entered the quire to receive Communion. He then received the Sacrament in his hands.[27] Within less than a month of becoming bishop, he began a visitation of his diocese. The chief object of the visitation was to remove the altars from the churches.

In his Articles, Ridley ordered his vicars to inquire diligently as to whether any persons in their parishes were speaking in favour of Papal supremacy, and whether any were agitating against the Book of Common Prayer by means of plays, songs or otherwise. They were also to inquire as to whether anyone was spreading sedition against the King, and whether anyone was saying that goods should be held in common, that there should be no magistrates, or condemning the taking of an oath, and lawsuits. They were to find out if anyone was denying that Christ took flesh of the Virgin. He particularly impressed upon them the need to unearth any secret Anabaptist conventicles. They were to suppress any private Masses which were being celebrated in defiance of the statute of 1547, and to report if anyone was saying grace in Latin at dinner or supper. They were to ascertain whether anyone was asserting that the Sacraments were valueless if administered by sinful priests. He also warned them to prevent any teaching that repentance was of no avail to a man who sinned after baptism. Finally, he directed the clergy to prevent any person from celebrating any of the suppressed holy days and from absenting himself from his lawful calling on such days, and gave a general instruction to the priests to perform their duties conscientiously.[28]

Ridley then sent a separate document to all his clergy, which was directed against Popish practices. This prohibited those ceremonies, such as the licking of the chalice and the elevation of the bread during the Sacrament, which were banned in the Book of Common Prayer. But among these injunctions Ridley inserted the one which shocked so many of his vicars to the core—for the removal of the altar from their church. The altar was to be replaced by a wooden Communion table, which was to be covered with a cloth, and must be set down in any part of the quire or chancel which the curates, churchwardens and questmen thought most suitable. The table was to be set in such a position that the minister and the communicants would be apart from the rest of the people. All by-altars and other tables were to be removed.[29]

Ridley began his visitation on 5th May.[30] It lasted seven weeks. He did not go into the more distant parts of his diocese, being content for the Council to instruct Sir John Gates, the Sheriff, to enforce his Injunctions in Essex;[31] but in the city of London, Ridley handled the business himself. This was much the most important part of the diocese, and it was here that the Catholic resistance had been greatest. Ridley therefore decided to visit every parish in the city in person. He summoned the vicar and curates, and six of the leading parishioners, to meet him in the parish church. Ridley always arranged for a suitable sermon to be preached; sometimes he preached himself. His Injunctions were then read out, and the audience enjoined to obedience. The

Catholic vicars were left in no doubt that the days of Bonner were past. If they had hoped to continue with their surreptitious celebrations of the Mass, they were now confronted with the peremptory order to remove the very altar from their church. Ridley was not content to address the vicars and leading parishioners in their churches; in Whitsun week, he summoned every vicar and curate to his palace at St. Paul's. He interviewed them all privately, and ordered each man to make a written submission to his Injunctions within four days;[32] and he made it perfectly clear that if any of them disobeyed his orders, he would be expelled from his benefice. By his ruthless energy, Ridley had convinced both friend and foe that he would brook no opposition from the Catholics. 'The new Bishop of London', wrote Christopher Hales to Gualter on 24th May, 'is now employed in his visitation, and threatens to eject those who shall not have come to their senses before his next visitation, and if I know the man he will be as good as his word'.[33]

At Whitsun, 25th May, Ridley preached at Paul's Cross. He was followed on the Monday by Hooper, and on the Tuesday by Cottisford. Ridley had not yet removed the altar from St. Paul's itself; he evidently thought it more impressive to delay this action until nearer the end of the visitation. On St. Barnabas' Day, as the Londoners were going home in the long summer evening annoyed that they had been forbidden by the Lord Mayor from celebrating it as a holy day, the altar was taken down and thrown out of the Cathedral. Ridley did not, as has been stated, pull down the wall in the upper quire, where the altar had stood, at this time; he was not to do this until nearly eighteen months later. Nor did he, on this occasion, move the position of the Communion table in the Cathedral. The table, in accordance with his Injunctions, was movable, but it was placed in the spot where the altar had stood.* When he had finished his visitation, not a single altar remained in any church in the diocese of London.

The Catholic bishops, who had reluctantly abandoned their opposition to the Book of Common Prayer and had been resigned to complying with it, were stirred to fresh resistance by Ridley's action. There was great indignation in many quarters, and the Catholics declared that Ridley was guilty of a praemunire in violating the canon law, and had indeed contravened the Act of Uniformity itself, for the Book of Common Prayer referred to the altar, and directed that certain ceremonies should be performed there. The Council had no intention of taking any action against Ridley, but Ridley submitted a document to the Council, stating the reasons which he relied upon to justify his action in removing altars.

Ridley gave six reasons to justify his action. The first of these contained the true explanation of the importance which Ridley attached to the removal of altars:

> The form of a table shall more move the simple from the superstitious opinions of the Popish Mass unto the right use of the Lord's Supper. For the use of an altar is to make sacrifice upon it; the use for a table is to serve for men to eat upon. Now, when we come unto the Lord's board, what do we come for? To sacrifice Christ up again, and to crucify him again, or

---

* See Wriothesley's *Chronicle*, vol. II, pp. 40–1, where it is stated that the altar was removed on 13th June and that the table was placed where the altar had stood; the table was not removed below the steps until March 1551 (see p. 242). *Greyfriars Chronicle*, p. 67, states that the altar was removed on St. Barnabas' Day at night and replaced by a table which was put below the steps. The *Greyfriars Chronicle* is probably right as to the date, and Wriothesley's *Chronicle* as to the position of the table. as it seems easiest to reconcile the conflicting statements on this basis, Gairdner, vol III, p. 310, accepts the *Greyfriars Chronicle's* version as to the position of the table.

to feed upon him, that was once only crucified and offered up for us? If we come to feed upon him, spiritually to eat his body, and spiritually to drink his blood, which is the true use of the Lord's Supper, then seeing no man can deny but the form of a table is more meet for the Lord's board than the form of an altar.[34]

His second reason was that in the Book of Common Prayer, the words 'altar' and 'table' were both used, and that consequently he had not contravened the Act of Uniformity in removing the altars. The third reason was that as the Papists considered that the Mass could only be performed on an altar, or on a super-altar, the removal of altars, and the substitution of tables, would bring home to the people that the new Communion was not a Romish Mass. His fourth reason was that the word 'altar', in Greek, denoted a place where sacrifices were performed; the fifth that Christ and the disciples had eaten the Last Supper from a table; and the sixth that since it was stated in the Book of Common Prayer that any ambiguity in the text should be resolved by the diocesan bishop, he had been entitled to interpret the Book of Common Prayer as permitting the removal of altars.*

The Council, however, were not prepared to leave it to every bishop to interpret the directions of the Book of Common Prayer on the question of the removal of altars. The Catholic bishops, and large numbers of the clergy and people, were profoundly shocked at Ridley's action, and considered it to be nothing short of sacrilege. When Ridley

---

* See Ridley's Register (London), f. 275, cited in *Works* p. 321, Gloucester Ridley, pp. 325–7, and Notes to Foxe, (vol. VI, *App.*, pp. 741–5, for proof that this document, which was sent by the Council to Ridley on 23rd November 1550, was written by Ridley himself at an earlier date, and possibly even before his visitation of May–June 1550.

condemned transubstantiation in a disputation at Cambridge, this was privately condemned as heresy by some of the learned doctors who heard him; but the removal of altars brought home to every subject in the kingdom that the central object which had stood in the churches for over a thousand years, and which they had watched with awe every Sunday since their early childhood, was condemned as idolatrous and thrown contemptuously away by the adherents of the new religion which had been forced upon them. If the suppression of altars in the diocese of London, where there were more Protestants than anywhere else, could lead to a public outcry, it was not difficult to see how it would be received in the dioceses of Exeter or York. Yet the Council decided to enforce this measure. On 23rd November 1550, an order was sent to every bishop to remove the altar from every church, and to replace it with a movable wooden table. The Council adopted the six reasons which Ridley had given them as a justification for his action in London, and sent them, along with the order, to all the bishops, including Ridley himself, who was now formally instructed to do the thing which he had already done for the reasons which he himself had provided.* This, though no doubt highly gratifying to Ridley, seems a somewhat curious proceeding, for two of Ridley's six reasons, while very relevant some months before in his justification of the action which he had taken in his diocese on his own

---

* Foxe, vol. VI, p. 5; for the evidence that this order, and Ridley's reasons in support of it, were sent to all the bishops, and not only to Ridley, as Foxe implies, see Strype, *Cranmer*, p. 326. Foxe is also wrong in stating that Ridley's visitation and the removal of altars in the diocese of London were after he had received this order from the Council (see Ridley's Register, cited in *Works*, p. 321). Earlier editions of Foxe, and *Works*, wrongly give the date of the Council's letter as 24th November.

initiative, were quite inappropriate to an order from the King in Council to all the Bishops in the country.

The Catholic bishops were so disheartened and over-awed by the developments in the previous eighteen months that only one of them dared make any resistance to the order. Day had been considered as something of a reformer in the days of Henry VIII, but after the accession of Edward he had clearly identified himself with the Catholic party, and had opposed every Protestant reform in the House of Lords. After the introduction of the Book of Common Prayer, however, he had abandoned his opposition to it, and had even gone so far as to preach a sermon against transubstantiation at Court. Now the overthrow of the altar aroused his resistance. During the summer of 1550, Day went to his diocese of Chichester, and preached against the new religious developments. When the Council got wind of his doings, they sent Cox to Sussex to counter the Bishop's activities, and summoned Day to come before them to explain his conduct. They ordered Day to take all necessary steps to remove the altars in his diocese, and when he demurred, he was required to submit a statement in writing giving the reasons for his opposition to the proposal.

Day presented his statement to the Council on 1st December. He based his arguments on the passage in Isaiah: 'In that day shall there be an altar to the Lord in the midst of the land of Egypt', and on the text from Paul's Epistle to the Hebrews: 'We have an altar, whereof they have no right to eat which serve the tabernacle'. Day's statement was shown to Ridley, and he and Cranmer argued with Day before the Council. They maintained that altars were not in use in the primitive Church, and that when Paul spoke of 'altar', he meant Christ himself. Day told the

Council that he would offer no opposition to their order, but that his conscience would not permit him to enforce it himself in his diocese, and he asked that they should find some other means of issuing the orders to the clergy of Chichester and not send them through him as Bishop. The Council refused to agree to this, and ordered Day to consult with either Cranmer, Goodrich or Ridley, who would be able to show him the error of his position. Day called at Lambeth Palace, but Cranmer was out; he was attending a meeting of the Council. Day made no further attempt to see either Cranmer, Ridley or Goodrich. The Council then ordered Day to issue the order for the removal of altars to all the priests in the diocese of Chichester before 7th December; but Day refused to comply. The time limit for obedience was extended to the 9th, but still the Bishop was adamant. He was then arrested, and sent to the Fleet.*

In the suppression of altars, Ridley had marched hand in hand with Hooper, who strongly supported Ridley's action, and had been employed by Ridley as a preacher at Paul's Cross on Whit Monday, at the height of Ridley's visitation. But Hooper was now to come into conflict with Ridley. Hooper's standing among the Protestants made it obvious that he should take his place on the episcopal bench, and Warwick proposed to appoint him Bishop of Gloucester. Hooper did not refuse to accept a bishopric, as Latimer had done a few years before; he decided to accept, and to put into practice his own ideas as to what a bishop should be. For Hooper, the duty of a bishop was to suppress Popery and vice in his diocese, not to waste his time in idle cere-

* *Acts of the Privy Council*, vol. II, pp. 137, 154, 168–70, 172–3, 176–8 (7th October, 8th and 30th November, 1st, 4th, 7th and 11th December 1550).

monies. He immediately adopted a position which led him
into his long controversy with Ridley over vestments.

As soon as he had been appointed bishop in July 1550,
Hooper told Cranmer that he objected to being consecrated
in the usual manner. He objected to the oath by the Saints
in the Oath of Supremacy, which ended with the words 'So
help me God and all Saints and the Holy Evangelist'.[35] He
also disapproved of the ceremonial in the ordination service
—particularly to the ceremony of carrying the Bible on his
shoulders, and turning round three times.[36] His chief objection, however, was to wearing vestments at his ordination,
or on any other occasion. He had three objections to vestments. Paul had said that the Levitical priesthood of Aaron
was no longer to continue, but to wear vestments was
Aaronical, and was thus restoring this priesthood in England. The vestments worn by the English clergy were the
same as those worn by the Papists, and had become the
garment of Antichrist. Finally, Hooper pointed to the fact
that Christ had been crucified naked in order to symbolise
that his truth needed no vestments.[37] The difficulty as to the
oath by the Saints was easily resolved, for in the summer of
1550, the King struck out the oath by the Saints from the
oath of Supremacy; but the question of vestments still remained. Cranmer pointed out to Hooper that to refuse to
wear the vestments prescribed by the canon law might
amount to a praemunire; but Hooper was adamant, and
announced that he would never consent to wear vestments
at his ordination.

The matter was then raised in the Council. Warwick was
quite prepared to permit Hooper to dispense with vestments,
and on 5th August he granted a royal pardon to Cranmer and Ridley with regard to any praemunire of which
they might be guilty in ordaining Hooper without vest-

ments.[38] Cranmer was not so happy about the position, but he was unwilling to displease Warwick, and would probably have given way had it not been for Ridley. Ridley strongly objected to Hooper's attitude, and urged the Archbishop to refuse to consecrate him without vestments. The wearing of vestments was prescribed by law, and Hooper must not be permitted to defy the law. Nor did Ridley weaken in his objection when he was shown the royal pardon granted to him. Thanks to Ridley, Cranmer stood firm against Warwick in the Council. The Council then agreed that Ridley should set down his views in writing, and send the document either to Hooper or to the Council. Hooper did not hear from Ridley for a month, and at the end of August was complaining that Ridley, instead of writing to him about the points in dispute, was intriguing against him at Court; but it appears that at some time in September Ridley met Hooper, and discussed the question with him.*

Ridley did not agree with Hooper's arguments that it was sinful to wear vestments. In Ridley's view, it was neither good nor bad in itself. There was no reason of doctrine either to wear or not to wear vestments; consequently, it was a matter which could be left to be regulated by the laws of the realm. As the regulations of the Church of England provided, however, that vestments should be worn, Hooper was guilty of the sin of disobedience in refusing to wear them. Ridley was only concerned in forcing Hooper to abandon his position of defiance to the regulations of the Church; he therefore stated that if Hooper would renounce his contention that it was sinful to wear vestments, he

* Micronius' letter to Bullinger, 28th August 1550 (*Original Letters*, p. 567). Strype, *Cranmer*, p. 303, states that Ridley had 'long arguings with Hooper'. If this is correct, they must have occurred between 28th August, when Micronius wrote to Bullinger, and 3rd October, when Hooper was summoned to the Council.

would be prepared to consecrate Hooper in the old merchant's cloak which he habitually wore, provided that the
King and the Archbishop of Canterbury consented.[39] Neither
Ridley nor Cranmer could move Hooper, and while Hooper
remained on friendly terms with the Archbishop, his relations with Ridley became very strained. The dispute had
now reached the stage at which the unity of the Protestant
movement was seriously endangered, for though every
effort was made to keep it secret, the news leaked out, and
caused great satisfaction among the Catholics at home and
abroad.[40]

By October 1550, the dispute had still not been resolved,
and Hooper had still not been consecrated. Warwick then
considered that the controversy must be ended at all costs,
and presumably hoped that if it were allowed to die down,
the matter of Hooper's ordination might be resolved without further friction in due course. On 3rd October, Hooper
was summoned before the Council, and ordered to refrain
from expressing his views about vestments; but he was permitted to submit a memorandum to the Council containing
a statement of his views. The Council then summoned Ridley to come before them on 6th October, at Richmond, and
ordered him to put a stop to his controversy with Hooper,
as disputes between learned divines were unseemly.[41] On
hearing that Hooper was submitting a statement of his
views to the Council, Ridley asked leave to do likewise, and
to reply to Hooper's treatise in his turn. He was permitted
to do so, and presented a treatise to the Council.

On 19th October, the Council brought Hooper and Ridley face to face before them, and a bitter dispute ensued.
According to Hooper, Ridley behaved in a most aggressive
and insulting manner, and in view of the tone of Ridley's
treatise against Hooper, it is not difficult to accept this as

true. When Hooper asked the Council to return to him the copy of the treatise which he had presented to them, Ridley objected, and persuaded the Council to hand over Hooper's treatise to him.[42] Perhaps he had not yet written his reply, and needed Hooper's manuscript for this purpose.

Warwick now began to lose patience with Hooper. He had no strong feelings in the matter, and faced with this strong opposition from Ridley, on a matter in which his private interests were in no way concerned, he urged Hooper to give way. The Council proposed a compromise to Hooper: if he would agree to wear vestments for his consecration, he need never wear them again, except when he preached in his cathedral or delivered a sermon at Court before the King, and on other public occasions.[43] Hooper refused to agree to this suggestion; nor was he willing to confine the controversy to the Council chamber and the houses of the bishops. He dealt with the issues in a number of public sermons, and tried to bring the force of his supporters in the capital to his aid. The Council thereupon ordered Hooper to be confined to his house, and only to leave it for the purpose of visiting Cranmer, Ridley, Goodrich or Holbeach for instruction by them on the truth in the matter of vestments. Hooper defied this order; he continued to preach sermons in London, and on 20th December he published a treatise, which he called his 'Confession of Faith'. In this he not only publicly stated his position with regard to vestments, which he condemned as Aaronical, but went on to denounce magistrates who strayed from the word of God. It was probably this reference to magistrates which led Warwick to abandon his efforts on Hooper's behalf. On 13th January 1551, Hooper was summoned before the Council, and placed under house arrest in Lambeth Palace; he was warned that if he continued in his

P

defiance, worse things would befall him. After a fortnight, Cranmer wrote to the Council informing them that Hooper was as obstinate as ever, and was determined to prescribe laws for the governance of the Church out of his own head; and on 27th January, the Council ordered Cranmer to convey Hooper from his palace to the Fleet.[44]

Hooper now found himself in prison along with his enemies Heath and Day, and prohibited from receiving any visitors or speaking to anyone except the prison chaplains. After a month he decided to submit. He had shown before, and was to show again, that he did not lack courage; but he had no wish to remain in prison at the orders of a government which, if he were prepared to surrender on this point, would help him to carry the Reformation beyond the stage where men like Ridley seemed eager to check it. He agreed to be consecrated wearing vestments. To complete his humiliation, Cranmer and Ridley were appointed to officiate at his ordination. On 8th March, Hooper was consecrated by the Archbishop at Lambeth, with Ridley assisting.[45] Ridley had won his fight with Hooper.

Yet the tide of Protestantism was moving in the direction in which Hooper wished it to go. Little more than a year later, the second Book of Common Prayer forbade the use of most of the vestments to which Hooper had objected. Hooper can hardly have been satisfied with the retention, in the second Book of Common Prayer, of the rochet for the bishop and the surplice for the priest and deacon; for it is difficult to accept the suggestion that Hooper objected, not to vestments in general, but only to Popish vestments,* in view of his own writings, which clearly condemn all vestments as Aaronical. But it is certainly true that one of the

* This suggestion is made by Neal, *History of the Puritans*, vol. I, p. 55.

three reasons which Hooper advanced against the vestments of 1550 was that they were the same as those worn by the Papists; and by abolishing most of the Popish garments, the book was certainly a step in his direction. The ritual to which he objected in the ordination service was also abolished in the second Book of Common Prayer.[46]

The struggle with Hooper over vestments is one of the most illuminating events in Ridley's life. It was not that he felt any respect or affection for vestments in themselves. He repeatedly stated, throughout the dispute, that he thought it was immaterial, from the point of view of doctrine, whether vestments were worn or not. Nor was it merely that he insisted that the laws of the land be obeyed, and feared that he would be guilty of a praemunire if he were a party to the ordination of Hooper without vestments. This was apparently Cranmer's original attitude, but it ceased to have any validity when he received the royal pardon in this connexion. It is certainly impossible to accept the suggestion that Ridley took the view that a royal pardon was insufficient in law to authorise disobedience to an Act of Parliament.* This theory was now being tentatively put forward by many of the common lawyers, and by Gardiner when it suited his purposes; but the Protestant leaders would have been the last to accept it. Ridley wrote in his treatise that he was ready to consecrate him in his old merchant's cloak if the King and Cranmer did not object—as he knew they did not—provided that Hooper would abandon his opposition to vestments. He was even prepared to consecrate priests and deacons without vestments when no royal pardon had been obtained. A year before the dispute with Hooper, Ridley had assisted at the consecration of Thomas Sampson by Cranmer when Sampson was per-

* The suggestion is made by Gloucester Ridley, p. 312.

mitted to be ordained in his ordinary dress on account of
his objection to vestments; and Ridley had been prepared
to ordain his chaplain Bradford on 10th August 1550, whilst
permitting Bradford to dispense with some of the requirements of the ordination service, at the very time when he
first raised his voice against the attitude of Hooper.[47] Yet
Ridley, at a time when the Council and Cranmer were prepared to let Hooper have his way, felt sufficiently strongly
about the vestments issue to enter into a controversy with
the chaplain of the Earl of Warwick, and to pursue it with
such determination as to threaten the unity of the Protestant
cause.

The explanation of Ridley's conduct in the controversy
with Hooper lies almost certainly in his mistrust and disapproval of the growing power of Hooper and the Protestant
extremists. In his struggle with Hooper, he was fighting, not
for the existing laws of England or in the interests of the
Council and the government, but for the idea of Authority
against the idea of anarchy in religion. He thought that
Hooper and the forces which he represented were leading
the country on the dangerous path of libertarianism, which
might even end in Anabaptism.[48] He was determined to
resist Hooper's attack on an established institution of the
Church, which, though he might not esteem it for its own
sake, nevertheless represented an ordinance laid down by
authority, and to defy it was something which was too close
to Anabaptism for Ridley's liking. The fact that he considered, and clearly said, that vestments were not necessary
through any rule of doctrine, only emphasized the necessity
for obedience to them as a sign of submission to the authority of Church and State. This explanation of Ridley's
attitude is fully borne out by the treatise which he submitted to the Council in reply to Hooper's document.

In the treatise, Ridley supplied his own interpretation of the texts which Hooper had cited, and put forward quotations from Paul and from Augustine in support of his own position. He argued that the vestments of the Church of England were not Aaronical, while he condemned Hooper's description of the priesthood of Aaron as 'pharisaical superstition' as being blasphemous; as for Hooper's argument that it was ordained that Christ should be crucified naked in order to show that his Truth needed no vestments, Ridley asked whether Christ's Truth was any the less true because he wore the white robe when he was mocked by Herod. For the most part, however, Ridley was arguing in a bitter polemical style that Hooper's views were dangerous and subversive.[49]

Ridley began by stating his position with his usual clarity:

> All the world knows I do grant the appointed vestments to be neither things to be regarded of necessity to our health and salvation, or yet as if without them the ministry might not be done; nor that this use of them is in Scripture, nor that the same doth justify the doer and user by God's holy word. For to say so were indeed to defend the Papistical and Aaronical priesthood both, against Christ's Gospel. But all our controversy is in this, whether the vestments as they be now appointed by the authority of the Church of England be things lawful to be used, or may be used without the breach of God's law; that is, whether they be things as of themselves indifferent, and not forbidden as sin against God's holy word, or no.[50]

In asserting that vestments were sinful, though God never proclaimed them to be such, Hooper was 'ungodly adding unto God's word'. In truth, whether or not vestments were worn was an indifferent matter. It did not follow from this, however, that because it was indifferent every man was free to choose whether he wore vestments or not; this would indeed have been the position, were it not for the fact that the wearing of vestments had been ordered by the magistrates; but having been ordered it must be obeyed.

> Then peradventure thou wilt say 'Ye bring us again in bondage of the law, and do deprive us of our liberty'. I answer, No, for I make it not a matter of justification, but of order; and to be under the law is another thing. For the Christian, liberty is not a licence to do what thou list, but to serve God in newness of thy mind, and for love, and not for servile fear.[51]

A little later, Ridley returned to the same theme:

> Lenity indeed is required in the law-maker, and all tyranny to be eschewed. Nevertheless, to teach that Christian liberty is free to use and not use, even as every man list, ordinances well made by lawful authority, is a seditious doctrine and liable to confound a good order.[52]

Hooper had given, as one of his reasons for addressing his treatise to the Council, his desire to warn the magistrates of their foes. To this, Ridley replied:

> This saying savoureth either of so great a presumption and confidence, as if a man should think that he is able to prove by his eloquence whatsoever he list (which is a perilous and a dangerous vice of a haughty stomach) or else of a too vile and too base an estimation of the magistrates, as though, otherwise than thus monished, they were not able to discern who are their friends, and who are their foes, who do maintain their estate by God's word in truth and in deed, and who can coll them and flatter them with glorious terms under the pretence of God's word, to maintain their own bold rashness, and to the subversion of all good and godly order.[53]

Ridley pointed out to the Council that Hooper, by his

attitude, was challenging the authority of State and Church:

> I pray you, who hath appointed now and instituted our vestments in the Church of England? And who hath established them? Hath not the Archbishop with his company of learned men thereunto appointed by the King his Highness and His Majesty's Council appointed them? Hath not the King His Majesty and the whole Parliament established them? If then this fourth note had been followed as it was proposed, what would have followed after, the wise may perceive. And, though it follow not in words, yet it is evident what followeth in meaning.[54]

Ridley had no doubt in his own mind that what followed was dangerously close to Anabaptism. He ended the treatise by warning the Council against his brother elect. 'Let His Highness take good heed with his doings'.[55]

The bitter struggle with Hooper over vestments reveals clearly the authoritarian opinions which Ridley held. There can be little doubt where he would have stood, if he had survived till Elizabeth's reign, in the vestments controversy which then broke out again within the victorious Protestant Church. Sampson and his followers did not hesitate to claim that Ridley would have given them his support in their struggle against vestments;* but it is difficult to accept any of the reasons which they advanced in support of their contention. His last message to Hooper from prison,† in which he referred to Hooper's wisdom and his own simplicity at the time of their dispute over vestments, may have

---

* See the statements of Nixon and Hawkins at their trial in 1567 (Grindal's *Works*, p. 211); see also Strype, *Ann als*, vol. II (ii), p. 222, citing an anonymous tract of 1565.

† Ridley's letter to Hooper (*Works*, pp. 355, 357); see Chapter IX, p. 366.

been no more than an expression of courtesy and humility at a time when his admiration for Hooper's heroism had led him to express his solidarity with him in the face of the common enemy. As for the fact that Ridley resisted the attempt to make him put on vestments at his degradation the day before his death, this can surely be explained by his disapproval of the whole ceremony, and of the vestments which he was required to wear—for these had been prohibited in the second Book of Common Prayer—and is no indication that he had changed his opinion that vestments were in themselves indifferent.

At the same time as Ridley was engaged in the vestments controversy, his authoritarianism led him into a conflict with the foreign Protestants in England. The aliens in England outside the Embassies were naturally subject to the laws of the realm, and consequently were obliged to comply with the Act of Uniformity under pain of incurring its penalties; but this raised a difficulty in the case of the foreign Protestants. Their services differed in a number of particulars from that prescribed in the Book of Common Prayer; and they consequently faced the prospect of prosecution in the country to which they had come for refuge. Cranmer was on terms of the closest friendship with Peter Martyr and many of the other foreign theologians, and he now intervened in their favour. He persuaded the Council to grant a licence to the aliens to hold their own services in a special church which was to be put aside for their use. It was of course necessary that these services should be carefully controlled, to make sure that no foreign Anabaptist was granted toleration; so it was arranged that both the German and Dutch communities, and the French refugees, should each appoint one minister to conduct their services, and that both should be under the control of John à Lasco, who was given the title of Superintendent of the foreigners' services. The Council agreed that the church of the old Austin Friars should be granted to the aliens for their use as soon as it had been repaired.[56]

When this matter was raised in the summer of 1550, Ridley opposed the whole project. The majority of the aliens in England had settled in London and the vicinity, and while most of them were living in Southwark,[57] which was in the diocese of Winchester, many others were in Ridley's diocese. Ridley took the same view which he had taken in the vestments controversy: as the differences between the foreign Protestant services and those laid down in the Book of Common Prayer concerned only inessentials, there was no justification for the aliens to disobey the laws of the realm in which they lived, and they should be forced to conform. Several other bishops supported him, but Ridley was the most determined of those who opposed the aliens, and his position and reputation as an ardent Protestant made him a particularly formidable adversary.[58]

The aliens, however, could rely on the friendship of Cranmer, and thanks to his influence could prepare to hold their services in the church of the Austin Friars. But they encountered continual difficulties about this, and attributed all their troubles to Ridley. As the church was in need of repair, the Council agreed to carry out the necessary work before handing over the church to the aliens; but the weeks dragged on, and the work was not completed. The foreign Protestants then decided to try to obtain the key of the church, as they were quite prepared to hold their services there before the workmen had finished the repairs; but this proved to be impossible. At the end of August 1550, à Lasco had an interview with the Lord Treasurer, the Earl of Wiltshire, and asked him to let them have the key of the church; but Wiltshire refused to hand over the key until the church had been repaired and formally granted to the aliens by the King. He took the opportunity to inform à Lasco that the aliens had no business to set up their own services, but should comply with the services in the Book of Common Prayer unless they could prove them to be contrary to God's word. The foreign Protestants were convinced that the delay was caused by deliberate obstruction, and that it was Ridley who had incited Lord Wiltshire to adopt this policy.[59]

In the middle of September, however, a number of London citizens agreed to set aside their own church to help the aliens. A Lasco immediately began to hold services there. At this, the church of the Austin Friars was made ready within a few weeks, and before the middle of October the aliens were worshipping in the fully repaired church. But this was not the end of their difficulties. The Council insisted, as a condition of permitting them to hold their services at all, that the Sacraments should be administered according to the provisions laid down in the Book of Common Prayer. This was reluctantly accepted by the foreigners, and while they continued to fear the worst, they were allowed to follow their own practices in other respects. Whenever any trouble arose, they saw in it the hand of Ridley, and considered him to be as much their enemy as Cranmer was their friend.[60]

In the summer of 1550, Ridley took action in yet another matter—though in this case the initiative did not come from him—in which he acted against libertarianism and extremism, and in the interests of order and discipline. He received an order from the Council to prohibit the preaching of any sermons in his diocese except on Sundays.[61] Ridley was active in seeing that this order was carried out. Many

Protestant preachers had begun to deliver lengthy sermons on all days of the week. The masters complained that these sermons drew away their servants from their work. In prohibiting all weekday sermons, the Council were able to please and assist the class on whom they relied for their support, and at the same time to prevent preaching by over-zealous extremists. Ridley instructed his clergy that while prayers should be held at all times, and on every day of the week, sermons ought only to be delivered on Sundays and on authorised holy days, when they would not distract the labourers and artizans from their lawful trades.[62]

Ridley was also occupied in the summer of 1550 in con-nexion with Gardiner. For two years, Gardiner had been imprisoned in the Tower by order of the King, without being brought to trial or charged with any offence. He now found an unexpected ally in the Duke of Somerset. In the spring of 1550, Warwick had felt strong enough to release Somerset from the Tower, and to reappoint him to the Council; he even married his eldest son to Somerset's daughter. But the old Protector was not content to take his place on the Council in a position of subordination to War-wick; he was determined to regain power, and he looked round to build up a party for himself. There was no hope now of reviving the force of the defeated tenants and small-holders; as for the Protestants, they were now more satisfied with Warwick than they had ever been with Somerset. Somerset therefore decided to rely on the Catholic faction, who, leaderless and dispirited, were eager to accept a prom-inent member of the Council as their leader.

Pursuing his new policy, Somerset proposed in the Coun-cil that Gardiner should be given an opportunity to make his submission with a view to his being released from prison. Somerset, Warwick, and other dignitaries were sent to visit

Gardiner in the Tower.* They presented Gardiner with a number of articles, to which he was required to subscribe; he was to declare that he believed in the royal supremacy over the Church, which was unabated during the infancy of the King, and that the King had full power to regulate the number of holy days and fast days; and he was to approve the repeal of the Statute of the Six Articles and the Book of Common Prayer. Gardiner agreed to accept all these articles; but he was also required to sign the preface, in which he was to admit that he had been suspected of working for Papal supremacy, and against the religious practices prescribed by the King, and to admit that he had been rightly punished. Gardiner still had spirit after two years in prison; he refused to sign the preface, and demanded that he be either released or put on trial for some offence.[63]

The Council decided to give Gardiner one last opportunity for submission. In the middle of July, they instructed Ridley, Petre, Cecil and Richard Goodrick, a common lawyer, to draft new articles for Gardiner to subscribe. Ridley and his colleages drew up twenty articles.† They were prepared to delete the preface to which Gardiner had objected, and to give him the opportunity of composing, in his own words, a full confession of his guilt; but they now required him to declare his approval of a much longer list of measures which he had always opposed. Gardiner was to recognise the royal supremacy and the authority of an infant King, to approve of the suppression of the monasteries and chantries, of images, holy water and holy

* Foxe, vol. VI, pp. 73–4, 115. Gardiner was visited by Somerset on 9th June and by Warwick on 9th July (see Muller, *Stephen Gardiner and the Tudor Reaction*, pp. 187, 190).

† See Foxe, vol. VI, pp. 82–4; *Acts of the Privy Council*, vol. III, pp. 70, 72–7 (11th and 13th July 1550); *King Edward's Journal*, 11th July 1550 (Burnet, vol. V, p. 24).

days, to consent to the marriage of priests, to the administration of the Sacrament in both kinds, and to the Homilies
and the Book of Common Prayer, and to condemn the
elevation of the Host.

On 14th July,* Ridley went with Petre, Sir William
Herbert and Richard Goodrick to visit Gardiner in the
Tower, and presented the new Articles to him. Gardiner's
attitude had hardened since his interviews with Somerset
and Warwick a few days before. He now refused even to
read the articles, and demanded that he be first set at
liberty, promising that if he were released he would consider them most carefully. Ridley, who probably thought
that the persecutor of Henry's reign was being treated far
too leniently by the Council, adopted a stern attitude
throughout the interview. He and his colleagues ordered
Gardiner to read the articles. Gardiner submitted to the
royal authority, and read them, but again demanded to be
set free. He tried to dispute with Ridley about the points at
issue, but Ridley said that he had not come to dispute. He
told Gardiner that the hand of God was to be seen in his
imprisonment, as he had inflicted so much hardship on
other men in former days; if he nevertheless wished for
mercy, he must sign the articles without discussion. Gardiner said that he wished for justice, not mercy, and Ridley
and his colleagues returned to report his contumacy to the
Council.[64] Soon afterwards, the revenues of the see of Winchester were sequestered.

* Foxe, vol. VI, p. 84, states that the twenty articles were drawn
up on 15th July; but Gardiner stated to the Commissioners at his trial
that Ridley and his colleagues visited him on the Monday, which was
14th July (cited in Foxe, vol. VI, pp. 75, 116); and this is confirmed
by the fact that the Council's order to Ridley to visit Gardiner was
given on the 13th, and Ridley's colleagues reported back to the
Council on the 15th (*Acts of the Privy Council*, vol. III, pp. 73, 78).

The Council now took measures to deprive Gardiner of his bishopric. In due course, a commission was appointed to try the case, and to determine whether he ought to be deprived. Nine commissioners were appointed: they were Cranmer, Ridley, Goodrich, Holbeach, Petre, Sir James Hales of the Court of Common Pleas, Richard Goodrick and two other gentlemen. The commissioners held their first session at Lambeth Palace on 15th December 1550; in the course of the next two months they sat for twenty-two sessions, taking verbal and written evidence at the houses of the members of the commission, in the Tower, and elsewhere. Ridley was present at fourteen of the twenty-two sessions; the sixth session on 17th January, at which Gardiner's witnesses were sworn, was held in his palace at St. Paul's.* The long official record of the proceedings does not give any indication of Ridley's part at the hearings, for while the written depositions and the verbal evidence of the witnesses are very fully reported, there is no mention made of any of the questions or comments of the commissioners; but apparently Ridley and Cranmer were the most active of all the commissioners, for the report of the trial which was sent to the Emperor singled out for mention the fact that Ridley and Cranmer had engaged in bitter arguments with Gardiner.[65]

There were eighty-five articles of accusation against

---

* See Foxe, vol. VI, pp. 64–266, for the deprivation proceedings against Gardiner. Ridley was absent from the seventh, fourteenth, fifteenth, sixteenth, seventeenth, eighteenth and nineteenth sessions. He was probably absent from the ninth session, for the record states that the Bishops of Ely and Lincoln and the other commissioners were present, and if Ridley had been there, the Bishop of London would presumably have been expressly mentioned along with his brother bishops (see Foxe, vol. VI, pp. 124–5). The last six sessions which Ridley missed were nothing more than interrogations of Gardiner by a few commissioners.

Gardiner. He was accused of disobedience to the King in having failed to urge his congregation, without equivocation, to accept the Book of Homilies and the Paraphrase of Erasmus in his sermons at Farnham and Winchester in the spring of 1548; in having failed to obey the royal command not to mention transubstantiation in his sermon before the King on St. Peter's Day in the same year; and in refusing to sign the articles and the preface in the Tower in the summer of 1550. Every action of Gardiner, both in and out of prison, including his appeal to be brought to trial, were listed as examples of his disobedience. Ironically enough, one of the charges in respect of which Ridley, with his colleagues, was sitting in judgment on Gardiner was Gardiner's refusal to co-operate with Somerset in the suppression of Trinity Hall and Clare Hall. The result of the proceedings was of course a foregone conclusion, but the commissioners were most scrupulous in observing all formalities, and thoroughly examined all the evidence, however long this might take them. They permitted Gardiner to be represented by a proctor, though his right to be represented was doubtful, and dutifully served *sub poenas* on all the witnesses whom Gardiner wished to call in his defence.

Gardiner conducted his defence with all the skill to be expected of the brilliant civil lawyer that he was. He challenged the jurisdiction of the commissioners, but he did not press the point. He did not create disorder, as Bonner had done; but he caused much embarrassment to his opponents by calling as witnesses several of the Lords of the Council, and by the skilful cross-examination to which he subjected the witnesses. Over seventy witnesses were called. Warwick, Somerset, Paget, Northampton, Tunstall, Thirlby and many other of the greatest dignitaries in the realm were called to give evidence with regard to the orders which the Council had issued to him, which he was alleged to have disobeyed. They unblushingly stated, upon oath, that Gardiner had been a zealous supporter of Papal supremacy in the days of Henry VIII, and how they had often heard Henry complain that Gardiner was thwarting his plans to break with Rome; and they adhered to their statements when Gardiner questioned them as to his important services to Henry in working for the divorce and the break with the Papacy. Only Tunstall and Thirlby and the Catholic bishops were prepared to say that Gardiner had supported Henry in these measures.

Gardiner insisted on calling many witnesses from Winchester and Farnham to testify that he had urged the people to accept the Book of Homilies three years before. These witnesses were not allowed to give evidence until they had been asked, and had answered on oath, whether they were Gardiner's servants or friends, and whether they hoped that Gardiner would be successful in the proceedings. In his defence to the charge of having mentioned transubstantiation in his sermon in June 1548, Gardiner referred to Ridley's sermon at Paul's Cross in November or December 1547, against the revilers of the Sacrament, and alleged that in this sermon Ridley had likewise defended the doctrine of the corporal Presence. This was not the last occasion on which Ridley was to be accused of having defended transubstantiation in that sermon. A number of witnesses were called to give evidence as to what Ridley had said on this occasion; but Ridley himself did not give verbal or written evidence about it, presumably because he was one of the commissioners. Had he done so, we should know more about his sermon at Paul's Cross, and also about the date of his birth, for all the witnesses began their evidence by stating their age if they knew it.

At the twenty-second session of the commission, on 14th February 1551, the commissioners gave their decision. They found that Gardiner had consistently opposed the godly reformations of abuses in religion set forth by the King's Highness' authority, and was a contemptuous disobeyer of the godly and just commandments of our Sovereign Lord the King. He was therefore deprived of his see of Winchester.[66] Ponet was translated from Rochester to Winchester. Scory was made Bishop of Rochester, and in August 1551, Ridley assisted at the consecration of his old Canterbury colleague.* Gardiner remained in the Tower.

In the spring of 1551, Ridley could look back with complete satisfaction to his first year in the see of London. Gardiner, Bonner, Heath and Day were in prison, and there was no sign of any renewal of Catholic resistance in the country. The peace with France in the spring of 1550, though it involved the loss of Boulogne and the fortresses in Scotland, had relieved the kingdom from any fear of a Papal Crusade, and had shattered the hopes of Cardinal Pole. The danger of faction in the Council had been greatly diminished through Warwick's reconciliation with Somerset. In religious matters, Cranmer and Ridley had met with unqualified success during 1550. Altars had been removed from every church in the country and the people dragooned into submission. The danger of extremism had been firmly checked by Ridley's stand against Hooper on the question of vestments. The Protestant leaders could now settle down to a period of slow consolidation of their successes.

---

* Ridley assisted at the consecration of Scory and Coverdale by Cranmer at Croydon on 30th August 1551 (Strype, *Cranmer*, p. 389, where it is incorrectly implied that the year was 1552. See Strype, *Memorials*, vol. II (i), p. 496).

NOTES

[1] *House of Lords Journal*, 14th January 1549/50.

[2] *Statutes of the Realm*, 3 & 4 Edw. VI, c. 16.

[3] *Statutes of the Realm*, 3 & 4 Edw. VI, c. 10.

[4] *Statutes of the Realm*, 3 & 4 Edw. VI, c. 12.

[5] *House of Lords Journal*, 31st January 1549/50.

[6] *Form and Manner of Making and Consecrating of Archbishops, Bishops, Priests and Deacons* (*Liturgies of King Edward VI*, pp. 161/86).

[7] See Burcher's letter to Bullinger, 21st November 1550 (*Original Letters*, p. 673).

[8] *Acts of the Privy Council*, vol. II, pp. 388, 403, 405 (8th and 28th February and 4th March 1549/50).

[9] *Acts of the Privy Council*, vol. II, pp. 385–6, 397, 400 (7th, 21st and 24th February 1549/50).

[10] *Cal. Pat. Rolls Edw. VI*, vol. III, p. 335 (12th April 1550). No further licences to bishops to hold their benefices *in commendam* were granted after June 1550 (see *Acts of the Privy Council*, vol. III, p. 57, 28th June 1550).

[11] Newcourt, *Repertorium*, vol. I, pp. 617–8, 737; vol. II, pp. 86, 159, 536.

[12] *Cal. Pat. Rolls Edw. VI*, vol. III, pp. 404, 423–4 (16th April 1550).

[13] Strype, *Memorials*, vol. II (i), p. 340.

[14] *Acts of the Privy Council*, vol. II, p. 400 (24th February 1549/50).

[15] *Cal. Pat. Rolls Edw. VI*, vol. III, pp. 262–3 (12th April 1550).

[16] Gloucester Ridley, p. 300.

[17] Thorold Rogers, *History of Agriculture and Prices*, vol. III, p. 632; vol. IV, p. 523; Hooper's letter to Cecil, 17th April 1551 (Bradford's *Works*, vol. II, p. 395).

[18] Ridley's letter to Queen Mary, 16th October 1555 (*Works*, pp. 428–9).

[19] *Acts of the Privy Council*, vol. II, p. 422 (30th March 1550).

[20] Foxe, vol. VII, pp. 408–9.

[21] Strype, *Cranmer*, p. 258; Burnet, vol. II, p. 204.

[22] See the Commissioners' sentence of excommunication on Joan Bocher (Burnet's *Records*, vol. V, pp. 246–7).

[23] Strype, *Memorials*, vol. II (i), p. 335.

[24] *Acts of the Privy Council*, vol. III, p. 19 (27th April 1550); *King Edward's Journal* (Burnet, vol. V, p. 17); *Greyfriars' Chronicle*, p. 66; Wriothesley's *Chronicle*, vol. II, pp. 37–8; Burnet, vol. II, p. 204.

[25] Foxe, vol. VII, pp. 6, 12.

[26] *Original Letters*, p. 79.

[27] *Greyfriars Chronicle*, p. 66.

[28] See Ridley's Articles in his Visitation (published in part in *Works* pp. 529–32, and in part in Foxe, vol. VI, *App.*, Document No. I).

[29] Ridley's Injunctions in his Visitation (*Works*, pp. 319–21).

[30] *Greyfriars Chronicle*, p. 66.

[31] *King Edward's Journal* (Burnet, vol. V, p. 22).

[32] Wriothesley's *Chronicle*, vol. II, p. 38.

[33] Christopher Hales' letter to Gualter, 24th May 1550 (*Original Letters*, pp. 187–8).

[34] *Reasons why the Lord's Board should rather be after the Form of a Table than of an Altar* (Foxe, vol. VI, p. 6; *Works*, pp. 321–4); and see Foxe, vol. VI, *App.*, p. 744.

[35] *Form and Manner of Making and Consecrating of Archbishops, Bishops, Priests and Deacons* (*Liturgies of King Edward VI*, p. 169).

[36] Burcher's letter to Bullinger, 21st November 1550 (*Original Letters*, p. 673).

[37] See extract from Hooper's treatise on vestments, cited by Gloucester Ridley, p. 316 n.

[38] Foxe, vol. VI, p. 640; see also Warwick's letter to Cranmer, 23rd July 1550 (Foxe, vol. VI, p. 641).

[39] Ridley's *Reply to Hooper on the Vestments Controversy* (Bradford's *Works*, vol. II, p. 390).

[40] Micronius' letter to Bullinger, 28th August 1550 (*Original Letters*, p. 567); Burcher's letter to Bullinger, 21st November 1550 (*op. cit.*, p. 673); Peter Martyr's letter to Bullinger, 28th January 1551 (*op. cit.*, p. 486); Scheyfve's Advices to the Imperial government, 9th April 1551 (*Calendar of Spanish State Papers*, vol. X, p. 261).

[41] *Acts of the Privy Council*, vol. III, p. 136 (6th October 1550); Gloucester Ridley, p. 314.

[42] Micronius' letter to Bullinger, postscript dated 20th October 1550 (*Original Letters*, p. 573).

[43] Burnet, vol. II, p. 286.

[44] *Acts of the Privy Council*, vol. III, pp. 199–200 (27th January 1550/1).

[45] Strype, *Cranmer*, p. 364.

[46] See *Second Book of Common Prayer* (*Liturgies of King Edward VI*, pp. 350–4).

[47] See Strype, *Cranmer*, p. 273; Gloucester Ridley, pp. 302–3. With regard to Bradford's ordination, see Ridley's Register (London), f. 319b; Sampson's *Preface to Two Notable Sermons of Bradford* (Bradford's *Works*, vol. I, p. 31).

[48] See Scheyfve's Advices to the Imperial government, 9th April 1551 (*Calendar of Spanish State Papers*, vol. X, p. 261).

[49] Ridley, *Reply to Hooper on the Vestment Controversy* (Bradford's *Works*, vol. II, pp. 375–95).

[50] Ridley, *op. cit.*, Bradford's *Works*, vol. II, p. 375.

[51] Ridley, *op. cit.*, Bradford's *Works*, vol. II, pp. 377, 382.

[52] Ridley, *op. cit.*, Bradford's *Works*, vol. II, p. 378.

[53] Ridley, *op. cit.*, Bradford's *Works*, vol. II, pp. 379–80.

[54] Ridley, *op. cit.*, Bradford's *Works*, vol. II, pp. 387–88.

[55] Ridley, *op. cit.*, Bradford's *Works*, vol. II, p. 394.

[56] Micronius' letter to Bullinger, 28th August 1550 (*Original Letters*, p. 568); Strype, *Cranmer*, pp. 335–8.

[57] Strype, *Cranmer*, p. 339.

[58] Micronius' letter to Bullinger, postscript dated 31st August 1550 (*Original Letters*, p. 569).

[59] Micronius' letter to Bullinger, postscript dated 31st August 1550 (*Original Letters*, p. 569).

[60] Micronius' letter to Bullinger, 13th October 1550, and postscript dated 20th October (*Original Letters*, pp. 570–1, 573); Utenhove's letter to Bullinger, 9th April 1551 (*op. cit.*, vol. III, p. 586).

[61] *Acts of the Privy Council*, vol. III, p. 53 (23rd June 1550).

[62] Wilkins, *Concilia*, vol. IV, pp. 62–3.

[63] Foxe, vol. VI, pp. 80–2; Muller, *Stephen Gardiner and the Tudor Reaction*, pp. 187–91.

[64] Foxe, vol. VI, p. 75. *Acts of the Privy Council*, vol. III, p. 78 (15th July 1550). Ridley himself did not attend this meeting of the Council.

[65] Scheyfve's letter to Charles V, 1st March 1551 (*Calendar of Spanish State Papers*, vol. X, p. 226).

[66] Foxe, vol. VI, p. 265.

VII

THE PROTESTANT REALM

By the beginning of 1551, England had been converted into as Protestant a state as any of the principalities and republics of Germany and Switzerland; it was the chief fortress of the Reformation in Europe. Cranmer and Ridley could now afford to relax a little, and Ridley had more time to devote himself to the routine administration of his diocese.

Ridley was now nearly fifty, but it is clear that he had lost none of his strength and vigour. Indeed, in his new office his assertive and dominating personality was able to express itself more fully than ever before. He was evidently an excellent preacher, and his skill in disputation was still unsurpassed, while his writings show both a remarkable lucidity of thought and expression and a vigorous and brilliant polemical ability which was no doubt equally manifest in his sermons. In conversation, he was in the habit of emphasizing his utterances with the expression 'Truly, truly';* for he strongly objected to blasphemous swearing. On one occasion, while he was Bishop of London, Ridley preached a sermon at Paul's Cross in which he told his congregation of the miserable end of a blaspheming gentleman of Cornwall. The gentleman was galloping through a town in Cornwall with a band of his companions, and insisted on uttering the most blasphemous oaths despite the remon-

* Grafton's *Chronicle*, vol. II, p. 529.

strances of some of his friends. His horse thereupon plunged over a bridge, and precipitated his rider to a dreadful death.[1]

While Ridley's contemporaries all refer to his gravity and courtesy,[2] there is no reason to believe that he was unduly solemn. If he lacked the boisterous humour of Latimer, he certainly had a keen sense of wit. On one occasion, when he had received a letter from Cecil, in which the Secretary had complained of the inadequacy of his house, Ridley wrote in reply that although he did not approve of unlawful beggars, he had been so moved by Cecil's description of his discomfiture that he was sending him ten trees—all pollards—from his woods for Cecil's house. He expressed the hope that the gift would have the effect of restraining the royal officers from doing as much damage in his woods as they had done when the see was vacant, and wrote that Cecil ought to have been an advocate on behalf of religious establishments since he could arouse such sympathy and extort gifts so readily for one house.[3] Ridley was also prepared to make a joke at his own expense. On one occasion when he was caught in a storm at sea—most probably while he was travelling between London and Rochester—he reassured his frightened companions by telling them that their ship was certainly in no danger of sinking, as it carried a bishop who was destined to be burned, not drowned.[4]

John Foxe, who was ordained a deacon by Ridley and knew him when he was Bishop of London, has left a detailed account of how Ridley passed an ordinary day in his life during these years. He probably rose at the usual hour of five in the morning, and as soon as his servant had dressed him—he usually wore a black furred gown—he passed half an hour on his knees in silent prayer. He then presumably had breakfast, and turned to his papers, working in his closet, unless he had other business to attend to, until ten o'clock. At ten, he attended morning prayers with his household. Ridley read aloud a chapter of the Acts or the Epistles, and often also a Psalm; he was particularly fond of reading the 101st Psalm. He distributed many copies of the New Testament to his household, and encouraged them to read it and learn passages by heart; and he gave gifts of money to those of his servants who could recite a chapter of the New Testament correctly at common prayers. He particularly encouraged them to learn and recite the thirteenth chapter of the Acts.

After morning prayers, Ridley dined in state with his household at about the usual hour of eleven. Dinner was a staid and sober affair. Ridley usually spoke little during the meal, but permitted both serious and merry talk at his table, and was prepared to participate in such conversation. He did not take as long over dinner as did most of his contemporaries. After dinner, he would allow himself an hour or so of relaxation. Foxe does not mention that he played handball or competed at archery, as he had done at Cambridge twenty years before; he was probably too old for this now. But he was a keen chess player, and usually managed to play a game of chess after dinner. He spent the rest of the afternoon in his closet at work with his secretaries, except on those days when he had to go by barge or ride to some other place in connexion with his duties. At five o'clock, he attended evening prayers with his household, and then had supper, which was as sober a meal as his dinner. After supper he played chess for about an hour. He then withdrew to his closet, and worked for about three hours, and after praying for half an hour on his knees, he went to bed at the very late hour of eleven. Every Sunday and holy day, Ridley preached a sermon either in St. Paul's, or in some church in his diocese, unless he was engaged in public duties elsewhere.[5]

This daily routine was varied to some extent when Parliament was in session. Parliament usually met for about two months in the year at some time between November and March. During the session, the House of Lords sat nearly every day of the week, except Sunday, at either eight or nine o'clock in the morning, rising in time for dinner at eleven; occasionally there was another sitting in the afternoon. Ridley was very regular in his Parliamentary attendances; during the six years that he was a bishop, the House of Lords sat two hundred and fifty-nine times, and Ridley was absent on only thirteen occasions.* Apart from the great controversial measures which furthered the Reformation, he dealt at these sittings with the usual batch of Parliamentary business—with bills to raise revenue; to regulate the manufacture of leather, yarn and caps; to prevent the stealing, and the export, of horses; to pave the streets of Calais; to levy fines in Chester; to reimpose the death penalty for sodomy; to punish merchants who made price-fixing agreements, and workers who combined to raise wages or shorten working hours, with the pillory and loss of an ear; to grant naturalisation to a number of aliens; to confirm grants of land to noblemen and gentlemen.[6] Ridley was certainly a loyal supporter of the government: during his time in Parliament there were only two occasions when he voted against a measure supported by the Council—on the bill to set up a commission for drafting a code of

---

* *House of Lords Journal* (4th November 1547–31st March 1553); Ridley is listed as being present on two hundred and forty-four occasions, and absent on thirteen occasions. On two occasions, no record of attendances has been preserved.

ecclesiastical law in 1550, and on the bill for the continuation of certain statutes in 1553.*

When he was Bishop of London, Ridley apparently saw a good deal of his family in Northumberland, and some of them seem to have been in residence with him in Fulham Palace comparatively frequently, for Foxe writes as if he regularly had some members of his family living with him. Old Sir Nicholas Ridley of Willimotiswick had died; he was succeeded at Willimotiswick by his son Nicholas.† The Bishop's eldest brother, Hugh, who had inherited Unthank Hall at the death of their father Christopher, had also died before 1555; his widow, Elizabeth, was living at Unthank with her children. The Bishop's favourite sister, Elizabeth, had married her cousin John Ridley of Walltown, and had a daughter called Elizabeth.‡ It is quite likely that some of these relatives in Northumberland visited Ridley at Fulham, and stayed with him for some time. What is certain, however, is that his sister Alice came to live in London with Nicholas.[7] Alice's first husband—who was apparently named Twydel,§ and was probably a gentleman of Northumberland—had died, leaving her to care for three young children. As Alice was in financial difficulties, she came to live with the Bishop. After a time, Ridley arranged for her to

* *House of Lords Journal*, 31st January 1549/50 (second session); 27th March 1553 (see pp. 256, 279).

† Sir Nicholas Ridley was dead by 1535, for in this year a report on the borders described Nicholas Ridley of Willimotiswick as a 'true sharp young man' (*L. & P. Henry VIII*, vol. IX, No. 1078).

‡ Ridley, *Last Farewell* (*Works*, p. 396). There is no indication of even the approximate date when Ridley's father and mother died.

§ See Gloucester Ridley, p. 211. Alice's first husband was almost certainly Twydel, for on 4th August 1547, the Fellows of Pembroke Hall granted land at Isleham to Ridley's sister, who is described as the mother of John Twydel. This sister can hardly have been Elizabeth, and we have no record of Ridley having any other sister except Alice.

marry his steward, George Shipside. It was unusual, though not unheard of, for well-born ladies to marry stewards; but evidently Ridley highly approved of the match, probably because Shipside was a devout Protestant. Ridley then promoted Shipside to be the keeper of his parks, and from the emoluments which he drew from this post, Shipside was able to maintain Alice and her children in comfort. Ridley also received a short visit from a young cousin, Ralph Whitfield, of whom he formed a very favourable opinion.[8] It is possible, however, that some of the other members of his family who visited him behaved occasionally in a way which Ridley considered to be frivolous or unseemly, for we are told that he checked impropriety in his family as severely as he did in his servants.[9]

Ridley was also in close contact with a number of friends and collaborators, several of whom were very able and learned men who were later to rise to prominent positions in the Church, or to win historical fame as martyrs. Edmund Grindal, John Bradford, John Rogers and John Lever were all of them Ridley's chaplains. Grindal was the Deputy Master of Pembroke Hall,[10] and Ridley knew him well. Rogers was also a Fellow of his own college. Bradford was a Lancashireman of humble parentage; but Ridley had a great respect for Bradford, and invited him to become a Fellow of Pembroke Hall, having persuaded Sandys, the Master of Katherine Hall, to refrain from inviting Bradford to be a Fellow of Katherine Hall.* Bradford had been involved in a fraud on the King when he was a servant with his master at the camp at Boulogne; but Latimer had induced him to repay the money, and he had quite repented of his earlier life. Whenever he saw a criminal under arrest,

---

* Bradford's letter to Treves, written probably in November 1549 (Bradford's *Works*, vol. II, p. 27).

he said: 'But for the grace of God, there goes John Bradford'.*

It was apparently in reply to a request from Bradford that Ridley gave his opinion on the validity of the decretal epistles of Clement, Anacletus, Lucius, Pontianus, Gelasius and Vigilius. This opinion was later reproduced in a manuscript, along with Ridley's judgment in the disputation on transubstantiation at Cambridge in 1549, as his Judgment on the Decretal Epistles. There is, however, no record that Ridley was ever called upon to deliver a judgment in any disputation, or on any similar occasion, on the subject of the forged decretals. This opinion was probably nothing more than a private expression of opinion which he put down on paper for the benefit of Bradford and of any other person who might be interested. Ridley pronounced the alleged epistles of Gelasius and Vigilius to be forgeries—particularly the passage which stated that a bishop could never be deposed; but he offered no objection to the text from Pontianus—'the priests with their mouths make the body of Christ'—which was to be understood as meaning that the priests made the Sacrament of the Lord's body. The document was probably written at some time between 1549 and 1553, for it was during this period that he was most closely associated with Bradford; and the fact that the opinion was concerned with the deprivation of bishops almost certainly indicates that it was written after the Protestant leaders had first begun to deprive their Catholic opponents of their sees in October 1549.†

---

* There appears to be no authority, other than tradition, for this famous saying of Bradford (see Editor's biographical Note, Bradford's *Works*, vol. II, p. xliii).

† See Ridley, *Judgment Concerning the Decretal Epistles* (*Works*, pp. 180–3). In the MS., Ridley is referred to as Bishop of London.

Ridley was also on terms of close friendship with Matthew Parker, the Master of Corpus Christi College, Cambridge. In July 1551, when the sweating sickness was raging, and preachers were required to bring home to the people that it was caused by the sin of covetousness, Ridley invited Parker to preach at Paul's Cross. The statutes of the University of 1490 laid down that all doctors of divinity, and other prominent persons at Cambridge, must regularly preach at Paul's Cross;[11] but Parker made difficulties about preaching at the Cross. Ridley thereupon wrote him a letter on 25th July, in which he insisted that Parker should preach on some day that suited his convenience. He wrote that he had more than enough preachers to choose from, but that many of them were unsatisfactory, some because they lacked soberness and discretion, by which Ridley probably meant that they showed extremist tendencies. While he praised Parker for his learning and ability, the disciplinarian in Ridley had been aroused by Parker's hesitancy in preaching, and he was prepared to insert a thinly veiled threat to report Parker to the Council if he did not preach in his turn at Paul's Cross.[12]

In his letter to Parker, Ridley sent his best regards to Mistress Parker, and told Parker that though he had never met his wife he had heard a great deal about her virtues. She was a charming, intelligent and devout woman, and her attributes were well known in Protestant circles. During his visit to Cambridge in August 1552, Ridley was a guest of Parker at Corpus Christi College, and there he met Mistress Parker. Ridley afterwards asked Parker whether Mistress Parker had a sister like herself; he told Parker that though he had never contemplated matrimony, he did not always think it wrong for priests to marry, and that if he himself were ever to marry, he could not hope for a better wife than a lady like Mistress Parker.*

In March 1551, Ridley took further steps to make the arrangements in St. Paul's more suited to his conception of the Lord's Supper. For nine months, a movable table had stood in the cathedral in place of the altar, but as the table had remained stationary where the altar had been, Ridley felt that the extent of the change had not been properly brought home to the people. Ridley was determined to make it clear that the Communion was a commemoration of the Lord's Supper by the communicants to be performed on a table, and in private. On the Tuesday in Holy Week —24th March—the iron gates on the north and south side of the quire were closed at Ridley's orders, and a wall was erected adjoining them, so as to close the upper quire to the north and south. The work was completed by Easter Eve, when Ridley attended the service at St. Paul's. After the singing of the Creed, the Communion table was carried down the steps into the middle of the upper quire, and set facing east and west. A curtain was then drawn across the quire to cut off the table from view, and Communion was celebrated in private, the priest standing on the south side of the table.[13]

While the danger of a Papist invasion or of a Catholic rising seemed more remote than at any time since the death of Henry VIII, the Protestant bishops were still greatly per-

---

* Strype, *Life of Parker*, vol. I, p. 48, vol. II, p. 27. Strype clearly implies that Ridley's meeting with Mistress Parker was during the Cambridge visitation of 1549, but this is certainly wrong, in view of Ridley's statement, in his letter to Parker in July 1551, that he had never met Mistress Parker. The article 'Matthaeus' in *De Antiquitate Britannica*, published by Strype (*Life of Parker*, vol. III, p. 294) states that the meeting was at Corpus Christi College when Ridley was Bishop of London. It therefore seems clear that it was during Ridley's visit to Cambridge in August 1552.

turbed by the danger of Anabaptism. In January 1551, a new commission for the suppression of Anabaptism was appointed. The commission was largely composed of the same dignitaries as had sat on the old commission, and Ridley was once again appointed a commissioner.[14] It was the start of a new drive against Anabaptism. In April, the commissioners were occupied with a serious charge in London. It was the case of George van Paris. Van Paris was a Dutch surgeon, who had probably fled to England to escape the persecution in the Netherlands. He could not speak English, and Coverdale had to act as an interpreter at his trial; but he had been spreading his heresy among his fellow countrymen in London, and they had condemned him, and handed him over to the authorities. He held the view that Jesus was not divine, but only a great religious teacher. Van Paris was certainly an extreme fanatic, and indulged in the greatest austerities; he ate a meal only once in two days, and prayed for a long time lying prostrate on the ground before the meal. He was not, however, abusive and violent like Joan Bocher, but was soft and mild in his behaviour, and prepared to endure all manner of suffering. Van Paris was brought before Ridley and the other commissioners, who tried hard to induce him to recant his heresy; but he remained meekly obstinate. On 6th April, the commissioners pronounced van Paris to be a heretic, and excommunicated him, declaring that he would be handed over to the secular powers to be dealt with according to law. Ridley signed the order with the others. It had now been clearly accepted that an excommunicated heretic could be burned at common law, apart from any statute, and within less than three weeks, on 25th April, van Paris was burned at Smithfield. He kissed the stake and the fagots before he was burned, and was calm and happy as they lit the fire.[15]

Van Paris was the last Anabaptist to be burned in the reign of Edward VI. He and Joan Bocher were the only two to suffer during the whole reign. This was certainly a striking record of mildness as compared with the number of victims who went to the stake in the time of Henry VIII and Mary, and it has naturally been proudly claimed by the admirers of Cranmer and Ridley as a noble achievement marred only by the two unfortunate exceptions. It is undeniable that, apart from the Anabaptists, religious dissenters were treated much less harshly under Edward than they were under Henry and Mary, and when prosecuted were dealt with as political offenders, not as heretics, and therefore were eligible for somewhat milder punishments. But this does not apply in the case of Anabaptism. The Protestant leaders were determined to stamp it out, and dealt with it as heresy; and we may be certain that Cranmer and Ridley were ready to send any number of unrepentant Anabaptists to the stake. If in fact they only burned two, this was simply because they could not lay their hands on any more. They had probably enormously exaggerated the danger of Anabaptism. Ridley was certainly greatly alarmed at the strength of the Anabaptists in London. In a letter to Cheke, in July 1551,[16] he informed him that he had found a preacher, whom he was sending all around Essex to expose the sin of the Papists and Anabaptists. This preacher was very poor, and had never been to a university, but he was excellent as a preacher for this purpose. No doubt Ridley thought that it was more fitting that a man of humble origin, who did not speak the language of the schools, should denounce the Anabaptists to the labourers, servants and artizans among whom the Anabaptists were spreading their propaganda.

If only a handful of the people of London and Kent were

susceptible to the arguments of the Anabaptists, far more of them had cause to be shocked at the spoliation of the Church by the courtiers and speculators. The looting had been bad enough under Henry VIII and in the days of Somerset's Protectorship, but it rose to new heights under Warwick. Having secured the spoils of the monastic lands and of the chantries, the speculators and spoilers now turned to the lands and revenues of the sees. Ridley and his brother bishops were powerless to stop or check these spoliations by the potentates on whom they entirely depended for their opportunity to consolidate the Protestant realm which they had brought into being; they could do no more than denounce, in their sermons, the prevalence of the sin of covetousness. Bradford now added his voice as a preacher on this subject to that of Latimer, and they were joined by Knox.

In the summer of 1551, the sweating sickness raged throughout England with a fury which had not been known since the terrible outbreak of 1517. It reached London at the beginning of July. In the first week, eight hundred people died; nearly all its victims were men between thirty and forty, and they died within a few hours of feeling the first symptoms.[17] The bishops persuaded the Council to announce that it was a divine punishment for the sin of covetousness, and orders were issued to the bishops to call for public prayer and repentance. Ridley issued his instructions to his preachers on 25th July, just after the plague had passed its height in London; he told them to preach that it was the punishment for sin, and especially for covetousness, and to press home to the people that the whole population of the kingdom might be wiped out if God's vengeance were not stayed. He told them to follow the commandment 'Tell unto my people their wickedness', and 'specially to beat down and destroy, with all your power and wit, that greedy and devouring serpent of covetousness that doth so now universally reign'.[18]

About the same time, Ridley was able to prevent a particularly flagrant attempt to plunder the revenues of the Church in his diocese. Some time before, William Thomas, one of the secretaries employed by the Council, had managed to persuade the Council to suggest that the Kentish Town Prebendary in St. Paul's Cathedral should assign the revenues of his prebend to Thomas. The Prebendary could hardly have resisted this suggestion from the Council had not Ridley intervened in the matter. He strongly opposed the plan. Ridley was then summoned before the Council, and taken to task for his opposition to their wishes; but he refused to submit, and the Council reluctantly agreed to abandon the idea for the present. They ordered Ridley, however, not to fill the vacancy which would occur if the Prebendary died or resigned his stall without first obtaining the permission of the King. In the summer of 1551, the Canon died. The Council at once suggested that the prebend should be suppressed, and the revenues made over to Thomas. On 23rd July, Ridley wrote a letter to Cheke about the matter. He told him that he wished to appoint Grindal to the Kentish Town stall, and was shocked at the suggestion that the revenues of the prebend be given to Thomas. He mentioned that the King had just sent orders to the bishops to preach against covetousness to stay the sweating sickness, and added: 'Sir, what preachers shall I get to open and set forth such matters and so as the King's Majesty and the Council do command them to be set forth, if either ungodly men, or unreasonable beasts, be suffered to pull away and devour the good and godly learned preachers'

R

livings?'[19] Ridley was one of the few men in England who was in a position to resist the Council. A few weeks later, he was permitted to collate whomsoever he pleased to the prebend. He did not, as it transpired, appoint Grindal, for he decided to appoint him to be Precentor of St. Paul's. He gave the vacant stall to Bradford. On St. Bartholomew's Day, he appointed Grindal Precentor and Bradford as the Kentish Town Prebendary, while on the same day he appointed Rogers as the Prebendary of St. Pancras, and his chaplain West as the Prebendary of Mora.[20] The unsuccessful Thomas was compensated for his disappointment with a gift of tolls and profits in Herefordshire and Wales.[21]

While Ridley was able on occasions to thwart an individual case of spoliation, he could not prevent the growth and increase of the looting of the sees throughout the country. After Warwick had beheaded Somerset in January 1552, he began to encounter opposition from Parliament, where the peers in the House of Lords had begun to fear his power. Unable to obtain supplies from Parliament, Warwick, who had made himself Duke of Northumberland in the autumn of 1551, determined to raise money by other means. The rapacity of Northumberland and his friends provided a further incentive to the Council to get rid of any bishop who opposed their policy, for the vacancy in the see was a great opportunity for plunder. In September 1551, the Council decided to deprive Day and Heath of their sees. A commission was appointed which consisted entirely of lawyers under the presidency of Sir Roger Chomley, the Chief Baron of the Court of Exchequer. The commissioners were instructed to deal with the cases of Day and Heath together, and not to delay proceedings by allowing the bishops to be legally represented. By 24th October, they had both been deprived.* While the trial was presumably conducted only by the six lawyers on the commission, it appears that Ridley had some part to play in the deprivation of the two bishops; for a contemporary diary records that on the afternoon of 10th October he deposed Heath and Day from their bishoprics at a ceremony in St. Paul's.[22] Heath and Day remained in the Fleet.

During the eighteen months which Day spent in prison, he was frequently visited by Ridley, who despite their strong doctrinal differences remained on terms of personal friendship with Day. Ridley's purpose was presumably to persuade Day to accept the new religious settlement. Four years later, when Day was not a prisoner but a judge, he was to tell Philpot that in the course of these discussions with Ridley in the Fleet, he had succeeded in shaking Ridley on the subject of the succession of bishops.† It is difficult to believe that Day was speaking the truth. Even if Ridley had any misgivings that he and his brother bishops could not claim to be the successors of Peter—and apart from Day's statement there is no reason whatever to believe that he had —it is inconceivable that he would have expressed them to Day when he visited him in prison, and equally unbelievable that Day, who had enough difficulties to face at the time, would have brought forward an argument which could only be used in support of Papal supremacy, which Day had never been accused of favouring. In 1555, Day was a Papist, and wished to force Philpot to recant by shak-

* *Acts of the Privy Council*, vol. III, pp. 368–9, 396, (28th September and 24th October 1551); on the latter date, the Council sent orders that the revenues of the dioceses of Chichester and Worcester should be seized pursuant to the judgment of the Commissioners depriving Day and Heath.

† See proceedings at Philpot's trial, December 1555 (Foxe, vol. VII, p. 674).

ing his faith in Ridley, whom Philpot revered as one greatly his superior in learning. If there is any truth at all in Day's story, it can only be that Day let fall some remark about the plausibility of this Popish argument, and that Ridley refused to discuss a question which was utterly irrelevant in 1551.

In November 1551, Ridley was required to place his palace at St. Paul's at the disposal of the Queen Regent of Scotland during her visit to London. Mary of Guise had visited her daughter, the Queen of Scots, in France, and on her return to Scotland, her ship was driven by winds into Portsmouth. She was granted a safe conduct to pass through England on her way home, and was invited to visit the King at Hampton Court. On 2nd November, she arrived in London, and was escorted in state to Ridley's palace in the city, where she stayed with all her attendants for four days before leaving on her three weeks' journey to Berwick. There is no record, however, that Ridley was presented to the Guise Princess, who was one of the most ardent Papist rulers in Europe, and it seems unlikely that he met her. His name is not mentioned among the lengthy list of dignitaries who received the Queen Regent at Baynard's Castle or who escorted her through Bishopsgate for a short distance along the Great North Road on her journey to Hertford; nor does it appear in the list of those who attended the dinner which was given in her honour by the King at Whitehall.[23] The Council probably thought it tactful for the Protestant bishops to absent themselves on these occasions, and Ridley may have taken care to be in Fulham from 2nd to 6th November.

In March 1552, Ridley was appointed to be a member of a committee of the Privy Council. The Council decided to reorganise the Council administration, and to lessen the increasing volume of work with which it had to deal, by appointing a number of committees to deal with different aspects of its work. A number of eminent personages who were not Lords of the Council were appointed to sit, along with the councillors, on these committees. Ridley was appointed to a committee which was to examine all the judicial business which was sent up to the Council from inferior courts, or brought there in the first instance, and to decide which of these cases were sufficiently important to be dealt with by the Council itself, and which should be sent back to be dealt with in other courts.[24]

About this time the Protestant leaders were engaged in three important tasks, and it is probable that Ridley was active in connexion with all of them. These were the preparation of the Articles of Religion, of the Second Book of Common Prayer and the Code of Ecclesiastical Law. Cranmer had for some time been under pressure from Bucer and other Protestants to draw up Articles of Religion which would authoritatively lay down the doctrines of the Church of England; but he had hitherto preferred to move less directly, by prescribing the form of service with its doctrinal implications, and to rely on periodical pronouncements on doctrine, rather than draw up a general body of Protestant doctrine. The time had now come when there was no longer any need to hesitate. There seems no doubt that the Articles of Religion were primarily the work of Cranmer; and we can say no more and no less than Strype and Burnet that it is very probable that he was assisted by Ridley. Ridley was much the most likely person for Cranmer to consult, and he and the Archbishop probably worked on the first draft together during the winter of 1551–2 without the assistance of anyone else. In May 1552, Cranmer submitted the draft to the Council, and in October it was sent to

Harley, Bill, Horn, Grindal, Perne and Knox for their comments. It is almost certain that the Articles were never submitted to Convocation; but Cranmer persuaded Edward to promulgate them by royal command a few weeks before he died.[25]

The forty-two Articles are certainly a statement of Ridley's views on all the fundamental doctrines of religion. They cover the same ground as the Thirty-nine Articles of 1562, except that the last four of the Articles of 1552 were omitted from the Thirty-nine Articles, while an additional article on good works was inserted in 1562. These last four articles of the forty-two Articles stated that the resurrection was not already passed, but that on the last day all men would rise for judgment with the bodies which they possessed on earth; that the souls of the dead do not sleep insensibly with their bodies from the time of their death to the Day of Judgment; that Millenarianism was a Jewish dotage; and that the doctrine of the Origenists, that after a longer or shorter period of suffering all men would be saved, was pernicious. The Articles endorsed the doctrine expressed in the Book of Homilies of 1547 that good works, though meritorious, were not an independent requirement for salvation. They condemned Purgatory, pardons, the invocation of Saints and the worship of images. They prescribed that all services should be conducted in English. The twenty-ninth article stated that transubstantiation was wrong, and that, as Christ's body was in Heaven and could not be in more than one place at the same time, he was not corporally present in the Sacrament of the Lord's Supper; and the elevation of the Host was condemned. The Articles laid down that there were only two Sacraments—baptism and the Lord's Supper—in place of the seven Sacraments of the old Church. The doctrine of grace was expounded, and it was stated that good works performed without grace were displeasing to God, and indeed sinful, as the works were not done in the manner that God had commanded. Excommunicated persons were to be considered as heathens. The Articles dealt with the doctrine of predestination, declaring that while it was true in the sense of God's election of those who were to be saved, it was liable to be misunderstood, and made an excuse for evil living. Some of the Articles were designed to strengthen the authority of the King, and to assist in the government of the State, whilst others were expressly or impliedly directed against the Anabaptists and the extremist sects. It was stated that General Councils of the Church could not lawfully be convened without the consent of princes; rash swearing was condemned, but it was lawful to take an oath when required by the magistrates; capital punishment was approved, and it was laid down that it was lawful for a Christian to fight in war at the command of the prince. The Articles also declared that the King was the Supreme Head of the Church under Christ, and that it was the duty of the subject to obey the secular powers, while the authority of the Bishop of Rome was repudiated. Only the clergy who had been ordained under the authority of the law were entitled to preach or administer the Sacraments. Infant baptism was approved, and the thirty-seventh article stated that, while men should give alms to the poor, it was wrong that all goods should be held in common, as certain Anabaptists did falsely boast. The thirty-third article was a declaration of the principles on which Ridley had taken his stand in his fight with Hooper over vestments and with the foreign Protestants: it was unnecessary that the ceremonies of the Church should be the same at all times and in all places, but whatever ceremonies were laid down by law must be obeyed, for the sake of law and order.[26]

The decision to revise the Book of Common Prayer was apparently taken as a result of discussions in Convocation in 1551. Here again there is no authoritative record as to the authorship of the second Book of Common Prayer; but it is certain that Ridley assisted Cranmer in the preparation of the book.[27] The new book made far-reaching alterations in the form of service laid down in the book of 1549, both with regard to ritual and to the words used in the prayers. Much of the ritual of the old service, which had been retained three years before in an attempt to appease the anger of the Catholics, was now abolished, and many ceremonies and prayers were eliminated altogether. These heavy blows at the old religion aroused much less hostility than the thin end of the wedge in the first Book of Common Prayer had stirred up in 1549; and the only open opposition to the second book was to come from those Protestants who thought that the innovations still did not go far enough. The book still provided that the congregation was to kneel when receiving the Sacrament of the Lord's Supper—a provision which was to cause much resentment among the Protestant extremists. But as a whole the book showed the growing influence of Hooper. All albs, copes and vestments were forbidden throughout the kingdom, though the bishop was still to wear his rochet, and the priest and deacon his white surplice.[28] There is no reason to believe that Ridley offered any opposition to this innovation; he had no objection to the abolition of vestments, provided that it was laid down by authority, and not introduced by Hooper and subversive agitators.

The new Book of Common Prayer was submitted to Parliament in the spring of 1552, and given force of law by the Second Act of Uniformity. The Act provided that the Book was to come into force on All Saints' Day, and increased the penalties on all who refused to officiate or attend at the prescribed service, or who officiated or attended at any other. They were now liable to six months' imprisonment for the first offence.[29] A number of priests and laymen had been prosecuted under the Act of 1549, and sentenced to fines and imprisonment; but the enforcement of the statute was as mild as the penalties laid down, in comparison not only with the treatment of Protestant heretics by Henry VIII, but with the punishment for sedition or non-political misdemeanours. Aldrich of Carlisle and Thirlby of Norwich were still free to oppose the Act of Uniformity, and every Protestant proposal, in the House of Lords, provided that they did not continue their resistance in their dioceses after the legislation came into force, while the deprived bishops in captivity were given every opportunity to win their pardon and release by submission. The Protestant leaders moved warily and hesitantly against the bastions of tradition, and shrank from the use against the established order of the iron hand which they applied to Anabaptism.

In the same session an Act was passed prohibiting usury. The statute of 1545, which had prohibited moneylenders from demanding interest at more than 10 per cent, had been ineffective to abolish the practice, and had resulted in moneylenders in every case raising their rate of interest to the permitted maximum. The new statute forbade usury altogether, enacting that anyone who lent money at interest was to forfeit the interest and the principal, and was liable to any fine which the King might impose.[30] At the same time an attempt was made to deal with the evils of simony. A bill was introduced into the House of Lords to prohibit the traffic in ecclesiastical offices, the reservation of pensions out of benefices, and the granting of advowsons during the lifetime of the incumbent. Ridley presumably interested himself in the bill, for he was appointed, along with Ponet, Thirlby and Hooper and four of the peers, to be a member of the commission which, in accordance with the usual practice, was directed to examine the bill before the third reading.[31] The bill passed both Houses, but owing to the complications which followed from the King's illness, it never received the royal assent[32]—either because of a simple oversight, or because some influence was exerted at Court to prevent it. Ridley was also appointed a commissioner to examine a bill which dealt with attempts by alien heretics to subvert the religion of the English people,[33] and doubtless did his best to intensify the provisions against the foreign Anabaptists; but the bill did not become law. At the same time, Ridley pursued his campaign against the old religion by prohibiting the people of London from celebrating St. George's Day.[34]

The proposal to draft a code of ecclesiastical law had been debated in the House of Lords two years before. This question had been under discussion in the reign of Henry VIII, and a commission of thirty-two persons had been set up in 1544 for the purpose of drafting a new code; but the commissioners had never carried out their duty.* In November 1549, the bishops submitted a bill to Parliament to increase the powers of the ecclesiastical courts to deal with vice and immorality and other misconduct; but the common lawyers viewed the proposal with misgiving, and the bill was thrown out by the House of Lords.[35] In January 1550, the common lawyers submitted their own bill. It provided that the King might appoint a commission of

* Strype, *Cranmer*, pp. 190–1; and see Gairdner, vol. II, pp. 48–9; Gloucester Ridley, pp. 161–2, deduces that Ridley was one of the commissioners appointed in 1544 from the fact that he was placed on the commission of 1552; but there appears to be no sound reason for this conclusion.

thirty-two persons to promulgate a code of ecclesiastical law within three years. The thirty-two commissioners were to consist of sixteen churchmen, of whom four were to be bishops, and of sixteen laymen, of whom four were to be common lawyers. The code, when drafted, was to have the force of law, provided that any part of it which conflicted with any statute, or with the common law, was to be void. The ecclesiastical courts were to be subject to all writs issued by the common law courts.[36]

The bill was opposed in the House of Lords by both the Catholic and the Protestant bishops, who made a common front against it. Ridley voted against the bill in the company of Cranmer, Holbeach, Goodrich, Aldrich, Tunstall, Thirlby, Heath and Day.[37] There has been some speculation as to the reason which led the Protestant bishops to oppose the measure, but it was almost certainly that they objected to the encroachments of the common lawyers. They would no more have approved of the presence of four common lawyers on the commission than of the provisions in the bill that no section of the code should conflict with the common law, and that the writs of the common law courts should issue to the ecclesiastical courts. Despite the opposition of the bishops, the bill became law.

It was probably in order to surmount the well-known opposition of the bishops, as well as of recollections of the delay in 1544, that the statute enacted that the commissioners were to promulgate their code of ecclesiastical law within three years. It was nevertheless nearly two years after the passing of the Act before the commissioners were even appointed—probably because of deliberate obstruction by Cranmer and his bishops at Court. It was then decided to appoint a commission of eight members—two bishops, two other divines, two civil lawyers and two common lawyers—who would work on the draft of the code, and that later a full commission of thirty-two would be appointed to consider their proposals. On 4th November 1551, Ridley was appointed as one of the eight commissioners, along with Cranmer, May, Cox and Peter Martyr; but a week later three changes were made in the composition of the commission. Ridley was withdrawn from the commission and replaced by Goodrich,* who soon afterwards was appointed Lord Chancellor. We do not know the reasons for this change; perhaps it was thought that Goodrich was superior as a canonist to Ridley; or possibly Ridley did not relish working together with the common lawyers, and succeeded in shifting the duty on to Goodrich, who had been as much opposed as Ridley to the statute under which the commissioners were acting. Ridley was, however, one of the thirty-two members of the full commission which was appointed in February 1552 to examine the draft of the eight commissioners.[38]

The Code of Ecclesiastical Law was probably largely the work of Cranmer, with the assistance of Peter Martyr, and it was drawn up in the recognised formulas of the civil law by Haddon and Cheke. The thirty-two commissioners approved the draft, which under the provisions of the Act of 1550 only required to be officially promulgated by the King to have the force of law; but the Code was never promulgated. This was apparently due to the opposition of the common lawyers. If Cranmer and the bishops had originally opposed the whole project of drafting the code because of the restrictions on the powers of the ecclesiastical courts which the common lawyers had inserted in the Act, they had nevertheless succeeded in persuading the commissioners

* Wilkins, *Concilia*, vol. IV, p. 69; *Cal. Pat. Rolls Edw. VI*, vol. IV, p. 114 (4th and 11th November 1551).

to endorse a code which gave too much scope to the ecclesiastical courts for the liking of the common lawyers. The
common lawyers were able to exercise sufficient influence
with Northumberland to hold up the promulgation of the
code until Edward's death eighteen months later, and the
code was never adopted.[39]

By the standards of the twentieth century, the code of
ecclesiastical law may seem to be very harsh; but for
sixteenth-century England, it was remarkably lenient and
merciful, and must take its place among the unsuccessful
attempts to humanise the law which have periodically been
made throughout our history. The code provided that anyone who denied the doctrines of Christianity, especially
belief in the Trinity, should be punished by death; but all
other heretics, along with blasphemers against God, and
witches and magicians, were only to be punished, if they
remained obdurate, with excommunication. Even the critics
of infant baptism were to suffer nothing worse than excommunication unless they coupled these views with a repudiation of the divinity of Christ. Excommunication was only to
be pronounced by a court composed of both the diocesan
bishop and the local justices of the peace; its consequences
were certainly to be unpleasant enough. The excommunicated man was to be unable to give evidence in any court,
was to lose his testamentary capacity, and no one, except
the members of his family, was to eat or speak with him on
pain of being excommunicated himself. If the excommuni-
cant did not repent, and make a public confession of his
guilt and repentance, within forty days, he was to be imprisoned until he did. The code abolished divorce *a mensa
et thoro*, and provided that a divorce *a vinculo* could be
granted by an ecclesiastical court on the grounds of adultery, desertion, prolonged absence without justification, or

ill-treatment of such a kind as to endanger life; but it was not to be obtainable for any cruelty falling short of this, or for any incurable disease. After a decree of divorce, which could be granted to either husband or wife, the innocent spouse was free to marry again during the lifetime of the former spouse; but the guilty party was not allowed to re-marry. If the divorce was obtained on the grounds of the adultery of the respondent, the guilty spouse was to be punished, as were all adulterers, by banishment or imprison-ment for life, at the discretion of the King, and was to forfeit half his goods to his spouse. The remainder of the thirty sections of the code were concerned with reiteration of principles of doctrine, and regulations for presentation and remuneration of priests, and the organisation of the Church.[40]

In May 1552, the Council ordered a royal visitation of Eton College. Eton had been included, along with Win-chester and the two Universities, in the scope of the com-mission issued to Ridley and his colleagues in November 1548; and now Ridley, Goodrich, Cheke, May and Wendy, or any two of them, were ordered to go to Eton to conduct the visitation. They apparently spent only a few days at Eton at the beginning of May. The Visitors decided that it was necessary to take action against Fawding, one of the Fellows, for uttering lewd words concerning the succession; they apparently placed him under arrest, and sent him to the Council. Fawding was unable to give a satisfactory ex-planation of his conduct, and the Council ordered him to be confined in the Fleet, where he was apparently held for over four months.[41] There is no record of what Fawding had been saying, but it is clear that he was guilty of a political offence; he probably shared the rising hatred of Northumberland which was felt by most of the people of England.

Soon after the visitation to Eton, Ridley was able to do an act of kindness to one of his adversaries. In June, the Council learned that Day and Heath, who were both of them still in the Fleet, were ill, and ordered that they should be released from the prison, and held in house arrest, for a month to enable them to recover their health. On 15th June, Day was sent to Goodrich's house, and Heath to Ridley's palace at Fulham, where he was to stay confined and to receive instruction from Ridley which, it was hoped, would lead him to repent his errors. At the end of the month he spent at Fulham, Heath's health was no better, and on 17th July, Ridley asked the Council to permit Heath to stay with him under house arrest indefinitely, and not to send him back to the Fleet. The Council agreed to permit both Heath and Day to stay in the charge of Ridley and Goodrich.[42] Ridley then sent Heath to his palace at St. Paul's, where he stayed for a year until he was released at Mary's accession.

In August, Ridley found time, while the King was on his progress with all the Court, to pay a short visit to Cambridge. He was not engaged, on this occasion, on any important business of Church and State, but could spend an agreeable time, which must have been something of a holiday, in the Master's lodgings at Pembroke Hall. Officially, the University had conformed in every respect to the requirements of the Council and the Protestant leaders; but beneath the surface there was an undercurrent of resistance which had caused some anxiety to Bucer until his death the previous year, and had led him to approach Ridley on two occasions, through the medium of Grindal and Parker, for advice and assistance. The opposition had centred round the issue of altars, and its most prominent spokesman was Young, who was one of Ridley's Fellows at Pembroke Hall, and had argued for the Catholics in the disputation in

1549.* The state of learning in the University was also a cause of anxiety. There were still very few new schools to replace the monasteries, and there were only about half the number of undergraduates at Cambridge there had been when Ridley was a young man,[43] though this was not the case at Pembroke Hall. Ridley could note with satisfaction that his College was thriving, and that its financial position was now much better than when he had been in residence fifteen years before. During his stay in Cambridge, Ridley was entertained to dinner by Parker at Corpus Christi College and made the acquaintance of Mistress Parker.†

It was probably while Ridley was in Cambridge in August 1552 that it was suggested to him that with all his other more important offices and duties he might resign his benefice of Soham in favour of Richard Hebb, who was the Treasurer of Pembroke Hall. Ridley must have known Hebb very well, but he apparently had a special talk with him in connexion with his presentation to Soham. Ridley made sure that Hebb had fully accepted the Protestant doctrines, and insisted that he sign a statement approving the Articles of Religion. Having satisfied himself of Hebb's reliability, he vacated the cure, and the College presented Hebb on 5th September 1552.[44] Ridley had already resigned his stall in Canterbury Cathedral in July 1550, and his prebend in Westminster Cathedral in November 1550.‡

---

* See Bucer's letters to Grindal, 31st August 1550, and (probably) to Parker at end of November or early December 1550 (Gorham, *Reformation Gleanings*, pp. 163, 209).

† See p. 252.

‡ *Cal. Pat. Rolls Edw. VI*, vol. III, p. 293 (15th July and 29th November 1550); Gloucester Ridley, p. 291, seems clearly to be in error in stating that Ridley resigned his stalls in Canterbury and Westminster Cathedrals respectively in July 1551 and July 1553.

While he was in Cambridge, Ridley obtained leave from Goodrich, who was the diocesan bishop, to ordain a number of divinity students as priests. One of them was John Whitgift, who was a member of Pembroke Hall. The Master of the College took an interest in his progress, and would not have been disappointed had he known of the zeal with which Whitgift would in after life pursue Puritans and sectaries who menaced the authority and discipline of the Church. Ridley ordained the students on St. Bartholomew's Day,[45] and then returned to London, having been able for a few weeks to leave the cares of his diocese and of public affairs and return to the College where he was always at his happiest.

On his journey back to London, Ridley was involved in an unpleasant incident which boded ill for him for the future. The Council had for some time been much concerned over the conduct of the Lady Mary. The Princess had been bastardised by statute in 1534, and had been forced by her father to recognise her own bastardy; but the Act of 1544 had made her eligible to succeed to the Crown if so appointed in King Henry's will, and Henry had devised the Crown to her if Edward died without issue. Mary was thus the heiress presumptive to the Throne. She made no secret of the fact that she was a Catholic, though she did not disclose that she was also a Papist, and in secret correspondence with her cousin, the Emperor. The difficulties with Mary began in June 1549, with the introduction of the Book of Common Prayer. She wrote a haughty letter to the Council, in which she informed them that she would never attend the new kind of service, and would continue to attend Mass in her house at Kenninghall in Norfolk, where she was residing.[46] By attending Mass, Mary was liable to a fine, and on the third offence to imprisonment, under the Act of Uniformity; but the Imperial Ambassador intervened on her behalf, and asked the Protector to permit Mary to continue attending Mass in her house, and to exempt her from the provisions of the statute. This was a small price to pay for the Emperor's neutrality in the dreadful summer of 1549, and Somerset agreed to allow Mary to attend her private Mass.

In January 1550, the King wrote a letter to his sister,[47] urging her to abandon the Mass and accept the Book of Common Prayer; but Mary remained adamant. Moreover, her chaplain celebrated Mass not merely in the presence of Mary herself, but with all the members of her household in the chapel. The Council therefore raised the matter with Mary, and again urged her to abandon the Mass. Mary reminded them of their promise to the Emperor in June 1549;* but the Council took the view that the promise to the Imperial Ambassador had been limited to permitting Mary herself to attend the Mass, and that this had never extended to the members of her household.[48] By the end of 1550, the situation was different from what it had been in June 1549: Warwick was now pursuing his strong Protestant policy, and in view of the peace with France, the Council were less concerned about angering the Emperor. They sent letters to Mary urging her to accept the truth in religion, and while not daring to touch the Princess herself, they proceeded against two of her chaplains under the Act of Uniformity. They were arrested for celebrating Mass in the presence of the ladies and gentlemen of Mary's household, for which they had not been granted a royal dispensation.

Mary wrote a letter of protest to the Council against the

* Mary's letter to the Council, 3rd February 1550 (Foxe, vol. VI, pp. 12–13).

prosecution of her chaplains, and again relied on the promise to the Imperial Ambassador.* On Christmas Day, 1550, the Council replied in a longer and sterner letter than any which they had yet written to the Princess. It was generally understood that the letter had been drafted by either Cranmer or Ridley.[49] Apart from justifying the policy of the Council, the letter contained passages rebutting the theological arguments which Mary had put forward in her letters to the King and to the Council. It is probable that either Ridley or the Archbishop drafted the passages in which the Princess was urged, with the help of texts from Paul and Leviticus, and from Augustine, Chrysostom and the Church History, to approve of church services in English, and to base her beliefs on Scripture rather than on the customs of the old Church;[50] but those parts of the letter which dealt with the promise to the Emperor and with the necessity of obeying the laws were probably written by the Lords of the Council, or their officials. Mary was still allowed to attend a private Mass alone, and continued to write letters, both to the Council and to the King himself, in which she demanded that her chaplains be released, and maintained that she would never abandon the Catholic religion in which she had been brought up by her father.†

In March 1551, the Council seem to have decided that the time had come to take firmer action against the obstinate Princess. In this they were encouraged by the King himself, for Edward, who was now thirteen and very precocious for his age, was an ardent Protestant, and indignant that his nearest and dearest subject was disobeying the law and

* Mary's letter to the Council, 4th December 1550 (Foxe, vol. VI, pp. 13–14).
† Mary's letters to the Council, 2nd May and 11th May 1551, and to Edward VI, 19th August 1551 (Foxe, vol. VI, pp. 18, 19, 21).

setting so evil an example to his people by her idolatrous beliefs. Mary was invited to come to Court, and on 18th March had an interview with the King at Whitehall. Edward strongly urged her to cease attending Mass, but Mary replied that her soul was God's, and that she would never change her faith. Her brother told her that she was his subject and must obey the law, for her defiance was an encouragement to sedition. Next day, the Imperial Ambassador requested an interview; he declared that if Mary were not permitted to attend Mass, the possibility of war with the Empire could not be excluded. No reply was given to the Ambassador, but the Council hastily considered the position. Even if Charles' threat of war was not to be taken seriously, the suppression of Mary's Mass would cause serious damage to English trade, and would interfere with the shipment to England of a large consignment of gunpowder which was held up at Antwerp. They therefore decided to take no action against Mary for the time being, and set about persuading the zealous young King that he must permit his sister to continue with her idolatrous ways for a little longer.

On 20th March, the Council sent Cranmer, Ridley and Ponet to the King, evidently with the object of inducing Edward to accept the necessity for retreat. Cranmer, Ridley and Ponet told Edward that they had considered whether it was permissible for him to allow Mary to hold her Mass, and that they had reached the conclusion that, though it was sin to licence sin, it was nevertheless justifiable to wink at evil for a short space of time where imperative necessity required it. They therefore urged him to permit the Lady Mary to continue with her Mass. Their answer caused Edward the greatest distress, and the boy cited passages from Scripture to the bishops to prove to them that

Mary's Papistry should immediately be suppressed. They naturally assured him that his arguments were unanswerable, but still urged him, in the interests of his realm and his merchants, to take no action for the present; after the gunpowder had arrived from Antwerp, and measures of defence had been taken, the matter could be reconsidered. The King reluctantly agreed, and the bishops withdrew, delighted with his Protestant zeal, while Cranmer congratulated Cheke on his achievements as royal tutor. The English Ambassador told the Emperor that he must not intervene in English internal affairs; but Mary's Mass was not prohibited.[51]

In September 1552, Mary was living at Hunsdon, in the diocese of London, which was only two miles away from Hadham, where Ridley had one of his country houses. Ridley stayed at Hadham on his journey back to London from Cambridge; he was probably in residence there for the whole of September. About 8th September, he rode over to Hunsdon in the morning to visit the Lady Mary.* He was received with all respect and hospitality by Sir Thomas Wharton and other officers of Mary's household, and spent all the rest of the morning in conversation with them. At eleven o'clock, the Princess received him, and they talked for a quarter of an hour until dinner was ready. Mary was most gracious; she told him that she remembered

* Foxe, vol. VI, p. 354, states that Ridley's visit to Mary was 'about 8th September 1552'; Gloucester Ridley, p. 379, states that Ridley was staying at Hadham on his journey back from Cambridge. Ridley probably stayed at Hadham for the whole of September, for he was in residence there on 2nd October 1552 (Ridley's Register (London), f. 295), and there is no record of his having been anywhere else during September. It should be noted that Strype's statement (*Cranmer*, p. 389) that Ridley was at Croydon on 30th August 1552 assisting at the consecration of Scory and Coverdale, is incorrect, as neither Scory nor Coverdale was consecrated on this day (see p. 241).

meeting him at Hampton Court when he was one of King Henry's chaplains, and remembered his excellent sermon at the marriage of Sir Anthony Browne to Elizabeth Fitzgerald, who had been one of her maids of honour, and was now Lady Clinton, the wife of the Lord High Admiral.

Ridley had dinner with Mary's household, and after dinner the Princess invited him again to her presence. Ridley then told her that he had not come merely to pay his respects, but to offer to preach before her next Sunday. This caused an embarrassed silence; when Mary spoke, she said that there was no need for her to make any reply, as he knew well enough what her answer would be. Ridley persisted that as he was her diocesan bishop he was under a duty to offer to preach to her; but to this, Mary replied that as he would not take a hint, she was obliged to speak frankly. He could, of course, preach, if he wished, in the parish church, but neither she nor any member of her household would attend the service. Ridley said that he hoped that she would not refuse to hear God's word. Mary replied that Ridley would never have dared say that his present beliefs were God's word if her father were still alive: what was God's word in King Henry's days was very different from what was God's word now. Ridley answered that God's word could never change, but that men were better able to understand it in certain epochs than in others. Mary said that she understood that Ridley was one of the Lords of the Council. Ridley pointed out that she was mistaken: he was not a member of the Council. The Princess said that she was surprised; he ought to be a Privy Councillor in view of the people who were Lords of the Council nowadays. Mary then thanked Ridley for his visit, but said that she thanked him not at all for his offer to preach to her; she said that she would never listen to any sermons or read any books in which new religious doctrines were expounded; she did not wish to know about them, and never would. She said that she would not obey the orders of a Council who acted for an infant King; when her brother came of age, she would obey him absolutely in religion as in all other matters. Ridley was then taken by Sir Thomas Wharton to the dining-room, and given a glass of wine before he rode back to Hadham. Ridley drank the wine, but as he put the glass down, he paused, deep in thought. He told the gentlemen that he regretted having drunk wine and eaten dinner in a household where God's word was despised, and denounced them all with such vehemence as to cause something of a panic amongst them. Then he rode away.[52]

Mary had defied the Bishop of London, as she had defied the Lord Chancellor and Northumberland himself; but she was allowed to continue attending her private Mass, and was not molested again during the rest of her brother's reign. The Protestant leaders did not believe in religious toleration; nor did anyone else, except for Somerset and a handful of visionaries. Yet they never inflicted on Mary herself even the comparatively lenient penalties provided by the first Act of Uniformity. Mary was protected by the friendship of the Emperor, the most powerful monarch in Europe; but she could rely on an even stronger defence against the projects of her enemies—her royal blood. The Council and the Protestant bishops dared not proceed with vigour against a royal princess, even if she was officially a bastard. They based their whole policy on the principle that the authority of the Council during the infancy of a king was as great as that of an adult king; but they showed, by their attitude to Mary, that they did not really believe it. Sixteen years earlier, with every possible brutality, Henry had forced Mary to submit to the divorce

of her mother and the break with Rome; but he was a king.
Northumberland was not prepared to use the same methods
to compel her to acknowledge the Book of Common Prayer.
Mary could defy him, and openly state that she believed
in the old Mass while she challenged him to vent his
hatred on her body;[53] but she did not breathe a word to
suggest that she believed in Papal supremacy. Mary was
more afraid of her father's ghost than of the Lords of the
Council.

The second Act of Uniformity was to come into force on
All Saints' Day. As the time approached, Hooper and Knox
and the Protestant extremists began an agitation against the
provision in the new Prayer Book that the people should receive the Sacrament of the Lord's Supper on their knees.
They denounced this as idolatrous worship of the bread and
wine which was nothing less than Popery. Cranmer and
Ridley were perfectly satisfied with the position, and at first
took no action to satisfy the critics; but as the vigour of
Protestant agitation increased, the Council shrank from in-
troducing the new service in the face of such determined
opposition. On 25th September,[54] Knox preached a sermon
before the King in which he denounced the kneeling
posture as idolatrous. The Council thereupon ordered
Cranmer to discuss with Ridley and Peter Martyr the possibility of changing this provision in the Book of Common
Prayer.

Cranmer was strongly opposed to Knox's proposal. Both
Ridley and Martyr, as well as the Archbishop, had approved
of the directive enforcing kneeling when they had drafted
the book, and Cranmer was particularly dubious over the
desirability of altering the provision now that it had been
approved by an Act of Parliament. The matter was very
urgent, as the new Prayer Book was to come into force in

less than a month; and Cranmer sent a messenger to Ridley —who perhaps was still at Hadham—to come at once to discuss the question with him and Martyr.* Ridley doubtless met Cranmer and Martyr in London on 8th, 9th or 10th October, and agreed with them to oppose any alteration in the book; but they were unable to resist the introduction of the black rubric. Five days before All Saints' Day, the Council took action to appease the extremists. On 27th October, they issued an order that a new provision was to be inserted in the Book of Common Prayer. It was hastily printed on slips, and stuck at random into all copies of the book which had not yet left the printers' hands. It stated that while communicants were to receive the Sacrament on their knees to show their humble and grateful acknowlegde-ment of the benefits of Christ and to avoid profanation and disorder, the kneeling posture did not signify any adoration of the bread and wine, which was idolatrous, as Christ, being in Heaven, could not be corporally in the bread and wine as he could not be in two places at the same time.[55]

Ridley had meanwhile been taking steps in his diocese to prepare for 1st November by perfecting the construction of St. Paul's. On 25th October, the Communion table was moved into the lower quire, and the workmen began abolish-ing the upper quire altogether. They removed the altar steps and levelled the floor of the cathedral, while the wall behind the spot where the altar had stood was taken down.

* See Cranmer's letter to the Council, 7th October 1552 (published in Lorimer, *John Knox and the Church of England*, pp. 103–5). Ridley was in Hadham on 2nd October (see p. 277 n.). He presumably met Cran-mer and Martyr in London after Cranmer wrote his letter of 7th October and before the Archbishop reported to the Council on 11th October (see *Acts of the Privy Council*, vol. IV, pp. 138, 140, 8th and 11th October, 1552).

All the chapels in the cathedral were done away with by structural alterations, and this necessitated the removal of a number of tombs. Ridley's enemies thought that he had intended, in the course of this work, to remove the tomb of John of Gaunt, and was only prevented by an order from the Council forbidding him to touch the royal sepulchre.*

On All Saints' Day, a service in accordance with the new book was held in St. Paul's, with Ridley officiating and all the notables of the city in attendance. In accordance with the new provisions, Ridley did not wear a cope, or any vestments except his rochet, while May and the canons wore no vestments except a surplice. Ridley preached in the quire in the morning, and then went to dinner. In the afternoon, he preached a second sermon at the Cross. He expounded at great length the doctrines in the new Book of Common Prayer, and did not finish his sermon till five o'clock. The dinner was probably a formal affair which took even longer than usual, but as it was presumably held at about eleven, Ridley's sermon probably lasted for well over three hours. Long sermons were in fashion at the time, but apparently the congregation had not expected Ridley to go on for quite so long; for his friend Dobbes, the Lord Mayor, had to send his servants to fetch tapers to light him on his way home. They had not brought the tapers with them, so it seems that the Lord Mayor had expected the sermon to finish before nightfall. The dignitaries of the city and the guilds did not enter the cathedral after the sermon

* *Greyfriars Chronicle*, p. 75, where the date is given as 25th October; the author of this diary obviously disapproved of Ridley. Wriothesley's *Chronicle*, vol. II, p. 79, and Stow's *Annals*, p. 1055, place the incident as occurring soon after All Saints' Day. The order for the suppression of the organ in St. Paul's had been given on 4th September 1552, not by Ridley, but by May (see *Greyfriars Chronicle*, p. 75).

was over, as was the usual practice, but went home as quickly as possible.[56]

The insertion of the black rubric at the eleventh hour into the Book of Common Prayer had shown how far Cranmer and Ridley could be compelled to go under the pressure of the radical elements. The mood of the hour was conducive to all forms of extremism, and at the end of September the Council received reports from Kent of the activities of David George and his followers. To the Protestant leaders, the Davidians were simply a pestilent Anabaptist sect, and new measures were immediately taken for the suppression of Anabaptism.[57] Ridley was still a member of the commission which had been set up to deal with the Anabaptists in January 1551. It does not appear that any important case was tried before the commissioners; but it has been suggested that Ridley accompanied Cranmer when the Archbishop went into Kent to investigate the activities of the sectaries there. Cranmer spent the greater part of the winter at Ford, from whence he conducted the examination of a number of malefactors, and it is possible that Ridley visited him there; but it seems improbable that Ridley took part in the trial of the fornicators at Ashford, where Cranmer was able to satisfy himself of the innocence of the defendants by his inspection of the house where the fornication was alleged to have occurred, and from his calculation of the position of the moon on the night in question. It is difficult to believe that the justices at Ashford, for all their readiness to discern an Anabaptist in every malefactor, could have referred a case of fornication to the commissioners who were dealing with Anabaptism; and it is much more likely that the case was dealt with by Cranmer in the course of his exercise of his ordinary episcopal jurisdiction, and that Ridley was not present in Ashford, if indeed he went into Kent at all.* Ridley was not wholly inactive, however, in his capacity as a commissioner, for at the end of December he was ordered by the Council to peruse the tracts of two men of Worcester, which were alleged to be heretical.[58]

Ridley was also concerned once more with the question of the services of the foreign Protestants in London. A Lasco's congregation had been continually pestered by the church-wardens of their parishes, who were threatening to prosecute them for their failure to attend the services in the parish church, and could not be persuaded that the aliens had been granted a licence by the King to hold their own services in their own church. There is no reason to believe that Ridley gave any countenance to the officiousness of the churchwardens, and indeed the parish priests never troubled the foreigners; but on 4th November, the Council instructed Ridley to meet à Lasco and discuss with him how best to smooth out the difficulties. The government machinery at length succeeded in conveying to the churchwardens an instruction to leave the aliens to worship in their church in peace.[59]

There was great distress among the London poor during the winter of 1552–3. The policy of converting arable into pasture land, which had proceeded unchecked since the autumn of 1549, had driven thousands of agricultural labourers out of work, and they flocked into London, to

* Strype, *Memorials*, vol. II (ii), p. 19, states that a commission was issued in October 1552 to Cranmer, Ridley and local dignitaries in Kent to deal with Anabaptists in the county, and that the case of the fornicators at Ashford was tried by the commissioners; but there is no official record of any new commission having been appointed to deal with Anabaptism in the autumn of 1552. In *Cranmer*, pp. 418–19, Strype states that the commission which had been appointed in January 1551 continued to deal with Anabaptism, and this is doubtless correct; and here Strype implies that Cranmer alone dealt with heretics in Kent.

roam the streets as vagabonds. In 1550, the authorities had rounded up all the vagabonds in London, and expelled them from the city and from Southwark; but they had drifted back again, and the problem was at its worst in 1552. Ridley had busied himself during the year in seeking to relieve the people in distress, and by the end of 1552 his efforts were producing most tangible results.

One Sunday early in 1552, Ridley preached a sermon before the King in the chapel royal at Whitehall.* In his sermon, Ridley dealt with the importance of Charity. After the service was over, the King summoned Ridley to his presence. He went with him into the gallery of the palace, and there paid him the signal honour of insisting that he be seated with his cap on his head. Edward then told him how impressed he had been with his sermon, and that he felt that a king above all was under an obligation to care for the relief of poverty and to set an example in the way of good works. He asked Ridley to advise him as to how the money should be spent. Ridley told the King that he would like time to consider the matter before replying, and Edward offered to send letters to the Lord Mayor commanding him to consult with Ridley on the relief of poverty

---

* Sir John Hayward, in his *Edward VI* (published in Kennet, vol. II, p. 323), states that the sermon and the subsequent interview with Edward VI occurred at the State opening of Parliament at Whitehall on 1st March 1552/3; he is followed by Gloucester Ridley (p. 397), and others, but this is certainly wrong, as Ridley's address to the Common Council occurred before the end of the term of office of Sir John Dobbes as Lord Mayor in November 1552 (see *Works*, p. 410), and the school of Christ's Hospital was opened in the old Greyfriars' church in November 1552 (Stow's *Annals*, p. 1055). In his *Survey*, vol. II, p. 24, Stow states that steps were already being taken for starting a school in the Greyfriars' church on 17th February 1551/2, in which case Ridley's sermon must have been preached before this date. Grafton's *Chronicle*, vol. II, pp. 529-31, clearly states that it was on a Sunday soon after the execution of Somerset on 18th January 1551/2.

in London. Ridley said that this was exactly what he wished
to suggest. The King told Ridley to wait until he wrote the
letter, and handed it to Ridley, who departed to see Dobbes,
the Lord Mayor. Dobbes invited Ridley to dine with him
next day, along with two of the aldermen and six of the
commonalty, and they discussed the question. Soon afterwards, Dobbes arranged for Ridley to address a special
meeting of the twenty-four aldermen of the Common Council, at which Ridley strongly urged his audience to take
advantage of the King's generosity, and do all they could
for the city poor.

After making inquiries, the city authorities sent their
suggestions to Ridley, who adopted them and submitted
them to the King. They explained that there were three
kinds of poor who were in need of assistance and each kind
was itself sub-divided into three. The first were the poor by
impotency—the fatherless, or poor man's child; the aged,
blind and lame; and those diseased by dropsy and leprosy.
The second kind were the poor by casualty—the wounded
soldier; the decayed householder; and those visited with
grievous disease. The third kind were the thriftless poor—
the rioter that consumeth all; the vagabond that will
abide in no case; and the idle person, as the strumpet and
other. If the King wished to help the poor, they suggested
that he should set up three establishments in London to
benefit each of these three classes—a school for the poor
man's children, a hospital for the sick, and a place of correction for the vagabonds and harlots, where they could be
cured, by harsh punishment, of their idle habits.[60] Edward
immediately acted to help a category in the first class. He
directed that the church of the Greyfriars should be used as
a school for the orphans of Christ's Hospital. The church of
the suppressed Franciscans had been set aside for this pur-

pose by Henry VIII a few weeks before his death,* but owing to administrative incompetence the design had not been carried out. The old church was now made ready, and the work on it began in July 1552; the school opened there in November.† On Christmas Day, three hundred and forty boys of Christ's Hospital lined the streets in Cheapside in the afternoon to cheer the Lord Mayor, George Barnes, on his way to St. Paul's, where Ridley preached the sermon, as he did on each of the following holy days.[61]

Ridley and Dobbes had one suggestion to make for the relief of poverty which it was necessary to put forward with a certain discretion. The royal palace of Bridewell had not been used for many years, and certain courtiers now used their influence to arrange for it to be sold at some nominal price to their friends. When Ridley heard this, he intervened in an attempt to get the King to hand over Bridewell for the use of the London poor. He wrote to Cecil:

> Good Master Cecil, I must be a suitor unto you in our good Master Christ's cause; I beseech you be good to him. The matter is, Sir, alas, he hath lain too long abroad, as you do know, without lodging, in the streets of London, both hungry, naked and cold. Now, thanks be to Almighty God, the citizens are willing to refresh him, and to give him both meat, drink, clothing and firing; but alas, Sir, they lack lodging for him. For in some one house I dare say they are fain to lodge three families under one roof. Sir, there is a wide, large, empty house of the King's Majesty's called Bridewell, that would wonderfully well serve to lodge Christ in, if he might find some good friends in the Court to procure in his cause. Surely I have such a good opinion of the King's Majesty that

---

* See p. 101.

† The work began on 26th July 1552 (Stow's *Survey* vol. II, p. 25), and the school first opened on these premises on 23rd November 1552 (Stow's *Annals*, p. 1055).

if Christ had such faithful and hearty friends who would heartily speak for him, he should undoubtedly speed at the King's Majesty's hands. Sir, I have promised my brethren the citizens to move you, because I do take you for one that feareth God, and would that Christ should lie no more abroad in the streets.*

Ridley's appeal to Cecil was successful in thwarting the intrigues of the courtiers to obtain the grant of Bridewell to their friends; but the palace was not immediately made over to the use of the poor. Ridley also wrote on this matter to Sir John Gates,[62] but without further success. This is hardly surprising: Gates, who was one of Northumberland's closest friends, was perhaps the most unscrupulous of all the courtiers. Ridley, however, did not abandon his attempts to obtain Bridewell for the poor, and he was helped in his efforts by Sir George Barnes, who succeeded Dobbes as Lord Mayor in November 1552. Bridewell was eventually made over for use as a house of correction for vagabonds and harlots in April 1553. As regards assistance to the sick, the King reopened St. Thomas's Hospital, in Southwark, in July 1552,† and soon after founded another hospital— St. Bartholomew's, in Smithfield. He also decided to grant the revenues from his property of the Savoy to the use of St. Thomas's Hospital; and though he died before he could complete the gift, it was confirmed, several years later, by Mary.[63]

Northumberland was now driven to resort to more ex-

* *Works*, p. 535. The letter was first published (apparently in full) by Strype (Stow's *Survey*, Part I, p. 176), who states that it was written in May 1552; but the references to the cold and to fuel suggest that it was written during the winter—that is to say, the winter of 1552–3.

† Work began at St. Thomas's at the end of July 1552 (Stow's *Annals*, p. 1053), and Bridewell was granted on 10th April 1553 (Wriothesley's *Chronicle*, vol. II, p. 83, Stow's *Annals*, p. 1057).

propriations and seizures of property, not only from greed, but from necessity. He had run into difficulties with Parliament, as the peers and gentlemen who had supported him against Somerset were afraid of his growing power. His rule became more and more unpopular, and many people were now being sentenced to have an ear cut off or nailed to the pillory, for seditious words; one man was sent to the pillory for using the words 'poor child' of the King. Northumberland therefore adopted any expedient in order to raise revenue for the Crown. In November 1552, he ordered the seizure of all the goods of the Church in London which were deemed to be no longer necessary for the use of the Church. In view of the suppression of copes and other vestments in the Second Book of Common Prayer, there was a large amount of linen available for Northumberland to seize, and these were commandeered, along with many cloths of the Communion tables. Ridley was powerless to stop the spoliation, but he appealed to the King and to the Council to grant any superfluous linen, over and above what the King might need, to the use of the poor in London.[64] Ridley did not venture to put his request any higher than this. The King granted his wish, and gave some of the linen to the use of the scholars of Christ's Hospital. The churchwardens were directed to organise relief for the destitute in London during the winter.

Faced with opposition and obstruction from Parliament, Northumberland decided to dissolve it, and writs were issued for a new election. Northumberland took elaborate precautions to ensure the return of candidates who would be friendly to him. He created a number of new Parliamentary boroughs, and directed the Lords Lieutenant to interview suitable candidates to ascertain if they would support Northumberland, and if satisfied that they would,

T

to make sure that they were elected. The new Parliament assembled on 1st March 1553. Ridley was chosen to preach the sermon at the state opening of Parliament by the King. But Edward had now fallen seriously ill, and he was unable to go to Westminster; the peers and commons were consequently summoned to the palace at Whitehall, and the King opened Parliament there, Ridley preaching the sermon in the royal chapel in the Palace.* The new Parliament, however, was hardly less refractory than the old, and it was prorogued after a month.

During this short session, Ridley, for the second time in the course of his six years in Parliament, voted against a bill supported by the Council. He voted, together with his colleague Scory, with Thirlby, with two Catholic peers—Arundel and Windsor—and with Paget, against the bill to extend the duration of a number of statutes which had been passed during the reigns of Henry VIII and Edward VI for a limited period only, and had now expired.† None of these statutes dealt with any religious issue, and only the Act against unlawful assemblies and resistance to enclosures—which Ridley had supported when it was originally enacted in 1549—had aroused any political controversy.

* Wriothesley's *Chronicle*, vol. II, p. 81. There seems to be no doubt that Ridley preached a sermon at the State opening of Parliament on 1st March 1552/3, though it was not this sermon which led to the grant of the charitable foundations (see p. 285 n).

† *House of Lords Journal*, 27th March 1553. See *Statutes of the Realm*, 7 Edw. VI, c. 11. The statute extended the duration, and in some cases slightly amended, existing statutes dealing with the export of horses, the making of cables and ropes, the winding of wools, the killing of weanlings, the punishment of perjury, the regrating of fish, the preserving of woods, the unlawful hunting of deer, the currying of leather, the making of malt, the tanning of leather, unlawful assemblies (the 1549–50 Act against resistance to enclosures), the sale of tanned leather, fortune telling, the sale of cattle, of butter and cheese, and relief of the poor.

The other Acts were concerned with the ban on the export of horses, with poaching, fortune-telling, perjury, and with the manufacture and sale of leather, malt, fish and other matters. We have no means of knowing why Ridley objected so strongly to these measures that he was prepared to go to the lengths of voting against the bill for the continuation of the statutes. Presumably some influential people—perhaps some of Ridley's friends among the London merchants—whose interests were adversely affected by one or other of these Acts, had succeeded in interesting Ridley in their grievances, and persuaded him to vote against the whole bill because of his opposition to some particular statute which was extended by the bill.

The Parliament of 1553 had failed to provide Northumberland with all the revenues which he required, and he was therefore driven to fresh spoliations. In February, the Council had ordered an inventory into the plate, bells and other property in the possession of the Church. Ridley was required to collaborate in this measure in the diocese of London. On 25th May 1553, he sat in the Guildhall, with Chief Justice Chomley and Barnes, the Lord Mayor, to receive the statements of the churchwardens as to the valuables of their churches.[65] The inventory was then presented to the Council to enable them to make further spoliations. Ridley was also a member, along with Thirlby and seven knights and lawyers, of a commission which had been set up to sell and dispose of the chantry lands which the King had appropriated under the statutes of 1545 and 1547.[66]

In the winter of 1552–3, Northumberland and Cranmer decided to translate Ridley from London to Durham. Tunstall had fallen into disgrace by his persistent opposition to all the Protestant measures, though he had so far been saved from arrest and deprivation by his personal friendship with Cranmer. An attempt had been made in the summer of 1550 to accuse him of complicity in the Yorkshire revolt of 1549, and while this was unsuccessful, he was arrested in December 1551 on a charge of participating in Somerset's conspiracy. Northumberland introduced a bill of attainder in the Parliament of 1552 condemning Tunstall for misprision of treason. The bill passed the House of Lords against the opposition of Cranmer—though Ridley and the other bishops voted in favour of it;* but it was thrown out in the Commons. Northumberland, however, had decided to divide the diocese of Durham into two bishoprics, and to take the opportunity of enriching himself in the process. Tunstall was deprived by a commission of lawyers in October 1552, and in March 1553 a statute was passed creating a new diocese of Newcastle out of the see of Durham. A large amount of property belonging to the see of Durham was appropriated by Northumberland himself and by other dignitaries; but it was provided that the see of Durham should have an annual income of two thousand marks, while the see of Newcastle was to receive a thousand marks a year.[67]

The Council decided to appoint Grindal to be the Bishop of Newcastle. On 18th November 1552, Ridley wrote to Cecil and Gates, requesting them to appoint either Bradford, Sampson, Harvey, Grimbold or his cousin Launcelot to succeed Grindal in the chantership of St. Paul's, though Ridley knew that Cecil and Gates were not well disposed towards him in view of the difficulties which had arisen in regard to the Kentish Town prebend in 1551. In this letter, Ridley expressed his satisfaction that Grindal was to be Bishop of Newcastle.[68] He made no reference to the fact that

* *House of Lords Journal*, 31st March 1552.

he himself was to be Bishop of Durham, but the decision to translate him had already been taken at this time, and was generally known in London.[69]

Ridley was evidently very pleased at the prospect of his translation to Durham, which would mean that he would now be the diocesan bishop of his countrymen in Tynedale.[70] As a child, he must have been brought up to look on the Bishop of Durham as the highest of dignitaries, and though the office was no longer what it had been fifty years before, there was no position which he could have been given which would more impress and delight his relations in the Marches. He would also have important work to do as Bishop of Durham. In Newcastle, his colleague Grindal would have to deal with Knox's Protestant extremists; but in the diocese of Durham, the old religion was as firmly entrenched in the people's mind as it had ever been. It was not an easy task to force Protestantism on the Catholic priests and laymen of the remote parishes in the north, and with a bishop like Tunstall, who was a Catholic at heart himself, the work had been only half-heartedly carried on. With Ridley there, things would be very different. This was probably the real reason for his translation to Durham. With the second Act of Uniformity in force and the Articles of Religion promulgated by the King, the immediate aim of the Protestant leaders was not to proclaim in Westminster some new religious reform, but to ensure that those which had already been decreed were enforced in the backward Catholic parts of the kingdom. There was no one better fitted than Ridley to effect the forcible conversion of the north to Protestantism. His visitation in the diocese of London in June 1550, when he had hurled the altar out of every church was remembered with horror by Catholics all over England. The rumours of his impending appointment as Bishop of Durham must have caused the deepest gloom in the parishes of the diocese.

With the adoption of the second Book of Common Prayer, the Reformation was now being extended further and further. On 2nd March, a meeting of Convocation was held in St. Paul's, which all the bishops attended wearing their full robes.* The new Catechism which Cranmer had written was adopted by Convocation, and Ridley, though he had played no part in drafting the Catechism, was active in inducing the clergy to approve it.† It appears, however, that the Articles of Religion were not submitted to Convocation, but were promulgated by the King in June, having first been submitted to the Universities and other leading churchmen. Indeed, Cranmer seems to have been contemplating at this time the suppression of Convocation altogether, replacing it with meetings of provincial synods, which were to be composed only of bishops, and were only to be called when the Archbishop thought fit.[71] The most satisfactory way of advancing the Reformation was for Cranmer to formulate new doctrines and practices in consultation with Ridley and a small number of his intimate collaborators, and then, after submitting the completed draft for approval to a somewhat larger number of dignitaries, to put it into force with the full approval of his Prince. But there was now a cloud on the horizon—the illness of the King.

---

* Wriothesley's *Chronicle*, vol. II, p. 82.

† See the argument between Ridley and Weston on this point during the Oxford disputation of 1554 (Foxe, vol. VI, p. 487). Foxe states that, in his conversation with Bourn and Feckenham in the Tower, Ridley also denied having written this Catechism (Foxe, vol. VI, p. 436, *Works*, pp. 160–1); but it seems more likely that the work to which Ridley was referring on this occasion was Cranmer's book against Gardiner on the Sacrament.

The appointment of Ridley and Grindal to their new sees was held up while Northumberland completed his spoliation of the diocese of Durham. Ridley was still Bishop of London on 6th July, when he issued the writs for a session of Convocation to be held in September.[72] On that day, the King died.

NOTES

[1] Foxe, vol. VIII, p. 645.

[2] Foxe, vol. VII, p. 408; Turner's letter to Foxe (*Works*, p. 493).

[3] Ridley's letter to Cecil, 16th September 1551 (*Works*, pp. 532–3). For the damage to Ridley's woods, see *Acts of the Privy Council*, vol. II, pp. 405, 411 (5th and 17th March 1549/50).

[4] Humphrey, *Life of Jewel*, pp. 258–9.

[5] Foxe, vol. VII, p. 408.

[6] *Statutes of the Realm*, 1 Edw. VI, c. 5, c. 6; 2 & 3 Edw. VI, c. 11, c. 15, c. 28, c. 29, c. 33, c. 38; 7 Edw. VI, c. 8; etc.

[7] Ridley's letter to Queen Mary, 16th October 1555 (*Works*, p. 428).

[8] Ridley, *Last Farewell* (*Works*, p. 397).

[9] Foxe, vol. VII, p. 408.

[10] Attwater, *Pembroke College Cambridge*, p. 37.

[11] *Collection of Statutes of Cambridge University*, pp. 97–8.

[12] Ridley's letter to Parker, 25th July 1551 (*Works*, p. 335).

[13] Wriothesley's *Chronicle*, vol. II, p. 47; *Greyfriars Chronicle*, p. 69, agrees that the table was moved on this occasion, though it seems to state that it had already been moved below the steps on St. Barnabas' Day. See p. 217 n. The procession of the choir had been suppressed at St. Paul's at Christmas 1550 (*Greyfriars Chronicle*, p. 68).

[14] Rymer, *Foedera*, vol. XV, pp. 250–2 (18th January 1550/1).

[15] Sentence of Excommunication on George van Paris (Wilkins, *Concilia*, vol. IV, p. 45); Burnet, vol. II, p. 205.

[16] Ridley's letter to Cheke, 23rd July 1551 (*Works*, p. 331).

[17] Stow's *Annals*, p. 1049.

[18] Ridley's letter to the Preachers of London, 25th July 1551 (Burnet's *Records*, vol. V, p. 346; *Works*, pp. 334–5).

[19] Ridley's letter to Cheke, 23rd July 1551 (*Works*, pp. 331–4); *Acts of the Privy Council*, vol. III, p. 319 (18th July 1551).

[20] Newcourt's *Repertorium*, vol. I, pp. 27, 171, 180, 196.

[21] Strype, *Memorials*, vol. II (i), p. 522.

[22] Wriothesley's *Chronicle*, vol. II, pp. 55–6. That Ridley played some

part in the deprivation of Heath and Day is confirmed by the fact that Edward VI made a note of Ridley's name on a document written by Cecil in September 1551 containing the names of the commissioners in the case of Heath and Day. Below the list of the commissioners, Edward wrote: 'The Bishop of London,' and next to it wrote a cross and the figure '4'. (*Literary Remains of Edward VI*, vol. I, p. 487). The commissioners who deprived Heath and Day sat in Ridley's palace at St. Paul's (*Greyfriars Chronicle*, p. 71).

[23] MS. Harleian, 290, art. 2; *King Edward's Journal*, 22nd October–6th November 1551 (Burnet, vol. V, pp. 52–5); *Machyn's Diary*, pp. 11–12.

[24] Edward VI, *Method for the Proceedings in the Council* (Burnet's *Records*, vol. V, p. 118); *King Edward's Journal*, 3rd March 1551/2 (Burnet, vol. V, p. 66).

[25] Burnet, vol. II, pp. 286–90; vol. III, pp. 368–73; Strype, *Cranmer*, p. 390. For the controversy with Knox over the Articles, and the reduction of the forty-five Articles in the original draft to forty-two, see Lorimer, *John Knox and the Church of England*, pp. 123–8. See also Dixon, vol. III, pp. 383, 480–4, 485 n., 513–8 n.

[26] *The Articles of Religion*, 1552 (Burnet's *Records*, vol. V, pp. 314–29).

[27] See Cranmer's letter to the Council, 7th October 1552, (published in Lorimer, *John Knox and the Church of England*, pp. 103–5) where Cranmer states that 'we'—meaning himself, Ridley and Peter Martyr—had approved the provision in the book that the people should kneel to receive Communion. See Smyth, *Cranmer and the Reformation*, pp. 246–7, for the probability that Ridley and his colleagues met to consider the draft of the Second Book of Common Prayer during the trial of Gardiner in January 1551.

[28] *The Second Book of Common Prayer* (*Liturgies of King Edward VI*) pp. 187–355.

[29] *Statutes of the Realm*, 5 & 6 Edw. VI, c. 1.

[30] *Statutes of the Realm*, 5 & 6 Edw. VI, c. 20.

[31] *House of Lords Journal*, 4th April 1552.

[32] Burnet, vol. II, p. 327.

[33] *House of Lords Journal*, 5th April 1552.

[34] *Greyfriars Chronicle*, p. 74.

[35] Burnet, vol. II, p. 248

[36] *Statutes of the Realm*, 3 & 4 Edw. VI, c. 11.

[37] *House of Lords Journal*, 31st January 1549/50 (second session.)

[38] *King Edward's Journal*, 10th February 1551/2 (Burnet's *Records*, vol. V, p. 64); *Cal. Pat. Rolls Edw. VI*, vol. IV, p. 354 (12th February 1551/2).

[39] Burnet, vol. II, p. 332.

[40] See *Reformation of the Ecclesiastical Laws*; Burnet, vol. II, pp. 332–40; Todd, *Cranmer*, vol. II, pp. 329–49.

[41] *Acts of the Privy Council*, vol. IV, pp. 35–6, 46–7 (6th and 14th May 1552); *King Edward's Journal*, 26th September 1552 (Burnet, vol. V, p. 85).

[42] *Acts of the Privy Council*, vol. IV, pp. 78, 80, 95 (13th and 15th June and 17th July 1552).

[43] Trevelyan, *English Social History*, p. 182.

[44] Ridley, *Last Farewell* (*Works*, p. 536).

[45] Strype, *Memorials*, vol. II (ii), p. 62; Cooper, *Annals of Cambridge*, vol. II, p. 64.

[46] Mary's letter to the Council, 22nd June 1549 (Foxe, vol. VI, pp. 7–8).

[47] Edward VI's letter to Mary, 24th January 1550 (Foxe, vol. VI, pp. 11–12).

[48] The Council's letter to Mary, 25th December 1550 (Foxe, vol. VI, pp. 14–15).

[49] Burnet, vol. II, pp. 296–7.

[50] The Council's letter to Mary, 25th December 1550 (Foxe, vol. VI, pp. 14–18).

[51] See *King Edward's Journal*, 18th–25th March 1550/1 (Burnet, vol. V, pp. 32–3); Morison's *Discourse* (published in *Literary Remains of Edward VI*, vol. II, pp. ccxxiv–xxx); Foxe, vol. V, pp. 700–1. The accounts of the incident by Edward, Morison and Foxe do not differ in any essential point.

[52] Foxe, vol. VI, pp. 354–5.

[53] Mary's letters to Edward VI, 3rd February 1550 and 19th August 1551 (Foxe, vol. VI, pp. 13, 21).

[54] See Gairdner, vol. III, pp. 334–5, for the probability that Knox's sermon was preached on 25th September.

[55] *The Second Book of Common Prayer* (*Liturgies of King Edward VI*, p. 283).

[56] *Greyfriars Chronicle*, p. 76; Wriothesley's *Chronicle*, vol. II, p. 78.

[57] *Acts of the Privy Council*, vol. IV, p. 131 (27th September 1552); Strype, *Cranmer*, p. 418.

[58] *Acts of the Privy Council*, vol. IV, pp. 197–8 (28th December 1552).

[59] *Acts of the Privy Council*, vol. IV, pp. 160–1 (4th November 1552); Strype, *Cranmer*, p. 339.

[60] With regard to the charitable foundations, and Ridley's part therein, see Grafton's *Chronicle*, vol. II, pp. 529–31; Ridley's *Last Farewell* (*Works*, p. 410).

[61] *Greyfriars Chronicle*, p. 76.

[62] Gloucester Ridley, p. 378.

[63] Gloucester Ridley, p. 399.

[64] Strype, *Memorials*, vol. II (ii), p. 15.

[65] *Acts of the Privy Council*, vol. IV, p. 219 (16th February 1552/3); Wriothesley's *Chronicle*, vol. II, p. 84; *Greyfriars Chronicle*, p. 77.

[66] The commissioners were appointed on 7th July 1552 (*Literary Remains of Edward VI*, vol. I, p. 414).

[67] Burnet, vol. II, p. 359; vol. III, pp. 356–8.

[68] Ridley's letter to Cecil and Gates, 18th November 1552 (*Works*, pp. 336–7).

[69] Scheyfve's Advices to the Imperial government, 20th November 1552 (*Calendar of Spanish State Papers*, vol. X, p. 591).

[70] Ridley, *Last Farewell* (*Works*, p. 397).

[71] Burnet, vol. III, pp. 373–4.

[72] Strype, *Memorials*, vol. II (ii), p. 114.

VIII

QUEEN MARY: THE TOWER AND
THE OXFORD DISPUTATION

On 19th June 1553, Ridley was summoned to Greenwich, where the dying King was in residence. There he found that all the leading officers of Church and State had likewise been called before the Council. They were all invited to sign their names to the King's will, by which he devised the Crown of England to the Lady Jane Grey.* They then understood why Northumberland had married his son Guilford to Jane Grey a fortnight before.

The document declared that King Henry VIII having by his will devised the Crown, in default of issue to King Edward, to the Lady Mary and her issue, or in default of these to the Lady Elizabeth and her issue, the King had decided to alter the settlement, and instead to devise the Crown to the Lady Jane Grey, the great niece of King Henry VIII. King Henry's marriages to both Catherine of Aragon and Ann Bullen were void in the eyes of God, and consequently both Mary and Elizabeth were bastards, and they were so declared to be by statute. Even if they had been legitimate, it was improper that they should succeed to the Crown, because they were only related by half-blood to the King, and it was a well-established law of custom and

* Ridley signed the will on 19th June, along with the Lords of the Council and the other dignitaries. The Lord Mayor and the London Aldermen signed on 8th July (see Froude, vol. V, pp. 507–8 and n.).

tradition that relatives of the half-blood could not succeed. If either Mary or Elizabeth came to the throne, they would probably marry a foreign prince, who would not only place the realm once more under the rule of the Bishop of Rome, but would subvert the laws of England and introduce the system of government in force in his country of origin. Edward had therefore appointed Jane to be Queen of England after his death.[1]

Many of the Lords of the Council were alarmed at the whole project. The common law judges were particularly dubious, and pointed out that Edward had not, like Henry, obtained statutory authority to devise the Crown by will. Moreover, under the statute of 1545 itself it was high treason to attempt to alter the succession established by Henry's will. But they all of them gave way under pressure from Northumberland, and signed the document.

The plot to put Jane Grey on the throne was unsuccessful, and in due course the Reformation was to be victorious in England under a Queen whom Ridley and his colleagues in 1553 attempted to exclude from the succession. The Protestant historians have therefore condemned Northumberland's action as severely as have the Catholics. It is very likely true, as his admirers have stated, that the cautious and timid Cranmer tried to persuade Northumberland to abandon his scheme to make Jane Queen, and only signed the will with great reluctance. It is unlikely that Ridley showed a similar hesitation. He was not the man to allow the Protestant settlement to die along with the King, and to see a Papist princess ascend the throne to undo the Reformation of the Church of England, without first putting up a fierce resistance, a desperate fight to preserve the new order which he had done so much to build. He knew that for him and all his followers there would be no mercy under

Mary, and he threw himself into this last struggle with all the vigour in his forceful nature.

Mary was at Hunsdon, chafing under the advice which the Emperor gave her to take no hasty action. On 4th July, she heard that the King was dying, and fled to Kenninghall, and from there to Framlingham in Suffolk. Edward died on 6th July. A few hours later, the dignitaries of the realm were summoned to Greenwich, and informed that the King was dead, having devised the Crown to Jane Dudley, whose husband Guilford would wear the Crown matrimonial. They were persuaded to swear allegiance to Jane, and told to keep the news of the King's death a close secret for the present. Northumberland seized the Tower and manned the fleet. On Monday the 10th, Jane arrived at the Tower, and was proclaimed Queen. The proclamation was received in silence—in ominous silence.[2] On the same day, the Council received a letter from Mary, commanding them to swear allegiance to her. They wrote in reply that Mary was a bastard, and must immediately swear allegiance to Queen Jane.* A few days later, they heard that Mary was preparing for resistance at Framlingham, and had been joined by thousands of people from Norfolk and Suffolk, to whom she promised that she had no intention of overthrowing the Protestant religion.[3] Several peers and gentlemen had also joined her. The Council sent the fleet to patrol the coast of Suffolk to prevent Mary from escaping abroad, and on 14th July Northumberland marched to Cambridge with six thousand soldiers to suppress the revolt. The people of London were silent. As Northumberland rode through Shoreditch with his army, the crowds pressed round him,

* The Council's letter to Mary is dated 9th July (Foxe, vol. VI, p. 386); but this is clearly impossible, as the letter states that it is being written in reply to Mary's letter of the 9th from Kenninghall.

but not a single cheer was raised. This caused him great anxiety;[4] but the Imperial Ambassador was much perturbed that there had not been a single demonstration in London against the daughter of Suffolk.[5]

The people of London were silent; but they were not impartial. They were quite unconvinced by the specious legal arguments in the pamphlets which were distributed throughout London by the Council. In their eyes, the Crown was hereditary; for them, Edward VI was King because he was his father's son. The attempt to give the Crown to Jane Dudley and her husband was a treasonable conspiracy by Northumberland to put his daughter-in-law and his son on the throne. In most cases, their traditional concept of hereditary monarchy went hand in hand with their loyalty to the old Catholic faith, and with their hatred of Northumberland and of covetous nobles and enclosing landlords. This last factor was probably the strongest: it was strong enough to make many Protestants flock to Mary in Norfolk and Suffolk, where the men who had fought with Ket had not forgotten how Northumberland had hanged their comrades. The people rose as one man against the nobles and landlords, and this time they were marching, not under a rebel leader, but at the call of their rightful Queen, the Princess who stood next in line of hereditary succession to a hereditary throne.

The Londoners had been silent on Friday, 14th July; by Sunday morning, they had found out that all their neighbours were loyal to Queen Mary. On that day, the Imperial Ambassadors realised that Mary was going to win if she could survive the first battle, and the Lords of the Council began to panic. They became convinced that London was on the verge of revolution, and they strengthened the guards at the Tower to protect them from the people.[6]

Cranmer was on the point of surrender. But while Queen Jane and her ministers were cowering in the Tower, Ridley went out to Paul's Cross to face the angry mob.*

For the last time, Ridley stood at the cross in the graveyard at St. Paul's and preached to the people of London. He had been ordered by the Council to retrieve the situation, and he castigated Mary in his most vigorous style. He said that both Mary and Elizabeth were bastards by the laws of God, as well as by Act of Parliament, and could not succeed to the Throne; but by now angry shouts began to be heard in the crowd. Ridley continued to speak above the rising clamour, and told his congregation what was in store for them if Mary came to the Throne. She was a Papist and would place them all once more under the sway of the Bishop of Rome; she would marry a foreign prince, and bring in foreign power to subvert the laws and government of England. He told them how he had visited her at Hunsdon in the previous September, and how she had refused to listen to him preach; she would undo all the work of her

---

* The historians have differed as to whether Ridley's sermon was preached on Sunday, 9th July or on Sunday, the 16th. The difference with regard to the dates is of course of the greatest importance, for if the sermon was preached a week earlier it assumes a completely different significance. The *Greyfriars Chronicle*, p. 78, states that it was on the 9th, and this is followed by Strype, *Memorials*, vol. III (i), p. 6, and by Gloucester Ridley, p. 414. The 16th is given by Wriothesley's *Chronicle*, vol. II, p. 88, Stow's *Annals*, p. 1063, Holinshed, vol. III, p. 1070, and Heylin (Part I) p. 162. It seems clear that the sermon was preached on the 16th, because of the letter of the Imperial Ambassadors to Charles V on 22nd July (*Calendar of Spanish State Papers*, vol. XI, p. 114), in which the Ambassadors wrote that the sermon was preached 'last Sunday', and make it plain, from its connexion with other events, that the 16th was the date, and that the sermon could not possibly have been preached on the 9th. It is not impossible, however, that Ridley may have preached another sermon of no historical importance at Paul's Cross on the 9th.

brother, the wise young King that they had lost, for she was an enemy of God's word.* By now the whole congregation was in uproar. The people of London had broken their silence.

Ridley obviously stayed in London during the next three days which saw the overthrow of the Protestant Reformation in England. The events of these three days ensured that Ridley would go down in history, not as a learned and able bishop who laid the foundations of the Reformation, but as a martyr and victim of the persecution of the Church of Rome. They meant, too, that Mary would be remembered, not as an unhappy princess who was cheated of her birthright because she remained true to her faith, but as one of the most ruthless monarchs who has ever occupied the Throne. In London they heard, during these three days, that Mary had been joined by forty thousand men at Framlingham; that Northumberland's men had deserted at Bury St. Edmunds; that the sailors who had been sent to patrol the coasts of Suffolk had mutinied, and had proclaimed Mary as Queen at Yarmouth; and that the levies which had been raised in Buckinghamshire had joined with Mary. On Wednesday the 19th, Paget, who had been working for Mary in London, decided that the time had come to approach the Lords of the Council and invite them to submit. On that day, seven of them swore allegiance to Mary, and begged her for mercy; they ordered the proclamation of Mary as Queen in London, and sent a messenger to Cambridge commanding Northumberland to surrender at

* Foxe, vol. VI, pp. 389–90; Wriothesley's *Chronicle*, vol. II, p. 88; but Wriothesley can hardly be right in stating that Ridley 'declared in his sermon of the death of King Edward', if, as is certain, and as Wriothesley himself states, the date of the sermon was the 16th, and not the 9th. He probably means no more than that Ridley referred to Edward's death in the sermon, as of course he must have done.

once to Mary. The seven Lords of the Council who had surrendered were among the most important of them all—Queen Jane's father Suffolk, the Marquis of Winchester, Bedford and Pembroke, Lord Chancellor Goodrich, Shrewsbury, and—foremost among the capitulators—Cranmer. After they had surrendered, resistance was hopeless; Northumberland proclaimed Mary as Queen in Cambridge, and rode off to Framlingham to submit. He was arrested on the road, and sent to the Tower. In London, the people greeted the proclamation of Mary as Queen with bonfires and celebrations.

By 20th July, it must have been clear to Ridley that all his hopes had been shattered by the events of the last three days. Mary was Queen, and could do her worst; a Catholic and a Papist sat on the Throne; the Caesar to whom they must render the obedience that was due unto Caesar was a Catholic Caesar who rejected the word of God; the Supreme Head of the Church of England wished only to use her supremacy over the Church to force it to its knees before the Pope. They had moved back at least to 1546, perhaps to 1533. And this Catholic Queen had come to power with the support of the overwhelming majority of her subjects, even if some of them had been tricked by her promise to uphold the religious settlement of Edward's reign. Mary had defeated what would now be considered to have been a treasonable Protestant revolt. King Edward's will would not, after all, be validated by Parliament; the statute of 1544 would remain in force, and those who had disputed Henry's will and his devise of the Crown to Mary would be guilty of high treason. Ridley, who had preached the sermon at Paul's Cross less than a week earlier, was in danger of being condemned and executed as a traitor.

As soon as it was known in London that Mary had been

victorious, all the nobles and courtiers who had supported Northumberland and Jane rode hastily to Framlingham to submit to Mary; the Suffolk castle, which Mary had regarded a fortnight earlier as being conveniently near the coast for an escape, was now thronged with peers and gentlemen acclaiming her as Queen and imploring her forgiveness. Ridley decided to go with all the rest to Framlingham. For this he has naturally been subjected to much criticism from hostile historians—that he, who a week earlier had condemned Mary as a bastard and Papist at Paul's Cross, should now fawn upon her and beg her forgiveness. Yet his action in going to Framlingham can surely be forgiven as readily as it can be understood. Everyone else was doing it, and Ridley may well have been guided in part by the instinct of self-preservation which he was afterwards to disregard so bravely; but his submission to Mary was probably sincere. He had always firmly believed in the Christian duty of obedience to the magistrates. At the beginning of the month, he had readily persuaded himself that Jane was his lawful Queen—a belief which coincided with the interests of the Reformation; now he probably thought that he had been wrong, and honestly repented of having committed the sin of rebellion.

Ridley left London for Framlingham on 20th or 21st July. He was accompanied by three or four of his servants. The reason for his departure was not generally known in London; the Imperial Ambassadors thought that he had fled from the capital to escape from the enraged populace.* But Ridley was riding to Framlingham—the last journey

* The Imperial Ambassadors' letter to Charles V, 22nd July 1553 (*Calendar of Spanish State Papers*, vol. XI, p. 114), which shows that Ridley had left for Framlingham by that date; and he would hardly have gone before the surrender of the 19th.

which he would ever make as a free man. He got as far as Ipswich—some twenty miles from his destination—where he was arrested by Mary's officers.[7] There is no reason to doubt this information, which was circulating in London when Ridley returned there as a prisoner less than a week later, and probably emanated from Ridley's guards, especially as there appears to be no real authority for the generally accepted tradition that he reached Framlingham, had an interview with Mary, and after imploring her mercy on his knees, was arrested in her presence.* Mary was surrounded with people who had come to beg for mercy, and on 21st July her Council, at Framlingham, gave orders that they were all to be detained by the Marshal until the Queen's pleasure was known, and not admitted to the Castle unless they were expressly sent for.[8] Ridley was probably seen and recognised in Ipswich by some of Mary's men, and on declaring that he wished to see the Queen, was detained until Mary had determined what his fate was to be.

Mary would not pardon Ridley. He was one of about a hundred to whom she was not prepared to show mercy. She was prepared to pardon the scheming courtiers who had been loyal to Northumberland and to Jane, and would, as she well knew, be equally loyal to her as long as she held the Crown and the power; but she would not forgive the heretic who had suppressed the altars in London and had upbraided her at Hunsdon less than a year before—least of all the man who had called her a bastard at Paul's Cross. Mary gave orders that he was to be taken back to London and imprisoned in the Tower. He travelled under escort on a lame horse,[9] along with the Marquis of Northampton and Lord

* This story seems to have been developed as a result of a series of embellishments of Foxe's statement that Ridley received a 'cold ewlcome' at Framlingham (vol. VI, p. 390).

Robert Dudley, who had also been exempted from the pardon. They reached London at two o'clock in the afternoon of Wednesday, 26th July, and were taken to the Tower. The streets were lined with soldiers to protect them from the angry crowds. Chief Justice Chomley was brought to the Tower the same evening.[10] Northampton and Chomley were soon to be released, and Robert Dudley had far to go; but Ridley was doomed.

There was a strange consortment of people in the Tower in the last week of July 1553. In the prisons lay the victims of Edward's reign, for Mary was more prompt in arresting her opponents than in releasing her friends; the officers of the Tower had offered to release them, but Gardiner, after more than five years in captivity, decided to wait for his ceremonial pardon when Mary reached London.[11] The old Duke of Norfolk was still there—he had been in the Tower since December 1546—and the Duchess of Somerset. There were also the new inmates of the prisons—Northumberland and his supporters, as well as all the judges who had so reluctantly supported Jane. And all the while Jane Dudley and her husband Guilford, with her father the Duke of Suffolk, were still living in the state apartments in the Tower, waiting, as were all the people in the prisons, for the Queen to decide their fate. Mary sent some officers on ahead to arrest Jane and the rest, and they were held in the Tower as prisoners. On 3rd August, Mary arrived in London. At the gates of the Tower, the Duke of Norfolk, Gardiner and the Duchess of Somerset were waiting on their knees to receive her pardon and release from prison.

Ridley did not participate in this ceremony. He was not to be released with his old enemies, but was just beginning his term of imprisonment. No one had any idea as to what was in store for him. The Queen had been quite arbitrary and capricious in pardoning and arresting her enemies. She had pardoned Cecil, who had drafted the letter to her of 11th July demanding her submission to Jane and proclaiming her to be a bastard, and all the Lords of the Council, except Northumberland and Gates, who had signed the letter; and Cranmer, the leader of the reformers, was still free, and was permitted by the Queen to officiate at King Edward's Protestant funeral along with Day, who had been released from house arrest. But Ridley had been sent to the Tower, and was no doubt anxiously awaiting the summoning of Parliament to see if his name was to be included in an Act of Attainder. Mary, however, did not wait for the meeting of Parliament to deal with her principal enemies; before the end of August, Norfolk had sentenced Northumberland to death in the Court of the Lord High Steward, and he had been executed along with Gates and Palmer.

In the matter of religion, Mary still moved with some caution. Within a week of her arrival in London, she had advanced a little from the position which she had taken in her hour of need at Framlingham. At Framlingham, she had proclaimed that the Protestant religion as established by law would not be altered, and that she merely reserved the right to keep her own private Mass. In London, on 12th August, she announced that she would introduce complete religious toleration in her realm, and added that she hoped, under these conditions, that her people would in due course be converted to her own Catholic viewpoint.[12] Next day, Gilbert Bourn, a Catholic doctor who had been Bonner's chaplain, preached a sermon at Paul's Cross which was the occasion for a riot organised by the London Protestants, from which Bourn was only rescued by the intervention of

Ridley's former chaplains, Rogers and Bradford;[13] and thereupon Mary prohibited all preaching except under licence. She also forbade any religious controversy, and the use of the terms 'Papist' and 'heretic'.*

About the middle of August, Bonner, who had been released from the Marshalsea a fortnight earlier, after nearly four years in prison, petitioned the Queen to set aside the sentence of the commissioners in 1549 depriving him of the bishopric of London. Bonner claimed, as he had done four years earlier, that the commissioners had had no jurisdiction to hear the case or to deprive him when he had appealed to be heard by the King himself. If Bonner's claim succeeded, it would mean that he had never been properly deprived, and was still Bishop of London, whereas Ridley had never been Bishop of London at all. On 22nd August, Mary appointed a commission of peers, dignitaries and civil lawyers, to hear Bonner's claim. The Queen's commission directed that all the members of the commission which had deprived Bonner in 1549, but especially Nicholas then Bishop of Rochester, should be served with notice of Bonner's claim, and given leave to appear before the commission in person or at least by proxy; but it also stated that the commissioners should not hesitate from proceeding with the case if the defendants did not appear.† The commissioners knew what was expected of them; they were

---

* In the proclamation from Richmond on 18th August 1553 (Foxe, vol. VI, pp. 390–1).

† *Cal. Pat. Rolls, Ph. & M.*, vol. I, pp. 74–5 (22nd August 1553); the commissioners were John Tregonwell; Roper; David Pole the Archdeacon of Derby; Draycot, the Archdeacon of Huntingdon; Bourn, the Archdeacon of Bedford; Cooke; Geoffery Glyn; Cole; Ermested; the Marquis of Winchester; Lord Arundel; Lord Derby; Lord Shrewsbury; Sir Richard Southwell; Sir Robert Southwell; Sir Edward Carne; Sir Richard Read; Griffith, the Archdeacon of Rochester; and John White, the Warden of St. Mary's College, Winchester.

prepared to ride roughshod over legal procedure, and gave their decision within a fortnight. Ridley was certainly not present in person at the hearing; he was supposed to be represented by proctors, but it seems quite likely that he was never notified of the proceedings at all, for he was never officially told of the decision which the commissioners had reached and was firmly convinced that he had been condemned unheard.* From a legal point of view, Bonner's arguments were weak in the extreme, for he did not put forward the only valid one—that the King had no power to deprive a Bishop; he realised that Mary intended to use the royal power of deprivation in the interests of their party. But in the new situation, the commissioners naturally gave judgment for Bonner, and pronounced on 5th September[14] that he had not been validly deprived, and was still Bishop of London, whereas Ridley had been a usurper. In due course—in March 1554—Ridley was dismissed from his position as Master of Pembroke Hall by the Fellows.[15] By this time, the authorities at Cambridge were requiring every member of the University to sign a statement repudiating Ridley, and expressing his disgust that a Cambridge man could be guilty of such heinous heresy.[16]

The return of Bonner as Bishop of London caused great legal difficulties in the diocese. As Ridley was now deemed never to have lawfully held the see, all the grants and leases which he had executed during his three years as bishop were declared void, and Bonner cancelled many of them. This invalidated the great spoliation of the see in the spring of 1550, but it also caused great hardship to many poorer people who had paid full consideration to the see for the grants and leases which Ridley had given them. Ridley

* 'Being (as I hear say I am) deposed and expulsed by judgment as an unjust usurper of that room' (Ridley, *Last Farewell, Works,* p. 408).

was very distressed when he heard how these tenants were being penalised for what was held to have been his usurpation of the see; and Protestant historians have contrasted it bitterly with Ridley's conduct when he had succeeded Bonner in 1550. Ridley had not ejected or mulcted a single tenant or grantee who held his title from Bonner. The cases were not in fact quite comparable. The Catholics now alleged that Ridley had never lawfully been Bishop of London, while the Protestants in 1550 did not dispute that Bonner had lawfully held the see until he had been deprived. But there can be no doubt that real hardship was caused to the tenants, and for some reason—probably for the most sordid financial motives—the authorities did not generally adopt the obvious solution of retrospectively confirming Ridley's grants.* This was the more inexcusable as Mary validated the grants which King Edward had made to Ridley as Bishop of London, and directed that they were to take effect as if they had been made to Bonner.[17]

Ridley could also with justice feel aggrieved at the treatment which his relatives received from Bonner. The kindness and hospitality which Ridley had shown, in his day of power, to Bonner's old mother and to his sister did not restrain Bonner from pursuing Ridley's brother-in-law Shipside and Alice with a malice which can have been dictated by no religious or political motive, but only by the bitterness which Bonner felt for the sufferings which had been inflicted on him in King Edward's days. His attitude is shown by the letter which he wrote on 6th September 1553 to Shirley and the Letchmores. He directed them to eject Shipside from his office as keeper of the Bishop's parks, and wrote:

* As to this, see Chapter X, pp. 405–6.

So I would ye did order all things at Kidmerley and Bushley at your pleasures; not suffering sheep's head nor Ship's side to be any meddler there, or to sell or carry away anything from thence; and I trust at your coming up now at the Parliament, I shall so handle both the said sheep's heads and the other calves' heads, that they shall perceive their sweet shall not be without sour sauce.[18]

Shipside and Alice and her three children were consequently plunged into poverty.[19]

In the middle of September, Cranmer was arrested and sent to the Tower. He was charged with high treason for his support of Jane Grey, and with sedition for having circulated a document protesting against the celebration of the old Mass in Canterbury Cathedral. Next day, Latimer arrived in the Tower; he had been arrested in Warwickshire, though he could easily have escaped abroad. Hooper and all the Protestant bishops, including Archbishop Holgate, were also arrested, as were increasing numbers of humbler Protestants. Some of the Protestants succeeded in escaping abroad, including Grindal and Cheke. Foreign Protestants, including Peter Martyr, Knox and John à Lasco, were allowed to leave the kingdom, and were deported during the autumn. In March 1554, all aliens were expelled from the realm. But the English Protestant leaders were caught in the trap. The King of Denmark, however, intervened on behalf of Coverdale, and he was eventually permitted to go to Denmark.

The Parliament which met in October 1553 found the Queen in a merciful mood. No Acts of Attainder were passed, and the statutes against treasons and unlawful assemblies of 1550 were repealed, while Mary, emulating for a brief period the liberalism of Somerset, again abolished all the new treasons and felonies which had been created since the accession of Henry VIII. The Queen would be merciful to everyone—except to Ridley. His sermon at Paul's Cross had roused the loyalists to fury, and everyone thought that he would be made an example. Three weeks after the execution of Northumberland and his friends, at the beginning of September, the Imperial Ambassadors wrote to the Emperor that Mary had decided to be merciful, and that Ridley would apparently be the only other person to be punished.[20] But when, in November, there came a sterner note, it was not Ridley who was selected as a victim. It was Cranmer who was tried for high treason in the Guildhall, along with Jane Grey and her husband. They all pleaded guilty, and were condemned to death; but the sentences were not carried out, and people still expected that Ridley would be executed. At the end of November, Ferdinand of Austria was informed by his agents that Ridley was about to be beheaded.[21]

But it soon became clear to Ridley what was likely to happen to him. He would not be executed for high treason, but would eventually be pardoned, along with the others, on this charge. He and the other Protestant bishops would be called to account for heresy, not for treason. For during the autumn the Queen's religious policy became clear. Parliament repealed all the statutes for the regulation of religion which had been passed in King Edward's reign, and restored the position which had existed at the death of Henry VIII.[22] This prohibited the administration of the Sacrament to the laity in both kinds and the marriage of priests. Married priests were driven from their benefices, and ruthlessly separated from their wives and children. Images, holy bread and holy water, and creeping to the Cross, were restored, and to the great delight of the people holy days were reinstated. Most important of all, the old service of the Mass was to be celebrated in every church in place of the service in the Book of Common Prayer. There was still no sign that Mary intended to burn the Protestants who did not attend the Mass; but it was clear that the doctrine of the Real Presence was to be reimposed, and that the authorities considered this to be much the most important issue between them and their opponents. At the session of Convocation in the autumn of 1553, a great disputation was held about transubstantiation. The Protestants were at a considerable disadvantage, as most of their ablest leaders had been arrested. They particularly wanted Ridley to dispute on their behalf, and they asked the Prolocutor, Weston, to permit Ridley to be brought from the Tower to Convocation to take part in the disputation along with Rogers and one or two others. Weston promised to refer this request to the Council, but if he did, Mary refused to permit it, and the Protestant case was most ably argued by John Philpot, the Archdeacon of Winchester. Six Protestants voted in Convocation against a resolution which affirmed the truth of transubstantiation, and which denounced a denial of the Real Presence as heresy; the rest of the members conformed, and made speeches in eulogy of Bonner, who was the hero of the hour.[23] Weston was brutally frank about the position: he is said to have ended the disputation by telling Philpot and his colleagues: 'You have the word, but we have the sword'.*

But if belief in the spiritual Presence was heresy, what was to happen to Ridley and the Protestant bishops? In Henry's reign, all heretics who were known to deny the truth of transubstantiation were burned. All over Europe burning was the recognized punishment for heresy. The

* Burnet, vol. II, p. 428; but the words are omitted from Foxe's full report of the disputation.

statute of 1401 had not yet been re-enacted, but under the new theory which the Protestant leaders themselves had laid down in Edward's reign, it was possible to burn heretics without statutory authority. There seemed to be no reason why the Queen should not start burning the Protestants as heretics again. The Protestant leaders expected nothing less. Ridley had long since realised that he would probably end his days at the stake.[24] Yet the situation was quite unprecedented; Mary was now confronted with heretics who had been bishops under Edward VI and had held high office in the State. The heretics who had suffered under Henry VIII were often men of humble origin, and while several people of gentle birth had been sent to the stake, it had never before been known for a bishop to be burned for heresy. To burn an artizan or labourer, or even a knight of the shire, was a different thing from burning an Archbishop of Canterbury and a Bishop of London, even a pretensed one, for the crime of expounding religious opinions which had been officially decreed in the previous reign by the King and his Council. The Emperor shrank from such a policy, and urged Mary to proceed against her enemies for treason.

Yet Mary had really no alternative except to burn the Protestant bishops if they refused to recant. The truths of the Catholic Church were again to be enforced in England; heretics who were condemned and excommunicated were again to die in the flames; and to deny the truth of the Real Presence in the Sacrament of the Altar was assuredly again to be heresy. How then could they spare the foremost champions of this heresy, the learned prelates and doctors who should have known better and had yet misled their flock, when the ignorant multitudes whom they had taught to err were to be punished for what was surely a more pardonable sin than that of Cranmer and Ridley? If the old religion was to be re-established in England and heresy was to be stamped out, then all the Protestant bishops must burn unless they would recant. From Mary's point of view, recantation was much the best solution of the difficulty. In the old days, the Catholic Church had always preferred to obtain a recantation from a heretic rather than to send him to the stake; and now the authorities were more than ever anxious to force Cranmer and Ridley and the other Protestant bishops to recant. The acid test was to be transubstantiation. A public recantation of their belief in the spiritual Presence would be enough to save them from the stake, and the Queen from the necessity of giving the unprecedented order to burn half a dozen bishops.

But Mary had another end in view which she had hitherto kept a close secret. She was not content for England to go back to the days of Henry VIII; she was determined to restore the supremacy of the Pope. So far the only hint which she had given of her intention was her declaration of 18th August 1553, when she had prohibited all preaching and religious controversy, that she herself would never renounce the religion to which she had adhered since her infancy—that is to say, since before the break with Rome. Mary was quite determined to reunite the realm with Christendom under Papal domination. She had taken Gardiner from the prison where he had lain to make him her Lord Chancellor; she would also take back his old enemy, Cardinal Pole, from the exile where he had lingered since 1532. Mary had been proclaimed as Supreme Head of the Church of England; she would use her position to purge the Church of heretical doctrine and practice, and to restore the Mass and the true faith, and then would humbly renounce the title and submit to the Pope.

Mary herself was about the only person in England who was really enthusiastically in favour of such a step. Nor were the calculating Catholic rulers of Europe in favour of it. Charles V warned Mary to be cautious, and Gardiner tried to cool her ardour. There was also a powerful body of opinion in England which otherwise supported Mary which viewed it with alarm. The nobles and gentlemen were for the most part quite ready to go to Mass again at the command of their sovereign; but a return of Papal supremacy might mean the invalidation of the grants of monastic lands which they had received by gift or purchase from Henry VIII. The confiscated property of the monks had been sold many times over in some cases, and the most Catholic landowner shrank from acknowledging the Papal supremacy over the Church if it meant that he might lose his land. Many of the most eminent of Mary's supporters, ardent Catholics though they were, had played the leading part in the suppression of the monasteries, and had been amply rewarded for it; they were prepared to support everything except the return of the monks.

Ridley was now being treated with great courtesy and attention by the Lieutenant and gaolers in the Tower. At first he had been confined under close arrest in his room, and had not been allowed to walk in the garden with the other prisoners; he had been informed that he could only leave his prison for the purpose of going to Mass. About the end of September, his treatment underwent a remarkable change. He was now permitted to go anywhere he wished in the Tower, and was in fact treated better than any of his fellow captives. This was evidently done in the hopes that he would be induced, by kind treatment, to go to Mass.[25] It was probably about this time that Mary decided not to execute Ridley as a traitor, but to treat him as a heretic;

and like all heretics, he was to be given every opportunity to recant and to attend the Mass.

According to Foxe, Ridley agreed on one occasion to attend Mass, but thereupon received a letter from Bradford, who was also imprisoned in the Tower, expostulating with him on the bad example which he was setting to all the humbler Protestants; after this, he refused to go to Mass again.[26] This statement by Foxe, who had every motive to deny, rather than to assert, the fact, cannot be lightly disregarded; but it is probably wrong. In his second conference with Latimer, Ridley stated his reasons for refusing to attend Mass even once,[27] which he would hardly have done if he had in fact already once been to Mass; while it is hardly conceivable that, after satisfying himself that he must never attend the Mass, he nevertheless went to the service. There is, however, a stronger argument, which appears to be almost conclusive, to show that Ridley never attended Mass in the Tower: his attendance at Mass was never brought out against him by his Catholic opponents and judges in any of the interviews, disputations and trials at which they sought to convert Ridley from his heretical opinions. It is certain that his judges, who repeatedly referred to the fact that he had been a pious Catholic in his youth, and had expressed sound Catholic doctrine as late as 1547 and 1548, would have confronted him with the fact that he had once attended Mass quite recently if they had known, as they would necessarily have done, that he had attended Mass in the Tower. We must therefore conclude that Ridley never went to Mass.

Some time in the late autumn of 1553, Ridley was invited by Bridges, the Lieutenant of the Tower, to dine with him at his table. There he found Sir John Bourn, the Secretary to the Council, along with Feckenham, one of

the royal chaplins, and Bridges, the brother of the Lieutenant. Chomley, the former Lord Chief Justice, who was
also imprisoned in the Tower, was likewise present. Bourn
and Feckenham began to talk about the wickedness of
heretics, and Ridley entirely agreed with them that anyone
who maintained an untrue religious opinion was a heretic.
Feckenham then went on to speak about transubstantiation,
and said that anyone who doubted it was unquestionably a
heretic. Ridley did not say a word, but ate in absolute
silence. The other Catholic doctors said that they noticed
that Ridley was saying nothing, and supposed that this was
because he agreed with Feckenham. Ridley said that he did
not agree, but that he did not feel free, in these circumstances, to express his opinions. They told him that they
were most interested to hear his views, and that he could
speak his mind quite freely; and Ridley then began to
argue with Bourn and Feckenham about the Real Presence
in the Sacrament. Bourn said that before Wyclif and Hus
no one had doubted the truth of transubstantiation; but
Ridley referred to the treatise of Bertram of Corbie, and
denied Bourn's suggestion that it was a forgery.* Bourn
then said that until about forty years ago, everybody in
Christendom had believed that Christ's Presence in the
Sacrament was carnal. Ridley replied that forty years ago
everybody accepted the supremacy of the Pope. Feckenham
at once said: 'What then?' Bourn may have thought that
this answer might convey the impression that he and Feck-

---

* This seems to have been Bourn's line of argument, unless
Bourn's words with regard to Bertram, as reported by Ridley: 'What
man was he? And when was he? And how do ye know?' (Foxe, vol. VI,
p. 436), merely indicate that Bourn had not heard of Bertram; but this
is unlikely, as Bertram's book had been published in England in 1548,
and in view of the later passages in Ridley's report of his talk with
Bourn.

enham believed in Papal supremacy, which was not yet official policy; so he hastily interrupted Feckenham, and explained that this was not a fair example: the question of Papal or royal supremacy was a positive law, not an article of faith. The discussion continued for some time, with Chomley taking the opportunity to earn his pardon by clumsy interventions on the Catholic side. At the end of the evening, Ridley complained that his books had been taken from him, and Bourn promised that he would try to arrange that they should be returned to him.[28]

While Ridley was now allowed to go wherever he would in the Tower, it was of course impossible for him to engage in any theological discussions with his fellow prisoners. He was, however, very anxious to exchange arguments with Latimer, and to formulate with his help the fundamental principles on which they would take their stand when they were charged with heresy, as it was now becoming increasingly clear that they would be. He therefore decided to enter into a secret correspondence with Latimer. Here both prisoners could rely on the fidelity of Latimer's servant, Augustine Bernher, who was in attendance on Latimer in his prison, and was most active and daring in smuggling their letters to each other.

Ridley therefore decided to put on paper his views on the Mass, which was certain to be the chief topic of argument with the commissioners who he knew would shortly be sitting in judgment on Latimer and himself. He put down his own views, and then arranged for Bernher to take the document to Latimer's prison and to return it with Latimer's comments. This furtive correspondence was published after Ridley and Latimer had been burned, and is known as the First Conference between Ridley and Latimer. Ridley formulated his reasons why they were opposed to the Mass

x

—because it was in Latin, a language which the people could not understand, and therefore precluded the people from being partakers in the Lord's Supper; and because in contravention of the commandment of Jesus and the words of St. Paul, the people did not drink the wine.[29] Both Ridley and Latimer attached great importance to the fact that the service was in a language which the people could not understand. Ridley wrote:

> There is also wanting the showing of the Lord's death, contrary to the mind of the Apostle 'As often as ye shall eat this bread and drink of this cup, ye shall show the Lord's death till he come'. What showing can be there whereas no man heareth, that is to say, understandeth what is said? No man, I mean, of the common people, for whose profit the prayer of the Church ought specially to serve.[30]

Latimer endorsed Ridley's arguments. In his long final message, he impressed upon Ridley the need for courage and steadfastness. He remembered how Shaxton, an able and learned reformer, had recanted in 1546 when they had both been arrested under suspicion of heresy. 'Fear of death', wrote Latimer, 'doth most persuade a great number. Be well ware of that argument, for it persuaded Shaxton'.[31]

During the winter, Ridley wrote a longer treatise. He smuggled this to Latimer, who returned it with his comments. This document was later published under the title of the *Second Conference between Ridley and Latimer*. It must have been written some time after the Mass was restored throughout the country on 21st December 1553, and before the date when Ridley and Latimer were put together in one prison at the beginning of February 1554. Ridley's treatise was in the form of an imaginary argument between himself and a fictitious character whom he portrayed as a follower of Antonius. Antonius had been an Arian bishop

who had persecuted Christians under King Hunericus dur-
ing the Vandal rule in North Africa in the fifth century.
Ridley obviously thought it likely that Latimer, whom he
knew to be far less learned than himself, had never heard of
Antonius, for he proceeded to tell him at some length who
Antonius was in case Latimer did not know.[32]

In his treatise, Ridley put into the mouth of the Antonian
every Catholic argument which he could think of against
the Protestant cause, and wrote his reply to them. He then
passed the document to Latimer for him to add his own
replies to the Catholic argument of the Antonian. The
Antonian is made to ask why Ridley, who has been so well
treated in prison, will not go to Mass when all men, and the
Queen herself, esteem it so highly; the reply is that he must
adhere to the truth of the Gospel. The Antonian then asks
why Ridley objects to the Mass when he used formerly to
celebrate it himself; he replies that he has publicly repented
of having once believed in the Mass, and objects to it
because it is in a language which the people cannot understand, because the Sacrament is not administered to the
laity in both kinds, and because of the false doctrine of the
Mass. On this, Latimer commented that he did not intend
to argue much at his trial, because they were both of them
certain to be burned whatever they said; they must trust to
prayer rather than to study, and bear the insults to which
they would be subjected with patience.

The third question of the Antonian was why Ridley, by
his obstinacy, endangered the unity of the Church, when he
himself had condemned the Anabaptists for doing the same
thing. Ridley replied that the unity of the Church should
certainly be preserved, but that the Mass was a Popish
device, not the Communion of the Church. As the Anabaptists had mischievously attempted to disrupt the unity of the

Church, they had been rightly condemned. Ridley was well aware that he would be asked how he could justify his resistance to authority when he had burned Anabaptists for doing the same thing; but even in his own day* there were people who asked this question in the form in which it was so often to be put by future generations—how could Ridley complain of the Catholic persecution when he himself had persecuted Anabaptists? Ridley's attitude was perfectly clear and logical. He did not object to the Church persecuting heretics, but he strongly condemned Papists for persecuting as heretics those who believed in the truth. Ridley agreed with the Catholics that heretics should be punished at the stake, but resented that he should be punished for heresy when he was innocent.

In his fourth question, the Antonian suggests that even if there is some small defect in the service of the Mass, Ridley should nevertheless attend the service, for Cyprian and Augustine had both said that a man was defiled, not by communion of Sacraments, but by consent of deeds. Ridley replied:

> If it were any one trifling ceremony, or if it were some one thing of itself indifferent, although I would wish nothing should be done in the Church which doth not edify the same, yet for the continuance of the common quietness I could be content to bear it. But forasmuch as things done in the Mass tend openly to the overthrow of Christ's institution, I judge that by no means either in word or deed I ought to consent unto it.[33]

This attitude was perfectly consistent with that which he had taken during the vestments controversy with Hooper, when he had required submission in inessentials. For Rid-

* See the pamphlet *The Displaying of the Family of Love*, published in London in 1579, and see Rogers, *On the Thirty-nine Articles*, p. 350.

ley, the Mass was not inessential, but fundamental. Latimer added a note in his usual forceful style: 'The marrow bones of the Mass are altogether there detestable'.

The Antonian asks Ridley whether he presumes to impeach the authority of Christ's Church and its General Councils.* Ridley answers that though the Church is the pillar of truth, it is composed of good men and bad men, and that if the majority of delegates at a General Council are bad men, then the decisions of the General Council will be bad; and he denies that Christ ever intended the articles of his Church to be laid down by General Councils.† The Antonian suggests that even assuming that the Mass is false, Ridley can nevertheless attend the Mass, because Jesus and the Apostles entered the Temple of the Jews; but Ridley replies that there is no authority to suggest that when Jesus and the Apostles went into the Temple they worshipped in any way which was repugnant to the word of God.[34] The Antonian asks why, if Ridley objects to the Mass because it is in Latin, he does not object to the baptism of infants being performed in Latin. To this Ridley says that while it is better for baptism to be performed in English, this is not so important as in the case of the Lord's Supper, as the new-born infant cannot in any case understand the meaning of the words.[35] Latimer added very little new to Ridley's points; he occasionally supplied an additional text, but for the most part he merely underlined Ridley's arguments, and expressed his admiration for Ridley's power of reasoning and exposition. To this last answer, however, he urged Ridley to reply that baptism too ought

* The Antonian's fifth, sixth, seventh, eighth, ninth and tenth objection (*Works*, pp. 122, 124, 125, 129–30, 131, 133).
† Ridley's answer to the fifth, eighth and ninth objection (*Works*, pp. 122–3, 130–2).

to be performed in English, though the child would be sufficiently baptised if the words were spoken in Latin.

Ridley then framed for the Antonian the last question, to which he gave the longest answer. Ought not Ridley to obey the laws of the realm and the Queen? If he does not, will he not be inciting to sedition and civil war, and must he not then expect to be punished as an enemy of his country? This was the most difficult of all the questions to answer for the authoritarian bishop who had forced Hooper to obey the State in the dispute over vestments, and who had denounced Hooper's opposition on very much the same grounds as he now put into the mouth of the Antonian. Ridley began his reply with a prayer:

> O heavenly Father, the Father of all wisdom, understanding and true strength, I beseech thee, for thy only Son our Saviour Christ's sake, look mercifully upon me wretched creature, and send thine Holy Spirit into my breast; that not only I may understand according to thy wisdom, how this pestilent and deadly dart is to be borne off, and with what answer it is to be beaten back; but also, when I must join to fight in the field for the glory of thy name, that then I, being strengthened with the defence of thy right hand, may manfully stand in the confession of thy faith and of thy truth, and continue in the same unto the end of my life, through the same our Lord Jesus Christ. Amen.*

He then turned to deal with the argument. It is right that the man who will not willingly obey God's laws should be punished; but there is a difference between a man who fails

---

* Answer to the fourteenth objection (*Works*, p. 142). This prayer became known as Bishop Ridley's prayer. It was not, as has often been stated, spoken by Ridley at the stake, but was written in the Second Conference with Latimer.

to do what is right and just, and he who refuses to obey laws which are contrary to God's word. A Christian should not respect all laws, but only such as are not contrary to God's word; he must obey his Prince, but in the Lord and never against the Lord. Elias and Christ himself were accused of sedition. The Christian must render unto the Prince that which is the Prince's, but unto God that which is God's. Ridley concluded the correspondence by telling Latimer how he was resolved to try his best to be steadfast. In his youth in Tynedale he had seen men buckle on their flimsy armour and stand ready with their spears to resist the Scots, and those who fell gave their lives in a just quarrel. So he was resolved to arm himself with spiritual weapons; they must both resist the Devil, and take up their cross and follow their captain Christ, who by his own blood had dedicated and hallowed that way which leadeth unto the Father; and he would try to suffer as manfully as the bishops who were martyred by Antonius.*

In the exchange of views between Ridley and Latimer, it was Ridley who had provided Latimer with nearly all the arguments. But Latimer had supplied Ridley with something more important. In the last resort, it was not argument, but courage, faith and constancy which were needed at this hour. The choice was clear: to recant on the Real Presence and live, or maintain their views and die; turn or burn. So many men were recanting. The Lady Elizabeth had led the way, and all the courtiers and politicians, and many of the Protestant clergy, had followed. Ridley knew the arguments in favour of this course; he had put them into the mouth of the Antonian in his treatise. He had created the character of the Antonian to represent the henchman of a persecuting bishop; but the arguments of the Antonian

* *Second Conference between Ridley and Latimer (Works, pp. 142–5).*

were not so much those of Gardiner as of the tempter Satan.
And against temptation it was not argument, but faith, that
was really needed. Here Latimer could inspire all his colleagues. It is very significant that in these days in the Tower,
when Ridley was steeling himself to face the ultimate ordeal
of the fire, it was not to his old friend Cranmer that he
turned, but to Latimer. Cranmer, too, was in the Tower,
and it would presumably have been as easy for Ridley to
get into secret communication with him as to do so with
Latimer. There may, of course, have been some factor of
which we know nothing, which made it impossible for
Ridley to write to Cranmer, and that consequently he
turned to Latimer instead. He may well have approached
Latimer and not Cranmer in the first place because of the
fact that Latimer's servant Bernher was the best available
courier, or because Ridley expected that Cranmer would
soon be executed for high treason, and would not have to
appear on a charge of heresy. But the fact that Ridley continued his correspondence with Latimer, with whom he had
never had much to do, rather than with any of the other
prisoners in the Tower is probably indicative of the help
which Latimer gave him. Ridley did not now need the
advice of Cranmer on how to manœuvre in Council or
Convocation; he wanted strength and fortitude which no
one could give him better than Latimer. Ridley had always
been a man of learning, and he would use this learning to
the last in the cause of Christ; but he had now imbued
something of the spirit of the simple artizans who in the
old days when he was still a Catholic had gone cheerfully to
the stake. The choice was Turn or Burn; he would burn.

For a short moment it seemed as if there might be a third
way out. In the first days of February, Wyatt and several
thousand Protestants from Kent were in arms on the other

side of London Bridge, and the prisoners were awaiting
their arrival at the Tower to release Ridley and his colleagues and to put Gardiner and the Catholics back in the
prisons again. But the rising failed, and the plight of the
Protestants was worse than ever. The Kent revolt against
Catholicism and the Spanish marriage drove all thoughts of
mercy from Mary's mind; a few days after Wyatt's surrender, Gardiner preached before the Queen, and begged her
to have mercy on the nation by cutting out the canker from
the Commonwealth and putting all traitors to death. Again
the life of Cranmer hung in the balance.* Jane Grey and
her husband, who had been condemned along with Cranmer, were beheaded. It was probably about this time that
the authorities ended their lenient treatment of Ridley, and
confined him once more in his prison; for he had refused to
avail himself of his opportunity to attend Mass. In one way,
however, Wyatt's revolt led to an immediate improvement
in Ridley's situation. At the beginning of February, a large
batch of prisoners arrived in the Tower, and the prisons
were so overcrowded that it was no longer possible to keep
the prisoners alone in separate rooms. Ridley was now
placed in a room together with Latimer, Cranmer and his
old chaplain Bradford.† This was a great solace to the

---

* Strype, *Cranmer*, p. 460, states that Cranmer received a pardon
in respect of his conviction for high treason; but it appears that a
pardon was never actually granted to him, and he could have been
executed for treason at any time. See Martin's statement at Cranmer's
trial for heresy in 1555, that he remained alive only by grace of the
Pope, and as a traitor was dead in law (Foxe, vol. VIII, p. 51). See
also *Acts of the Privy Council*, vol. V, p. 17 (3rd May 1554).

† Ridley's letter to Grindal, 31st May 1555 (*Works*, p. 390); but
Ridley had evidently lost his sense of time to some extent in prison. He
states that he was first in close prison for two months, then at liberty in
the Tower for about half a year, and then again returned to close
prison; but he was only in the Tower for a little over seven months.

four of them. There was no longer any need for Bernher to carry notes surreptitiously between Ridley and Latimer; they could now discuss their position, and work out a common line to put forward at their trial. Together they pored over the New Testament, making sure that there was no passage in the text which gave countenance to the doctrine of the corporal Presence.*

The four men were together for a month. The decision to put them in one room was probably a hurried one taken by someone in authority as a way of solving a pressing administrative problem. It was a great blunder. If Cranmer had not been together with his colleagues in February 1554, he would probably have recanted his heretical opinions. Until this time he had far exceeded all the other traitors in his cringing self-abasement and piteous appeals for mercy. After a month with Ridley, Latimer and Bradford, he bravely defied the commissioners at Oxford and again and again refused to recant; he only recanted after all the other three had been put to death. This was a great defeat for Mary. There was nothing which she wanted so much as Cranmer's recantation, and if Cranmer had recanted before the Commissioners in Oxford in April 1554, his life would probably have been spared and he would never have withdrawn his recantation. It has become an accepted maxim among historians that Mary was resolved to execute Cranmer for his part in the divorce of her mother, and that the heresy proceedings against him were only a means of achieving this end. This can hardly be true. No doubt the memories of Cranmer's part in the divorce did not endear him to Mary, and may well have been largely responsible for her

* Latimer's protestation at the Oxford disputation, published in Strype, *Memorials*, vol. III (ii), pp. 292–3. The relevant passage is omitted from the report of the disputation in Foxe, vol. VI, pp. 501–3.

barbarous decision at the end to burn him despite his recantation; but Mary was quite prepared to sacrifice her
personal feelings to the interests of Church and State. She
showed no resentment against Gardiner, who had played at
least as important a part as Cranmer in the divorce of
Catherine of Aragon; she had released from prison the old
Duke of Norfolk, who had treated her with such brutality
at Henry's orders in 1536, and had restored him to his
former office; she was surrounded by advisers who had
eagerly worked for the divorce at Henry's bidding. Whatever her personal feelings might be, Mary could understand,
and indeed approve, the obedience which these men had
shown to their monarch in her father's days. Cranmer was
singled out from all the rest because he was the leader of the
Reformation; he was now being proclaimed as the author
of the divorce in order to excuse the Lord Chancellor and
to show that a king could do no wrong. But as the leader
of the Reformation, the Queen was more interested in
obtaining his recantation than his death. His arrest for
treason, when so many men who had been far more prominent in their support of Jane were forgiven, his trial and
sentence as a traitor, and the failure to carry out the
sentence when Mary had only to fix the date, were all
dictated by a desire to force a recantation from him.
Nothing would have demoralised the Protestants so much
as a recantation by their leader; but when the recantation
came at last, it was too late to be of much value to the
Queen.

On 8th March 1554, the authorities decided that Ridley,
Latimer and Cranmer should be sent to Oxford to hold a
disputation on the Real Presence with the most learned
Catholic doctors of Oxford and Cambridge.[36] This was
doubtless welcome news to Cranmer and Ridley; it meant a

temporary reprieve for Cranmer, who would not, after all, be executed for treason, and Ridley must have been delighted to have an opportunity of publicly vindicating his belief in the spiritual Presence, which no one had been able to defend in public since it had been discussed in Convocation in the autumn. Latimer was not so happy; he was nearly seventy, and tired and ill, and though he was more ready than any of them to suffer for his faith, he did not trust his skill in disputation with the most learned of his opponents.

The Queen and the Council had planned this great disputation to discredit the Protestant leaders and their doctrine of the spiritual Presence, and if possible to induce them to recant. From the Catholic point of view, Cranmer and Ridley had done much harm. For four years they had spread this heresy throughout the kingdom to mislead the people, and many erring sheep had strayed from the flock as a result of their teaching. The humble artizans and labourers who denied the truth of transubstantiation could not hold their own in argument with their learned inquisitors, but they could all endorse the views and arguments of the leading Protestant champions even if they did not fully understand them. In the old days, the ignorant heretics had always been told that unlettered labourers such as they could not understand the subtleties of theological argument, but should accept the conclusions which learned doctors had reached, and not presume to challenge them. But now they could reply that men like Cranmer and Ridley, who were as learned as any of their examiners, agreed with them; they could base their faith on the fact that the learned Protestant prelates had decided, after examining all the books, that Christ was not carnally present in the Sacrament of the Altar. It was therefore necessary for the government to show them all that Cranmer and Ridley were wrong, and to announce to the people that after a full and solemn disputation the views of the ablest Protestant leaders had been found to be false and heretical. It was for this reason that transubstantiation had been debated at such length in the session of Convocation in 1553; but there the Protestants had not been represented by their foremost disputants, and they had suggested that if Ridley had been allowed to participate in the disputation in Convocation, they would have proved their case beyond all doubt. The Council therefore decided that Cranmer, Ridley and Latimer must be forced to participate in the disputation at Oxford.

It seemed, however—despite some ambiguity in Bonner's commission to the commissioners who were to hold the disputation—that the commissioners would be entitled to condemn Ridley, Cranmer and Latimer as heretics, and to excommunicate them. This would mean that, as excommunicated heretics, they would be liable to be burned. The disputation was therefore something very different from that other disputation which had been held before Ridley in Cambridge in 1549, when neither side risked anything more than to be condemned as wrong by the Prolocutor; this time, one side was to appear at the disputation as prisoners to face the danger of the stake. The Oxford disputation of 1554 was something without precedent during the century—an extraordinary mixture of a disputation and a trial. But whatever the niceties of the position in law, the three Protestant leaders were well aware that if they refused to recant in the disputation, they would burn.

On 10th March, Cranmer, Latimer and Ridley were taken from the Tower to Oxford in the custody of Sir John

Williams.* They were not allowed to send on any of their personal effects or books, but were permitted to take with them anything which they could carry on their horses. They rode to Windsor, where they spent the night, and went on to Oxford next day. There they were all three placed in the common gaol, which was known as Bocardo.† The Protestant historians have been very indignant at the fact that Cranmer, Ridley and Latimer were imprisoned in Bocardo along with thieves and harlots; but the three were much too important prisoners to be put together with the common criminals, and it is quite clear that they never came into contact with them.

In Bocardo, Ridley, Cranmer and Latimer were allowed the use of their personal servants. They were also permitted pen and paper. It is not certain whether they were imprisoned together in the same place of confinement, as they

* Foxe gave the date as 10th April (see Foxe, vol. VI, *App.*, p. 761), having stated that the order to bring them to Oxford was received by the Lieutenant of the Tower on 10th March; but this is clearly wrong, and it is probably a mistake for 10th March—two days after the order to take them to Oxford was sent to the Lieutenant of the Tower. Ridley, in his letter to Grindal (*Works*, p. 390) states that they were brought to Oxford 'a little before Easter', which was on 25th March, though Ridley was certainly wrong in writing that the disputation was held about Whitsun, this shows clearly that he was not brought to Oxford only four days before the disputation opened. Peter Martyr in Strasburg had heard the news of their journey to Oxford by 3rd April. Lever in Geneva was told the news by a man who left London on 13th March, though his informant was wrong in telling him that Sir James Hales had gone with them to Oxford. See Martyr's letter to Bullinger, 3rd April 1554, and Lever's letter to Bullinger, 11th April 1554 (*Original Letters*, pp. 515, 154). See also *Machyn's Diary*, p. 57.

† Ridley's letter to Grindal, 31st May 1555 (*Works*, p. 390); Foxe, vol. VI, p. 439. There is no doubt that all three prisoners were originally imprisoned in Bocardo; see Ridley's letters to Bradford (*Works*, p. 360), and to West, dated from Bocardo, 8th April 1554 (*Works*, p. 342). This is also implied by Foxe, vol. VI, p. 440.

had been in the Tower; but they were certainly permitted to walk together on the parapet on the northern side of Bocardo, which was on the northern wall of the city. Here they could be seen by people in the street, and their friends and supporters could approach them, and perhaps make some sign of support if they dared to do so. But within less than a month, the conditions of their captivity became harsher. One night a piece of coal fell out of the fireplace in the bailiff's house, and burned a hole in the floor before the servants could extinguish it, and a few nights later there was a drunken brawl in the street outside, and a man was arrested for his part in it. These incidents gave rise to rumours in the town that Ridley, Cranmer and Latimer had been trying to escape, and that their attempt had only been thwarted by the energy of the bailiffs. Soon afterwards, the prisoners were forbidden to take exercise on the wall of Bocardo.

Apparently the doctors of the University, who were losing no chance of vilifying Ridley and his colleagues in their daily conversation, had something to do with this; they apparently feared that the Protestant sympathisers in Oxford would get into contact with their leaders on the parapet. Cranmer, Ridley and Latimer were strictly forbidden to receive any visitors, and their servants were not allowed to go out into the town and the surrounding country as they had previously been permitted to do.* A few days after-

* Ridley's letter to Bradford (*Works*, pp. 359–60), where the letter is reprinted from Coverdale's *Letters of the Martyrs*, and more fully in Foxe, vol. VII, pp. 424–5. Gloucester Ridley, p. 554, places the date of this letter as the end of November 1554, and considers that the Bishop of Worcester's journey through Oxford referred to by Ridley was the occasion when Heath passed through Oxford on his way from Worcester to London to attend Parliament in November 1554; but this seems impossible in view of the fact that Ridley was in Bocardo

wards, their servants were removed altogether; but they were each supplied with another man—a stranger—to act as their servants.* The presence of a servant might facilitate their attempts at escape and their communications with the other Protestants; but it was unthinkable that men of rank, even if they were the worst of heretics, should be deprived of the use of a servant.

Ridley had not yet been deprived of pen and paper,† and about the beginning of April he wrote to Bradford, whom he had left behind in the Tower. He told him about their conditions in Bocardo; it was now, he wrote, a college of quondams. He mentioned that Heath, who had been restored as Bishop of Worcester, had travelled through Oxford, but had not visited them in prison, and he noted that it was on the very day that Heath had been in the town that the conditions of their imprisonment had become so much worse, and that the Book of the Communion Service had been taken from them at the orders of the Mayor. Ridley evidently had no idea of what the authorities had in

with Cranmer and Latimer when he wrote this letter, because in his letter to Grindal in May 1555, Ridley wrote that since the disputation of April 1554, he and Cranmer and Latimer had been kept in different prisons. See also the references in Ridley's letter to Bradford to the examination of Taylor and (in the fuller version in Foxe) to Hooper's deprivation; and see Notes to *Bradford's Works*, vol. II, pp. 82–3, where however, the Notes are certainly wrong in stating that 'my Lord of Worcester' mentioned in Ridley's letter, is Pates.

* Ridley's letter to Grindal, 31st May 1555 (*Works*, p. 390); Ridley's *Account of the Disputation at Oxford* (*Works*, p. 306). Both passages make it clear that the servants were changed before the disputation, and this must therefore have occurred during the period of about a week which elapsed between the date of Ridley's letter to Bradford (*Works*, pp. 358–60), and the beginning of the disputation on 14th April 1554.

† Ridley was not deprived of pen and paper until after the disputation (see *Account of the Disputation at Oxford, Works*, p. 306).

store for them; he had heard from Bradford that there was a rumour in London that the three Protestant leaders were to be brought back from Oxford to London, but Ridley had heard that other eminent Protestant prisoners were going to be brought to join them in Oxford.[37]

At about the same time, Ridley received a letter from West, who had been one of Ridley's chaplains when he was Bishop of London. West had recanted, and had retained his preferments, and now, probably at the suggestion of the authorities, he wrote to Ridley urging him to recant to save his life. Ridley wrote a long reply on 8th April. The tone of his letter was friendly, but firm. He told West that he did not fear death, but that if he recanted he would have much to fear hereafter. He admitted that he had never been in favour of unnecessary innovation in religion for its own sake, and that he still considered confession to be a beneficial practice. West had written that he had always greatly admired Ridley's doctrine and preaching, except on the matter of the Sacrament; on this subject, West wrote, he had never really been convinced by Ridley. Ridley replied that if it were not for the changed circumstances he would be amazed at this statement of West. West had never before given the slightest indication of this, and Ridley would not write what he thought about the reasons for West's statement, as West would not care what he said, as he could do him neither good nor harm; but he did mention that West had promised him in the past that he would set forth the word of God, and that formerly all learned men had believed that common prayer in the Church should be held in a language which all men could understand. He ended his letter:

And because, I dare say, you wrote of friendship unto me this short, earnest advertisement, and, I think, verily wishing me

Y

to live and not to die; therefore, bearing you in my heart no
less love in God than you do me in the world, I say unto you
in the word of the Lord (and that I say to you I say to all my
friends and lovers in God) that if you do not confess and
maintain, to your power and knowledge, that which is
grounded upon God's word, but will, either for fear or gain
of the world, shrink and play the Apostata, indeed you shall
die the death; you know what I mean. And I beseech you all,
my true friends and lovers in God, remember what I say;
for this may be the last time peradventure that ever I shall
write unto you.*

While Ridley, Cranmer and Latimer were in Bocardo, in
complete ignorance as to what was going to happen to them,
the preparations for the disputation had been completed.
The commissioners for the disputation were presided over
by Dr. Weston as Prolocutor. He had spent several years in
prison under Edward VI, and was a singularly unpleasant
man. The other commissioners and disputants were all Oxford or Cambridge doctors. The Cambridge doctors included many of Ridley's old acquaintances. There was old
Croke, from whom Ridley had learned Greek as an undergraduate thirty-five years before; Young, who was now
Master of Pembroke Hall and Vice-Chancellor of the
University; and Glyn, who with Young had disputed before

* Ridley's letter to West (*Works*, pp. 337–42). In Coverdale's
Letters of the Martyrs, f. 43, the date is given as 8th April 1554. Foxe
(vol. VII, p. 433) gives the date as 8th April 1555; Gloucester Ridley,
p. 582, gives it as 18th April 1555. But Strype, *Cranmer App.*, pp.
964–8, publishing the copy from Foxe's MSS. gives the date as 8th
April 1554, and this seems much more likely. It is dated 'from Bocardo'
in all editions, and there is no reason to believe that Ridley was taken
back to Bocardo in April 1555; indeed, this possibility seems to be
excluded by Ridley's letter to Grindal in May 1555, written from
Irish's house (*Works*, p. 390), where Ridley states that since the disputation he has been kept separate from Cranmer, who was in Bocardo.

Ridley in the disputation at Cambridge in 1549. Feckenham
was one of the Oxford doctors. Cranmer, Ridley and Latimer were kept in prison while their adversaries received
honorary degrees from the University and took part in
formalities and feasts; but after five weeks together in
Bocardo, the three were separated on 13th April. Ridley
was removed to the house of Master Irish, who was one of
the Aldermen of Oxford; Latimer was taken to another
house, while Cranmer remained in Bocardo. Next day, on
Saturday, 14th April, they were brought before the commissioners, who were sitting in St. Mary's Church.[38]

The three prisoners were called before the commissioners
one by one—first Cranmer, then Ridley, then Latimer.
When it was Ridley's turn, he entered, bowed to Weston
and his colleagues, and stood before them. Weston then read
out three propositions which were to be the subject of the
disputation: the first, that in the Sacrament of the Altar, by
the virtue of God's word spoken of the priest, the natural
body of Christ, born of the Virgin Mary, and his natural
blood are really present under the forms of bread and wine;
the second, that after the consecration there remaineth no
substance of bread and wine, neither any other substance,
than the substance of God and man; the third, that in the
Mass is the lively sacrifice of the Church, propitiable and
available for the sins as well of quick as of the dead. Ridley
was asked whether he admitted or denied these propositions; he said that they were all false, and sprung from a
sour and bitter fruit. He was then asked whether he could
deny that in his sermon at Paul's Cross in 1547, when he
attacked the Protestant sects who reviled the Sacrament,
he had stated that Christ was corporally present in the
bread and wine. Ridley denied that he had said this at
Paul's Cross, and challenged the Prolocutor to produce a

witness who could say that he had heard Ridley say any such thing. He was also confronted with his conversation with Gardiner in February 1548. Weston then told him to write out his arguments against the propositions that evening, and to be ready to dispute on Tuesday the 17th.* Ridley asked for more time to prepare for the disputation, and complained that he had not got enough books to prepare his case. Weston promised to provide him with all the books he required, but refused to postpone the date of the disputation. Ridley then withdrew, and Latimer was brought in.[39] A similar procedure had been adopted with Cranmer, and was now adopted with Latimer, but Cranmer's disputation was fixed for the Monday, and Latimer's for the Wednesday.

The commissioners, the Catholic disputants and the three prisoners themselves seem to have realised that Ridley would be the most formidable of the three in the disputation. He was more learned than Latimer, and more skilful in disputation even than Cranmer, and he had also the advantage of his two friends in age. He was now fifty, and well advanced into middle age, but he was still active in mind and body, and neat and smart in his appearance and dress. Cranmer and Latimer were about fifteen years older than Ridley;† unlike Ridley and Latimer, Cranmer had been utterly dejected in spirit a few months earlier, while Latimer, ever since his accident ten years before, had suffered badly in his health. But Cranmer and Latimer had both benefited considerably from their discussions with Ridley in the Tower.

* Different editions of Foxe give different dates, but it was almost certainly on Tuesday, 17th April that Ridley disputed (see Cranmer's letter to the council, 23rd April, 1554, Cranmer's *Works*, vol. II, p. 445).

† For the conflict of evidence as to Latimer's age, see Chester, *Hugh Latimer*, pp. 2–3.

The three prisoners were at a considerable disadvantage in the disputation. The commissioners and the Catholic disputants together numbered some twenty leading doctors of divinity, and all were arrayed against each of the Protestant leaders, who were to argue alone against them. Their opponents had obviously been given much longer notice of the exact terms of the propositions to be disputed, and they had none of the difficulties which the prisoners had in getting hold of the books which they needed. The disputation was to take place before an audience of several hundred doctors and undergraduates of Oxford, who were all good Catholics now, whatever they might have been a year ago, and were eager to show their detestation of heretical doctrines by hissing and insulting the prisoners. For Latimer, there was the further disadvantage that the disputation was to be held in Latin, and he no longer felt sufficiently at home in the language to dispute in Latin. As it turned out, the commissioners allowed Latimer to dispute in English.

Cranmer disputed on the Monday. He showed none of the hesitation which his adversaries probably expected in view of the cringing attitude which he had adopted in the autumn; he argued with great skill, and greatly angered his opponents, while the audience interrupted and hissed him repeatedly. On Tuesday, it was Ridley's turn. He was brought before the commissioners, who were now sitting in the Divinity Schools.[40] He began by objecting that he had not had enough time to prepare his statement of his case, and asked for leave to amend the statement if necessary. Weston said that he could amend it at any time before next Sunday. He was then told that he could choose two notaries to assist him by taking notes of what was said at the disputation, and was offered the two who had assisted

Cranmer the day before. Ridley agreed to take them, and said that he hoped that they were honest men. They were honest, and brave men too. They were Mounson and Jewel. It needed courage to act for Cranmer and Ridley in a disputation at Oxford. The University had already begun a vigorous campaign against heresy. Undergraduates suspected of holding Protestant views were being whipped, and any Fellow or doctor who showed heretical tendencies ran the risk of more serious punishment. Soon after the disputation, Jewel thought it prudent to slip away from Oxford, and escape abroad, and it seems that the authorities were considering arresting him at the time of his flight.[41]

At the beginning of the disputation, Ridley started to read out a statement of his reasons for opposing the three propositions and denying the corporal Presence. He was soon stopped by Weston, who told him that he had already submitted his views in writing, and was here today to dispute with his opponents. Ridley said that he had only a few words which he wished to say, and persisted in summarising his objections to the propositions. Despite the protests of the Catholic disputants, Weston allowed him to continue, but he urged him to be brief. Ridley then continued to read out his reasons for denying the propositions. They were contrary to the writings of the Gospels; they contravened the true significance of the Lord's Supper; they taught the people to believe in unnecessary miracles for which there was no authority in Scripture, and strengthened the views of the heretics who erred concerning the two natures of Christ; they led to the belief that dogs and swine, who might chance to eat the consecrated Host, were partakers of the Sacrament; and if true, they meant that the congregation who partook of the Lord's Supper were cannibals like the Anthropophagi of Africa. At this there was a great uproar among the audience, and one of the Catholic disputants cried out that Ridley was speaking blasphemies. Weston then said that he had spoken far too long already, and he was not allowed to continue. Ridley had hardly been accurate when he told Weston that he only wished to read out a 'few words'; his statement was about six thousand words in length. It seems that he was stopped at the point when he referred to the cannibalism of the Catholic doctrine. This means that Weston allowed him to continue for about five minutes after the Catholic doctors had first protested against Ridley reading out the statement.

Dr. Smith, the first of the Catholic spokesmen, then began to dispute with Ridley about the Real Presence. Ridley said that there was some ambiguity in the phrase the 'Real Presence'; he thought that Christ was really present in the consecrated bread and wine, because something appertaining to his body was present by grace; but he was not present in a corporal sense. Weston may have thought that Ridley was trying to find a loophole for escape, for he intervened to make the issue clear; although he wanted a recantation from Ridley, it must be an unequivocal, not an evasive, one. Weston said that when they spoke of Christ's body being present in the Sacrament, they meant that body which he took of the Virgin. Ridley had no intention at all of evading the issue; he merely wanted it clearly defined. He was perfectly prepared to oppose the propositions when they were clarified in this fashion.

The disputation then continued for the rest of the morning, chiefly on the question of the authority of the early Fathers. They cited Augustine, Chrysostom, Bernard, Theophylact, Justin, Tertullian and Cyprian; but when Ridley attempted to cite a passage from Theophylact to support his view that the bread was converted into the flesh of

Christ, not by transubstantiation but by sacramental converting or turning, the uproar in the hall was so great that
he was compelled to abandon his line of argument. The
Catholic doctors also argued with Ridley on the basis of
reason. They discussed whether Christ could be carnally
present in the Sacrament when he was in Heaven, and
whether, when seen by Paul, he was on earth, or, being in
Heaven, revealed himself to Paul on earth; and they disagreed in their interpretation of the passage from Augustine:
'He was carried in his own hands'.

The commissioners and the Catholic doctors grew increasingly impatient with Ridley during the course of the
disputation, while the University men in the audience were
continually interrupting Ridley's arguments with jeers and
insults. Weston does not seem to have made the slightest
attempt to check the interruptions; but for several hours
Ridley stood his ground alone against his twenty opponents
and their jeering followers without once weakening in his
argument. It was worst of all when Tresham was disputing
with him. Tresham said that he dishonoured his Father in
Heaven and polluted his mother the Church on earth;
Ridley replied that Tresham polluted his school by such
words. Tresham then referred to the decision of the Council
of Lateran in favour of transubstantiation, and mentioned
that three hundred bishops and seventy metropolitans had
attended the Council of Lateran, along with many other
churchmen, and that if anyone contradicted their pronouncement he was no child of the Church, but a heretic.
Ridley said that while it was true that all these bishops had
been present at the Council, it had also been attended by
eight hundred abbots, priors and friars. At this, one of the
notaries who was writing down what was said could not
contain himself; he shouted out: 'What! Will you deny then

the authority of that Council for the multitude of those priors?' Ridley answered that he denied the authority of the Council of Lateran, not so much for this reason, as because its decision did not agree with God's word, and was held under Innocent III, whom the historians showed to be most pernicious to the Church and Commonwealth of Christ. Tresham seized on this damning statement and cried: 'What! Do you not receive the Council of Lateran?' Then, turning to the notaries, he said: 'Write! Write!' Ridley was unperturbed; he answered: 'No Sir, I receive not that Council; write, and write again!'

Eventually the time arrived for Weston to close the hearing. He did so by stating the truth of the corporal Presence in the Sacrament: 'That which the woman did hold in her womb, the same thing holdeth the priest'. Ridley replied by immediately summarizing his own position: 'I grant the priest holdeth the same thing, but after another manner. She did hold the natural body; the priest holdeth the mystery of the body'. Weston then ended the day's proceedings with these words: 'Here you see the stubborn, the vainglorious, the crafty, the unconstant mind of this man. You see today that the strength of the truth is irresistible. So let us cry together: "Truth is victorious!"'*

And they all called out together: 'Truth is victorious!'

Latimer was called next day. He was unable to dispute in the way in which Cranmer and Ridley had done, but he defiantly asserted his belief in the spiritual Presence, and enraged his opponents and the audience beyond measure. At the end of the day, Weston told him that he would not

---

* '*Videtis praefractum hominis animum, gloriosum, vafrum, inconstantem; videtis hodie veritatis vires inconcussas. Itaque clamate, Vicit veritas.*' This passage has been translated, in the text, into more modern English than that used by Foxe. All the other passages cited in the account of the disputation are in Foxe's translation.

be so happy when he had a fagot stuck in his beard, but that the Queen might well show mercy if he would turn. Latimer said that he would never turn, but that he prayed continually that the Queen would turn.

Three days after he had argued before the commissioners, on Friday the 20th, Ridley was again called before them, this time together with Cranmer and Latimer in St. Mary's Church. They were all informed that their opinions were heretical, and that unless they recanted and accepted the three propositions they would be condemned as heretics and excommunicated. Cranmer tried to argue, but was told that he could only answer 'Yes' or 'No' to the questions as to whether they would agree to the propositions. Weston then earnestly entreated them to turn and remain in the bosom of the Church. They each refused. Ridley said: 'Although I be not of your company, yet doubt I not but my name is written in another place, whither this sentence will send us sooner than we should by the course of nature have come'; and Cranmer and Latimer made similar statements. Weston concluded the proceedings by saying: 'If you go to Heaven in this faith, then I will never come thither, as I am thus persuaded'. The prisoners were then separated and taken back to their places of detention.[42]

The three Protestant leaders had been condemned; they were now to be humiliated. Next day, on Saturday, 21st April, the proceedings terminated with a procession through the streets of Oxford, with Weston carrying the Host aloft, and all the people kneeling to adore it. Ridley, Cranmer and Latimer were forced to watch the procession, to see the Host adored again by the people of Oxford, to witness the utter defeat of all their hopes and the triumph of their enemies. Ridley was taken to the door of his prison in Alderman Irish's house, and Cranmer watched from the gaol of Bocardo; it had been specially arranged for the pro-procession to pass by these places so that the two arch-heretics could see it. Latimer was taken by his guards to watch the procession from the Carfax, but as it passed he broke loose from his escort, and rushed into a shop so that he could not see.[43]

NOTES

[1] *Letters Patent for the Limitation of the Crown* (published in *Queen Jane's Chronicle*, pp. 91–100).

[2] Letter of the Imperial Ambassadors to Charles V, 10th July 1553 (*Calendar of Spanish State Papers*, vol. XI, p. 80).

[3] Foxe, vol. VI, p. 387.

[4] *Chronicles of Queen Jane*, p. 8.

[5] Letter of the Imperial Ambassadors to Charles V, 11th July 1553 (*Calendar of Spanish State Papers*, vol. XI, p. 83).

[6] The Imperial Ambassadors' letter to Charles V, 16th July 1553 (*Calendar of Spanish State Papers*, vol. XI, pp. 91–2).

[7] *Greyfriars Chronicle*, p. 81.

[8] *Acts of the Privy Council*, vol. IV, p. 301 (21st July 1553).

[9] Foxe, vol. VI, p. 390.

[10] *Greyfriars Chronicle*, p. 81; Wriothesley's *Chronicle*, vol. II, p. 91; letter of the Imperial Ambassadors to Charles V, 27th July 1553 (*Calendar of Spanish State Papers*, vol. XI, pp. 119–20); *Machyn's Diary*, p. 38.

[11] The Imperial Ambassadors' letter to Charles V, 22nd July 1553 (*Calendar of Spanish State Papers*, vol. XI, p. 114).

[12] Foxe, vol VI, pp. 387, 392; Burnet, vol. II, pp. 382, 393–4.

[13] Foxe, vol. VI, pp. 391–2.

[14] See Bonner's letter to Shirley and Richard and Roger Letchmore, 6th September 1553 (Burnet's *Records*, vol. V, p. 373).

[15] Attwater, *Pembroke College Cambridge*, pp. 40–1.

[16] See the account of the Oxford disputation by an anonymous eye-witness, published in Foxe, vol. VI, *App.*, Document No. III.

[17] *Cal. Pat. Rolls Ph. & M.*, vol. I, p. 121 (2nd March 1553/4).

[18] Bonner's letter to Shirley and the Letchmores (Burnet's *Records*, vol. V, p. 373).

[19] Foxe, vol. VII, p. 409.

[20] The Imperial Ambassadors' letter to Charles V, 9th September 1553 (*Calendar of Spanish State Papers*, vol. XI, p. 216).

[21] Games' letter to the King of the Romans, 28th November 1553 (*Calendar of Spanish State Papers*, vol. XI, p. 398).

[22] *Statutes of the Realm*, 1 Mary, st. 2, c. 2.

[23] Foxe, vol. VI, pp. 395–411.

[24] Humphrey, *Life of Jewel*, pp. 258–9. (See Chapter VII, p. 246.)

[25] Ridley's letter to Grindal, 31st May 1555 (*Works*, p. 390); *Chronicles of Queen Jane*, p. 27.

[26] Foxe, vol. VIII, p. 708.

[27] Second Conference between Ridley and Latimer (*Works*, pp. 118–9).

[28] Ridley, *Conferences between Ridley and Secretary Bourn and Others* (Foxe, vol. VI, pp. 434–8; *Works*, pp. 155–65).

[29] See *First Conference between Ridley and Latimer* (*Works*, pp. 103–10).

[30] *First Conference between Ridley and Latimer* (*Works*, p. 104). The passages cited are taken from the 1556 edition, with the spelling modernised.

[31] *First Conference between Ridley and Latimer* (*Works*, p. 115).

[32] *Second Conference between Ridley and Latimer* (*Works*, p. 147).

[33] *Second Conference between Ridley and Latimer* (*Works*, p. 121).

[34] The twelfth objection (*Works*, pp. 137–40).

[35] The thirteenth objection (*Works*, pp. 140–1).

[36] *Acts of the Privy Council*, vol. IV, p. 406 (8th March 1553–4).

[37] Ridley's letter to Bradford (*Works*, pp. 358–60).

[38] Foxe, vol. VI, pp. 439–41.

[39] Foxe, vol. VI, pp. 442–3.

[40] See Foxe, vol. VI, pp. 470–500, for the report of the disputation.

[41] Mallet, *History of Oxford University*, vol. II, p. 96.

[42] Foxe, vol. VI, pp. 533–4.

[43] Foxe, vol. VI, p. 534.

IX

OXFORD

The three prisoners in Oxford now prepared themselves for death. They had no idea how long they would be kept alive, but there was reason to believe that their execution would not be long delayed. It would take at least a week for the Queen to sign the warrant and fix the date for their death; but at any time after the end of April, they must expect to die in the fire. They must often have wondered what would happen when the fagots were lit. Death by burning varied greatly with the circumstances. The condemned heretic was allowed to get some gunpowder from his friends, and hang it in a bag around his neck, so that when the flames reached the bag it would explode, and blow the victim at once to oblivion. Even without the gunpowder, the sufferer might be suffocated quite rapidly by the smoke. But sometimes the fire burned slowly, and did not reach the gunpowder, or if the powder was damp, it did not always explode. Death at the stake might well be comparatively easy, or it might be a prolonged and most horrible agony; it all depended on the state of the fagots, and on the wind and smoke.

Ridley and Latimer had resigned themselves to death in the fire however it might come to them; and Cranmer, too, was steadfast at this time. Ten years before, in Henry's reign, Ridley and Cranmer had dissembled and manœuvred; they had spoken only when they thought it safe to do so, and then had said only a little of what they thought; they had defended the Mass, and had themselves held up the Host for adoration, for some years after they became convinced that it was wrong, while they waited for the right tactical moment for publicly professing their views. Latimer had always been more outspoken; but he had recanted twenty-three years before, when he had been arrested on a charge of heresy, and had accepted a bishopric against his conscience in order to further the Reformation. But things were very different now. In King Henry's time, the royal policy had chopped and changed, moving at one time against the Pope and at another against the Protestants; Cranmer was high in favour then, and there was much to be gained by courting the royal pleasure. Now the Queen and Gardiner and Bonner were their bitter enemies, and the time for compromise had gone. They had led the realm to a Protestant Reformation under Edward, and had nailed their colours to the mast; and a submission and recantation, to which Mary was so eager to force them, would have dispirited all the growing number of Protestants who looked to them for leadership. To suffer martyrdom was the best service which they could now render to their cause. And each of them derived strength and fortitude from the example of his colleagues, even when they were no longer together. Alone, any of them—and certainly, as events were later to prove, their leader Cranmer—might have weakened; together none could desert his brothers, and all three were firm and resolute. Neither Ridley nor Latimer ever thought of turning to escape the fire.

On 23rd April 1554—three days after he had been condemned—Ridley wrote to Weston, who had already left Oxford. He reminded Weston that he had promised to send Ridley a copy of the transcript of the disputation which his notaries Jewel and Mounson had taken down, but that Weston had not kept his promise, perhaps because of his hasty departure from Oxford. Ridley also sent Weston some

written submissions on the second and third of the propositions which had been discussed in the disputation, pointing
out that Weston had promised that he could submit a
further statement in writing. He stated that he was now
doing so because he had not been able to develop his case
to the full at the disputation, and he asked Weston to present his document to the higher house of Convocation, and
especially to Gardiner, Tunstall, Thirlby, Heath and Day,
and also to Goodrich, who had submitted to Mary and had
been permitted to retain his see of Ely. It appears that
Weston did not submit Ridley's statement to the bishops,
and he certainly did not send him a copy of the transcript
of the disputation.[1] He was not the man to do anything to
oblige a heretic, and was perhaps annoyed at the tone of
Ridley's letter; for the letter, though courteous, was not
submissive. Ridley wrote that a righteous judge performed
his promises, and informed Weston that Alderman Irish and
the bailiffs were witnesses to the fact that he was sending
his written statement to Weston.[2]

A few days later, Ridley wrote a letter to Cranmer, which
was carried by Ridley's servant. He wrote that he regretted
that he had not been able to discuss with Cranmer his
written statement on the points at issue in the disputation.
He mentioned that he had heard a rumour that Morgan,
the judge who had condemned Lady Jane Grey and Cranmer for treason, had gone mad; and he put forward suggestions as to how they could communicate with one
another through their servants. At the foot of his letter,
Ridley expressed the problem which confronted all of them
in three words: Turn or Burn.[3]

Meanwhile the Queen and the Council were considering
what to do with Ridley, Cranmer and Latimer. There were
certain legal difficulties in the way of burning them. The

statute of 1401 had not yet been re-enacted, and while the Protestants had burned Anabaptists under the common law, the legality of this procedure was not free from doubt. There was, moreover, some doubt as to whether Bonner's commission to Weston and his colleagues for the Oxford disputation had authorised them to excommunicate the three Protestant leaders. The Council decided, on 3rd May, to ask the judges and Queen's Counsel for an opinion as to the legal position of the three men.[4] Presumably the judges and Queen's Counsel were doubtful whether Cranmer, Latimer and Ridley could be burned, and advised against it. Weston was indignant that the extirpation of heresy should be held up by legal subtleties, and suggested that all heretics should be burned, and their friends left to bring an action about it afterwards;[5] but Mary evidently decided that she could not order the heretics to be burned until the legality of so doing was more clearly established. The three men in Oxford knew nothing of this. They were daily expecting to be told the date of their death.*

Ridley was now imprisoned in the house of Alderman Irish, who became Mayor of Oxford at Michaelmas 1554.[6] The house was situated on the north side of Oxford, a little to the south of Bocardo and the city walls.† Ridley, like

* Ridley's letter to Cranmer, April 1554 (*Works*, p. 363). Latimer expected—very unreasonably—to be burned the day after the conclusion of the disputation, when he was taken out to watch the procession of the Host through Oxford (Foxe, vol. VI, p. 534).

† When Ridley walked from Irish's house to the stake, he passed Bocardo (Foxe, vol. VII, p. 548), which shows that the house must have been on the south side of Bocardo. Irish had a garden near the site of the old priory of the Austin Friars in the parish of St. Mary Magdalene; see sale of house by Owen to Martyn on 10th July 1550 (Salter, *Oxford City Properties*, p. 258), where the house is described as being opposite the old priory and bounded on the west side by Alderman Irish's garden.

Extract from a letter (in Latin) to Bradford, written by Ridley from prison early in 1555. It is the letter published in *Works* pp. 537–41

Preaching at Paul's Cross. The Cross was situated much closer to the Cathedral than is shown in this picture painted in 1616

An old engraving showing the Martyrdom of Latimer and Ridley

Latimer in the bailiff's house and Cranmer in Bocardo, was
kept at the expense of the city of Oxford, which was peti-
tioning the Council to be repaid the cost of maintaining
the three prisoners. They were well supplied with food,
eating regularly goose, larks, and all kinds of meat and
poultry, and cheese and fruit, and each drinking a penny-
worth of wine with each meal—that is to say, about a pint
—as well as ale.* They also received food and other gifts
from their friends and admirers who were at liberty—particularly from the Duchess of Suffolk, from Lady Vane, and
other ladies.[7] But in other respects the conditions were
harsh. Ridley was forbidden to receive any visitors, and on
at least three occasions his friends who called at Irish's
house to see him were prevented from doing so.† He was,
however, occasionally visited by people who had obviously
been sent by the authorities to see him. Immediately after
the disputation in April 1554, Ridley was visited by Glyn

---

* *Acts of the Privy Council*, vol. V, p. 17 (3rd May 1554); *Oxford City
Records*, pp. 228–32; Strype, *Cranmer*, pp. 562–3. Strype (*op. cit.*, p. 562)
and Gloucester Ridley, p. 514, state that Ridley, Cranmer and Latimer
all dined and supped together; but there is no indication in Ridley's
letters that he ever saw Cranmer or Latimer between April 1554 and
October 1555, and it seems very unlikely that they ate their meals
together. The suggestion seems to be based on the fact that the accounts
for their meals were in many cases made up together. The three men
drank threepence worth of wine between them at almost every dinner
and supper. In 1555, the price of red Bordeaux wine seems to have
ranged from about threepence to a shilling a gallon in Oxford; malm-
sey cost 2s. 4d. a gallon (see Thorold Rogers, *History of Agriculture and
Prices*, vol. III, p. 516, vol. IV, p. 652).

† See Ridley's letters to Bernher, to Punt, and to 'A Friend that
came to visit him in prison but could not speak with him' (*Works*,
pp. 372, 376, 385). In all these cases, Coverdale states in the head-
notes to the letters that the persons to whom Ridley was writing had
called at his prison and had been refused permission to see him. In none
of these letters is there any indication in Ridley's text that this had
happened.

z

and Young. They came to see him before they left Oxford, with Dr. Oglethorpe. No doubt they were supposed to be visiting Ridley in order to attempt to convert him; but Glyn, who had been very aggressive during the disputation, took the opportunity of apologising to Ridley for the insults which he had hurled at him in public. Ridley told Glyn that he forgave him, and hoped that all his adversaries would repent themselves of their ways, so that they might all of them meet reconciled in Heaven.[8] In January 1555, he received a visit from Croke, who had dinner with Ridley.* He had presumably been sent to persuade Ridley to recant.

As soon as Ridley had been condemned as a heretic, Weston gave orders that he was to be deprived of pen and paper; he was not going to have Ridley writing heretical tracts in prison. The order was not immediately enforced, but some time later Ridley's writing materials were removed.[9] He nevertheless succeeded in obtaining pen and paper, and in maintaining regular contact with Shipside and with Latimer's servant Bernher, who were able to smuggle out, not only letters, but also treatises and pamphlets. Ridley apparently managed to do this by the simple and necessary expedient of bribing his new servant to break the regulations laid down by the authorities, and he wrote to Cranmer in Bocardo, urging him to do the same.[10] Sometimes he was unable to obtain pen and paper; on these occasions, he cut out the lead from the window-panes, and

* Ridley's letter to Bernher (Bradford's *Works*, vol. II, pp. 172–3), which, by reference to Ridley's letter to Bradford (*Works*, pp. 371–2) dates Croke's visit as having been on 19th January 1555, or thereabouts, owing to the reference in Ridley's letter to Bradford to the dissolution of Parliament. In Coverdale's *Letters of the Martyrs*, f. 70–1, the passage relating to Croke's visit appears in identical words in the text of a letter from Ridley to Bernher (*Works*, pp. 372–5); which in part is entirely different in substance from the letter published in Bradford's *Works* from the MS. in Emmanuel College, Cambridge.

sharpening it so as to form a pencil, wrote in the margin of harmless books which he was allowed to possess.[11] He then presumably sent out the books by his servant to Bernher, and thus smuggled his treatises out of prison.

As week after week passed by, and there was no news as to when he would be burned, Ridley decided to write as many treatises as possible in order that his opinions might be preserved at a time when the authorities were continually seizing and burning Protestant books, and many of the official records of the things which the Protestants had done when they had been in power. Weston had failed to keep his promise to send him the report of the disputation; and Ridley consequently wrote out, to the best of his excellent memory, a report of the disputation at considerable length.* He wrote a short preface to the report,[12] in which he described the insults to which he had been subjected by the Prolocutor and the audience, how he had been baited and interrupted, and the uproar and disorder which had marked the disputation: even the Sorbonnical clamours which had disgraced the disputations at the University of Paris had been nothing compared to this. Ridley was anxious for his account of the disputation to be secretly distributed amongst the Protestants, for he was afraid that the disputation had been grossly misrepresented by official propaganda, and that his followers would be dismayed by the versions which they would hear of how he had been worsted and exposed as an ignorant heretic. This indeed was the story which the authorities were spreading. Seyton told Bradford that Ridley had completely failed to make

---

* Ridley, *Disputatio habita Oxonii* 1554 (*Works*, pp. 433–81); this is a slightly shortened report as compared to the transcript which Foxe discovered after the accession of Elizabeth I (see Strype, *Cranmer*, pp. 487–88).

out his case in the disputation, and Story told Philpot, who admired Ridley so greatly, that Ridley had admitted that he had learned all he knew from Cranmer, and had trembled when confronted by an unknown Bachelor of Divinity; while Dr. Smith told his congregation at Whittington College in London that in the disputation at Oxford he had reduced Ridley to silence by his brilliant arguments.*

Ridley then began to write treatises. He wrote a pamphlet on the Lord's Supper, in which he summarized the views which he had formed at Herne nine years before, and for which he was now ready to be burned. This work was written in English, and intended for the less learned reader; it contained many texts from the Gospels and from Paul and the writings of six of the early Fathers—three of the Greek, and three of the Latin, Church.† He wrote a reply to a book by Tunstall on transubstantiation,‡

* See Ridley, *Account of the Disputation at Oxford* (*Works*, pp. 303–4); Seyton's conversation with Bradford on 29th January 1555 (Bradford's *Works*, vol. I, p. 494); and Story's words at the fifth examination of Philpot (Foxe, vol. VII, p. 628). But it seems much more likely that there is an error in the report, and that it was Ridley—not, as reported, Latimer—whom Story described as a 'sophister', and Latimer—not Ridley—whom he accused of learning all he knew from Cranmer, and trembling with the palsy at the sight of a Bachelor of Divinity. On the other hand, it is possible that Story lied and reversed the roles of Ridley and Latimer in order to demoralise Philpot, for the authorities were always trying to undermine Philpot's admiration for Ridley. For Smith's sermon in Whittington College, see Carlile, *Discourse wherein it is proved that Peter was never at Rome*, pp. 9–10.

† Ridley, *Brief Declaration of the Lord's Supper* (*Works*, pp. 5–45); it has also been published under the title 'Treatise against the Error of Transubstantiation'. The Latin version is Ridley's *Collectanea ex Evangeliis et D. Paulo, tribus doctoribus Ecclesiae Graecae, sc. Origene, Chrysostome, et Theodoreto, et tribus Ecclesiae Latinae, sc. Tertulliano, Augustino et Gelasio de verbis Institutionis Coenae Dominicae figurative intelligendis.*

‡ Ridley, *Annotationes in Tonstalli Libros de Transubstantiatione*. This has been lost (see Strype, *Cranmer*, p. 492).

which he had no doubt been permitted and encouraged to read by his gaolers; but it seems unlikely that he was the author of a reply to a book by Gardiner, for this was probably written by Cranmer.* He wrote some comments on two sermons which Watson, who had been one of his adversaries in the disputation in April, had delivered before the Queen during Lent.† He also wrote messages of encouragement to all the Protestants who were standing firm at this dreadful time.‡ These treatises were secretly carried by Bernher and Shipside to Protestants in London, who arranged for them to be smuggled to the English emigrants in Strasbourg, Zurich and Frankfurt. There they would be safe, and would be preserved for future generations; but it was agreed that they should not be published abroad until after Ridley had been burned, for if they were published the authorities in England would hear of it, and would take steps to prevent Ridley from writing any more.[13]

The summer of 1554 wore on, and still Ridley, Cranmer and Latimer were allowed to live. The Queen had now decided to postpone their burning indefinitely until Papal supremacy had been re-established. She was resolved, whatever the Emperor might say, to reunite the realm to Rome, and bring Pole to England as Papal Legate. The heretics would then be excommunicated under the auth-

* According to Foxe, vol. VII, p. 597, Ridley was the author of the short treatise *Certain Matters wherein Stephen Gardiner, Bishop of Winchester, varieth from other of the Papists touching the Sacrament of the Lord's Supper* (Foxe, vol. VII, pp. 597–602); (*Works*, pp. 307–15); but see Notes to *Works*, p. 543, for evidence that the treatise was probably written by Cranmer.

† Ridley, *Annotationes in duas Watsoni conciones quadragesimales coram regina.* This work is lost; for references to its existence, see Ridley's letter to Bradford (*Works*, p. 538, 540).

‡ *To the Brethren remaining in captivity of the flesh* (*Works*, pp. 342–8); and *To the Brethren which constantly cleave unto Christ* (*Works*, pp. 349–55).

ority of the Roman Church, and they would be condemned, not only for their denial of transubstantiation, but also for their refusal to submit to the authority of the Pope. Mary had no intention of penalising those who, in the past, out of obedience to her father, had renounced the Pope and had imprisoned and killed the faithful adherents of the Holy See. None of these men need fear for their lives or positions if they supported Mary's policy now; the presence of Gardiner on the woolsack was sure proof of that. Nor need the peers and gentlemen who were living on the spoils of the monasteries fear for their wealth when the Pope's supremacy was restored, for only some of the Crown lands would be restored to the monks. It was the suppression of the monasteries which more than anything else had caused the popular opposition to the Reformation, and the Catholic revolts against Henry VIII and Edward VI; but this was the only result of the religious policy of the last twenty-five years which was not to be undone. In all else, things would be put back to 1533. Mary resolved to brush aside for ever the compromise of Henry's reign, and his idea of a Catholic Church of England; henceforth the issue was to be clear between the Universal Church of Christ, under its head on earth in the Chair of St. Peter, and the heretics who denied the doctrines of that Church and refused to bow to its Pontiff.

At the end of July 1554, Prince Philip of Spain arrived at Southampton, escorted by a whole fleet of a hundred and fifty Spanish ships, and carrying five hundred thousand pounds in gold and silver from the Indies, as a gift to his bride. He was married to Mary by Gardiner in his cathedral at Winchester. If Mary could no longer style herself the Supreme Head of the Church of England, she was compensated for this by the addition of eleven new titles in its place. England was now closely linked with the Empire, and many Spanish priests and friars appeared in London. But while official propaganda proclaimed the incalculable advantages of the Spanish alliance, which would enable England to share in the vast wealth of the Indies, the people bitterly resented the presence of the Spaniards. The Protestant prophecies as to what would happen if Mary came to the throne seemed to be completely vindicated. Hatred of the Spaniards turned quickly to hatred of the King and Queen, and this in its turn passed over into hatred of their religion. Nearly every week some new outrage on the Catholic religion was perpetrated at dead of night in London.

It now only remained to submit to Rome, and for Pole to arrive as Papal Legate. He landed at Dover in November, and made his triumphal progress to London. On 29th November, the realm submitted to the spiritual supremacy of the Pope, and Pole absolved the nation of its twenty-one years of sin. A few days later, Gardiner preached a sermon at Paul's Cross in which he confessed his sin in supporting the break with Rome, and praised the saintly Cardinal Pole; for twenty years he had been vilified and exiled, but now he had come, not to punish, but to forgive. Gardiner was no doubt sincere in his repentance; the divorce and the break with Rome which he had done so much to foster had led to the Reformation of Edward's reign which had placed him in the Tower. Like Bonner and many others, Gardiner had come to believe that only a reunion with Rome could prevent the total subversion of Church and State by Protestantism.

Ridley heard something about all these events from his gaolers and from the letters from his friends which reached him. He was well informed as to the religious and political developments in the outside world. Then in the autumn of 1554 came disaster: Shipside was arrested. He had been sending Ridley's pamphlets and letters to Grimbold, who had been one of Ridley's chaplains when he was Bishop of London, and the rumour spread throughout all the prisons where the Protestants were confined that Grimbold had betrayed them. It was said that he had been promised his life and liberty, and to be allowed to retain his preferments, if he worked as a spy for the Council among the Protestants in prison and their friends outside. Ridley managed to write a letter to Cranmer and Latimer telling them the facts about Shipside's arrest. He wrote that he refused to believe that Grimbold had played a Judas' part, and that he understood from Shipside, who had evidently managed to get a letter to Ridley after his arrest, that they had been betrayed, not by Grimbold, but by a man whom Shipside had used as a contact with Grimbold. Ridley wrote that so far Shipside had refused to answer any questions which the authorities had put to him, and had insisted on being shown the authority for his arrest before he told them anything at all; but Ridley was sure that they would break Shipside in the end, and that all his manuscripts would be seized and burned. This must have been a heavy blow to him, but he resigned himself to it if it was the will of God.[14] But nearly all his works escaped the authorities. Some were already safe in Germany and Switzerland, and the others were well hidden somewhere in England. Four of his works have never been found;* they were presumably discovered and destroyed by the government. But all his other writings were preserved.

---

* Ridley's *De Abominationibus Sedis Romanae*; his book against Tunstall; his Treatise on Predestination and Election; and his *Annotationes in duas Watsoni conciones quadrigesimales.*

It seems that Ridley was now being treated more harshly than either Cranmer or Latimer. The increased vigilance of his gaolers and the arrest of Shipside made it much more difficult for Ridley to communicate with his friends and supporters. In any case, most of them were now in prison themselves; but the Protestants still managed to smuggle letters from one prison to another from time to time. Ridley was worried about his brother-in-law, and asked his friends who were still at liberty to send their gifts to Shipside rather than to him: he had everything that he needed. He did not like to risk sending a letter to Shipside in case this made matters worse for Shipside.[15] The new difficulties about correspondence made it much harder for Ridley to hear news of what was happening outside, and he now heard many rumours which he could not believe to be true. Irish and his wife were always telling him of leading Protestants who had recanted. They told him that Bradford, whom he had left behind in the Tower, was now high in favour with Gardiner; and Mistress Irish reported that Hooper had been hanged, drawn and quartered for high treason.[16] But Ridley did not believe a word she said, and he wrote to Bradford not to believe any rumours which he might hear that Ridley, Cranmer and Latimer had recanted.

While the three Protestant leaders in Oxford were held in the strictest isolation, most of their followers were confined in the common gaols. Many of the Protestants were herded together in the King's Bench prison in London. Here Bradford was chosen to act as their leader, and to organise the financial assistance which was necessary to keep the prisoners from starvation. He arranged for gifts to be sent to those Protestants, whether free or under arrest, who were most in need of them.[17] Ridley was in no need of any financial help,

and on the contrary was able to send gifts to Bradford for
distribution to the poorer brethren.[18]

But Bradford, in the King's Bench prison, was now confronted with a new cause of anxiety. Mary made no distinction between different brands of heretics, and was of
course especially eager to strike at Anabaptists and extremists. The outspoken violence of the sectaries and their
low social class made them the primary target for the royal
officers, and they soon formed the majority of the inmates of
the King's Bench prison. These were the old type of heretic
—low-born fanatics, who led saintly lives and uttered the
wildest opinions, and who despised and condemned all
learning and doctrinal argument. Many of them were
followers of Harry Hart; they rejected the doctrine of grace
by election, and ardently believed in free will. Bradford and
the rest of Ridley's friends and followers tried to show the
Freewillers their error, and bitter arguments developed in
the prison. The Freewillers accused Bradford of discriminat-
ing against them in the matter of financial assistance, and
of preventing them from receiving gifts—a charge which he
strongly denied. Some of the heretics denied the divinity of
Christ, and with them matters were even worse. The authorities seem to have viewed the quarrels between the heretics
with indifference and no doubt with satisfaction, until in
1556 they reached the point where they interfered with the
discipline and good order of the prison, and the Council
intervened to stop them.[19]

Bradford was determined to get the advice and assistance
of the men whom he considered to be, from their prisons,
the leaders of the Church. A letter was drawn up by the
prisoners in the King's Bench, and signed by Ferrar, Taylor,
Bradford and Philpot, and copies were secretly sent to
Cranmer, Latimer and Ridley. In this letter, the four Pro-

testants told their leaders of the activities of the Freewillers in the King's Bench. Bradford enclosed a treatise which he had written against them, along with one of Harry Hart's pamphlets, and asked Ridley to read his own treatise to see whether it was correct; he also asked Ridley to write a reply to Hart.[20] Ridley received the letter and the documents about 20th January 1555. It was just at a time when Ridley's gaolers were being particularly vigilant. Ridley was ill at the time;* but he studied Bradford's treatise, and returned it to him within three days, for he was afraid that the authorities would search his prison and discover it; in his letters to Bradford and to Bernher, who as usual was acting as the courier, he made only hidden references to Bradford's treatise, and directed Bernher to burn his letter as soon as he had read it. He refused, however, to write a reply to Hart. He told Bernher that, in the existing circumstances, it would be impossible for him to write a treatise without his gaolers finding out what he was doing, and taking effective steps to prevent him from writing in the future. He thought that Hart's treatise was such nonsense that it was not worth while taking risks in order to reply to it.[21] He did, however, write a treatise on predestination a short time afterwards.[22] This treatise has been lost, but there is no reason to doubt that in it Ridley expressed, in a more forceful and brilliant style, the opinions which Bradford had put forward in his treatise,†—rejecting both free will and predestination in favour of the doctrine of God's election and justification by faith in Christ.

* The date is fixed by the relation of the letter to one of Ridley's letters to Bradford, where reference is made to the dissolution of Parliament (*Works*, p. 371). Ridley refers to his illness in his letter to Punt (*Works*, pp. 376–7), which appears to refer to the time when Ridley received Bradford's treatise against the Freewillers.

† Bradford, *Defence of Election* (Bradford's *Works*, vol. I, pp. 307–30).

In January 1555, Parliament passed an Act which provided that the three Lollard statutes of 1382, 1401 and 1414 were again to be in force. With Papal supremacy re-established, and the heresy statutes re-enacted, Mary could now proceed at once with excommunicating heretics under the commission of the Papal Legate, and burning them under statutory powers. Within a fortnight, Gardiner and Bonner and others were sitting in commission in the Marshalsea by the authority of Cardinal Pole. Ridley heard all kinds of rumours as to what was going to happen to him and his colleagues in Oxford. Someone told him that they were each to be taken to a different college in Oxford for some unknown purpose which he could not imagine. But Ridley had no doubt that they would be burned almost immediately.[23] Everyone thought that the three arch-heretics in Oxford would be the first to suffer;[24] but though the burnings started at the beginning of February, the authorities chose other victims. Rogers, Bradford and Hooper were tried in Southwark. They all refused to recant, and were condemned and excommunicated. But Cranmer, Latimer and Ridley were spared.

There was now no reason at all why Ridley and Latimer should not be burned; that they were not was probably because they were thought of by the authorities together with Cranmer, and there was a special reason why Cranmer should not yet die. Alone of all the Protestant bishops, Cranmer had been consecrated before the final break with Rome, and had been appointed Archbishop with the consent of the Pope. For this reason, Mary, who had used her temporary position as Supreme Head of the Church of England to deprive the reformers of their sees, as well as ejecting as usurpers those of them who had replaced the Catholic bishops, hesitated to deprive Cranmer. He had been suspended from exercising his duties at the time of his arrest, but he was still Archbishop of Canterbury. Now that it was possible for him to be excommunicated and degraded under the authority of the Papal Legate, there was another reason for permitting him to retain his archiepiscopal see a little longer. Mary did not want the primacy vacated by Cranmer's degradation and death until she had decided whom to appoint as his successor. About this time, Pope Julius III died, and Mary was working hard to secure the election of Pole as Pope. If Pole was chosen, she intended to appoint Gardiner as Archbishop of Canterbury, but if Pole was unsuccessful, he was to be the Archbishop, while Gardiner was to remain Lord Chancellor. This gave an incentive to Gardiner to work for Pole's election, and his efforts were supported by all his subordinates who expected to move up a step in the hierarchy of State and Church if Pole secured the Papal diadem. Pole was unsuccessful, and Marcellus was chosen Pope; but three weeks after his election, Marcellus died, and the whole matter was reopened. Cranmer was kept alive, and Ridley and Latimer with him, until Pole had been defeated a second time. It had been rumoured in Rome that Pole had been too soft to heretics in his province of Viterbo. He was determined not to lay himself open to this charge again.

Rogers was the first to die. He was burned at Smithfield on 4th February; death came quickly and easily to him. Ridley wrote to Bernher, telling him how glad he was that Rogers, who had shown such constancy and had been chosen to be the protomartyr of the age, had been a Prebendary of St. Paul's, and that he himself had appointed him to the stall.[25] Bradford and Hooper had also been condemned and excommunicated at the same time as Rogers. Ridley was particularly eager to write to Hooper before he died, in view of their bitter controversy over vestments in King Edward's reign. He had already received two letters from Hooper, and had also read the writings which Hooper had smuggled out of prison; but he had not been able to reply to them. About 18th January, he wrote to Hooper:

My dearly beloved brother and fellow Elder, whom I reverence in the Lord, pardon me, I beseech you, that hitherto, since your captivity and mine, I have not saluted you by my letters; whereas, I do indeed confess, I have received from you (such was your gentleness) two letters at sundry times, but yet at such times as I could not be suffered to write unto you again; or, if I might have written, yet was I greatly in doubt lest my letters should not safely come unto your hands. But now, my dear brother, forasmuch as I understand by your works, which I have yet but superficially seen, that we thoroughly agree and wholly consent together in those things which are the grounds and substantial points of our religion, against the which the world so furiously rageth in these our days, howsoever in time past in smaller matters and circumstances of religion your wisdom and my simplicity (I confess) have in some points varied; now, I say, be you assured, that even with my whole heart (God is my witness) in the bowels of Christ, I love you, and in truth, for the truth's sake which abideth in us, and (as I am persuaded) shall by the grace of God abide with us for evermore. And because the world, as I perceive, brother, ceaseth not to play his pageant, and busily conspireth against Christ our Saviour, with all possible force and power, exalting high things against the knowledge of God, let us join hands together in Christ; and if we cannot overthrow, yet to our power, and as much as in us lieth, let us shake those high things, not with carnal, but with spiritual, weapons; and withal, brother, let us prepare ourselves to the day of our dissolution; whereby after the short time of this bodily affliction, by the grace of our Lord Jesus Christ, we shall triumph together with him in eternal glory.[26]

Ridley then asked Hooper to extend his warmest salutations to Crome, who nine years before had been examined by Ridley on a charge of denying the corporal Presence. He went on to tell Hooper that he still had his disagreements with him on a number of points about which Hooper had written to him in prison. We do not know what these issues were. Ridley then proceeded, in his letter, to urge Hooper not to attempt to write to him, in case his letters were intercepted. He strongly advised him not to consent to the publication of any of his treatises, certainly not under his own name, lest the authorities took reprisals against the other prisoners and prevented them from writing any more. He ended his letter:

> Farewell, in the Lord, my most dear brother; and if there be any more in prison with you for Christ's cause, I beseech you, as you may, salute them in my name; to whose prayers I do most humbly and heartily commend myself and my fellow prisoners, concaptives in the Lord; and yet once again and for ever in Christ, my most dear brother, farewell.*

The authorities thought it fitting that Hooper should be burned in his old diocese. He was taken from London to Gloucester, and burned there on 9th February. The wind blew the flames away from him, and twice put out the fire, and the gunpowder around his neck and under his armpits did not explode. Hooper was seen to move after one of his arms had been burned off. He took three-quarters of an hour to die.

Ridley also wrote to Bradford a final letter of farewell.

* Ridley's letter to Hooper. It was written in Latin (*Works*, pp. 355–8, for the original and the translation). The date of this letter can be deduced approximately from a passage in Ridley's letter to Bradford (*Works*, p. 372), the date of which can be ascertained by the reference to the dissolution of Parliament.

Bradford was to be taken to Lancashire to be burned, as he had originally come from the county. Ridley wrote to him that God would pour forth benefits on Lancashire because of Bradford's martyrdom there. He ended the letter by telling Bradford of the fear which he himself had sometimes felt at the prospect of being burned:

> We do look now, every day, when we shall be called on, blessed be God. I ween I am the weakest, many ways, of our company; and yet I thank our Lord God and heavenly Father by Christ, that since I heard of our dear brother Rogers' departing, and stout confession of Christ and his truth, even unto the death, my heart, blessed be God, so rejoiced of it, that since that time, I say, I never felt any lumpish heaviness in my heart, as I grant I have felt sometimes before. O good brother, blessed be God in thee, and blessed be the time that ever I knew thee. Farewell! Farewell!
>
> Your brother in Christ, N.R.
>
> Brother, farewell.[27]

But Bradford was not burned. He was not taken to Lancashire, where Bernher had gone to give him this farewell letter. He remained in prison in London. Ridley heard that Bradford was still alive, and wrote other letters to him. He told him that he had heard a rumour that Bradford's life had been spared because he had saved Gilbert Bourn from being lynched by the Protestant mob at Paul's Cross when Bourn had preached there in August 1553; and he assured Bradford that he did not believe the tales that Irish told him of how he was high in favour with Gardiner. Ridley wrote to Bradford that he was sure that God had spared him, as he had for a time spared Peter and Paul, because he had work for Bradford to do; and he commented on how remarkable it was that he and Cranmer and Latimer had not been the first to be burned, as everyone expected.[28] It was only in July that Bradford was burned at Smithfield. By then, Protestants were being burned all over the south of England.

Ridley had heard that Papal supremacy had been re-established in England; no doubt his gaolers took care to tell him about it. It was a vindication of all the Protestant arguments in the last twenty years. They had always denounced their Catholic opponents as Papists, and had said that Gardiner and Mary, though they might profess to believe that the King was the Supreme Head of the Church, were in fact working for Papal supremacy. Now they were proved right. If Gardiner was convinced that only a return to Rome could prevent the victory of heresy, the Protestants were certain that images, Latin services and above all transubstantiation led inevitably to Popery. The news of the return of Papal supremacy led Ridley to write a pamphlet. This was his *Piteous Lamentation of the Miserable Estate of the Church of Christ in England,* which he must have written during the winter of 1554–5. The Lamentation was written in English; he also wrote a treatise in Latin on *The Abominations of the Roman See and the Roman Pontiffs* which may have been no more than a Latin version of his Lamentation. He smuggled out the treatise by Bernher. Ridley was very worried when Bernher failed to return to him a few days later at the time when he had arranged to come. He was afraid that Bernher had been arrested with the manuscript on him.[29] But Bernher was not arrested, and the *Piteous Lamentation* was safely sent abroad, though the Latin treatise was probably discovered and destroyed. *

* Ridley's *De Abominationibus Sedis Romanae et Pontificum Romanorum* has been lost. If, as is generally assumed, it was a different work from the *Piteous Lamentation on the Miserable Estate of the Church of Christ in England,* it would appear from the title of the treatise to be a work of a very similar nature.

2A

The *Piteous Lamentation* was not a dispassionate theological treatise with abundant quotations and interpretations and closely reasoned arguments; it was a splendid piece of stirring invective against the Popish Antichrist. England had recently been a realm where the true religion was taught and practised; now Antichrist reigned in England. Ridley wrote:

> Of late all that were endued with the light and grace of understanding of God's holy mysteries did bless God, which had brought them out of that horrible blindness and ignorance, whereby in times past, being seduced by Satan's subtleties, they believed that the Sacrament was not the Sacrament, but the thing itself whereof it is a Sacrament; that the creature was the Creator; and that the thing which hath neither life nor sense (alas! such was the horrible blindness!) was the Lord himself, which made the eye to see, and hath given all senses and understanding unto man. But now, alas! England is returned again like a dog to her own vomit and spewing, and is in worse case than ever she was: for it had been better never to have known the truth, than to forsake the truth once received and known. And now, not only that light is turned into darkness, and God's grace is received in vain; but also laws of death are made by High Court of Parliament, masterfully to maintain by sword, fire and all kind of violence, that heinous idolatry, wherein that adoration is given unto the lifeless and dumb creature, which is only due unto the everliving God. Yea, they say they can and do make of bread both Man and God by their transubstantiation—O wicked men, and Satan's own brood![30]

Of late the Lord's cup was distributed at his table to the laity as well as to the clergy, as Christ had commanded; now the cup was denied to the laity, and the commemoration of the Lord's Supper had been converted into a blasphemous sacrifice. Of late God's commandment not to

worship images was engraved in most of the churches; now
God's holy word was erased, and images had been restored.
Of late the ministers admitted to the priesthood had made
solemn promises before the congregation that they would
teach nothing that was not in Scripture or clearly grounded
thereon; now all the wicked traditions of man had been
restored. And what else was to be expected, as Rome was
the Babylon of the Apocalypse? When John wrote, Rome
was the only city which ruled over the kings of the earth,
and it was to Rome that he referred; and the abominations
in the cup of the whore were the whole trade of the Romish
religion.[31]

> What word of God hath that devillish drab, for the mainten-
> ance of her manifold abominations, and to set to sale such
> merchandise, wherewith (alas! the madness of man!) the
> wicked harlot hath bewitched almost the whole world? Did
> not Peter, the very true Apostle of Christ (of whom this stink-
> ing strumpet beareth herself so high, but falsely and without
> all just cause) did not he, I say, give all the world warning of
> her pelf and trash, of her false doctors and apostles? For this
> whore and beast will be called Dominus Apostolicus. . . .[32]

And Ridley went on to describe the iniquities of pardons
and dispensations which had been sold by the old Church
before the break with Rome; now the flattering friars and
the false pardoners would come in again.

Ridley then turned to consider how it was that this plague
of God had fallen upon England, and declared that it was a
punishment for the covetousness that had disgraced the
nation in the reign of King Edward.

> Alas! my dear country, what hast thou done, that thou hast
> provoked the wrath of God and caused him to pour out his
> vengeance upon thee for thine own deserts? Canst thou be

content to hear thy faults told thee? Alas! thou hast heard oft, and wouldst never amend. England, thy faults of all degrees and sorts of men, of magistrates, of the ministers, and of the common people, were never more plainly told, since thou bearedst that name, than thou didst hear them of late, even before the magistrates, in King Edward's days, but thou heardest them only, and didst amend never a whit. For even of thy greatest magistrates, some (the King's Highness then, that innocent, that godly-hearted and peerless young Christian Prince excepted) evermore unkindly and ungently, against those that went about most busily and most wholesomely to cure their sore backs, spurned privily, and would not spare to speak evil of them, even unto the Prince himself; and yet would they towards the same preachers outwardly bear a jolly countenance and a fair face.

I have heard that Cranmer, and another whom I will not name, were both in high displeasure, the one for showing his conscience secretly, but plainly and fully, in the Duke of Somerset's cause,* and both of late, but specially Cranmer, for repugning as they might against the late spoil of the Church goods, taken away only by commandment of the higher powers, without any law or order of justice, and without any request or consent of them to which they did belong. As for Latimer, Lever, Bradford and Knox, their tongues were so sharp, they ripped in so deep in their galled backs, to have purged them, no doubt, of that filthy matter that was festered in their hearts, of insatiable covetousness, of filthy carnality and voluptuousness, of intolerable ambition and pride, of ungodly loathsomeness to hear poor men's causes, and to hear God's word, that these men, of all other, these magistrates then could never abide. Others there were, very godly men and well learned, that went about by the wholesome plasters of God's word, howbeit after a more soft

* It seems clear that this is a reference to Ridley's action in opposing Somerset's intention of suppressing Clare Hall in 1549.

manner of handling the matter; but alas! all sped alike. For all that could be done of all hands, their disease did not minish, but daily did increase, which, no doubt, is no small occasion in that state, of the heavy plague of God, that is poured upon England at this day.[33]

Under Edward, the Protestant religion had been established and upheld by the authorities, but now the same men who had then been Protestants were ardent Catholics, which showed that their Protestantism had been insincere.

Ridley then turned to the question of what the Protestants should do in the existing situation. He strongly urged all those who had not yet been arrested to escape abroad. He wrote that some of the Protestants would agree with this advice, but that others would condemn it, and refuse to flee, on the grounds that it would be cowardly to do so, and that the most noble thing that a Christian could do was to give his life in Christ's cause. Ridley replied that the best thing for one person was not necessarily the best for another. A child should not learn to run before he could walk. While those reformers who were in prison must not yield an inch, and must unhesitatingly go to their deaths, it would be wrong for those who could escape to seek martyrdom before their time; if God willed it, they would be given the opportunity to die for his cause at the appropriate hour. He warned these over-zealous martyrs by the example of Quintus in the writings of Eusebius, and illustrated his argument with examples from Scripture. Paul had escaped from Damascus, and Elias fled from the fury of Jezebel; and Christ had said: 'When they persecute you in one city, fly unto another'. Let all who were at liberty flee from the plague while there was yet time. But there was a third class of Protestants. They thought that it was impossible to flee abroad, to abandon all their property and relatives in

England, and to face the tremendous difficulties of the life of a refugee in a foreign country where they could not speak the language. They argued that it was permissible to recant, while retaining their Protestant beliefs in their hearts. Ridley told them that Satan's subtleties were deep, and that this argument was of his doing. They should flee abroad, where the Lord would provide for them. He warned them to rid themselves of any illusions that, if they stayed in England, they could stay away from the Popish public worship, and worship devoutly in private; if they stayed, they would be forced, in order to avoid falling under suspicion, to worship images, to sprinkle themselves with holy water, and to contribute to the maintenance of the pardoners and flattering friars; above all, they would be forced to worship the creature as the Creator.[34]

For all the violent and polemical language of Ridley's Lamentation, his pamphlet shows clearly that in the dreadful position in which he was placed he had not lost any of his reasoning powers which now as always guided his actions. Latimer and Bradford and the other Protestant leaders had not made any attempt to escape before their arrest, and their refusal to fly was later glorified by Foxe and his successors, and elevated to be the hall-mark of the true martyr. But Ridley saw no value in courting martyrdom, and urged them all to flee the country. He took the view, however, that while flight was justifiable, recantation was not. Other Protestants did not share his opinion; they thought that it was justifiable to pretend to recant, and to worship at the Mass of which they did not approve, as Ridley himself had done in the reign of Henry VIII. Many of the lesser men had recanted, and had returned to the bosom of the Roman Church. The politicians were now all good Catholics again, protesting that they had only taken the

Oath of Supremacy under duress, and at heart had always been loyal to the Pope. Most of the parish priests were once more officiating at Mass, and had put away their wives. Launcelot Ridley is said to have recanted,* along with so many others. Nicholas never referred to Launcelot in any of the letters which have been preserved; perhaps, if he heard what Launcelot had done, he refused to believe it, as he had refused to believe that Grimbold was a government agent. But he probably came to accept the fact of Launcelot's apostasy before he died, for he made no mention whatever of Launcelot in his 'Last Farewell'. Launcelot had only done what all the others were doing. These men did not wish to be martyrs; after all, the Queen would not live for ever, and when she died the realm might once again have need of Protestants.

Ridley did not agree. He had never been one of the fanatics who rushed eagerly to a cruel death in a mood of rapture and exhaltation. Ridley's beliefs were all based on reason and logic. It was this logic which had led him, on the basis of his fundamental assumptions, to renounce the doctrine of transubstantiation when he was already well advanced in years; and now it led him to the conclusion that, while men who could still do so ought to escape abroad, he himself had no option but to be burned alive. He knew better than anyone the powerful arguments in favour of a feigned recantation; but his penetrating mind could not overlook the weaknesses in these arguments, and made him realise that to accept them would be to use reason as a cloak for cowardice. His keen imagination made

* Launcelot Ridley was deprived of his preachership in Canterbury Cathedral and of his cure of Willingham in Cambridgeshire in 1553 or 1554 as a married priest; but he is said to have later recanted (see Cooper, *Ath. Cant.*, vol. I, pp. 354, 563).

him well aware of what it meant to die in the fire; and he was afraid. He had told Bradford that he was weaker than his colleagues;[35] certainly he had none of the fervour of the natural martyr to assist him. But though he could see clearly that for those Protestants who were fortunate enough to be free, flight was justifiable, he could also see that for him the only possibility was the stake. His attitude is a remarkable tribute to his intelligence and to his bravery. And he had the courage of Latimer and the example of Rogers and Hooper to inspire him. He knew that a recantation by the three Protestant leaders in Oxford, which the Queen was so eager to obtain, would heavily demoralise all the Protestants in England; while the sight of the three of them, who had all held high office in the State and Church and had lived a life of pomp and comfort, going bravely to the flames for their beliefs, would rally all their supporters and would strike such a blow against Popery as would not be forgotten for centuries. If Cecil and Lord Robert Dudley, who were going to Mass and loyally serving the King and Queen, were able, by their recantation, to live to fight another day, and to render great services to the Protestant cause, it was Ridley and his colleagues who ensured the defeat of Popery in England under Elizabeth, and who crushed in the bud the first signs of its revival in 1688.

Ridley would not accept any excuse for recantation, and on this point he was as hard on others as on himself. Bernher asked his advice about the case of a Protestant, who had presumably fled abroad, whose wife was confronted with the choice of recantation, flight or death. The husband had advised her to recant in a letter he had written to her. Ridley condemned his action, and said that he had been prompted by a too tender zeal for his wife's welfare rather than by the contempt for all carnal and worldly affections which he ought to feel in Christ's cause, and he condemned the wife for making public a letter which could be used by the authorities to demoralise the reformers.[36] Ridley also wrote to Mistress Glover, a niece of Latimer, whose husband had been excommunicated as a heretic and was awaiting death. He referred to old father Latimer as having been placed by the Lord to be his standard bearer in their age and country against his mortal foe, Antichrist. He told Mistress Glover that she must encourage her husband in his glorious death, and not hinder his cause in any way, for it was Christ's cause.[37] Glover was burned at Coventry in September 1555. By this time, more than fifty Protestants had been burned, including Ferrar and Taylor.

Ridley was still expecting to be burned any day;[38] but the spring passed, and he faced another summer in his Oxford prison, where he had now been confined for over a year. During the summer, he was able to enter into correspondence with Grindal, who was in Frankfurt. On 6th May, Grindal wrote his first letter to Ridley; it apparently took only about three weeks to smuggle the letter from Frankfurt to Ridley's prison, for Ridley is said to have replied on 31st May.[39] Grindal told Ridley that there were many English Protestants in Frankfurt, where they were well treated by the authorities; others were in Zurich with Bullinger, others in Strasburg with Peter Martyr, and a few were with Scory in Friesland. He told Ridley that they had received a copy of his arguments in the Oxford disputation, his treatise on his discussion with the imaginary Antonian, and his treatise on the Lord's Supper, which they intended to translate into Latin. Grindal saluted Ridley for his brave stand against Antichrist.[40]

Ridley wrote and thanked Grindal for his letter, and his news, and asked for more news of Scory, Cheke and the other emigrants. He wrote that if the account of the Oxford disputation which Grindal had received was any other except the account which he had written himself, it was no doubt a complete misrepresentation of what had actually occurred. He told Grindal that he did not think it worth while to translate his treatise on the Lord's Supper into Latin—he had not written it for the learned reader; but in any case he urged Grindal not to publish anything in any language under Ridley's name until his fate had been settled. He then gave Grindal all the news about what was happening in England—of how he had been imprisoned in the Tower; of how Rogers, Hooper and Ferrar had been burned, along with many others, especially in Essex and Kent, but that for some extraordinary reason Bradford was still alive, although he had been handed over to the secular powers; of how Shipside had been arrested but had been released after nearly six months in prison; of how their University of Cambridge had been purged of all traces of Protestant teaching, and the heads of colleges who were Protestants, or married, had been expelled, along with many Fellows; and of how Gardiner had gone abroad to negotiate peace between France and the Empire. He also told him that the Queen was pregnant, and commented: 'May God prosper her to the glory of his name'. He added that he was sure that he and his friends would be burned as soon as Gardiner returned from abroad and the royal child was born, and asked Grindal to pray, not only for him, but also for Cranmer and Latimer.

Ridley also told Grindal of the trials which he was experiencing with Mistress Irish. He wrote:

Of all us three concaptives at Oxford, I am kept most strait, and with least liberty, either because the man in whose house I am a prisoner is ruled (though he be the Mayor of

the city) by his wife, an old ill-tempered and most superstitious woman, who indeed takes it to herself as a matter of
praise, that she is said to guard me most strictly and cautiously. The man himself, however, whose name is Irish, is
good tempered enough to everybody, but to his wife most
obsequious. Now although, as you know, I have never myself
had a wife, yet from my daily association with this couple I
seem in some measure to understand how great an evil and
intolerable a yoke it is to be joined in wedlock with a bad
woman. Rightly therefore has the wise man said, A good wife
is the gift of God, and again, Blessed is the husband of a good
woman. Either, I say, this is the cause, or because this has
been so commanded them by the higher powers (from what
causes I know not)—which they, if ever I complain of my too
strict imprisonment with them, often and diligently impress
upon me.*

Soon afterwards, Ridley received another letter from
Grindal, giving him more news of the position of the English fugitives in Frankfurt. The authorities in Frankfurt
were Protestants, but in certain details their church services
differed from those laid down in the Book of Common
Prayer. The authorities had ordered the English to conform
to the services applied in Frankfurt, and Grindal and his
colleagues had complied. Grindal also told Ridley of the
controversies which they were having with Knox, who was
also in Frankfurt, and had attacked the provision in the

* Ridley's letter to Grindal (*Works*, pp. 388–95). Part of the passage
cited (pp. 391–2) was written in Latin—presumably in case Mistress
Irish saw the letter. According to Gloucester Ridley, p. 586, the letter
was written on 31st May 1555; if this is correct, Grindal's letter of 6th
May must have reached Ridley in Oxford from Frankfurt remarkably
quickly in the circumstances. In the letter, Ridley mentions that
Thomas Ridley, of the Bull Head in Cheapside, who had been a great
friend to him since he had been in prison, had died. He was not a relation of Nicholas.

Book of Common Prayer that in some cases infants could be baptised in private. In his reply to Grindal, Ridley said that he thought that the authorities in Frankfurt had been quite right to insist that the English fugitives should adopt the church services of the city, and that the English had been right to conform. Where the only difference in the services related to inessentials, all aliens in a country should adapt themselves to the services in use there; and Ridley added that if he had had his way, John à Lasco and the foreign Protestants in England would have been compelled to observe the Act of Uniformity in King Edward's reign. As for the dispute with Knox, Ridley pointed out that the Book of Common Prayer had laid down that baptism should be performed in public except in cases of urgency, when it could be performed in private. What did Knox propose to do in cases of urgency? Did he wish to leave the infant to die unbaptised? Ridley wrote that Knox was a learned and zealous man, but that he hoped that in future Knox would only use these gifts for the glory of God.*

Ridley had heard that the Queen was pregnant. The whole country knew it; at the beginning of May, they heard that she was in labour, and began to celebrate the birth of a prince. At the end of January, Ridley had written

* Ridley's letter to Grindal (*Works,* pp. 533–5). The letter is undated, but can hardly have been written before the beginning of August 1555, for it was written in reply to a letter from Grindal, which was evidently written in answer to Ridley's letter of 31st May. This correspondence with Grindal about Knox and the exiles in Frankfurt cannot have been written at an earlier period, for Grindal states in his letter of 6th May 1555 that this was the first time that he had been able to write to Ridley.

The controversies between Grindal and his friends and Knox grew so bitter that the English fugitives denounced Knox to the authorities in Frankfurt as a traitor to the Emperor. Knox thereupon hastily left Frankfurt, and went to Calvin in Geneva.

to Bradford telling him that he had heard a rumour that King Philip had been appointed Protector for the infant in the event of the Queen dying during childbirth.* By the end of July it was known that it had all been a mistake: the Queen had never been pregnant at all. The news spread in no time through the prisons; and while to most of the Queen's subjects it was the occasion for coarse jokes, to the Protestant prisoners it was an act of God. The first-born had been struck down. This confirmed them in their faith and constancy. To the less heroic Protestants, it was a new reason for prudence and feigned recantation. The Queen was thirty-nine years old, and the King returned to Spain in August; it was clear that Mary would never have a child, and would be succeeded by Elizabeth. The Princess was now regularly attending Mass, but she had formerly been a Protestant, and when she came to the throne things would be very different. A year before, she was a prisoner, and the Emperor and Gardiner were strongly urging Mary to put her to death; now she alone stood between Mary Queen of Scots, the wife of the heir to the throne of France, and the throne of England. The Emperor was the last person to desire to end her life, and she could rely on the friendship of Philip. The future for those Protestants who could survive the Queen was bright.

But Ridley does not seem to have had any thought of the future of Protestantism in England. In one of his letters from prison, he wrote that the forces of Satan had been too quick for them, and had stamped out the Reformation before the Protestants could compel the children of England to learn Cranmer's Catechism, which would have ensured

---

* Ridley's letter to Bradford (*Works*, p. 371); this letter must have been written about 18th January 1555, in view of the references in it to the dissolution of Parliament.

its continuation.[41] Ridley was convinced, as he wrote in his *Piteous Lamentation*, that the end of the world was near at hand.[42] He was thinking of salvation, and all his splendid powers of reasoning rejected the subtle arguments of the tempter who strove to convince him that he could recant and yet be saved. He could never betray Latimer, and the memory of Rogers and Bradford. He was afraid, but he had steeled himself to face death in a dreadful form. Fortunately he did not know quite how horrible that death would be.

NOTES

[1] See Ridley's *Account of the Disputation at Oxford* (*Works*, p. 305).

[2] Ridley's letter to Weston, 23rd April 1554 (*Works*, pp. 375–6). Foxe, vol. VI, pp. 534–5, publishes the letter as two separate letters.

[3] Ridley's letter to Cranmer (*Works*, pp. 362–3).

[4] *Acts of the Privy Council*, vol. V, p. 17 (3rd May 1554).

[5] Strype, *Cranmer*, p. 501.

[6] Foxe, vol. VI, p. 440. For Irish's election as Mayor, see *Oxford City Records*, p. 221.

[7] Ridley's letters to Bradford and Bernher (*Works*, pp. 365, 374, 382).

[8] Ridley, *Disputatio habita Oxonii* (*Works*, p. 468); Foxe, vol. VI, pp. 491–2.

[9] Ridley, *Account of the Disputation at Oxford* (*Works*, p. 306).

[10] Ridley's letter to Cranmer, about 23rd April 1554 (*Works*, p. 363).

[11] Foxe, vol. VIII, p. 35.

[12] Ridley, *Account of the Disputation at Oxford* (*Works*, pp. 303–6).

[13] Grindal's letter to Ridley, 6th May 1555 (*Works*, p. 388).

[14] Ridley's letter to Cranmer and Latimer (*Works*, pp. 361–2).

[15] Ridley's letters to Bernher and to Bradford (*Works*, pp. 382, 541).

[16] Ridley's letters to Bradford and to Bernher (*Works*, pp. 365, 370, 373, 379).

[17] Strype, *Cranmer*, p. 503.

[18] See Ridley's letter to an unknown Correspondent (*Works*, p. 385).

[19] Strype, *Cranmer*, pp. 503–5.

[20] Letter of Ferrar, Bradford, Taylor and Philpot to Cranmer, Ridley and Latimer (Bradford's *Works*, vol. II, pp. 169–71).

[21] See Ridley's letters to Bernher and to Bradford (Bradford's *Works*, vol. II, pp. 172–5), and to Punt (*Works*, pp. 376–7).

[22] See Ridley's letters to Bradford (*Works*, pp. 537–42); Strype, *Cranmer*, p. 502.

[23] Ridley's letters to Bernher and to Bradford (*Works*, pp. 371, 373).

[24] Ridley's letter to Bradford (*Works*, p. 370).

[25] Ridley's letter to Bernher (*Works*, pp. 380–1).

[26] Ridley's letter to Hooper (*Works*, pp. 355–8).

[27] Ridley's letter to Bradford (*Works*, pp. 377–8).

[28] Ridley's letter to Bradford (*Works*, pp. 369–71).

[29] Ridley's letter to Bradford (*Works*, pp. 371–2).

[30] *A Piteous Lamentation of the Miserable Estate of the Church of Christ in England* (Foxe, vol. VII, pp. 568–9; *Works*, p. 51).

[31] *Piteous Lamentation* (*Works*, pp. 51–3).

[32] *Piteous Lamentation* (Foxe, vol. VII, pp. 569–70; *Works*, p. 53).

[33] *Piteous Lamentation* (Foxe, vol. VII, pp. 572–3; *Works*, pp. 58–9).

[34] *Piteous Lamentation* (Foxe, vol. VII, pp. 575–7; *Works*, pp. 62, 65–7).

[35] Ridley's letter to Bradford (*Works*, p. 378).

[36] Ridley's letter to Bernher (*Works*, pp. 382–3).

[37] Ridley's letter to Mistress Glover (*Works*, pp. 383–4).

[38] Ridley's letter to Grindal, 31st May 1555 (*Works*, p. 394).

[39] Gloucester Ridley, p. 586.

[40] Grindal's letter to Ridley, 6th May 1555 (*Works*, pp. 386–8).

[41] Ridley's letter to the Brethren which constantly cleave unto Christ (*Works*, pp. 350–1).

[42] *Piteous Lamentation* (*Works*, p. 75).

X

THE STAKE

Ridley has gone down in history, not as a bishop, but as a martyr. People who know nothing about his career, or about his work as a leader of the Reformation, remember—many of them with every detail—his last hours and his dreadful death. This is right and proper, for it was the greatest moment of his life. He deliberately decided, after many months of consideration, to die in the fire rather than save his life by a recantation, which he was given the opportunity to do on many occasions, and even at the stake itself. He had no reason to doubt that he would be spared if he recanted; it was only some five months after his death that Mary cheated Cranmer.* If he had recanted before his second excommunication, he would certainly have been spared; and it is probable that a recantation at the stake would in fact have obtained him the pardon that was promised. He did not want to die, and if he could have survived three more years he would have had much to live for; but he did not flinch from the ordeal.

Perhaps for a few months, in the spring and summer of 1555, he could not repress a gleam of hope. While he prayed for the Queen in her pregnancy,[1] as a Christian and a loyal subject, the desire for life within him may have made him

* On 19th January 1556, the Council ordered their officers to proceed immediately with the burning of excommunicated heretics without referring the matter to the Council with a view to a pardon being offered to the heretic if he recanted, as had previously been the invariable practice (*Acts of the Privy Council*, vol. V, p. 228, 19th January 1555/56).

dare to speculate on the possibility that both Mary and her child might die in her childbirth, and that Elizabeth would come to the throne in the nick of time to save the three Oxford prisoners. But he was not so lucky as the mean and brutal Norfolk. The task of rebuilding the Protestant Church was left to those younger men who had escaped the full fury of Mary's persecution by following Ridley's advice and fleeing the realm, and who looked to Ridley and his fellow prisoners for their inspiration. By his death, Ridley won a place in history far higher than theirs.

As the summer turned to autumn, the men who had waited for eighteen months in Oxford were told that their turn had come at last. They were to be tried in the Court of the Papal Legate. A commission was issued by Cardinal Pole, Legate in England of Pope Paul IV, to Bishop White of Lincoln, Bishop Brooks of Gloucester and Bishop Holyman of Bristol, to hear the cause in Oxford. The commissioners were instructed to ascertain whether Cranmer, Ridley and Latimer still adhered to the views which they had expressed in the disputation in Oxford in April 1554 that there was no transubstantiation of the consecrated bread and wine in the Sacrament—views which had already been held to be heretical on that occasion by Dr. Weston. If the heretics recanted these views, they were to be received again into the Church; if not, they were to be pronounced heretics and excommunicated.[2] On 12th September 1555,* Cranmer was brought before the commissioners; he

---

* See Cranmer's letter to Queen Mary (Jenkyns, *Cranmer*, vol. I, p. 369), which shows that it was on Thursday, 12th September, that Cranmer appeared before Brooks and the commissioners for his trial, although it was on 7th September that Cranmer was summoned to appear in Rome within eighty days. Froude, vol. VI, p. 372, evidently misunderstood this passage in Cranmer's letter, and wrongly states that Cranmer's trial was on the 7th.

refused to recant, was adjudged a heretic, and excommunicated. Still Ridley and Latimer were left in prison, and not
brought to trial. But they had only just over a fortnight to
wait. On 30th September, they were brought again to the
Divinity Schools,[3] where they had argued in the disputation
in April 1554. Again they were to be separately examined
before the commissioners.

Ridley was tried first. At eight o'clock in the morning,
he was brought before the commissioners. Among the audience was Weston, who had presided at the disputation of
1554. The proceedings began with the reading of Cardinal
Pole's commission. Ridley had naturally removed his cap
when he entered the hall, but when the Legate's name was
mentioned, he put it on his head. Bishop White immediately
stopped the reading of the commission. He told Ridley that
he and his brother commissioners were quite indifferent as
to whether Ridley showed any respect to them in their personal capacity; but they must insist that he remove his cap
out of respect to the Legate of the Pope. Ridley replied that
he would gladly do honour to them as individuals, and also
to Cardinal Pole, because he was of royal blood and a most
learned and virtuous man, but that he had sworn never to
recognise the authority of the Bishop of Rome. White told
him that however much Pole might be deserving of respect
on account of his royal blood and learning, it was as Legate
of the Pope's Holiness that they required Ridley to honour
him. As White referred to Pole's royal blood, Ridley removed his cap; but when he spoke of the Pope, Ridley put
it on again. White said that if he refused to take off his cap
it would be forcibly removed from his head. He ordered
Ridley three times to remove the cap, and then told the
beadle to remove it; and Ridley inclined his head to assist
the beadle in the operation.

White then made a long statement, in which he urged
Ridley to recant his heresies. He reminded Ridley that he
would be doing no new thing in adhering to the Church of
Rome, as he had once been a faithful member of that
Church. He referred him to his most effective and Catholic
sermon at Paul's Cross in November 1547, when he had
denounced the heretics who reviled the Sacrament; and
he said that the Lord Chancellor had told him of a conversation he had had with Ridley when Ridley was sent by
the Council to examine him on his opposition to the Book
of Homilies. Gardiner had told White that Ridley had said:
'Tush, my Lord, this matter of Justification is but a trifle,
let us not stick to condescend herein to them; but for God's
love, my Lord, stand stoutly in the verity of the Sacrament;
for I see they will assault that also'.

In his reply, Ridley gave his reasons for opposing the
Papal Supremacy. He said that when Jesus said: 'Thou art
Peter, and upon this stone I will build my Church', he was
referring, not to Peter the mortal man, but to his belief in
the divinity of Christ. This belief was the foundation of all
Christianity, and if anyone denied this, he did not have
Christ in him. Ridley declared that the Bishop of Rome
was the Antichrist of St. John. Turning to Augustine, Ridley said that his words 'All the Christian countries beyond
the sea and far regions are subject to the see of Rome'
applied only to Europe, for Augustine had been in Africa
when he wrote this passage, and as the sea to which he
referred was undoubtedly the Mediterranean, he meant
that the Pope's jurisdiction was limited to the mainland of
Europe, as was the jurisdiction of the Patriarch of Rome in
the days of the four Patriarchs. White strongly contested
this interpretation of the passage, and asserted that when
Augustine spoke of the 'whole world' he meant more than

Europe; but Ridley said that the words the 'whole world' were limited by the following words. Ridley ended his statement by admitting that he had once been a Catholic and a believer in Papal supremacy, and mentioned that St. Paul had once been a persecutor of Christ. But while admitting that he had been a Papist, he strongly denied that he had supported transubstantiation in his sermon of November 1547, or in his conversation with Gardiner: he had merely urged Gardiner to be zealous in pursuing Anabaptists; and in the sermon at Paul's Cross he had defended the Sacrament from the revilers, and had asserted the spiritual Presence of Christ in the Sacrament, but had been misunderstood by the ignorant, who thought that the Presence was carnal.

White again urged Ridley to recant, and to accept the supremacy of the Pope. God had given two symbols of power to the world—the sword and the keys. The sword he gave to princes, and the keys to the successors of Peter. The King and Queen themselves, though rightly jealous of their temporal prerogative and primacy, were the first to acknowledge the spiritual supremacy of the Pope; so why should Ridley claim for the King and Queen a supremacy which they themselves repudiated? In his reply, Ridley condemned the Roman Church for not administering the Sacrament to the laity in both kinds. He did not deal with White's point about the repudiation of the royal supremacy by Philip and Mary themselves; but this does not necessarily mean that he had no answer to it. The trial was not conducted like a disputation, and White had made a long speech; when he came to reply, Ridley dealt with other points that White had raised, and may well have overlooked this argument.

White accused Ridley of heresy in having denied the

doctrine of the Real Presence in the disputation the previous year. He asked him to declare whether he still adhered to the heretical views which he had then expressed. Ridley said he would prefer to deal with transubstantiation to-morrow—it was nearly time for the adjournment—and White said that by replying to his question then, Ridley would not prejudice his opportunity of going into the question more fully tomorrow, which he promised that he would be able to do. Ridley said that he had had many promises made to him at the disputation in April 1554, but that they had not been kept; and he added that White was treating him with great courtesy, but would shortly hand him over to the secular power to be burned, as the high priests had handed over Christ to Pilate. At this Weston, who was probably enraged by Ridley's references to his broken promises at the time of the disputation, shouted out in indignation from his seat in the audience that Ridley was saying that the King was like Pilate; but Ridley replied that he was merely saying that Weston was like Caiaphas. White then stopped these exchanges by asking Ridley to reply to the questions. Ridley replied that he would answer the questions, but only subject to his protest against the jurisdiction which the commissioners derived from the Pope, and he asked leave to state the reasons why he ob-jected to this jurisdiction. White said that they had received instructions not to permit Ridley to challenge their juris-diction in public. Ridley persisted in his request, and asked to be allowed to speak three words on this matter. White then agreed that he might speak not three, but forty words, next day, but as it was long past the time for the adjourn-ment he must now reply to the questions. Ridley then gave his answers, making a short statement on his opinion with regard to the Real Presence; Christ's body was really present in the Sacrament, spiritually, by grace and efficacy, but it was not present as a lively and movable body under the forms of bread and wine. After further argument, White ordered Ridley to prepare a statement in writing as to his views for next day, and directed that he should be supplied with books, pen and paper. The hearing was then adjourned, and the commissioners proceeded to deal with Latimer.

Next day, on 1st October, Ridley was brought before the commissioners, who on this occasion were sitting in St. Mary's Church. The hall was crowded with spectators; nearly everyone of note in the University and the city was there, along with many of the justices from the county who had come to Oxford for the Michaelmas Sessions. They sat on benches along all four sides of the church. Ridley was placed at a table quite a little distance away from the dais where the commissioners sat; for Ridley, but not for Lati- mer, it was covered with a silk cloth to denote that Ridley had taken his doctor's degree at a University. This was the only rank which he still held. The proceedings started soon after eight o'clock in the morning. White began by telling Ridley that he hoped that today he would remove his cap when the Legate's commission was read; but Ridley said that he did not intend to do so. White said that in this case they would have to do as they did yesterday, and without waiting for further orders, the beadle quickly snatched the cap from Ridley's head. White then produced some new arguments which had occurred to him about Augustine's '*totus orbis*' statement, and he and Ridley argued about this and the meaning of '*in transmarinis*' for a long time. At last White turned the discussion to the question of altars. He quoted Cyril's words: 'Altars are erected in Christ's name in Britain and in far countries: ergo, Christ is come'. He asked someone to fetch him a book by Melanchthon, in which the German Lutheran had defended altars on the strength of this passage from Cyril;* but none could be found, for all Melanchthon's books had been destroyed as heretical. If anyone in Oxford had a copy, he obviously thought it wiser not to produce it even at the behest of the Bishop of Lincoln. White said that the words of Cyril might well be reversed, for under Edward VI they could say: 'Altars are plucked down in Britain: ergo, Christ is not come'. Ridley replied that by 'altar', Cyril did not mean the Jewish altar, but the table of the Lord, and added that the Lord's Supper had never been better ministered or more duly received than after the removal of altars. White then said:

A goodly receiving, I promise you, to set an oyster table instead of an altar, and to come from puddings at Westminster to receive; and yet, when your table was constituted, you could never be content, in placing the same now east, now north, now one way, now another, until it pleased God of his goodness to place it clean out of the church.

Ridley replied:

Your Lordship's unreverend terms do not elevate the thing. Perhaps some men came more devoutly from puddings than other men now do from other things.

White then asked Ridley if he had prepared his answers to the questions as to whether he still adhered to the views which he had expressed in the disputation in 1554, warning him that if his reply dealt with any matter other than these questions he would not be allowed to read it. Ridley began to read out his answers, but White stopped him, and refused to allow him to read it aloud until the commissioners

* It was Melanchthon's *Loci Communes rerum Theologicarum seu Hypothyposes Theologicae*, which was published in 1521.

had first examined it to make sure that it was fit to be read out to the public. Ridley protested, but passed the document up to White, who read it, and showed it to his colleagues; he refused to read it out aloud, because it contained blasphemies, and challenged the jurisdiction of the Pope's commissioners, though Ridley protested that it contained virtually nothing except quotations from the early Fathers. White then asked Ridley to reply to the questions, but Ridley answered that his reply was contained in the document, and repeatedly called on White to read it out; but White read out only a few selected passages, omitting all the parts which he considered to be irrelevant and blasphemous.

The Bishop of Gloucester then made an earnest appeal to Ridley to recant, and to accept the authority of the Church in place of his own reason. Brooks said that Ridley and his colleagues had no solid basis for their beliefs: Latimer looked to Cranmer, Cranmer looked to Ridley, and Ridley looked to the singularity of his own wit. He said that he and Ridley could argue for ever as to the meaning of the texts of the Scriptures and of the early Fathers; these texts could be interpreted either way, and who was to determine which interpretation was right? It could only be determined by the Church. Brooks urged Ridley not to be wise in his own conceit, and said that the Arians had not been condemned by the superior arguments of the Catholics, but by the authority of the Church. If the Church's authority were not accepted in such matters, there would be no end to arguments and disputations. Ridley answered that he tried to avoid conceit, and said that it was not true that Cranmer looked to him, for Cranmer had been a doctor at Cambridge when Ridley was only an undergraduate; Cranmer had been his teacher rather than his pupil. Brooks replied that Latimer had told them yesterday that he derived all his opinions from Cranmer's books, and that Cranmer had said to them that Ridley had inspired him with all his doctrinal views. White then also urged him most earnestly to recant; he took off his cap as he spoke to Ridley, presumably to show that he was speaking as a friend and adviser rather than as a judge.

Ridley said that he could not recant, because he was convinced that the religion which he held was grounded upon God's word, and asked leave to state why he would not acknowledge the supremacy of the Pope. White refused to let him do this, and Ridley then reminded him of his promise yesterday that he would be allowed to speak forty words. This prompted Weston to intervene in the trial once more: he shouted out that Ridley had spoken four hundred words already. White agreed to let him speak exactly forty words and no more, and told him that they would count his words on their fingers. Ridley began to speak, but after a few sentences the commissioners stopped him. It seems clear that it was Weston's intervention that suggested to the commissioners the idea of limiting Ridley to precisely forty words. But despite the meanness of this trick, Ridley could not really complain that he had been denied an opportunity to state his case; the previous day, White had allowed him to make a lengthy statement about the Papacy, and had not intervened even when Ridley called the Pope Antichrist. Perhaps White had been taken to task for this overnight, and was conscious that the Queen and Gardiner might receive an unfavourable report from Weston on the way in which he had handled the proceedings; for he had certainly not shown throughout the trial the bias and intolerance which Weston had displayed at the disputation in 1554. He felt bound, however, to comply with his instructions not to permit Ridley to challenge the jurisdiction which the commissioners derived from the Pope, or to use the trial as an opportunity to utter heresies against the Pope in public.

Without further discussion, White now proceeded to pass sentence on Ridley. He told him that as he was an obstinate heretic, he would have to give his judgment, but that he was very sorry to have to do so. Ridley interjected that he could well believe this, as it would certainly be burdensome to White's immortal soul. White then condemned him as a heretic, and excommunicated him, and told him that he would be dealt with by the secular powers according to the law of the land.

Ridley was taken back to Irish's house. The commissioners then resumed their examination of Latimer, and he too refused to recant, and was condemned. Ridley knew that at last the end was near. Throughout eighteen months of solitary confinement, Ridley had known that one day, when all the delays and disputations were over, the time would come for the men to light the fagots; now he knew that there were only a few more days to wait. In these favourable circumstances, Ridley was confronted with the arguments of a supreme exponent of orthodoxy. The Spanish friar, Soto, paid a visit to Ridley and Latimer. He came on the same mission which five years before had sent Ridley to Joan Bocher two days before her death—to effect a conversion under the shadow of the stake. There can be little doubt that it was Latimer who refused to talk to Soto, and that Ridley agreed to see him and discuss the points at issue with him.* He probably argued with Soto for many

* Cardinal Pole wrote to King Philip that Soto had been to Oxford to see the two heretics, but that one of them had refused to speak with him, while Soto spoke to the other, but could make no progress with him (*Letters of Cardinal Pole*, vol. V, p. 47). Our knowledge of the characters and attitudes of Ridley and Latimer is quite sufficient to enable us to identify each of the two heretics referred to.

hours, but did not yield an inch. Soto was doubtless parti-cularly eager to save Ridley from the stake, for the Spanish friars, and Philip himself, used their influence on the side of mercy and moderation. They thought it inadvisable to use in England the drastic methods which could profitably be applied to heretics in Spain and the Netherlands; and they had no need, like most of their English colleagues, to atone for having tortured Papists by burning Protestants. But the Spaniards were the principal target for the hostility of the English people. In 1553, in his last sermon, Ridley had warned his congregation that Mary would marry a foreign prince who would bring in foreign agents to rule in England. Soto in Oxford was the vindication of Ridley's sermon at Paul's Cross.

In the last few days before 16th October, Ridley's rela-tives made desperate efforts to save him. Old Latimer, who came from a yeoman family in Leicestershire, had no in-fluential friends to help him; but Ridley was more fortunate here. His kinsmen were gentlefolk, and they lived in North-umberland, where the feelings of family loyalty of an earlier age were still strong enough to outweigh religious differ-ences, and where the Tudor absolutism was weak enough for men to venture to intervene in such a matter. Mabel Ridley, the wife of Nicholas Ridley of Willimotiswick, was the grand-daughter of old Lord Dacre.* Dacre had been a most powerful figure in Northumberland for the last thirty years. He had no sympathy whatever with Ridley's views, and had regularly voted against him in the House of Lords; he had, indeed, spent a few months in the Fleet under Northumberland's administration. But to this relic

* Gloucester Ridley, p. 630. For Ridley's letter to a cousin of his, whom Gloucester Ridley thinks was Mabel Ridley, see *Works*, pp. 385–6.

of the feudal era, it was much more important that Ridley was a relative than that he was a heretic; and now, according to Foxe, he offered Mary £10,000* if she would commute the death penalty to which Ridley was subject by law. There is nothing improbable in this story, even if we can hardly believe that the sum could have been so large; Dacre, who had defied Henry VIII with impunity,† was about the only man in England who could dare to make such a suggestion to the Queen. Presumably the proposal was made discreetly, through unofficial channels; it was turned down.[4] Mary was not the woman to compromise the dignity of her position by accepting such an offer, even though it was made by the only subject whose property she could not seize whenever she wished. It is unlikely that Ridley, in his Oxford prison, knew anything about the enormous sum that Dacre was prepared to pay to save his life. If the offer had been accepted, we may be sure that Ridley would not have relished being spared on this account, while his colleague and inspirer, Latimer, went alone to the stake.

As soon as the trial before the Legate's Court was over, Ridley hastened to write two messages of farewell. The one was addressed to all his friends, and to the places and institutions with which he had been connected during his life; it is known as his 'Last Farewell'. It is, at the same time, a farewell letter to his relatives, a short autobiographical survey, and a statement of his views on the counter-Reformation in England. The second was a special message to the

* Foxe, vol. VIII, p. 707, implies that Dacre offered ten thousand marks—£6,666—in the first instance, and then raised the offer to £10,000. These sums represent about £200,000 and £300,000 in terms of present-day currency.

† Lord Dacre of Gilsland was arrested in 1534, and a bill of attainder on a charge of high treason was introduced into Parliament, but was rejected, and Dacre was released.

Protestant prisoners and to those who had fled abroad, and was a shorter document; it is known as his 'Farewell to the Prisoners and Exiles'.

In his 'Last Farewell', Ridley first bade farewell to his relations. He referred to the loyalty and kindness which Shipside had always shown him, particularly since his arrest, and to his Protestant zeal; he told his sister Alice that she must bear her cross in good part, and must honour and obey her good husband, according to God's law, and also her mother-in-law. He was sure that Shipside would care for her three children as if he had been their father. He bade farewell to his sister Elizabeth and her husband, John Ridley of Walltown; he reminded Elizabeth that people had always said that she had loved him more than any of her other brethren. He regretted that he had not been able to do more to help them, and commended the meek and gentle spirit of their daughter Elizabeth. He told the widow of his brother Hugh of Unthank that he had intended to act as a father to her many children, but that now they would have to look to God for a father. He greeted Nicholas Ridley of Willimotiswick and his wife, and said that Nicholas had been chosen to be the bell-wether of the Ridley family. He told his young cousin, Ralph Whitfield, that he regretted his stay with him had been so short, and that he had suffered a loss during his visit.[5]

Ridley then addressed himself to the inhabitants of Tynedale in general, and said that he had greatly looked forward to coming among them and preaching to them when he had been chosen as Bishop of Durham just before King Edward died. Ridley no doubt was well aware that his attitude would not be easily understood in Catholic Northumberland, so he told his fellow-countrymen not to be shocked at the manner of his death. He was as certain that he was dying for the truth of God as he was of the truth of the Gospel of John and the Epistles of Paul. It was a noble death to die in battle against the thieves of the Marches, but it was equally and indeed more worthy to fall in battle for God's cause against the robbers of the Church. The authorities now in power were Church robbers; they had robbed the Church of England of its service in English, of its Homilies and Articles of Religion, of the Lord's cup and of the Lord's table, replacing it with a thing they called their Mass. The Church robbers were worse than the poor, simple thieves of the border; for the border robbers did not deny that their actions were evil, and came to sessions only to be hanged; while the Church robbers were able to persuade the people that their evil was good, and came to Court to sit in judgment upon all who denounced their lies, to condemn them to burn alive in flaming fire. The Church robbers could not be fought with spear and lance, with bow and bill, but only with spiritual weapons. He told the people of Tynedale that they must not be dismayed if Ridley, whom they had admired as a successful dignitary of the realm, was now to die as a criminal; for he was more honoured at the prospect of martyrdom in Christ's quarrel than ever he had been by his elevation to the sees of Rochester and London, or by his selection as Bishop of Durham.[6]

He then bade farewell to the University of Cambridge, which had bestowed so many offices and honours upon him, and where he had found more friends than even in his homeland of Northumberland, and had received more benefits than from anyone except his father and mother. He referred particularly to Pembroke Hall, which had been in his charge. He hoped that he could say that he had left the college in as good a state of learning and piety as he had found it, though he had no idea of what was happening now at Pembroke Hall. Then he turned to Herne, his first cure, to which Cranmer had appointed him. He lamented that his efforts to convert his parishioners there had not been more successful, but mentioned that it was at Herne that God revealed to him the doctrine of the Lord's Supper. He paid tribute to the memory of Lady Fyneux, and hoped that many other people in Herne had been equally receptive to his preaching. With regard to Canterbury Cathedral, he said that he could not honestly say anything pleasant about the time when he had been a Prebendary there, though he mentioned that he had a few friends in Canterbury. He bade farewell to Soham; he stated that he had only held the benefice for a short time, but that this was nevertheless too long in view of the fact that he had not been able to live in the parish. He lamented the fact that the present Vicar, Hebb, had apostasised and submitted to Rome, despite the promises which he had made to Ridley when Ridley had resigned the cure in his favour in 1552. He bade farewell to the see of Rochester, which he had found an agreeable and obedient diocese, and lamented its present state; but he had nothing to say to Westminster Cathedral beyond what he had said with regard to Canterbury Cathedral.[7]

He had harsher things to say of London:

O London, London! To whom now may I speak in thee, or whom shall I bid farewell? Shall I speak to the Prebendaries of Paul's? Alas, all that loved God's word, and were the true setters forth thereof, are now (as I hear say) some burned and slain, some exiled and banished, and some holden in hard prison, and appointed daily to be put to most cruel death, for Christ's Gospel sake. As for the rest of them, I know they could never brook me well, nor could I ever in them delight.

Shall I speak to the see thereof, wherein of late I was placed
almost, and not fully, by the space of three years? But what
may I say to it, being (as I hear say I am) deposed and expulsed by judgment as an unjust usurper of that room? O
judgment, judgment! Can this be just judgment to condemn
the chief minister of God's word, the pastor and bishop of
the diocese, and never bring him into judgment, that he
might have heard what crimes were laid to his charge, nor
never suffer him to have any place or time to answer for
himself. . . .

O thou now wicked and bloody see! Why dost thou set up
again many altars of idolatry, which by the word of God were
justly taken away? Why hast thou overthrown the Lord's
table? Why dost thou daily delude thy people, masking in thy
Masses, instead of the Lord's Holy Supper, which ought
to be common as well (saith Chrysostom, yea, the Lord himself) to the people as to the priest? How darest thou deny to
the people of Christ, contrary to his express commandment
in the Gospel, his holy cup? Why babblest thou to the people
the common prayer in a strange tongue, wherein St. Paul
commandeth, in the Lord's name, that no man should speak
before the congregation except it should be by and by
declared in their common tongue, that all might be edified?
Nay, hearken, thou whorish bawd of Babylon, thou wicked
limb of Antichrist, thou bloody wolf: why slayest thou down
and makest havoc of the prophets of God? Why murderest
thou so cruelly Christ's poor silly sheep, which will not hear
thy voice because thou art a stranger, and wilt follow none
other but their own pastor Christ's voice? Thinkest thou
to escape, or that the Lord will not require the blood of his
Saints at thy hands? Thy god, which is the work of thy hands,
and whom thou sayest thou hast power to make—that thy
deaf and dumb god (I say) will not, indeed, nor cannot
(although thou art not ashamed to call him thy Maker)
make thee to escape the revenging hand of the High and
Almighty God. But be thou assured, that the living Lord our

Saviour and Redeemer, which sitteth on the right hand of his Father in glory, he seeth all thy wicked ways and cruelty done to his dear members, and he will not forget his holy ones; and his hands, O thou whorish drab, shalt thou never escape. Instead of my farewell to thee, now I say: Fie upon thee, fie upon thee, filthy drab, and all thy false prophets.[8]

But Ridley went on to say that he could not leave London without remembering those secret mourners who would never consent to the league between their see and the seat of Satan, and to refer to Sir Richard Dobbes and Sir George Barnes, both of whom had been Lord Mayor of London when he was Bishop; and he praised them for their good works in the city, and especially for having helped him, not without difficulty, to obtain the grant of the palace of Bridewell for charitable uses.*

Finally, he bade farewell to the House of Lords. He said that he could now speak freely to the temporal peers, because by the time they read his message he would be dead, and they would therefore not be able either to reward or harm him for what he said. The House of Lords had passed the bills for restoring the Papal supremacy and for re-enacting the heresy statutes under which the Protestants were now being burned; and Ridley warned them that they could not relieve themselves of responsibility for this by arguing that, in these spiritual matters, they had followed the directions of the Church, any more than Pilate would be forgiven the death of Christ because he had washed his hands of him, and had been prompted by Annas and Caiaphas. He declared that the see of Rome was the see of

* In his *Last Farewell* (*Works*, pp. 410–12), Ridley lamented the fact that King Edward's gift of the revenues of the Savoy to these charitable uses had not been carried through owing to Mary's accession; but it was, in fact, confirmed by Mary. See Gloucester Ridley, p. 399.

Satan, and that the Bishop of Rome was Antichrist himself. He reminded the Lords that they had often listened to his sermons before the King and to his speeches in Parliament with apparent approval, and that now they should listen to him all the more, as there was no possibility now that he was influenced in his views by ambition or fear of the authorities. He told them that they could not justify their action on the grounds that the question of Papal supremacy was only a matter of policy, and not of religion, because the new instructions to the curates in the diocese of York laid down that to believe in Papal supremacy was necessary for salvation. The merits of the question of Papal supremacy had not changed since the days of Henry VIII and Edward VI, and if the Lords believed that it was a matter of salvation, how was it possible that they had ever approved of the break with Rome, merely in order to please their mortal Prince?[9] He ended his 'Last Farewell' with these words to the peers:

The whore of Babylon may well for a time dally with you, and make you so drunken with the wine of her filthy stews and whoredom (as with her dispensations and promises of pardon *a poena et culpa*) that for drunkenness and blindness ye may think yourselves safe. But be ye assured, when the living Lord shall try this matter by the fire, and judge it according to his word, when all her abominations shall appear what they be, then ye, my Lords (I give your Lordships warning in time), repent if ye will be happy, and love your own soul's health; repent, I say, or else without all doubt ye shall never escape the hands of the living Lord for the guilt of your perjury and breach of your oath. As ye have banqueted and lain by the whore in the fornication of her whorish dispensations, pardons, idolatry, and such like abominations; so shall ye drink with her (except ye repent betimes) of the cup of the Lord's indignation and everlasting wrath, which is prepared for the beast, his false prophets, and all their partakers. For he that is partner with them in their whoredom and abominations must also be partner with them of their plagues, and in the latter day shall be thrown with them into the lake burning with brimstone and unquenchable fire. Thus fare ye well, my Lords all. I pray God give you understanding of his blessed will and pleasure, and make you to believe and embrace the truth. Amen.[10]

He then wrote a message of farewell to his followers in prison and in exile. To them, he could speak in a different language from that which he had adopted to his other friends and to his enemies. He told them of the eternal glory which they would win if they suffered bravely in Christ's cause, and ended his letter:

Farewell, dear brethren, farewell! And let us comfort our hearts in all troubles, and in death, with the word of God! For Heaven and earth shall perish, but the word of the Lord endureth for ever.

Farewell, Christ's dearly beloved spouse here wandering in this world, in a strange land, far from thine own country, and compassed about on every hand with deadly enemies, which cease not to assault thee, ever seeking thy destruction!

Farewell, farewell, O ye the whole and universal congregation of the chosen of God, here living upon earth, the true Church militant of Christ, the true mystical body of Christ, the very household and family of God, and the sacred temple of the Holy Ghost. Farewell.

Farewell, O thou little flock of the high heavenly pastor Christ! For to thee it hath pleased the heavenly Father to give an everlasting and eternal Kingdom. Farewell.

Farewell, thou spiritual house of God, thou holy and royal priesthood, thou chosen generation, thou holy nation, thou won spouse! Farewell, farewell!

N.R.[11]

Ridley then wrote a final letter of a very different kind. It was a petition to the Queen on behalf of the former tenants of the see of London, who had been granted their leases by Ridley and had been ejected by Bonner. In his letter, which was couched in most respectful terms, Ridley told Mary that many of these tenants, whose leases had been made without any fraud or collusion, had on entry to their lands or on renewal of their leases paid fines, both to him and to the Chapter of St. Paul's. They had apparently surrendered their former holdings on entry into the lands from which Bonner had ejected them. Ridley made a humble supplication to the Queen to permit these tenants to continue to hold the leases which Ridley had granted them, or, if she felt unable to do this, at least to give them back their former holdings and to repay the fines which they had paid on entry to the forfeited lands. He mentioned that when he had left the see he had left behind a large quantity of plate in his offices—chiefly in an iron chest in his bedchamber—and that half of this plate should be enough to cover the cost of repaying to the tenants the proportion of their fines which had been paid to Ridley. Ridley also mentioned the plight of Alice and her children, who had been deprived of the property which he had granted them, and begged that their case might be mercifully considered, especially as he had not taken any of Bonner's personal goods when he entered into the see, but had, on the contrary, paid for the lead which he had found, and had paid Bonner's debts to his servants for their livery and wages to the amount of £53 or £55*—he could not remember which. Ridley asked the Queen to hear the views of Archbishop Heath, who had been confined in Ridley's house for a year before Ridley's arrest, and who knew Alice, with regard to the requests in his petition.[12]

* It was, in fact, £54. See Chapter VI, pp. 208-9.

In these last days before his death, Ridley's anxiety was not for the dreadful fate which lay ahead of him, but for the well-being of those tenants of the see of London who had been the incidental victims of the venomous hatred which Bonner and Mary felt towards him. It is difficult to know what really happened with regard to the tenants' leases. The authorities had not forgotten the transactions of April 1550, when with Ridley's connivance the four manors of the see had been presented as a gift to the courtiers, and doubtless they attempted to justify their attitude by assuming that all the leases granted by Ridley had been equally questionable. It is significant that Ridley expressly stated, in his petition to Mary, that the leases of which he wrote had not been granted by virtue of any fraudulent or collusive arrangement, which suggests that he was aware that his enemies might allege that they had been. Moreover, he also mentioned in his petition that in many cases the true value of the fines paid by the tenants had not been stated in the leases,[13] which makes it seem likely that in some of these cases the stated fines were inadequate. But clearly not all the tenants who held leases from Ridley were unscrupulous courtiers. Ridley had not petitioned the Queen to recognise his grants to Wentworth, Darcy and Rich. He had approached Mary on behalf of the tenants who, as he stated in his letter, had all paid fines to the see, and had been guilty of no fraud or collusion. It is possible, however, that the plight of these tenants was not as bad as Ridley had been led to believe from the rumours which he had heard in prison. There is no doubt that some of the tenants who held leases from Ridley were allowed to continue in possession under Bonner; for we know that even the Protestant Hutchinson was permitted to retain his lease of the priory of St. Helen's Bishopsgate and the advowson of Rickmansworth, which must have been granted to him by Ridley, as the property was only acquired by the see of London when it was granted to the see, along with the other property of the old abbey of Westminster, in April 1550; for Hutchinson bequeathed this lease in his will, a few weeks before his death, in May 1555.[14] Some of the leases, however, were cancelled, and a bill to restore them was defeated in the House of Lords in 1559, though some years later the tenants were in some cases given back their leases.[15]

The execution of Ridley and Latimer was fixed for 16th October. Cranmer was to be kept a little longer. As an Archbishop and Metropolitan, he had been given the right to appear before the Papal Court in Rome within eighty days—a right which he was effectually prevented from exercising by being detained a prisoner in Bocardo—and further efforts were to be made to persuade him to recant. For Ridley, the hour of martyrdom was at last at hand. But first there was a ceremony to perform: he must be degraded from the priesthood. Ridley had been ordained a priest under the ordinal of the old Church before the break with Rome; and now that he had been excommunicated as a heretic, he must be formally unfrocked from the spiritual office which he had so shamefully abused. He was not, however, degraded from the office of a bishop, for Brooks, at the degradation ceremony, refused to recognise him as being a bishop.

There has been much dispute and speculation as to the reason for Brooks' attitude. Ridley had been consecrated a bishop in 1547, before the ordinal of the old Church had been replaced by the ordination services of 1550 and 1552. The authorities took the view that he had usurped the see of London, and had vacated the see of Rochester in 1550; but as there seems no reason to believe that they considered the office of bishop to be one of jurisdiction only, and not of order, this cannot explain their failure to recognise Ridley as being a bishop. Ridley had been consecrated while the realm was in schism from Rome, and in the Oath of Supremacy had repudiated his duty to the Pope; but this also applied to many of the Catholic bishops, including Bonner, and Pole had taken the view that despite the schism these bishops had been validly ordained. There seems to be no reason whatever for the suggestion that some of the requirements of the old ordinal had been illegally dispensed with at Ridley's consecration, and in view of the caution with which the Protestant leaders were proceeding in the autumn of 1547 this is very unlikely; for even if this was done at the consecration of Ferrar a year later—nearly eighteen months before the old ordinal was abolished—the reformers were much less likely to venture on such a step in September 1547 than in September 1548. Moreover, White himself, at Ridley's trial only a fortnight before his degradation, had stated—in Brooks' presence—that Ridley had been properly ordained a bishop, and in passing sentence had ordered him to be degraded from the order.*

The explanation is probably simple enough. In the case of Cranmer, Pole was not likely to forget how the Pope had been tricked by Henry VIII into agreeing to his consecration as Archbishop of Canterbury. Cranmer was therefore treated as a special case, as a renegade Metropolitan. In the case of the other Protestant bishops, it is probable that no deliberate decision was taken. Hooper had been consecrated under the ordinal of 1550 which, if too orthodox for him,

---

* For the various explanations which have been put forward for the authorities' refusal to recognise Ridley as being a bishop, and their inadequacy, see Gloucester Ridley, pp. 659–61; Dixon, vol. IV, p. 437 n.

was too radical to be recognised by the Church of Rome; he was the first of the Protestant bishops to be degraded, and as he was clearly not recognised as a bishop by the authorities because of his improper ordination, the decision was taken to degrade him only from the priesthood. This would have been sufficient for the idea to gain ground among the authorities that all the Protestant bishops, apart from Cranmer, were to be degraded only from the priesthood. Once this was accepted, the authorities would have hesitated before adopting a different procedure, and the matter was probably never referred to Pole or Gardiner, who alone were high enough to take the initiative in reversing it. It was probably for this reason that Ridley and probably Latimer, who had both been consecrated under the old ordinal, were treated as being only priests. White knew that Ridley was a bishop in the eyes of the Church of Rome, and passed the proper sentence upon him; but at the last moment, Brooks, though he knew that his action was wrong, thought it safer to err by showing an excess of zeal.

On the morning of Tuesday, 15th October, a body of dignitaries came to Ridley's prison in Alderman Irish's* house to perform the degradation ceremony. They included Brooks, the Bishop of Gloucester, and Dr. Marshal, the Vice-Chancellor of the University, as well as several other doctors and officials of the University.† Brooks told Ridley why they had come, and urged him to recant

* Foxe, vol. VII, p. 542, states that Irish was the Mayor of Oxford. In fact, however, Irish had just relinquished his office, having been Mayor from Michaelmas 1554 to Michaelmas 1555 (*Oxford City Records*, pp. 221, 227).

† For the account of Ridley's degradation, see Foxe, vol. VII, pp. 542–7. Foxe presumably acquired his information from Shipside, who was present.

and accept the Queen's pardon; but Ridley said that he would never recant as long as his tongue could wag in his head and there was breath left in his body, and that he was ready to seal his beliefs with his blood. They then began the degradation ceremony. They had brought priest's vestments with them for the ceremony, but Ridley refused to put on the vestments, presumably because they had been condemned as Popish in the second Book of Common Prayer.* Brooks ordered him to dress, and told him that the vestments would be forcibly put on him if he did not put them on himself. Ridley refused to comply, but said that if Christ had been so cruelly dealt with, it was not for him to complain if he were treated in similar fashion, and he allowed the officials to dress him without resistance. Then they handed him a wafer which was to represent the Host, in order that it might be taken from the hands which were no longer worthy to hold it. Ridley absolutely refused to take the wafer, and Brooks ordered an attendant to hold it forcibly in Ridley's hands. They removed the garments and the wafer from him while Brooks spoke the appropriate words; but Ridley meanwhile was denouncing the Popish fopperies which he had been forced to wear as foolish and abominable and too fond for a vice in a play. Brooks ordered him to be silent, and as Ridley went on, declaring that the Bishop of Rome was Antichrist, he warned him that if he persisted in uttering these blasphemies and disturbing the ceremony of unfrocking, he would have to be gagged. Edridge, the University Reader in Greek, suggested to Brooks that by law he ought to be gagged at once; but at this Ridley sighed, and fell silent, and Brooks did not order

* For the suggestion by Sampson and his followers that Ridley refused to wear the vestments because he had come to the conclusion that all vestments were sinful, see Chapter VI, pp. 231–2.

him to be gagged. As the ceremony continued, Ridley interrupted it from time to time by some new interjection against the Papal Antichrist. When they declared that they deprived him of the right to preach the Gospel, Ridley said: 'O Lord God, forgive them this their wickedness'.

When the ceremony was over, Ridley asked Brooks to stay behind for a moment, as he wished to say something to him. Brooks said that he could not talk to Ridley, because he had been excommunicated, and that he was precluded, by his religion, from talking with a man who was not a member of the Church. Ridley then urged Brooks to read Bertram's book on transubstantiation, and Brooks, without replying, began to leave the room; but Ridley then told him that he wished to present a petition to the Queen. Brooks at once agreed to stay and listen. Ridley thereupon read out the letter which he had written to the Queen about the tenants of the see of London; but when he came to the passage referring to his sister Alice, he broke down, and his eyes filled with tears. He quickly pulled himself together, and said: 'This is nature that moveth me, but now I have done', and finished reading the petition. He then handed the letter to Shipside, who was present, and directed him to present it to the Queen on behalf of himself and of all the other tenants of the see of London. Brooks told Ridley that the petition did him great credit, and promised to speak to the Queen about it; he said that he thought the petition would have been granted were it not for the fact that Ridley had resisted the Queen's policy, which made it unlikely that she would accede to his supplication. Ridley sighed, and said that in that case there was nothing to be done, and Brooks promised to do all he could. Brooks knew his Queen too well. Alice and Shipside got no relief at all from Mary. They had to wait until a Protestant Queen sat on the throne before Bonner made restitution in full to Ridley's executors in a vain attempt to avoid the Tower.[16]

Brooks then called the bailiffs, and ordered them to see to it that Ridley spoke to no one before his execution, and was brought to the stake at the appointed hour. Ridley then said that he thanked God that no one could accuse him of having committed any serious crime or misconduct, for if he had done so it would certainly have been brought up against him now. Brooks commented that Ridley was a proud Pharisee to praise himself in this manner, and Ridley denied it, and stated that he was well aware that he was a miserable sinner. The head of one of the Oxford Colleges then tried to persuade Ridley to recant; but he was unsuccessful, and left declaring that Ridley was the most obstinate and wilful man that he had ever heard talk since he was born.

On the last evening, Ridley sat down to supper in Irish's house with Shipside and the Alderman and Mistress Irish. Irish provided them with an excellent supper, and evidently charged the cost of it on the public funds. They ate a shoulder of mutton, a pig, a plover, bread and cheese and pears, and they had both ale and wine to drink, at a total cost of two shillings and sixpence halfpenny.* Ridley had quite recovered from the unpleasant experience of the morning, and was unperturbed by thoughts of the morrow. He had washed his beard and legs, and was in the best of spirits. He said that he considered his burning next day would be his wedding, and he asked them all to be present.

* The total of 2s. 6½d. was made up as follows: bread and ale, 3d.; shoulder of mutton, 9d.; a pig, 11d.; a plover, 4d.; wine, 1½d.; cheese and pears, 2d. Gloucester Ridley, p. 662, states that this was the meal at Ridley's last supper; but according to *Oxford City Records*, p. 232, an identical bill of account was drawn up in respect of Latimer's supper on 15th October.

He added that he hoped that Alice would come, as he wanted his sister to be present at his marriage, and he asked Shipside whether he thought that Alice could bring herself to be there. Shipside said that he was sure that she would be there, and Ridley said that he was glad to hear that her spirit was so stalwart. At this, even Mistress Irish, who had been so hostile to Ridley when he was first her prisoner, began to cry; but Ridley told her not to weep, and said that he feared that this meant that she would not be present at his wedding. Ridley said that though he would perhaps find his breakfast somewhat sharp and painful, yet he was sure that his supper would be more pleasant and sweet. After supper, Ridley announced that he was going to bed, and Shipside offered to sit up with him all night; but Ridley would not hear of it, and said that he intended to sleep as well as he had ever done in his life.[17]

Next day—16th October 1555—Ridley was led to his death* They were to be burned in the ditch just outside the walls on the north side of the town, near Balliol College.† Ridley had dressed himself in the black furred gown he usually wore; he had a fur tippet around his neck, and wore his cap over a velvet nightcap.‡ He had put on his slippers. He walked from Irish's house

* It is always assumed that Ridley and Latimer were burned in the morning, and this is almost certainly correct, though there does not appear to be any evidence of this apart from Foxe's story that Gardiner in London received the news of their death at four o'clock in the afternoon of the same day (Foxe, vol. VII, pp. 592–3); and Foxe's story is obviously fictitious. There is a record of the items and cost of Latimer's dinner on 16th October (*Oxford City Records*, p. 232), which suggests that they were burned in the afternoon; but this was probably a mistake.

† For the conflicting views as to the exact spot where Ridley and Latimer were burned, see Hurst, *Oxford Topography*, pp. 123–4.

‡ See Foxe, vol. VII, pp. 547–51, for the description of Ridley's execution. Foxe apparently obtained his information from Shipside.

between the Mayor and one of the Aldermen. Latimer followed a little way behind, in the custody of the Sheriff; he wore shoddy old clothes, and a handkerchief round his head. On their way to the stake, they walked past Bocardo, where Ridley knew that Cranmer was imprisoned, and he looked up at the windows of the prison; he hoped that Cranmer might be looking out of the window of his room, and that they could exchange a few hasty words of farewell. But Cranmer was not at the window; he was in his prison, engaged in talk with Soto. The friar, however, had arranged for Cranmer to be brought out on to the northern parapet of the prison to see Ridley and Latimer burned.

As they walked, Ridley looked back, and saw Latimer and his escort a little distance behind him. 'Oh, be ye there?' he shouted. Latimer was old and ill, but his spirit was unbroken; he answered: 'Yea; have after as fast as I can follow'. When they reached the stake, Ridley looked up to Heaven, and held up his hands. Then Latimer joined him, and they embraced; and Ridley said: 'Be of good heart, brother, for God will either assuage the fury of the flame, or else strengthen us to abide it'. Ridley knelt down, and kissed the stake, and prayed, and Latimer knelt beside him, and prayed too; and the two men stood together and talked, and waited for a little while, presumably because some hitch had held up the proceedings. It was eighteen months since they had been able to speak to each other. Now they could talk together for the last time where no one could overhear them, and speak words which they knew could never be repeated.

Lord Williams was in charge of the execution; he had gained his peerage since he had brought Ridley and his colleagues from the Tower to Oxford in March 1554. He sat on a platform, and the University and city officials took their places by his side. They were surrounded by their officers and men, who were apparently there in some strength, as the authorities anticipated the possibility of disorder. Shipside was there, but it seems that Alice had not after all been able to face the ordeal, for there is no mention that Ridley spoke any word to her. There was a great crowd of onlookers who had come to see Ridley and Latimer burned—Catholics who were there to see them rightly punished, doctors of the University who had come to approve and to be seen approving, Protestants who revered the martyrs, and crowds of men and women who had come merely to enjoy a spectacle. There were probably many who were enraged against the Government and admired the victims of the Church of Rome—far more than there had been at the burning of Bilney or Frith some twenty-five years before. Three months later, the Queen would be forced to order the Sheriffs to arrest any person who demonstrated at a burning in sympathy with the heretics.[18] Among the spectators was a Fellow of Magdalen College, Oxford—Julins Palmer. Palmer had always been a zealous Catholic; he had denounced the Reformation in King Edward's days, and had consequently been expelled from his Fellowship. Now that he had been welcomed back as a Fellow he was becoming more and more disgusted with the methods which his Church was using to extirpate heresy —most of all, perhaps, with the jubilation and gloating of the doctors at Oxford at the agonies of every Protestant victim. Soon after he had witnessed the death of Latimer and Ridley, Palmer declared himself a Protestant, and in due course was burned as a heretic.[19] There were men like Palmer in England as well as men like Rich.

The stake was an iron post standing some eight feet high.

It was surrounded, at a distance of a foot or so, by bundles of fagots and gorse. The soldiers kept the crowd at a safe distance from the stake, but Shipside was permitted to stand close by the stake, within the ring of soldiers, to be with Ridley at the end, and to assist in any way he could in shortening his sufferings.

The sermon was to be preached by Richard Smith, who had been the leading Catholic disputant at the disputation of April 1554. Smith chose as his text: 'If I yield my body to the fire to be burned, and have not charity, I shall gain nothing thereby'. He said that some misguided people might think that because Ridley and Latimer were prepared to be burned for their heretical views there was something meritorious in their action; but it was the sanctity of the cause for which a man died, not the manner of his death, which made him righteous. In fact, by obstinately refusing to recant and thus suffering a death from which recantation would have saved them, Ridley and Latimer were in effect committing the sin of suicide, like Judas and a woman who had just hanged herself in Oxford. Smith said that the prisoners were excommunicated heretics, because they denied the Real Presence of Christ in the Sacrament of the Altar, an incontestable truth of the Catholic Church which was denied by both Lutherans and Zwinglians. Smith said that Ridley and Latimer were Zwinglians, and that of all heretics the Zwinglians were the worst. He then earnestly urged them to recant, to save their lives and souls —Smith himself had certainly set them an example in this direction. His sermon was shorter than was expected; it only lasted a quarter of an hour.

While Smith had been speaking, Ridley and Latimer had been raising their hands and eyes to Heaven, and making other signs of disapproval. As soon as the sermon was over,

Ridley asked Latimer whether Latimer or he should reply first to Smith. Latimer, of course, said that Ridley should speak first. They both of them then approached Lord Williams, and knelt to him; and Ridley asked permission to say two or three words in reply to the sermon. Williams hesitated, and consulted Irish and other dignitaries; but Marshal, the Vice-Chancellor, immediately intervened, and said that if Ridley wished to recant he could speak for as long as he liked but that otherwise he could not speak. He also told him that if he recanted his life would be spared. Ridley replied: 'Well, so long as the breath is in my body, I will never deny my Lord Christ and his known truth. God's will be done in me'; and he cried out in a loud voice that he committed his cause to God. He then asked Lord Williams to approach the Queen on behalf of Alice and the tenants of the see of London, and told him that Shipside had his petition to the Queen which he would give to Lord Williams.*

They were told to get ready for death. Ridley distributed presents which he had brought with him to the officers and gentlemen of Williams' escort, and to people in the crowd; he gave a groat, some nutmeg, and other small gifts. Then he proceeded to undress; he gave his gown to Shipside, and told him to treasure it, and gave other garments which he was wearing to the onlookers, leaving the rest of his clothes with the bailiffs. The people clustered around, and fought to secure some part of his garments; some of them plucked the points off his hose. They clamoured to obtain some object in memory of the martyr. Ridley kept on the long

* According to Foxe's account, Ridley did not mention his petition to the Queen to Lord Williams until he was fastened to the stake with the gunpowder round his neck; but it seems unlikely that he would have forgotten to mention the matter when he spoke to Williams before he undressed.

truss which he wore beneath his gown, and said that it
would be better to go in his truss; but Shipside urged him
to take it off, and be burned only in his shirt. The truss
would delay death, and prolong the pain of the fire, while
it would be of use to some poor man. Ridley then took off
his truss, and stood only in his shirt, and said: 'O heavenly
Father, I give unto thee most hearty thanks, for that thou
hast called me to be a professor of thee, even unto death.
I beseech thee, Lord God, take mercy upon this realm of
England, and deliver the same from all her enemies'. A
smith fastened him to the stake with a chain fixed tightly
round his waist. Ridley shook the chain, and felt it was
tight, and said to the smith: 'Good fellow, knock it in hard,
for the flesh will have his course'. He did not delude himself
into thinking that he could stand patiently in the fire unless
he was securely fastened.

At the same time, Latimer, who had no gifts and fine
clothes to give away, was fastened to the same stake on the
other side with the same chain that was holding Ridley.
Now all was ready; but Shipside came forward with a bag
of gunpowder, and gave it to Ridley to hang around his
neck. The Catholic doctors who were watching said that
Ridley was no true martyr to take this means of lessening
his sufferings;* but Ridley took the gunpowder, and
said that he accepted it as a gift from God. He asked Shipside if he had any more powder for Latimer, and Shipside
told him that he had brought another bag for Latimer. The
soldiers were now all ready to light the fire, and Ridley
told Shipside to hurry to take the gunpowder to Latimer
before they lit the fagots, for he was afraid that he would
reach him too late. Shipside went quickly round to the

* This was the attitude of Dorman, who was present at the execution; see Dorman, *Disproof of Master Nowell's Reproof*, p. 19.

other side of the stake, and gave a bag of gunpowder to Latimer. They waited till Latimer had tied the bag around his neck; then they lit a fagot, and flung it at the foot of the pile of fagots and gorse. It was then that Latimer called out to Ridley: 'Be of good comfort, Master Ridley, and play the man; we shall this day by God's grace light such a candle in England, as I trust shall never be put out'.

The gorse and the fagots flared up, and the flames rose rapidly on Latimer's side of the stake. He held out his hands into the flames, and stroked his face with his burning hands; and in a very short time he was overcome by the smoke, and died. As the flames began to rise on Ridley's side, Ridley called out, in Latin: 'Into thy hands, O Lord, I commend my spirit!', and then he again called out the words in English. But the fire around Ridley burned slowly, for the fagots were piled so thick on the gorse that, while the gorse was burning well, the flames could not rise higher than the knees. Soon they burned fiercely at Ridley's feet and legs, and he screamed in pain. 'I cannot burn', he cried, and then fell again to calling loudly on God. Shipside rushed forward to try to shorten his torments, and maddened by the horror of it all, seized fagot after fagot, and threw them high around Ridley's face and head, as he wildly tried to add fuel to make the fire burn faster. But the fagots which Shipside piled on only deadened the flames still more; they could not rise, while the burning gorse set fire to the bottom of the fagots and burned off Ridley's legs. Ridley was leaping up and down under the fagots which covered him, and he shouted out: 'For God's sake, let the fire come unto me!' As he turned and writhed in his pain, the people could see that he was not burning at all above the waist, and that even his shirt was still untouched. He was still quite conscious, and called out 'I cannot burn', and then found relief in his faith, and cried: 'Lord have mercy upon me'. But still he could not die, and with the lower part of his body burned clean away, he swayed over the chain which held him to the stake by the waist, and seemed about to fall into the flames right over on Latimer's side. Then one of the soldiers saw the flames breaking through under one of the fagots, and he hauled the fagot away with his bill, and the flames leaped upwards. Ridley could see what was happening, and he knew what to do. He swung what was left of him towards the rising flames, and the summit of the fire reached the bag around his neck. It touched the gunpowder, and he died, and his body fell at Latimer's feet.

NOTES

[1] Ridley's letter to Grindal (*Works*, p. 394).

[2] Foxe, vol. VII, p. 518.

[3] The account of Ridley's trial is taken from Foxe, vol. VII, pp. 518–29 (first day's session), and pp. 534–40 (second day's session).

[4] Foxe, vol. VIII, pp. 707–8.

[5] Ridley, *Last Farewell* (*Works*, pp. 395–7).

[6] *Works*, pp. 397–405.

[7] *Works*, pp. 406–8, 536.

[8] Foxe, vol. VII, pp. 558–9; *Works*, pp. 408–9.

[9] *Last Farewell* (*Works*, pp. 412–18).

[10] *Last Farewell* (Foxe, vol. VII, p. 563; *Works*, p. 418).

[11] Ridley, *Farewell to the Prisoners and Exiles* (Foxe, vol. VII, p. 567; *Works*, pp. 426–7).

[12] Ridley's letter to Queen Mary, 16th October 1555 (*Works*, pp. 427–9).

[13] Ridley's letter to Queen Mary (*Works*, p. 428).

[14] See *Hutchinson's Works* (Editor's Biographical Note), pp. viii–x.

[15] Strype, *Annals*, vol. I (i), pp. 86, 94–5; Foxe, vol. VII, p. 546 n.

[16] See Jewel's letter to Peter Martyr, 26th January 1559 (*Zurich Letters*, vol. I, p. 7).

[17] Foxe, vol. VII, p. 547.

[18] *Acts of the Privy Council*, vol. V, p. 224 (14th January 1555/6).

[19] Foxe, vol. VIII, pp. 201–18.

BIBLIOGRAPHY OF WORKS CITED

Acts of the Privy Council of England (ed. Dasent; London, 1890–1907).

ATTWATER: *Pembroke College Cambridge: a Short History* (Cambridge, 1936).

BASS-MULLINGER: *The University of Cambridge from the earliest times to the Royal Injunctions of 1535* (Cambridge, 1873).

The University of Cambridge from the Royal Injunctions of 1535 to the Accession of Charles I (Cambridge, 1884).

BELLOC: *Cranmer* (London, 1931).

BRADFORD: *The Writings of John Bradford* (Parker Society; Cambridge, 1853).

BRAND: *History and Antiquities of Newcastle-upon-Tyne* (London, 1779).

BUCHANAN: *Memorials of Herne* (London, 1887).

BURNET: *History of the Reformation of the Church of England* (ed. Pocock; Oxford, 1865).

Calendar of Letters, Documents and State Papers relating to the Negotiations between England and Spain in Simancas and elsewhere (ed. Tyler; London, 1862–1916).

Calendar of the Patent Rolls, Edward VI (London, 1924–7).

Calendar of the Patent Rolls, Philip and Mary (London, 1936–9).

Calendar of State Papers (Domestic), Edward VI, Mary and Elizabeth 1547–80 (ed. Lemon; London, 1856).

CAIUS: *Works of John Caius, M.D.* (Cambridge, 1912).

CARLILE: *A discourse wherein it is plainly proved by the matter of time and place that Peter was never at Rome* (London, 1572).

CHESTER: *Hugh Latimer, Apostle to the English* (Philadelphia, 1954).

Chronicles of Queen Jane and of two years of Queen Mary (ed. Nichols; Camden Society No. 48, London, 1850).

Collection of Statutes of Cambridge University (Cambridge, 1840).

COLLIER: *Ecclesiastical History of Great Britain* (ed. Barham; 1840-41).

COOPER: *Annals of Cambridge* (Cambridge, 1843).
Athenae Cantabrigienses (Cambridge, 1858–61).
County History of Northumberland (Northumberland County History Committee; Newcastle, 1893–1940).
COVERDALE: *Certain most godly, fruitful and comfortable letters of such true saints and holy martyrs of God* (London, 1564).
CRANMER: *The Works of Thomas Cranmer* (Parker Society; Cambridge, 1844–6).
CREVIER: *Histoire de l'Université de Paris* (Paris, 1761).
DARBY: *Hugh Latimer* (London, 1953).
DE RAM: *Anecdotes pour servir à l'histoire de l'Université de Louvain, No. 10* (Louvain, 1847).
DIXON: *History of the Church of England* (London, 1878–1902).
DORMAN: *A disproof of Master Nowell's Reproof* (Antwerp, 1565).
FAULKNER: *An Historical and Topographical Account of Fulham* (London, 1813).
FOXE: *Acts and Monuments of these latter and perilous days touching matters of the Church* (ed. Pratt; 1877).
FRANKLIN: *Paris et les Parisiens au Seizième Siècle* (Paris, 1921).
FROUDE: *History of England from the fall of Wolsey to the death of Elizabeth* (ed. 1860).
FULLER: *History of the Church of England* (London, ed. 1868).
FULLER: *History of the University of Cambridge* (ed. Prickett and Wright; 1840).
GAIRDNER: *Lollardry and the Reformation in England* (London, 1908).
GARDINER: *Letters of Stephen Gardiner* (ed. Muller; Cambridge, 1933).
GARDINER: *Obedience in Church and State* (ed. Janelle; Cambridge, 1930).
GASQUET and BISHOP: *Edward VI and the Book of Common Prayer* (London, 1890).
GILDAS: *Opus novum Gildas Britanus Monachus* (1st ed., London, 1525).
GORHAM: *Gleanings of a few scattered ears during the period of the Reformation in England* (London, 1857).
Grace Book A containing the Proctors' Accounts and other records of the University of Cambridge for the years 1454–88 (ed. Leather: Cambridge, 1897).

Grace Book B, Part II, containing the Accounts of the Proctors of the University of Cambridge, 1511–44 (Luard Memorial Series, No. III), (ed. Bateson; Cambridge, 1905).

Grace Book Γ, containing the Records of the University of Cambridge for the years 1501–42 (ed. Searle; Cambridge, 1908).

GRAFTON's *Chronicle* (London, ed. 1809).

Greyfriars Chronicle (Camden Society, No. 53) (ed. Nichols, London, 1852).

GRINDAL: *Remains of Archbishop Grindal* (Parker Society; Cambridge, 1843).

HALL's *Chronicle* (London, ed. 1809).

Harleian MSS.

HASTED: *History and Topographical Survey of the County of Kent* (Canterbury, 2nd ed., 1797–1800).

HEYLIN: *Ecclesia Restaurata, or History of the Church of England* (London, 1661).

HODGSON: *History of Northumberland* (Newcastle, 1858).

HOLDSWORTH: *History of English Law* (London, 1st ed., 1903–9).

HOLINSHED: *Chronicles of England, Scotland and Ireland* (London, ed. 1807–08).

House of Lords Journal.

HUMPHREY: *Iuelli vita* (London, 1573).

HURST: *Oxford Topography* (Oxford Historical Series, No. 39; Oxford, 1899).

HUTCHINSON: *Works of Roger Hutchinson* (Parker Society; Cambridge, 1842).

JANELLE: *l'Angleterre catholique à la veille du schisme* (Paris, 1935).

JENKYNS: *Remains of Thomas Cranmer, Archbishop of Canterbury* (Oxford, 1833).

KENNET: *A complete history of England* (London, 1706).

LAMB: *Collection of Letters and Statutes from Corpus Christi College MSS.* (London, 1838).

LANGDALE: *Catholica Confutatio impiae cuiusdem determinationis D. Nicolai Ridlei* (Paris, 1556).

LATIMER: *Sermons of Hugh Latimer* (Parker Society, Cambridge, 1844).

LEINSTER, DUKE OF: *The Earls of Kildare and their Ancestors from 1057 to 1773* (Dublin, 1864).

LELAND: *The Itinerary of John Leland* (London, 1906–10).

Letters and Papers (Foreign and Domestic) of the Reign of King Henry VIII (London, 1862–1910).

Literary Remains of King Edward VI (ed. Nichols; Roxburgh Club, London, 1857).

Liturgies of King Edward VI. The Two Liturgies with other documents set forth by Authority in the reign of King Edward VI (Parker Society; Cambridge, 1844).

London Chronicle in the times of Henry VII and Henry VIII (ed. Hopper; Camden Miscellany, Camden Society No. 73; London, 1859).

LORIMER: *John Knox and the Church of England* (London, 1875).

The Lord Chamberlain's MSS.

MACHYN: *Machyn's Diary* (ed. Nichols; Camden Society No. 42; London, 1848).

MACKENZIE: *A descriptive and historical account of Newcastle-upon-Tyne* (Newcastle, 1827).

MACKENZIE and DENT: *A historical and descriptive view of the County of Northumberland* (Newcastle, 1811).

MALLET: *History of the University of Oxford* (London, 1924–7).

MAYNARD SMITH: *Henry VIII and the Reformation* (London, 1948).

MICHELET: *Histoire de France* (Paris, ed. 1898).

MORE: *The correspondence of Sir Thomas More* (Princeton, 1947).

MOULE: *Bishop Ridley on the Lord's Supper* (London, 1895).

MULLER: *Stephen Gardiner and the Tudor Reaction* (London, 1926).

NAMÈCHE: *Cours d'Histoire Nationale* (Louvain, 1853–94).

Narratives of the Days of the Reformation (ed. Nichols; Camden Society No. 77; London, 1859).

NEAL: *History of the Puritans or Protestant Nonconformists* (ed. 1755).

NEF: *Rise of the British Coal Industry* (London, 1932).

NEWCOURT: *Repertorium Ecclesiasticum Parochiale Londinense* (ed. 1710).

Original Letters relative to the English Reformation (Parker Society, Cambridge, 1846).

Oxford City Records: Selections from the Records of the City of Oxford 1509–83 (ed. Turner; Oxford, 1880).

PARKER: *Correspondence of Matthew Parker, Archbishop of Canterbury* (Parker Society; Cambridge, 1853).

PEACOCK: *Observations on the statutes of the University of Cambridge* (London, 1841).

Pembroke College, Cambridge MSS.

PILKINGTON: *The Works of John Pilkington, Bishop of Durham* (Parker Society; Cambridge, 1842).

POLE: *Epistolarum Reginaldi Poli* (Brixiae, 1744–57).

POLLARD: *Thomas Cranmer and the English Reformation* (London, 1927).

Public Record Office Lists and Indexes (London, 1892–1931).

Reformation of the Ecclesiastical Laws as attempted in the reigns of King Henry VIII, King Edward VI and Queen Elizabeth (ed. Cardwell; Oxford, 1850).

REID: *The King's Council in the North* (London, 1921).

RIDLEY, GLOUCESTER: *Life of Dr. Nicholas Ridley* (London, 1763).

RIDLEY, NICHOLAS: *Register* (London).

Register (Rochester).

Works of Bishop Ridley (Parker Society; Cambridge, 1843).

RIDLON: *History of the Ancient Ryedales*—Riddell, Riddle, Ridlon, Ridley Families (Manchester, New Hampshire, 1884).

ROGERS, THOMAS: *The Catholic Doctrine of the Church of England —An Exposition of the Thirty-nine Articles* (Parker Society; Cambridge, 1854).

ROGERS, THOROLD: *History of Agriculture and Prices* (Oxford, 1872).

ROSE-TROUP: *The Western Rebellion of 1549* (London, 1913).

Rotuli Parliamentorum (ed. Strachey; London, 1767–77).

RYMER: *Foedera, Conventiones, Literae et cujuscunque generis Acta Publica inter Reges Angliae* (London, ed. 1704–17).

SALTER: *Oxford City Properties* (Oxford Historical Society, No. 83; Oxford, 1926).

SELVE: *Correspondance politique de Odet de Selve* (Paris, 1888).

SIMPSON: *St. Paul's Cathedral* (Camden Society, New Series, No. 26, London, 1880).

SMYTH, C. H.: *Cranmer and the Reformation under Edward VI* (Cambridge, 1926).

State Papers during the reign of Henry VIII (London, 1831–52).

Statutes of the Realm (London, 1810–24).

STONE: *History of the doctrine of the Holy Eucharist* (London, 1909).

STOW: *The Chronicle of England from Brute unto this present yeare, 1580* (Annals, 1st ed., London, 1580).

STOW: *Survey of the cities of London and Westminster* (ed. Strype; London, 1720).

Survey of London (1603 edition) (ed. Kingsford; Oxford, 1908).

STRYPE: *Annals of the Reformation* (ed. 1824).

    Ecclesiastical Memorials (ed. 1822).

    Life of Archbishop Parker (ed. 1821).

    Life of Sir John Cheke (ed. 1821).

    Memorials of Archbishop Cranmer (ed. 1840).

TODD: *Life of Archbishop Cranmer* (London, 1831).

TREVELYAN: *English Social History* (London, 1944).

Trevelyan Papers prior to 1588 (ed. Collier; Camden Society, No. 67; London, 1857).

TROLLOPE: *History of Christ's Hospital* (London, 1834).

University College Oxford MS.

Valor Ecclesiasticus tempore Regis Henrici Octavo (ed. Caley; London, 1810–34).

Victoria County History of Oxfordshire (London, 1939–54).

WILKINS: *Concilia Magnae Britaniae et Hiberniae* (London, 1737).

WRIOTHESLEY: *Chronicle of England during the reigns of the Tudors, 1485–1559* (ed. Hamilton; Camden Society, New Series, Nos. 11, 20; London, 1875–77).

Zurich Letters: Letters of the Reformers (ed. Robinson; Parker Society; Cambridge, 1842–45).

ABBREVIATIONS USED IN NOTES

Bass-Mullinger: University of Cambridge, vol. I—*Bass-Mullinger, University of Cambridge from the earliest times to the Royal Injunctions of 1535.*

Bass-Mullinger: University of Cambridge, vol. II—*Bass-Mullinger, University of Cambridge from the Royal Injunctions of 1535 to the Accession of Charles I.*

Bradford's Works: *The Writings of John Bradford.*

Burnet: *Burnet, History of the Reformation of the Church of England (Parts I, II and III).*

Burnet's Records: *Burnet, History of the Reformation of the Church of England (Appendix).*

Cal. Pat. Rolls, Edw. VI: *Calendar of Patent Rolls, Edward VI.*

Cal. Pat. Rolls, Ph. & M.: *Calender of Patent Rolls, Philip and Mary.*

Calendar of Spanish State Papers: *Calendar of Letters, Despatches and State Papers relating to the Negotiations between England and Spain in Simancas and elsewhere.*

Cooper: Ath. Cant.: *Cooper, Athenae Cantabrigienses.*

Dixon: *Dixon, History of the Church of England.*

Foxe: *Foxe, Acts and Monuments of these latter and perilous days touching matters of the Church.*

Gairdner: *Gairdner, Lollardry and the Reformation.*

Gildas' History: *Gildas, Opus novum Gildas Britanus Monachus.*

Gloucester Ridley: *Ridley, Gloucester: Life of Dr. Nicholas Ridley.*

Grindal's Works: *The Remains of Archbishop Grindal.*

Heylin: *Heylin, Ecclesia Restaurata or History of the Church of England.*

Holinshed: *Holinshed, Chronicles of England, Scotland and Ireland.*

Humphrey: Life of Jewel—*Humphrey, Iuelli vita.*

Kennet: *Kennet, A complete history of England.*

Lemon: Calendar of State Papers (Domestic) Edward VI, etc. : *Calendar of State Papers (Domestic) Edward VI, Mary and Elizabeth, 1547-80, ed. Lemon.*

L. & P. Henry VIII: *Letters and Papers (Foreign and Domestic) of the Reign of King Henry VIII.*

Letters of Cardinal Pole: *Epistolarum Reginaldi Poli.*

Rogers, On the Thirty-nine Articles: *Rogers, The Catholic Doctrine of the Church of England—an Exposition of the Thirty-nine Articles.*

Rot. Parl.: *Rotuli Parliamentorum.*

Stow's Annals: *Stow, Chronicle of England from Brute unto this present yeare, 1580.*

Stow's Survey: *Stow, Survey of London (ed. Kingsford, 1908).*

Strype: Cranmer—*Strype, Memorials of Archbishop Cranmer, vol. I.*

Strype: Cranmer App.—*Strype, Memorials of Archbishop Cranmer, vol. II.*

Strype: Memorials—*Strype, Ecclesiastical Memorials.*

Strype, Stow's Survey: *Stow, Survey of London (ed. Strype, 1720).*

Works: *The Works of Bishop Ridley.*

INDEX